WHITE-COLLAR CRIMINAL

THE EDITOR

GILBERT GEIS is currently professor of sociology at California State College at Los Angeles. He studied at Colgate University, the University of Stockholm, and Brigham Young University, and received his doctorate from the University of Wisconsin in 1953. He was a Fulbright and Social Science Research Council Fellow in Norway, 1951–52, taught at the University of Oklahoma from 1952 to 1957, and was a Liberal Arts Fellow in Law and Sociology at the Harvard Law School in 1965–66. He has been project director on grants from the National Institute of Mental Health and the Walter E. Meyer Research Institute of Law, and research director of an Office of Economic Opportunity program employing former narcotic addicts in street work with addicts and as classroom assistants in junior high schools.

Professor Geis' major publications include *The East Los Angeles Half-way House for Narcotic Addicts, Juvenile Gangs* (President's Committee on Juvenile Delinquency and Youth Crime, 1965), *The Longest Way Home*, with William E. Bittle, and *Man, Crime, and Society*, with Herbert A. Bloch, as well as many articles on crime and delinquency.

Professor Geis has served as chairman of the section on Crime and Delinquency of the Society for the Study of Social Problems and as secretary-treasurer of the criminology section of the American Sociological Association. He has been a consultant to the President's Commission on Law Enforcement and Administration of Justice; in this capacity he was responsible for draft statements on white-collar crime and on compensation to victims of violent crime.

WHITE-COLLAR

THE OFFENDER

Edited, with introductions and notes,

CRIMINAL

IN BUSINESS AND THE PROFESSIONS

by Gilbert Geis

Atherton Press   New York   1968

White-Collar Criminal
The Offender in Business and the Professions
Gilbert Geis, editor

Copyright © 1968 by Atherton Press, Inc.

Address all inquiries to:
Atherton Press, Inc., 70 Fifth Avenue, New York 10011

Library of Congress Catalog Card Number 68-16407

FIRST EDITION

Manufactured in the United States of America
Designed by JoAnn Randel

For Robley

PREFACE

Issues involved in the description and study of white-collar crime—loosely defined as those offenses committed by persons in government, business, and the professions in their occupational roles—are marked at the moment by their tentative, uncertain condition. White-collar crime provides material that is often absorbing, tantalizing, offensive, and intellectually challenging. The issue of proper treatment for white-collar criminals is but one of a range of items capable of arousing intense debate and disagreement. White-collar crime raises questions that confront and seriously challenge sociological and psychological views regarding the cause of criminal behavior. Studies of white-collar crime provide material for penetrating appraisal of the moral and ethical standards of our society, and for re-examination of ideas regarding the relationship between a social structure and the behavior of persons involved in it.

Readers of the following selections will likely be impressed by the rather cozy fellow-feeling that exists among many of the contributions reprinted here, with numerous citations being to readings also reprinted in the volume. In fact, readers may enjoy noting as they proceed how writers of later articles select conclusions from earlier pieces which fit their purposes, and how they rephrase conclusions to provide empirical or speculative fuel for issues which concern them but which might not have been of as much importance to the prior writer, who touched upon them only obliquely. The relatively delimited nature of material at the moment means that the literature of white-collar crime can rather readily be comprehended, its viewpoints absorbed, and its boundaries and border disputes distinguished and addressed.

This encapsulated state of affairs is not likely to last for long and it was for this reason, in addition to the intrinsic value and interest of the subject, that it appeared particularly desirable to bring together basic materials regarding white-collar crime which have been published in the United States and Great Britain, the two jurisdictions where such studies have most systematically been carried on.

Increased public focus on white-collar crime is clearly foreshadowed by President Johnson's special message on crime to Congress in February, 1967. Mr. Johnson had earlier appointed a group—the President's Commission on Law Enforcement and Administration of Justice—to investigate "street crimes" and acts of violence and depredation that had pushed the subject of crime into the political arena as a major campaign issue during 1964. Despite the circumscribed nature of its charge, the Commission felt obliged to extend its investigation into the area of white-collar crime in order to place its findings and recommendations into proper perspective. Taking note of one of his Commission's conclusions, the President told Congress: "The economic cost of white-collar crime—embezzlement, petty theft from business, consumer frauds, antitrust violations, and the like— dwarfs that of all crimes of violence."

In the same vein, James V. Bennett, in a message marking his retirement after thirty-four years as director of the Federal Bureau of Prisons, predicted growing concern with white-collar crime as he reviewed those things which he believed would take place in crime control in the coming years:

> The criminal laws of the Federal government and the states can be expected to bring about many changes that will in the future affect our corrections system just as they have in the past. It is likely that the trend toward more Federal involvement in crime control will continue and that more and more offenders will be brought within the purview of Federal statutes. But the emphasis can be expected to shift sharply, and much more will be done to control white-collar crime. Even now, according to competent criminologists, white-collar crime composes the vast bulk of our crime problem. Its large mass lies unseen and iceberg-like below the lesser bulk of such visible crimes as auto theft, bank robbery, burglary, and the like. A recent study, for example, indicates that less than one out of ten embezzlers is ever reported to the police or brought into court for

prosecution. Other studies suggest that only a tiny fraction of the crimes of fraud ever come to official attention. Our burgeoning economy will greatly enlarge the possibilities for white-collar crime, and we will have to make energetic efforts to prevent its spread.

Increased attention to white-collar crime, predicted by Bennett, is partly reflected by the material included in the present volume, although, in itself, a preference for more recent material was not our primary consideration. Rather, the chronological distribution reflects the greater amount of material on white-collar crime being published every year. Quite notable has been the convergence of legal and sociological interest in the subject, though perhaps equally notable has been the absence of writings in the discipline of economics on social and human aspects of white-collar crime. Legal scholars often take sociological writers to task for what they view as a cavalier disregard for the niceties of legal definitions of crime and legal procedures for determination of culpability. It is particularly noteworthy that the two major critiques of sociological studies of white-collar crime are written by academicians with degrees in both law and sociology—Paul W. Tappan and Robert G. Caldwell. Though neither writer himself chose to turn his sociological interests to empirical study of the subject, both took pains to point out their fundamental sympathy with considered extension of the term "criminal" (and of theories of crime causation) to at least some persons included in the broader definitions used by a number of their sociological colleagues.

The matter of definition will play an important role throughout many of the following pages as various writers struggle to formulate the concept of "white-collar crime" in manageable and acceptable form. It is moot whether the term has scientific validity and value, but it is not arguable that Edwin H. Sutherland, the sociologist who coined the phrase, placed the concept squarely into the public domain from whence even the most persuasive strictures have been unable to dislodge it. By concentrating upon a variegated range of offenses undertaken for highly diverse reasons and involving discrepant kinds of acts and patterns that were prosecuted under differing statutes and codes, and by ignoring the offender himself to focus on his social position, Sutherland may have saddled the study of such behavior with an awkward and unmanageable definition—more of a handicap, perhaps, than an asset. Many persons argue for the use of terms such as "economic crime" or "occupational crime" as being more descriptive of the subject matter now embraced by "white-collar crime." Nonetheless, pending its ultimate clarification or discard, if such is to be its intellectual fate, popular understanding and usage seemed compelling arguments at the moment for retention of the term "white-collar crime." The appeal of "white-collar crime" as a term cannot be gainsaid, and the thrust of the label in creating a universe of "reality" (in much the manner that the term "juvenile delinquency" tends to create and perpetuate a distinct group of offenders falling within a defined age bracket) cannot be underestimated.

It is not only the definition of white-collar crime that has caused difficulty, but even the rendition of the term itself has been the subject of variant usage. In his first article on the subject, Sutherland employed the hyphenated form of "white-collar crime." He omitted the hyphen, however, in his monograph, *White Collar Crime*, and in his later writings. In fact, Sutherland miscited his first article at least once in later years, dropping the hyphen, an act that, considering his reputation for extraordinary scholarly meticulousness, may have indicated the strength of his grammatical conversion. On the other hand, critics possessed of more wryness than respect, mark such action as merely further manifestation of Sutherland's routine failure to take a consistent definitional stand on his subject. For present purposes, the hyphen has been retained purely out of personal preference. Presumably, considering the direction of English usage, this issue will be resolved when the two words become joined together as "whitecollar."

Another note needs to be entered, one regarding the criteria employed for selecting the readings. After the initial definitional and polemic groundwork had been set in place, preference was invariably given to articles that contained empirical material derived from the study of one or another aspect of white-collar crime. Several good overviews of the subject were not included, though after they have read the source material, those interested in comparing their judgments and interpretations may find value in pursuing summary statements cited in the Selected References. Priority was also always given to systematic inquiries, particularly when they proceeded from one or several hypotheses; but, lacking such investigations, the search was extended to popular sources so that large gaps of significant material would not occur.

Some editorial license was taken with several of the articles. Legal writings, for understandable reasons—primarily their relevance to future litigation—tend to be suffused with footnotes. Often text material in law reviews runs but one or two lines on a page otherwise taken up with documentation. The tendency here was to trim such material, especially when it was highly technical or referred to sources not readily available. The same criteria of relevance, duplication, and accessibility were applied to the nonlegal writings as well, though the need for cutting was not as pronounced. Extensive omissions in text material, made for reasons of space or in regard to direct relevance to the subject of white-collar crime, are indicated by ellipses.

Finally, gratitude is expressed to the writers and to the copyright holders for their kind permission to reprint material. I also want to acknowledge the excellent job of typing by Shirlee Repath, who advanced photostatic reproductions into manuscript form.

Los Angeles   GILBERT GEIS

CONTENTS

V

WHITE-COLLAR OFFENSES AND THE LEGAL PROCESS

295

VI

CONTROVERSY REGARDING THE CONCEPT OF WHITE-COLLAR CRIME

347

INTRODUCTION

I

A sense of injustice, provoked by examples of inequities in the legal treatment of the powerful and the weak, has often led to imprecations against the crimes and sins of members of the upper classes—persons in government, business, and the professions. Often, those in power and those with professional training and social position are held to higher standards than their less fortunate brethren, on the ground that their background demands added social responsibility. It is these ideas, coupled with the view that no behavior is beyond scrutiny and appraisal, that have provided much of the impetus for the study of acts now grouped as "white-collar crime," "occupational crime," and "economic crime."

It is an intriguing enterprise to attempt to locate in different historical periods the sources of the most powerful forms of social criticism directed against the entrenched classes. Nay-saying prophets, as well as disenchanted members of the ruling classes and free-swinging muckrakers, have at various times led crusades against those they believed were deviating from acceptable standards of conduct.

In the United States social censure and caricature have long been the territory of novelists. If, for instance, Mark Schorer's biography of Sinclair Lewis is an accurate appraisal, some of these writers, exiles from a world to which they longed to belong, stood outside, jeering and casting diabolically well-aimed brickbats. Others, undoubtedly motivated by a sincere desire for social reform, found the literary license of fictional creation the most hospitable milieu for the advocacy of their .ideals.

Rather subtly, however, the function performed by novelists in the United States began to be assumed by sociologists, members of a newly emergent academic discipline. Writers of fiction then turned more toward clinical dissection of individual motivation and toward portraiture of their protagonists—people responding to given social conditions which, however deplorable they might be, nonetheless demanded their due and, failing to exact it, took their reasonable psychic and social toll.

The early sociological scholars came together from a wide diversity of sources, but few would miss the strong ministerial tone that pervaded their ranks. They were persons of evangelical bent who believed that they had found the resolution of man's difficulties in a moral fervor buttressed by the dictates and metaphors of science. They were marked by a distaste of fuzzy speculation, a devotion to principles that can best be called "quasi-empirical," and by an insistent thrust to the roots of society where they intended to work their will, fortified by the tools of their trade and the trappings of their academic positions.

In 1896, when sociology was barely out of swaddling clothes, Edward A. Ross, author of the first significant sociological statement made in the United States about white-collar crime, could condescendingly describe sociology before his time as "a turgid mass of stale metaphysics, dark sayings, random historical illusions, and mawkish ethical raptures."[1] Ross' intense interest in social reform is clearly evident in his tribute to Lester F. Ward, his uncle by marriage, and the first president (1906–1907) of the American Sociological Society. "Suckled on the practicalism of Ward," wrote Ross, "I wouldn't give a snap of my fingers for the 'pussyfooting' sociologists."[2]

Sociology was a field, Ross noted, that "does not meekly sidle in among the established sciences dealing with the various aspects of social life"; it "aspires to nothing less than suzerainty."[3] In his turn, Ward told how the new science would operate: Society, he wrote, "should not drift aimlessly to and fro, backwards and forwards, without guidance. Rather, the group should carefully study its situations, comprehend the aims it desires to accomplish, study scientifically the best methods for attainment of these, and then concentrate social energy to the task set before it."[4] In these terms, Ward found agencies such as legislatures well on their way toward senescence. Perhaps they would have to be maintained, he noted, "but more and more they will become a merely formal way of putting the final sanction of society on decisions that have been worked out in the . . . sociological laboratory."[5] For Albion W. Small, a third pioneering sociologist, even the question of social values was readily susceptible to resolution by means of science. "The most reliable criterion of human values which science can propose," Small wrote, "would be the consensus of councils of scientists representing the largest possible variety of human interest, and cooperating to reduce their special judgments to a scale which would render their due to each of the interests of the total calculation."[6]

It is from this heritage that the present-day study of white-collar crime emerged. Edwin H. Sutherland, who in 1940 gave white-collar crime its label and a set of posulates, reflects both the early traditions of sociology and its subsequent development. His formal training had been in economics, his entrance into sociology a matter of later preference and academic exigency. Sutherland s approach was clearly one of scientific muckraking. Though he eschewed melioristic statements and stressed that his interest lay not in the reform of society but merely in reform of criminological theory, no contemporary reader is apt to regard this as anything other than a patent disingenuousness very similar to the disclaimers of eighteenth-century satirists faced with ostracism or excommunication were their professional heresies to become manifest.

Sutherland was, in fact, also deeply interested in making an impress on criminological theory; he had a vested interest in supporting his "differential association" theory, and in protecting its special vulnerability by demanding that a theory of crime explain *all* crime. It was Sutherland's fclt professional obligation to present a facade of disengagement that merits special note, however, because the history of the ethos of sociology runs parallel to the history of study of white-collar crime, and the latter cannot readily be understood without comprehension of the former.

The early rationale of sociology, arising from "that general groping for social betterment produced by the misery that came in the wake of the industrial revolution and the factory system,"[7] was to be ridiculed by later sociologists as a preoccupation with "sex, sin, and sewage."[8] By 1939, Ward's biographer could plaintively label him "A Buried Caesar" and note that "most American teachers of sociology will smile tolerantly at the mention of his name as one who lived in the dim nineties and has been left far behind."[9] "As far as American sociology is concerned," another writer stated, "Ward was dead long before he died."[10] The work of Small and Ross was similarly denigrated. Of Small it was said that his "permanent influence upon sociology through his writings will ultimately prove slight and ephemeral as compared with the impress of his personality and personal activities upon the development of the sociological movement."[11] So, too, it was believed unlikely that Ross' "system as such will ever have a great deal of importance for formal social theory."[12] The nontheoretical work of the early sociological mainstays received even shorter shrift; it was an ephemeral kind of output, beneath comment. Sociologists were now beginning to accord respect to the work of those later caricatured by David Riesman as pedants who, "with no philosophical training, consume their time affixing exact degrees of significance to insignificant correlations and never get around to discovering anything new about society."[13]

The polemical and theoretical return of American sociologists to matters of immediate social concern coincided with the conclusion of World War II; this approach has gained considerable momentum in the 1960s, though the tendency marked by Riesman also remains a major motif in a field of study now able to absorb relatively comfortably a panorama of working ideologies. The postwar ethos was aptly indicated by Louis Wirth in a survey of sociological developments between 1895 and 1947:

> In recent years sociology seems to have begun to move into a phase closely resembling the period of initial enthusiasm for sociology in America. This phase is marked by a return to the original interest of sociologists in the actual problems of man in society. The presently emerging orientation of sociology differs from that of a generation ago, however, in several important respects: In Small's day the passion for solving the practical problems of society was supported by little more than faith that sociology could discover a scientific foundation for ethics and social policies and was guided in its investigations largely by unproved but intuitively plausible broad philosophical notions concerning human nature, the social order and social dynamics.
>
> The contemporary return of sociology to the original interest of its intellectual progenitors in contrast is distinguished by more tempered expectations. . . . Rather than aspiring to the role of value-setter, the contemporary sociologist is increasingly sensitive to the fact that science, or at least science alone, cannot set values.[14]

Explanations for the shift in stress may be found in changes in the surrounding political and social atmosphere, conditions which inevitably influence what subjects are studied and how they are approached. Matters of personnel recruitment, availability of funds for certain kinds of research, and differentiated rewards from colleagues and others—all play into the formation of a pattern of work in an academic discipline. For sociology, its chronological position vis-à-vis other defined areas of study and its own movement from infancy through adolescence may have aided in eliminating some self-consciousness and contributed to a breakdown of occupational immurement.

These items must be taken into account, at least partially, in reviewing the development and present position of studies of white-collar crime. There are also matters of personal influence, items generally difficult to assess and weigh properly. Much work regarding white-collar crime was clearly generated from a pattern of respect and discipleship accorded to Sutherland. Contributors to the present volume, for instance, include Marshall B. Clinard and Donald R. Cressey, both students and friends of Sutherland. Frank Hartung, in turn, has worked closely with Clinard, and both Donald R. Newman and Richard Quinney, while students at the University of Wisconsin, wrote doctoral dissertations under Clinard's supervision.

It is interesting as well, in this respect, to note that some of the writers represented here rounded out their sociology work with legal studies in order to complement their understanding of the issues involved in matters such as culpability and deterrence, items of basic importance to legal scholarship. Edward A. Ross and Roscoe Pound, the latter perhaps the most pre-eminent legal scholar of his time, were colleagues at the University of Nebraska, and Pound later dedicated one of his books to Ross, while Ross, for his part, pressed hard to obtain the presidency of the University of Wisconsin for Pound. Jerome Hall, the distinguished professor of jurisprudence at Indiana University, and Sutherland, who spent the major part of his academic career at Indiana, engaged in an exchange of information and ideas that enriched study and discussion of white-collar crime. Newman was a student at the University of Wisconsin Law School, earning credits to fulfill the minor requirement for his Wisconsin sociology doctorate and Harry Ball participated in summer Social Science Research Council seminars involving social scientists and law professors. From the field of legal scholarship, Sanford Kadish, Lawrence Friedman, and Alan Dershowitz, among those writers represented in this volume, have been deeply involved in collaborative work with behavioral science colleagues.

These personal influences and cross-disciplinary roots have undoubtedly provided studies of white-collar crime with direction and sophistication. The impact of secularization on an intellectual endeavor is like the impact of foreigners on a previously isolated geographical area—a seaport city, for instance, almost invariably becomes more cosmopolitan than its hinterland neighbors. Sociologists have responded to charges of "fatuous liberalism" raised from legal circles by attempting to buttress their conclusions and recommendations with sounder data. Riesman observed that "When a law professor comes to a sociologist because he is worried about the unequal distribution of justice, and regards legal aid work as a drop in the bucket, the latter's preoccupation with methodology and lack of reformist concern may surprise him and send him back to his own devices";[15] barbs like that exert real suasion on sociological thought. On the other hand, the sociologist's scorn for legal conclusions that appear to be jerry-built on untested and unwarranted assumptions about human behavior and social activity provide pressure for experimental materials and for the acquisition of the complex and delicate skills essential for the collection of impregnable data.

It is developments such as these that have placed the study of white-collar crime in the position it occupies today and which portend the direction in which such studies are apt to move. Many gaps remain to be filled of course. Virtually the only psychological consideration of white-collar crime, for instance, is Walter Bromberg's clinical analysis of Richard Whitney, president of the New York Stock Exchange, who in 1933 was convicted of grand larceny for manipulating corporate funds;[16] such a study needs additional psychological support from other investigations before its conclusions can safely be generalized. Moreover, articulation between inquiries into organization structures and studies of white-collar crime has only barely gotten underway. Finally, the necessity to relate white-collar crime to theories of deviance and to general theories of human behavior has persistently challenged scholars and remains a major issue which must be carefully addressed.

II

The foregoing are but a few of the currents which have played upon popular and academic discourse regarding white-collar crime. The individual writers represented in this volume themselves highlight and address additional issues and, on occasion, undertake to adjudicate them. Rather than repeat such material, these introductory remarks will be confined to a more general overview of considerations emanating from studies of white-collar crime and to a notation of views not otherwise represented in the readings. The consequences of white-collar crime for the integrity of a society and the commission of "ordinary" kinds of crime, the importance of distinguishing between illegal and other kinds of meretricious behavior, the historical emergence of conditions that gave rise to laws defining white-collar crime, the need for typologies of such crime, and a summary review of general merits and shortcomings of Sutherland's pioneering position provide substance for the remaining introductory remarks.

It is important, initially, to realize that Sutherland, by virtue of his position in American sociology, the attractiveness of his terminology, and the illustrations he used to support his views, broadened the horizons of criminological research well beyond their traditional limits. The tendency to generalize about crime and criminals on the basis of the more readily visible forms of criminal activity, such as murder, assault, and robbery, was irreversibly affected by Sutherland's analysis that the propensity to violate the law is not confined to the stereotyped "criminal." That differential opportunities to commit different kinds of crime must be included in criminological analysis represents a major contribution of the Sutherland focus on white-collar offenses and should not be undervalued. In his foreword to the 1961 edition of *White Collar Crime,* Donald R. Cressey also observes that "the lasting merit of this book . . . is its demonstration that a pattern of crime can be found to exist outside both the focus of popular preoccupation with crime and the focus of scientific investigation of crime and criminality."[17] For Cressey, a paramount problem is the determination of why white-collar crime was able to remain beyond popular and criminological purview for so long.

Justice Oliver Wendell Holmes provided an approach to this issue when he pointed out that matters which a society chooses to study and acts which it decides to proscribe are telling indications of fundamental values. "It is perfectly proper to regard and study law simply as a great anthropological document," Holmes noted, continuing:

> It is proper to resort to [law] to discover what ideals of society have been strong enough to reach that final form of expression, or what have been the changes in dominant ideas from century to century. It is proper to study it as an exercise in the morphology and transformation of human ideas. The study pursued for such ends becomes science in its strictest sense.[18]

The same idea has been stated in the metaphorical language of Justice Cardozo: "Life casts the molds of conduct, which will some day become fixed as law," Cardozo wrote. "Law preserves the molds, which have taken form and shape from life."[19]

Few scholars have directed their attention to the charting of circumstances giving rise to statutes designed to discourage and to punish certain derelictions by members of the more powerful and entrenched segments of the society, though many have noted the striking increase in such rules and have marked signposts along the way. Holmes, for instance, has observed:

> When we read in the old books that it is the duty of one exercising a common calling to do his work upon demand and do it with reasonable skill, we shall see that the gentleman is in the saddle, and means to have the common people kept up to the mark for his convenience. We recognize the imperative tone which in our day has changed sides, and is oftener to be heard from the hotel clerk than from the guest.[20]

The growing concentration of statutory law on principles such as *caveat vendor*—"let the seller beware"—undoubtedly represents a function of, among other things, population growth, the development of cities, greater life expectancy, and enhanced technology, the last rich in its potential and awesome in its threat. As Pound has noted, "The points at which the claims and desires of each individual and those of his fellows conflict or overlap have increased enormously. Likewise, new agencies of menace to the general security have developed in profusion."[21]

Two dominant motifs mark the history of response to acts now considered white-collar crime. On the one hand, throughout time there has been a broad sweep of denunciation based almost exclusively on moral principles, usually deemed as self-evident and part of a natural, immutable code. Witness, for example, the diatribes of the Biblical prophets, such as Micah, the yeoman farmer of the eighth century before Christ who bespoke the doom of Judah because of its low ethical level;[22] note, too, the uncompromising verdict of the Book of Ecclesiastes regarding commercial activities:

> A merchant shall hardly keep himself from doing wrong, and a huckster shall not be freed from sin. . . . As a nail sticketh fast between the joinings of the stones, so doth sin stick close to buying and selling.[23]

On the other hand, there has been a rambling and variegated response in the law to conditions such as those denounced in Biblical writings. Part of the explanation for the discrepancy between moral and legal codes can be found in the nature and the function of law. Law, for instance, may be employed to maintain the status quo as well as to establish new ground rules. The latter situation, as de Tocqueville has pointed out, is not likely to occur when conditions are at their worst, but rather when they are in the process of change to the better.[24] It is then that people come to taste potential gains and to stir restively about the rate of change. Through most of history, with highly segmented and compartmentalized class patterns and strong authoritarian rule, those on the lower rungs of the social order were not likely to insist that they be treated fairly or decently or that their resources not be unreasonably exploited.

The reading of the legal record, however, is not merely a question of rote perusal of provisions with the assumption that absence equals indifference. Failure to outlaw certain behavior may represent espousal of goals likely to be compromised if lesser aims are accentuated. Legal statements may also stand for quite fanciful positions, and the discrepancy between the law on the books and the law in fact may be substantial. In addition, the oft-repeated dictum that law tends to be a reflection, however belated, of customary conditions fails to do justice to the basic question of *whose* customary ways will prevail and for what reason they will do so.

In such terms, a major thesis regarding white-collar crime is that the legal delineation of such offenses can be said to represent, though not in a direct or simple manner, social views that, for complex reasons, have come to be embodied in official codes. One facet of this development may be briefly summarized by reference to extension of the law of theft into white-collar realms.

Anthropological evidence makes clear that a sense of rightful possession of private property is far from an innate human characteristic. Sociologists have suggested that for Western civilization the doctrine of predestination, arising with notable intensity in countries persuaded to Calvinistic dogma, became translated into a belief that material possessions indicated divine approval, manifest in their bestowal.[25] Extratheological precepts also obviously contributed to a belief in the sovereignty of ownership. In the United States, the early entrenchment of this thesis is marked in the ringing words of John Adams, the country's second President:

> Property is surely a right of mankind as really as liberty. . . . The moment the idea is admitted into society, that property is not as sacred as the laws of God, and that there is not a force of law and public justice to protect it, anarchy and tyranny commence.[26]

It was from such an ideological perspective that the law of fraud, fundamental in white-collar crime, emerged. In his meticulous tracing of this development in *Theft, Law, and Society*, Jerome Hall concentrates initially upon the decision in the Carrier's Case in 1473, a decision which for the first time included within the definition of theft the appropriation of goods by a middleman. Prior to 1473, virtually all theft involved cattle, and the law covered only direct acts. By the time of the Carrier's Case, however, manufacturing had begun to replace the feudal system. The new middle class had started to take shape, and its trade interests coincided with those of the Crown. In addition, the Carrier's Case involved wool and textile products, and these goods had recently become England's most significant exports. It was these conditions which coalesced in 1473 to change the Anglo-Saxon definition of theft.[27]

The slow, erratic, but nonetheless inexorable expansion of the concept of commercial fraud during the almost half-millenium since the Carrier's Case provides fascinating material on the interplay between those in possession of goods seeking to protect them and place themselves in a position to acquire more and other groups seeking their own advantage—with the state in the middle attempting to set rules by which the game will be played.

A few landmarks along the way may be noted briefly.[28] The thirteenth-century English courts, for instance, provided that there was to be "no remedy for the man who to his damage had trusted the word of a liar."[29] Even in the eighteenth century, a British Chief Justice could rhetorically ask: "When A got money from B by pretending that C had sent for it, shall we indict one man for making a fool of another?"[30] It was only in 1757 that a statutory provision for the punishment of "mere private cheating" was placed into English law. It was such judicial sentiments that led Jonathan Swift to locate an ancient Hebrew tradition in a land visited by Gulliver:

> [The Lilliputians] look upon fraud as a greater crime than theft, and therefore seldom fail to punish it with death; for they allege that care and vigilance, with a very common understanding, may preserve a man's goods from theft, but honesty has no defense against superior cunning.[31]

In the United States, the law of fraud developed too, and was fought each step of the way by those who held the view, expressed in the words of Chief Justice Stone, that "any interference with the operation of the natural laws of greed" was "subversive of liberty."[32] Some of the underlying factors that encouraged state interference with commerce provide keys to present enactments against white-collar crime. Herman Mannheim noted some of these items: (1) movement from an agricultural to a commercial and industrial society; (2) increasing inequality in the distribution of property, and the amassing of great wealth by the few; (3) the growing need to leave property in the hands of other persons; (4) transformation of ownership of visible property into intangible powers and rights, such as corporate shares, including a system of social security in place of ownership of goods; and (5) passage of property from private to corporate ownership.[33]

The present state of this movement—a movement that demands concentrated attention from students interested in understanding the roots of white-collar crime—is epitomized by a recent popular panegyric on the relationship between the activities of federal regulatory agencies and the better life that we presumably all live: "You may never meet an investigator for the United States Government," it begins, "but you are safer, more comfortable, and more secure because thousands of Federal agents labor unceasingly in the background of American life." It proceeds to praise "kilocycle cops" who patrol radio and television airwaves, guardians of drug and advertising standards, enforcers of wage-and-hour laws, and similar federal agents.[34] It requires only a comparison between such sentiments and John Adams' equally self-righteous view on private property and its divine attributes to appreciate the extraordinary social revolution that provides the historical background of acts now designated as white-collar crime.

III

Use of white-collar crime statistics and case studies to take the moral temperature of the nation is a tempting enterprise. *Life* magazine, for instance, declared that white-collar crime represents a "moral lightheaded-ness" that "whatever its cause, is potentially far more dangerous than any number of juvenile 'rumbles.' "[35] C. Wright Mills also thought he dis-cerned great social malaise in reactions to announcements of white-collar crimes. "As news of higher immoralities breaks," Mills wrote, "people often say, 'Well, another one got caught today,' thereby implying that the cases disclosed are not odd events involving occasional characters but symptoms of widespread conditions."[36]

The accuracy of such statements and their basic meaning is not readily apparent. Note, for instance, a Biblical commentator's summary of conditions at the time that Micah was inveighing against the scandals he saw in Hebrew life:

> Morals were appallingly low. Government officials were dishonest. A low ethical level prevailed in most areas of life. Because the nation had lost her moral integrity, she had become sinful, soft, and ripe for conquest.[37]

The tone has not changed in almost three thousand years, and the following observations can be made about contemporary American society:

> There is much evidence of a widespread apathy toward the traditional values of American life. The ideas of strict honesty have become out of date in many fields of endeavor, public as well as private. The fall of certain television quiz heroes led to a widespread suspicion that a sick industry built them up, and that the commercialism which underwrites its programs is cynical and defiant. The crass disregard of the elemental essentials of straightforward dealing has invaded many areas of our society. One investigation after another reveals blunted moral sensibilities on the part of certain public officials and some of the agents of private enter-prise who deal with them. Furthermore, the accused seem genuinely to feel justified in their actions, proclaiming one after another that no wrongdoing was involved nor intended. The victims of the deception, while diverse in their reactions, show surprisingly little moral indignation.[38]

In the same vein, early Greece, we are told, had its predators who in violation of its codes bought up land that they had learned would subse-quently be acquired by the government; the Alcmaenoids, a leading Greek family, are reported to have contracted to build a solid marble temple, but instead to have employed concrete, veneering it with marble.[39] It is a rather long step, however, to maintain that ancient precursors of present-day white-collar crime underlay the demise of the Greek state, unless one employs such data to fill out Durant's skeletal commentary, built on an analysis of the bones of departed civilizations, that "a nation is born stoic and dies epicurean,"[40]—which, if translated into white-collar crime terms, indicates that self-indulgent, exploitative, and unprincipled behavior ultimately dooms a society. The paradox implicit in Durant's observation is that stable, stoic societies, while they may persist longer than their epicurean counterparts, often do so at the expense of items such as vitality and enterprise, freedom and opportunity for self-determination. On the other hand, societies providing scope for such values, all of which in some measure are considered fundamental in American life, also appear to encourage deviation, variation, and innovation among some persons often at the expense of others.

The necessity for historical and comparative cross-cultural studies of white-collar crime, relating its forms and its intensity to measures of social vitality, is clearly indicated before a better evaluation can be made of the meaning of such crime for a nation's survival or demise.

IV

The relationship between white-collar crime and "ordinary" or "traditional" kinds of crime seems somewhat better established than that between white-collar crime and cultural well-being. Perceptions regarding the ubiquitous nature of white-collar crime are said to have consequences for other kinds of crime, particularly in terms of permitting an individual to "rationalize" or "neutralize" his behavior; that is, to provide an explanation for his offense satisfactory to himself and to his presumed or real accusers. Lacking such an explanation, the offender may be forced to regard himself as an alien and abject creature, unable to control his behavior and incapable of acting in a manner which he has introjected as desirable. The role of white-collar crime in the rationalization of traditional crime is summarized by Gibbons:

> It is not unlikely that the existence of white-collar criminality, along with differential handling of the individuals involved in it, provides run-of-the-mill offenders with powerful rationalizations for their own conduct. The latter can argue that "everyone is crooked" and that they are the "little fish" who are the victims of a corrupt and hypocritical society. In the same way, some rather obvious problems for treatment of conventional offenders may arise from their perception of widespread illegality among individuals of comfortable economic standing. Although definitive evidence on this matter is lacking, it is possible to gather up an abundance of statements by articulate criminals and delinquents in which these individuals allude to the facts of white-collar crime as one basis for their grievances against "society."[41]

Perhaps the best-known piece of research on this subject is by Sykes and Matza; they categorized the rationalizations of delinquents into several types, including an "appeal to higher loyalties" (loyalty to gang friends, for instance, is considered a more important moral obligation than respect for private property) and "condemnation of the condemners."[42] It is with this latter explanation, insisting that the delinquent is but one among many predators in the society, that the issue of white-collar crime comes into focus. Well-versed in newspaper reports of chicanery in high places, the juvenile may maintain that he is no worse, and in some respects much better, than so-called "respectable" citizens, who not only commit crimes but also compound their offenses by being hypocritical about them. A personalized version of this phenomenon is found in the remarks of one delinquent gang member:

> Wherever you look, wherever you turn, authority is there in the shape of parents, teachers, priests, and policemen, social workers and truant officers—a great Greek chorus of do's and dont's chanting about how you goofed and you've failed. And man, you can't stand that for long. After a while you've got to cut out or go nuts—or turn it all around and tell yourself that it's you who are right and the Greek chorus that is wrong. That's easy enough to do because half the time the chorus doesn't practice what it preaches anyway.[43]

The same point is made more formally by Sheldon and Eleanor Glueck, noted investigators of juvenile delinquency, who point out that "the demands made upon the growing boy by every vehicle of modern life are numerous, involved, often subtle, sometimes inconsistent." The Gluecks draw the following implications from this situation:

> The child is told that he must be honest, non-aggressive, self-controlled, but on every hand he runs into vivid contradictory attitudes, values, and behavior in an environment that—both in and out of politics—seemingly rewards selfishness, aggression, a predatory attitude, and success by any means. It does not require the wisdom of a Seneca to convince the child, as it convinced that wise statesman, that "successful and fortunate crime is called virtue."[44]

Research probes into the less favored economic segments of the society reinforce the suggestion that in such groups individuals tend to regard others as exploitative and hostile, and to take comfort in such perceptions as justification for their own behavior. Cohen and Hodges, for example, found the ideas that "people are no good" and that the world "resembles a jungle" pervading responses to a questionnaire given persons in the "lower- blue-collar" class. Particularly notable was the cynicism concerning merchandising and service occupations:

> Economic and occupational success, they most often agreed, is accomplished by "friends or connections," "luck or chance," "pull or manipulating," or "cheating or underhanded dealing" (in contrast to "daring

and taking risks," "education," or "hard, day-by-day work"). [In contrast to members of other classes] they most often agree that television repairmen, politicians, doctors, auto mechanics, butchers, union officials, and businessmen are not trustworthy.[45]

Lower- blue-collar class members were found to be the most credulous members of the society regarding the accuracy of the written or printed word. Cohen and Hodges believe that limited experience, both direct and vicarious, makes such individuals particularly vulnerable to messages seeming to emanate from trustworthy sources. The researchers suggest that there is no conflict between their findings of credulity and misanthropy. "It is one thing to feel a generalized distrust of human beings, their motives and their claims," they write. "It is another to form an attitude on a specific claim or message where one has few independent criteria for evaluating the content of the message, little awareness of specific alternatives and little disposition to weigh evidence."[46]

The data necessary to refine the observations presented by Gibbons are as yet not available. It would be informative to learn about the perceptions regarding the prevalence of white-collar crime that are held by different kinds of traditional offenders and to determine the views on white-collar crime among individuals raised in social strata which produce a disproportionately high percentage of traditional offenders—and to do so *before* such individuals separate into essentially law-abiding or criminal categories. An informal California survey suggests the possibility that prison inmates in that state usually do not have recourse to white-collar crime as justification for their own offenses.[47] Persistent demands by the state parole board that offenders accept categorically their own guilt and personal responsibility for their acts—a thesis based upon Freudian principles of therapeutic grace—may condition verbal responses by prisoners. Group therapy, widely practiced in California correctional institutions, tends to divert attention from expressions of social cynicism and concentrate it upon psychic inadequacies. The California study, for instance, found expressions such as "I do my own number" and "I have myself to worry about" the most common answers to questions regarding the influence of knowledge and beliefs concerning white-collar crime upon the individual's own violation.

V

Most causal explanations of white-collar crime derive from an "evil causes evil" view based on the belief that only deplorable conditions of person or place can give rise to criminal behavior. There is neglect of the fact that perfectly adequate human beings and perfectly adequate social situations, judged by reasonable criteria, may produce untoward consequences, in the manner that both kindness and murder kill.

One of the earliest and hardiest explanations of white-collar crime is suggested by Aristotle in *Politics*. "Men may desire superfluities in order to enjoy pleasure unaccompanied with pain, and therefore they commit crimes," he noted. "The greatest crimes are caused by excess and not by necessity."[48] Sutherland, however, in perhaps the most telling of his observations on crime causation, laid to rest the Aristotelian postulate and its contemporary kin. "Though criminal behavior is an expression of general needs and values," Sutherland emphasized, "it is not explained by those general needs and values, since non-criminal behavior is an expression of the same needs and values."[49] The financially pressed corporate executive, Sutherland's view points out, may embezzle or he may move to a cheaper house, send his wife to work, himself take a weekend job, or borrow money from an uncle. Each of these alternatives may be able to satisfy his necessity adequately. The need alone, shared by untold numbers of other individuals who resolve it both legally and illegally, offers little clue to the precise method that will be selected for its satisfaction.

Sutherland's focus was on the enunciation of a theory to explain all crime. In an article on corporate violations, for instance, he noted mockingly that General Motors does not have an inferiority complex, United States Steel does not suffer from an unresolved Oedipus problem, and the Duponts do not desire to return to the womb. It was a clever piece of invective, designed to decimate the position of clinical theorists in criminology. "The assumption that an offender may have some such pathological distortion of the intellect seems to me absurd," Sutherland wrote, "and if it is absurd regarding the crimes of businessmen, it is equally absurd regarding the crimes of persons in the lower economic classes."[50]

To substitute for partial explanations and for psychological theses regarding criminal behavior, Sutherland advanced his own hypothesis which, "for reasons of economy, simplicity, and logic," was to be used to explain both white-collar criminality and lower-class criminality. This was his theory of differential association. "Criminality is learned," it stated in part, "in direct or indirect association with those who already practice the behavior." Since criminality is so learned, Sutherland observed, it can be and is learned at all social levels.[51]

It appears likely that Sutherland was led by his theoretical preconceptions into a number of intellectual traps which rendered the concept of white-collar crime of dubious utility for theoretical purposes. Having at hand an explanatory scheme which could embrace virtually the entire range of human conduct, Sutherland felt no need to differentiate carefully among an extraordinarily wide range of offenses—criminal, ethical, and moral—engaged in by persons who were "respected" and "socially accepted and approved." All would fit neatly into his interpretative scheme for white-collar crime in the same manner that professional crime, aggressive crime following encephalitis, and a host of other highly divergent forms of behavior could be "explained" by differential association.

It is important to realize that no one, of course, had ever maintained that General Motors or its management personnel suffered from an inferiority complex, any more than any serious scholar would have taken the position that all criminals, of either the lower or upper class, are driven by an unrequited yearning to return to the womb. Sutherland was obviously flailing a theoretical nonesuch, and it was, in fact, Sutherland himself who, in one vital respect, came nearest to the theories he was belaboring, with his insistence that all criminals could, and should, be analyzed in terms of a single theoretical interpretation.

It was this commitment that inevitably tended to blur action distinctions for Sutherland. As Merton has noted, "the decision to encompass a great variety of behaviors under one heading naturally leads us to look for an all-encompassing set of propositions which will account for the entire range of behavior." "This is not too remote," Merton points out, "from the assumption of a John Brown or a Benjamin Rush that there must be *a* theory of disease, rather than distinct theories of disease —of tuberculosis and of arthritis, of typhoid and syphilis—theories which are diverse rather than single."[52]

A present need in regard to the concept of white-collar crime appears to be to separate those types of activity that fall within the range of criminal statutes and then to gather together into less ubiquitous groupings those forms of behavior which analytically resemble one another, both in their manifestations and in the ingredients that enter into their origin. As a starting point, it might be desirable to separate white-collar crimes committed (1) by individuals as individuals (for example, lawyers or doctors), (2) by employees against a corporation or business (embezzlers), and (3) by policy-making officials for the firm (for example, in antitrust cases).

It would seem desirable that studies of embezzlers, for instance, should at first be evaluated on their own merits (as Cressey did[53]) rather than as investigations into a type of behavior similar to the crimes of corporate officials. Sutherland himself pointed out that "the ordinary case of embezzlement is a crime by a single individual in a subordinate position against a strong corporation,"[54] and Daniel Bell, after declaring that Sutherland's *White Collar Crime* is "misleadingly entitled," goes on to remark that bank embezzlers, as a group, are not upper-class individuals, but members of the middle class.[55] Embezzlers, to carry the point somewhat further, usually work alone, while antitrust violators must work in compact with others. The embezzler benefits himself directly, and harms his employer. On the other hand, offenders such as antitrust violators, though they undoubtedly most often operate in terms of personal advantage, can rationalize their offense as contributing to the fiscal health of their employer. These may not be crucial variations, but it would seem preferable to examine offenses such as embezzling, tax evasion, corporate violations, and fee splitting as distinct forms of crime which may be related to each other in some ways and to other offenses in different ways. It would also appear reasonable to concentrate initially on the elements of the criminal act for purposes of grouping it rather than upon the social characteristics of the perpetrators of the acts, and to group behavior in terms of the latter item only for the most compelling pragmatic or interpretative reasons. The crimes of medical doctors, for instance, would appear to be susceptible to differentiation on more meaningful terms than the professional status of their perpetrators. The offenses of fee splitting and abortion, both committed by doctors, seem about as related in most essential respects as the offenses of infanticide and adultery, both of which may be committed by mothers.

Until this analytical impasse is more fully resolved, the concept of white-collar crime may stand indicted on Tappan's charge that it soars "into vacuity, wide and handsome,"[56] and on Vold's allegation that it is at the moment "ambiguous, uncertain, and controversial."[57]

It may be noted in conclusion that the need for white-collar crime to be studied in terms of more homogeneous units represents a requirement common to the field of criminology. "It should be abundantly clear that theories which treat crime as though it were a unitary concept are particularly prone to failure and that the search for something which explains crime in general is the blind spot in criminology," Gibbs has written, pointing out that "if our concern is with causal homogeneity, as it should be, we can ill afford to deal with broad categories of behavior; it is far better to look within these broad categories and delimit specific types of behavior for investigation."[58]

Notes

1. Edward A. Ross, Review of Giddings, "Principles of Sociology," *Educational Review*, 12 (June, 1896), p. 92.

2. Edward A. Ross, *Seventy Years of It* (New York: Appleton-Century, 1936), p. 180.

3. Edward A. Ross, *Foundations of Sociology*, 5th ed. (New York: Macmillan, 1926), p. 8.

4. James Quayle Dealey, "Lester Frank Ward," in Howard W. Odum, ed., *American Masters of Social Science* (New York: Holt, 1927), p. 82.

5. Lester F. Ward, *Applied Sociology* (Boston: Ginn, 1906), pp. 338–339.

6. Albion W. Small, *The Meaning of Social Science* (Chicago: University of Chicago Press, 1910), p. 242.

7. Harry Elmer Barnes, "The Development of Sociology," in Harry Elmer Barnes, Howard Becker, and Frances Bennett Becker, eds., *Contemporary Social Theory* (New York: Appleton-Century, 1940), p. 3.

8. Howard Becker, "Anthropology and Sociology," in John Gillin, ed., *For a Science of Man* (New York: Macmillan, 1954), p. 145.

9. Samuel Chugerman, *Lester F. Ward: The American Aristotle* (Durham, N.C.: Duke University Press, 1939), pp. 67, 70.

10. John C. Burnham, *Lester Frank Ward in American Thought* (Washington, D.C.: Public Affairs Press, 1956), p. 10.

11. Harry Elmer Barnes, "Albion Woodbury Small: Promoter of American Sociology and Expositor of Social Interests," in Harry Elmer Barnes, ed., *An Introduction to the History of Sociology* (Chicago: University of Chicago Press, 1948), p. 788.

12. William L. Kolb, "The Sociological Theories of Edward Alsworth Ross," in *ibid.*, p. 831.

13. David Riesman, *Thorstein Veblen: A Critical Interpretation* (New York: Scribner, 1953), p. 48.

14. Quoted in Leon Bramson, *The Political Context of Sociology* (Princeton, N.J.: Princeton University Press, 1961), pp. 93–94.

15. David Riesman, "Law and Sociology," in William M. Evan, ed., *Law and Sociology* (New York: The Free Press, 1962), pp. 30–31.

16. Walter Bromberg, *Crime and the Mind* (New York: Macmillan, 1965), pp. 384–389.

17. Donald R. Cressey, "Foreword," *White Collar Crime* (New York: Holt, 1961), p. xii.

18. Oliver Wendell Holmes, "Law in Science and Science in Law," in *Collected Legal Papers* (New York: Harcourt, Brace, 1921), p. 212.

19. Benjamin N. Cardozo, *The Nature of the Judicial Process* (New Haven, Conn.: Yale University Press, 1921), p. 64.

20. Holmes, *op. cit.*, pp. 213–214.

21. Roscoe Pound, *Criminal Justice in America* (New York: Holt, 1930), p. 12.

22. Micah 1:1–16 and 2:1–12.

23. Ecclesiastes 27:2.

24. Alexis de Tocqueville, *The Old Regime and the French Revolution*, trans. by Stuart Gilbert (Garden City, N.Y.: Doubleday, 1955), pp. 176–177.

25. Max Weber, *The Protestant Ethic and the Spirit of Capitalism*, trans. by Talcott Parsons (London: G. Allen, 1930).

26. John Adams, *Works*, vol. 6 (Boston: Little, Brown, 1853), pp. 8–9.

27. Jerome Hall, *Theft, Law and Society*, 2d ed. (Indianapolis: Bobbs-Merrill, 1952), pp. 1–33.

28. Much of this material is drawn from Hermann Mannheim, *Criminal Justice and Social Reconstruction* (London: Routledge, 1946), sect. 3; and Hermann Mannheim, *Comparative Criminology* (Boston: Houghton Mifflin, 1967), chap. 21.

29. Frederick Pollock and Frederic William Maitland, *History of English Law*, vol. 2 (Boston: Little, Brown, 1909), p. 535.

30. Quoted by Hermann Mannheim, *Criminal Justice and Social Reconstruction*, *op. cit.*, p. 121.

31. Jonathan Swift, "A Voyage to Lilliput," in *Gulliver's Travels*, pt. 1, chap. 6 (1735).

32. Alpheus T. Mason, *Harlan Fiske Stone: Pillar of the Law* (New York: Viking, 1956), p. 380.

33. Mannheim, *Criminal Justice and Social Reconstruction*, *op. cit.*, pp. 86–87.

34. Miriam Ottenberg, *The Federal Investigators* (Englewood Cliffs, N.J.: Prentice-Hall, 1962), pp. xi–xii.

35. Frank Gibney, "The Crooks in White Collars," *Life*, 43 (October 14, 1957), p. 176.

36. C. Wright Mills, *The Power Elite* (New York: Oxford University Press, 1956), pp. 343–344.

37. Rolland W. Wolfe, "The Book of Micah," in *The Interpreter's Bible*, vol. 6 (Nashville, Tenn.: Abingdon Press, 1951), pp. 898–899.

38. Leroy Bowman, *Youth and Delinquency in an Inadequate Society* (New York: League for Industrial Democracy, 1960), p. 21.

39. John McConaughy, *From Cain to Capone: Racketeering down the Ages* (New York: Brentano's, 1931), p. 24.

40. Will Durant, *Our Oriental Heritage* (New York: Simon and Schuster, 1954), p. 259.

41. Don C. Gibbons, *Changing the Lawbreaker* (Englewood Cliffs, N.J.: Prentice-Hall, 1965), p. 271.

42. Gresham M. Sykes and David Matza, "Techniques of Neutralization: A Theory of Delinquency," *American Sociological Review*, 22 (December, 1967), pp. 664–670.

43. Kitty Hanson, *Rebel in the Streets* (Englewood Cliffs, N.J.: Prentice-Hall, 1964), p. 132.

44. Sheldon Glueck and Eleanor Glueck, *Ventures in Criminology* (Cambridge: Harvard University Press, 1965), p. 20.

45. Albert K. Cohen and Harold M. Hodges, Jr., "Characteristics of the Lower Blue-Collar-Class," *Social Problems*, 10 (Spring, 1963), p. 323.

46. *Ibid.*, p. 325.

47. The conclusions were reached by James H. Cosby in 1966 after more than a dozen discussions of the subject with groups of inmates of a California prison.

48. Aristotle, *Politics*, trans. by J. E. C. Welldon (London: Macmillan, 1932), book II, chap. 7, p. 65.

49. Edwin H. Sutherland and Donald R. Cressey, *Principles of Criminology*, 7th ed. (Philadelphia: Lippincott, 1966), p. 82.

50. Edwin H. Sutherland, "Crimes of Corporations," in Albert Cohen, Alfred Lindesmith, and Karl Schuessler, eds., *The Sutherland Papers* (Bloomington, Ind.: Indiana University Press, 1956), p. 96.

51. See Sutherland and Cressey, *op. cit.*, chap. 4.

52. Robert K. Merton, in Helen L. Witmer and Ruth Kotinsky, eds., *New Perspectives for Research on Juvenile Delinquency*, Washington, D.C.: Children's Bureau Publication No. 356, 1956, p. 27.

53. Donald R. Cressey, *Other People's Money: The Social Psychology of Embezzlement* (New York: The Free Press, 1953).

54. Edwin H. Sutherland, *White Collar Crime* (New York: Dryden Press, 1949), p. 231.

55. Daniel Bell, "Crime As an American Way of Life," in *End of Ideology* (New York: The Free Press, 1960), p. 382.

56. Paul W. Tappan, "Who Is the Criminal?" *American Sociological Review*, 12 (February, 1947), p. 98.

57. George B. Vold, *Theoretical Criminology* (New York: Oxford University Press, 1958), p. 253.

58. Jack Gibbs, "Needed: Analytical Typologies in Criminology," *Southwestern Social Science Quarterly*, 40 (March, 1960), p. 323.

1

WHAT IS "WHITE-COLLAR CRIME"?

Formal study of white-collar crime as a distinct, separable kind of criminal behavior got clearly underway with the publication of Sutherland's "White-Collar Criminality," the third reading in this part, though earlier writers (notably the two represented at the beginning of the part) had paid special attention to "criminaloid" behavior, as Edward A. Ross called it, and to the "crimes of the upperworld," in the designation of Albert Morris.

Sutherland was fifty-seven at the time he delivered his paper—his first published work on the subject—as the presidential address to the American Sociological Society in 1939. He later reported that he had been at work for more than a quarter of a century on the topic. He was born in 1883 in Gibbon, Nebraska, and taught briefly at Grand Island College before obtaining his doctorate at the University of Chicago in 1913. In 1924, Sutherland published his highly regarded *Principles of Criminology*, a text which, with revisions by Donald R. Cressey, is now in its seventh edition. The high personal esteem in which Sutherland was held is reflected in an obituary notice at the time of his death in 1950 by John Mueller, a colleague of Sutherland's at Indiana University:

Sutherland was amazingly open-minded, and his seminars constituted a collaborative inquiry rather than a transmission of information. He would spend hours with a student in office or home, discussing the problems which he was resolving in his own mind. With his soft-spoken demeanor, his readiness to listen to critical rebuttal, he impressed the student as a man of paternal wisdom. He never taught in terms of sarcasm, ridicule, or abuse. He never "taught" at all, but presided over a Socratic inquiry into human relations.

"White-Collar Criminality" is a rather informal paper, tailored to oral presentation. Although its sources are not indicated, it is evident that Matthew Josephson's The Robber Barons (1934) had exerted considerable influence on Sutherland. The polemical undertone of the paper, noted earlier, is apparent in arguable phrases, such as that which maintains that "white-collar crimes . . . create distrust, which . . . produces social disorganization on a large scale."

The initial reading in this part represents the work of a man who as late as 1948 could still be described as "the most dramatic and effective classroom teacher in the history of American sociology." Physically prepossessing (he stood 6 feet 6 inches tall and weighed more than 250 pounds), Edward A. Ross (1866–1951) was, in the words of a former student, "always a person whom one held in awe," and "to have been associated with him was a supremely choice life experience." Ross' extraordinary erudition and the unusual force and grace of his language, even with its now old-fashioned ring, bespeak the impact that he exerted both on his discipline and on his times. Ross' Social Control, for instance, was read in 1906 by Justice Oliver Wendell Holmes who, in typical fashion, then plunged into another Ross volume, Foundations of Sociology and, in equally typical fashion, felt impelled to communicate his enthusiasm to the President of the United States—Theodore Roosevelt—who, also apparently excited by the books, conveyed his appreciation to Ross.

Ross' observations in "The Criminaloid" were later incorporated into a book, Sin and Society (1907) which, according to William Jennings Bryan's biographer, was bound in scarlet and read surreptitiously by the nation's undergraduates, most of them first misled by the title into sampling the volume and later excited by the prose and the ideas into finishing it.

Albert Morris' article on "criminals of the upperworld" stands as the initial prolonged examination in textbook form of what came to be known as "white-collar crime." It should be noted that Sutherland employed essentially the same approach that Morris used to establish his theory and a worldwide reputation in criminology; first, concentrating intensive attention on the subject and, then, generalizing the wealth of information into theoretical relevance. For Morris, now retired after a distinguished career at Boston University, these early writings are looked back upon as words put down "when I was a child''—"Both criminology and sociology have grown since then," Morris observes, "as, I hope, I have too." Particularly noteworthy is Morris' declaration in the *Journal of Criminal Law, Criminology, and Police Science* (June, 1965) that "the attributes of white-collar crime that constitute the most significant characteristic are shared by offenders who wear blue collars, coveralls, uniforms and even dresses."

THE CRIMINALOID

Edward Alsworth Ross

The Edda has it that during Thor's visit to the giants he is challenged to lift a certain gray cat. "Our young men think it nothing but play." Thor puts forth his whole strength, but can at most bend the creature's back and lift one foot. On leaving, however, the mortified hero is told the secret of his failure. "The cat—ah! we were terror-stricken when we saw one paw off the floor; for that is the Midgard serpent which, tail in mouth, girds and keeps us the created world."

How often today the prosecutor who tries to lay by the heels some notorious public enemy is baffled by a mysterious resistance! The thews of Justice become as water; her sword turns to lath. Though the machinery of the law is strained askew, the evildoer remains erect, smiling, unscathed. At the end, the mortified champion of the law may be given to understand that, like Thor, he was contending with the established order, that he had unwittingly laid hold on a pillar of society and was therefore pitting himself against the reigning organization in local finance and politics.

Reprinted from *The Atlantic Monthly*, 99 (January, 1907), pp. 44–50.

The real weakness in the moral position of Americans is not their attitude toward the plain criminal, but their attitude toward the quasi-criminal. The shocking leniency of the public in judging conspicuous persons who have thriven by antisocial practices is not due, as many imagine, to sycophancy. Let a prominent man commit some offense in bad odor and the multitude flings its stones with right goodwill. The social lynching of the self-made magnate who put away his faded, toil-worn wife for the sake of a soubrette proves that the props of the old morality have not rotted through. Sex righteousness continues to be thus stiffly upheld simply because man has not invented *new* ways of wronging woman. So long ago were sex sins recognized and branded that the public, feeling sure of itself, lays on with promptness and emphasis. The slowness of this same public in lashing other kinds of transgression betrays, not sycophancy or unthinking admiration of success, but perplexity. The prosperous evildoers that bask undisturbed in popular favor have been careful to shun—or seem to shun—the familiar types of wickedness. Overlooked in Bible and prayer book, their obliquities lack the brimstone smell. Surpass as their misdeeds may in meanness and cruelty, there has not yet been time enough to store up strong emotion about them; and so the sight of them does not let loose the flood of wrath and abhorrence that rushes down upon the long-attainted sins.

The immunity enjoyed by the perpetrator of new sins has brought into being a class for which we may coin the term "criminaloid." (Like "asteroid," "crystalloid," "anthropoid," the term "criminaloid" is Latin–Greek, to be sure, but so is "sociology.") By this we designate those who prosper by flagitious practices which have not yet come under the effective ban of public opinion. Often, indeed, they are guilty in the eyes of the law; but since they are not culpable in the eyes of the public and in their own eyes, their spiritual attitude is not that of the criminal. The lawmaker may make their misdeeds crimes, but, so long as morality stands stock-still in the old tracks, they escape both punishment and ignominy. Unlike their low-browed cousins, they occupy the cabin rather than the steerage of society. Relentless pursuit hems in the criminals, narrows their range of success, denies them influence. The criminaloids, on the other hand, encounter but feeble opposition, and, since their practices are often more lucrative than the authentic crimes, they distance their more scrupulous rivals in business and politics and reap an uncommon worldly prosperity.

Of greater moment is the fact that the criminaloids lower the tone of the community. The criminal slinks in the shadow, menacing our purses but not our ideals; the criminaloid, however, does not belong to the half-world. Fortified by his connections with "legitimate business," "the regular party organization," perhaps with orthodoxy and the *bon ton*, he may even bestride his community like a Colossus. In his sight and in their own sight the old-style, square-dealing sort are as grasshoppers. Do we not hail him as "a man who does things," make him director of our banks and railroads, trustee of our hospitals and libraries? When Prince Henry visits us, do we not put him on the reception committee? He has far more initial weight in the community than has the arraigning clergyman, editor, or prosecutor. From his example and his excuses spreads a noxious influence that tarnishes the ideals of ingenuous youth on the threshold of active life. To put the soul of this pagan through a Bertillon system and set forth its marks of easy identification is, therefore, a sanitary measure demanded in the interest of public health.

The key to the criminaloid is not evil impulse, but moral insensibility. The director who speculates in the securities of his corporation, the banker who lends his depositors' money to himself under divers corporate aliases, the railroad official who grants a secret rebate for his private graft, the builder who hires walking delegates to harass his rivals with causeless strikes, the labor leader who instigates a strike in order to be paid for calling it off, the publisher who bribes his textbooks into the schools, these reveal in their faces nothing of the wolf or vulture. Nature has not foredoomed them to evil by a double dose of lust, cruelty, malice, greed, or jealousy. They are not degenerates tormented by monstrous cravings. They want nothing more than we all want—money, power, consideration —in a word, success; but they are in a hurry and they are not particular as to the means.

The criminaloid prefers to prey on the anonymous public. He is touchy about the individual victim and, if faced down, will even make him reparation out of the plunder gathered at longer range. Too squeamish and too prudent to practice treachery, brutality, and violence himself, he takes care to work through middlemen. Conscious of the antipodal difference between doing wrong and getting it done, he places out his dirty work. With a string of intermediaries between himself and the toughs who slug voters at the polls or the gang of navvies who break other navvies' heads with shovels on behalf of his electric line, he is able to keep his hands sweet and his boots clean. Thus he becomes a consumer of custom-made crime, a client of criminals, oftener a maker of criminals by persuading or requiring his subordinates to break the law. Of course, he must have "responsible" agents as valves to check the return flow of guilt from such proceedings. He shows them the goal, provides the money, insists on "results," but vehemently declines to know the foul methods by which alone his understrappers can get these "results." Not to bribe, but to employ and finance the briber; not to lie, but to admit to your editorial columns "paying matter"; not to commit perjury, but to hire men to homestead and make over to you claims they have sworn were entered in good faith and without collusion; not to cheat, but to promise a "rake-off" to a mysterious go-between in case your just assessment is cut down; not to rob on the highway, but to make the carrier pay you a rebate on your rival's shipments; not to shed innocent blood, but to bribe inspectors to overlook your neglect to install safety appliances—such are the ways of the criminaloid. He is a buyer rather than a practitioner of sin, and his middlemen spare him unpleasant details.

Secure in his quilted armor of lawyer-spun sophistries, the criminaloid promulgates an ethics which the public hails as a disinterested contribution to the philosophy of conduct. He invokes a pseudo-Darwinism to sanction the revival of outlawed and bygone tactics of struggle. Ideals of fellowship and peace are "unscientific." To win the game with the aid of a sleeveful of aces proves one's fitness to survive. A sack of spoils is nature's patent of nobility. A fortune is a personal attribute, as truly creditable as a straight back or a symmetrical face. Poverty, like the misshapen ear of the degenerate, proves inferiority. The wholesale fleecer of trusting, workaday people is a "Napoleon," a "superman." Labor defending its daily bread must, of course, obey the law; but "business," especially the "big proposition," may free itself of such trammels in the name of a "higher law." The censurers of the criminaloid are "pin-headed disturbers" who would imitate him if they had the chance or the brains.

The criminaloid is not antisocial by nature.   Nationwide is the zone of devastation of the adulterator, the rebater, the commercial freebooter, the fraud promoter, the humbug healer, the law-defying monopolist. Statewide is the burnt district of the corrupt legislator, the corporation-owned judge, the venal inspector, the bought bank examiner, the mercenary editor. But draw near the sinner and he whitens. If his fellowmen are wronged clear to his doorstep, he is criminal, not criminaloid. For the latter loses his sinister look, even takes on a benign aspect, as you come close. Within his home town, his ward, his circle, he is perhaps a good man, if judged by the simple old-time tests. Very likely he keeps his marriage vows, pays his debts, "mixes" well, stands by his friends, and has a contracted kind of public spirit. He is ready enough to rescue imperiled babies, protect maidens, or help poor widows. He is unevenly moral: oak in the family and clan virtues, but basswood in commercial and civic ethics. In some relations he is more sympathetic and generous than his critics, and he resents with genuine feeling the scorn of men who happen to have specialized in virtues other than those that appeal to him. Perhaps his point of honor is to give bribes, but not to take them; perhaps it is to "stay bought," that is, not to sell out to both sides at once.

This type is exemplified by the St. Louis boodler, who after accepting $25,000 to vote against a certain franchise was offered a larger sum to vote for it. He did so, but returned the first bribe. He was asked on the witness stand why he had returned it. "Because it wasn't mine!" he exclaimed, flushing with anger. "I hadn't earned it."

Seeing that the conventional sins are mostly close-range inflictions, whereas the long-range sins, being recent in type, have not yet been branded, the criminaloid receives from his community the credit for the close-in good he does, but not the shame of the remote evil he works.

Sometimes it is time instead of space that divides him from his victims. It is tomorrow's morrow that will suffer from the patent soothing syrup, the factory toil of infants, the grabbing of public lands, the butchery of forests, and the smuggling-in of coolies. In such a case, the short-sighted many exonerate him; only the far-sighted few mark him for what he is. Or it may be a social interval that leaves him his illusion of innocence. Like Robin Hood, the criminaloid spares his own sort and finds his quarry on another social plane. The labor grafter, the political "striker," and the blackmailing society editor prey upward; the franchise grabber, the fiduciary thief, and the frenzied financier prey downward. In either case, the sinner moves in an atmosphere of friendly approval and can still any smart of conscience with the balm of adulation.

It is above all the political criminaloid who is social. We are assured that the king of the St. Louis boodlers was "a good fellow—by nature, at first, then by profession. . . . Everywhere Big Ed went, there went a smile also and encouragement for your weakness, no matter what it was." The head of the Minneapolis ring was "a good fellow—a genial, generous reprobate . . . the best-loved man in the community . . . especially good to the poor." "Stars-and-Stripes Sam" was the nickname of a notorious looter of Philadelphia, who amassed influence by making "a practice of going to lodges, associations, brotherhoods, Sunday schools, and all sorts of public and private meetings, joining some, but making at all speeches patriotic and sentimental." The corrupt boss of another plundered city is reported to be "a charming character," possessing "goodness of heart and personal charm," and loved for his "genial, hearty kindness." He shrank from robbing anybody, but was equal, however, to robbing everybody. Of this type was Tweed, who had a "good heart," donated $50,000 to the poor of New York, and was sincerely loved by his clan.

It is now clear why hot controversy rages about the unmasked criminaloid. His home town, political clan, or social class insists that he is a good man maligned, that his detractors are purblind or jealous. The criminaloid is really a borderer between the camps of good and evil, and this is why he is so interesting. To run him to earth and brand him, as long ago pirates and traitors were branded, is the crying need of our time. For this Anak among malefactors, working unchecked in the rich field of sinister opportunities opened up by latter-day conditions, is society's most dangerous foe, more redoubtable by far than the plain criminal, because

he sports the livery of virtue and operates on a Titanic scale. Every year
that sees him pursue in insolent triumph his nefarious career raises up a
host of imitators and hurries society toward moral bankruptcy.

The criminaloid practices a protective mimicry of the good.   Because
so many good men are pious, the criminaloid covets a high seat in the
temple as a valuable private asset. Accordingly he is often to be found
in the assemblies of the faithful, zealously exhorting and bearing witness.
Onward thought he must leave to honest men; his line is strict orthodoxy.
The upright may fall slack in devout observances, but he cannot afford
to neglect his church connection. He needs it in his business. Such simu-
lation is easier because the godly are slow to drive out the open-handed
sinner who eschews the conventional sins. Many deprecate prying into
the methods of any brother "having money or goods ostensibly his own
or under a title not disapproved by the proper tribunals." They have, indeed, much warrant for insisting that the saving of souls rather than the
salvation of society is the true mission of the church.

The old Hebrew prophets, to be sure, were intensely alive to the
social effect of sin. They clamor against "making the ephah small and
the shekel great," falsifying the balances, "treading upon the poor." "Sensational," almost "demagogic," is their outcry against those who "turn
aside the stranger in his right," "take a bribe," "judge not the cause of
the fatherless," "oppress the hireling in his wages," "take increase," "withhold the pledge," "turn aside the poor in the gate from their right," "take
away the righteousness of the righteous from him." No doubt their stub-
born insistence that God wants "mercy and not sacrifice," despises feast
days, delights not in burnt offerings, will not hear the melody of viols, but
desires judgment to "run down as waters and righteousness as a mighty
stream," struck their contemporaries as extreme. Over against their antiquated outlook may be set the larger view that our concern should be for
the sinner rather than the sinned against. He is in peril of hell fire whereas
the latter risks nothing more serious than loss, misery, and death. After
all, sin's overshadowing effect is the pollution of the sinner's soul; and so
it may be more Christian not to scourge forth the traffickers from the
temple, but to leave them undisturbed where good seed may perchance
fall upon their souls.

Likewise, the criminaloid counterfeits the good citizen. He takes care
to meet all the conventional tests—flag worship, old-soldier sentiment,
observance of all the national holidays, perfervid patriotism, party regu-
larity and support. Full well he knows that giving a fountain or a park
or establishing a college chair on the Neolithic drama or the elegiac poetry
of the Chaldeans will more than outweigh the dodging of taxes, the
grabbing of streets, and the corrupting of city councils. Let him have his
way about charters and franchises, and he will zealously support that

"good government" which consists in sweeping the streets, holding down the "lid," and keeping taxes low. Nor will he fail in that scrupulous correctness of private and domestic life which confers respectability. In politics, to be sure, it is often necessary to play the "good fellow"; but in business and finance a studious conformity to the *convenances* is of the highest importance. The criminaloid must perforce seem sober and chaste, "a good husband and a kind father." If in this respect he offend, his hour of need will find him without support, and some callow reporter or district attorney will bowl him over like any vulgar criminal.

The criminaloid, therefore, puts on the whole armor of the good. He stands having his loins girt about with religiosity and wearing the breastplate of respectability. His feet are shod with ostentatious philanthropy; his head is encased in the helmet of spread-eagle patriotism. Holding in his left hand the buckler of worldly success and in his right the sword of "influence," he is "able to withstand in the evil day and, having done all, to stand."

The criminaloid plays the support of his local or special group against the larger society. The plain criminal can do himself no good by appealing to his "Mollies," "Larrikins," or "Mafiosi," for they have no social standing. The criminaloid, however, identifies himself with some legitimate group, and when arraigned he calls upon his group to protect its own. The politically influential Western land thieves stir up the slumbering local feeling against the "impertinent meddlers" of the forestry service and the land office. Safe behind the judicial dictum that "bribery is merely a conventional crime," the boodlers denounce their indicter as "blackening the fair name" of their state, and cry, "Stand up for the grand, old commonwealth of Nemaha!" The city boss harps artfully on the chord of local spirit and summons his bailiwick to rebuke the upstate reformers who would unhorse him. The law-breaking saloon keeper rallies merchants with the cry that enforcement of the liquor laws "hurts business." The labor grafter represents his exposure as a capitalist plot and calls upon all Truss Riveters to "stand pat" and "vindicate" him with a re-election. When a pious buccaneer is brought to bay, the Reverend Simon Magus thus sounds the denominational bugle: "Brother Barabbas is a loyal Newlight and a generous supporter of the Newlight Church. This vicious attack upon him is, therefore, a covert thrust at the Newlight body and ought to be resented by all the brethren." High finance, springing to the help of self-confessed thieves, meets an avenging public in this wise: "The integrity trust not only seeks with diabolical skill a reputation to blast, but, once blasted, it sinks into it wolfish fangs and gloats over the result of its fiendish act"—and adds, "This is not the true American spirit." Here twangs the ultimate chord! For in criminaloid philosophy it is "un-American" to wrench patronage from the hands of

spoilsmen, un-American to deal federal justice to rascals of state importance, un-American to pry into arrangements between shipper and carrier,
un-American to pry the truth out of reluctant magnates.

The claims of the wider community have no foe so formidable as the
scared criminaloid. He is the champion of the tribal order as opposed to
the civil order. By constantly stirring up on his own behalf some sort of
clannishness—local, sectional, partisan, sectarian, or professional—he re-
kindles dying jealousies and checks the rise of the civic spirit. It is in line
with this clannishness that he wants citizens to act together on a personal
basis. He does not know what it is to rally around a principle. Fellow
partisans are "friends." To scratch or to bolt is to "go back on your
friends." The criminaloid understands sympathy and antipathy as springs
of conduct, but justice strikes him as hardly human. The law is a club
to rescue your friends from and to smite your enemies with, but it has
no claim of its own. He expects his victims to "come back" at him if they
can, but he cannot see why everything may not be "arranged," "settled
out of court." Those inflexible prosecutors who hew to the line and cannot be "squared" impress him as fanatical and unearthly, as monsters who
find their pleasure in making trouble for others. For to his barbarian eyes
society is all a matter of "stand in."

So long as the public conscience is torpid, the criminaloid has no
sense of turpitude. In the dusk and the silence, the magic of clan opinion
converts his misdeeds into something rich and strange. For the clan lexi-
con tells him that a bribe is a "retaining fee," a railroad pass is a "courtesy," probing is "scandal mongering," the investigator is an "officious
busybody," a protest is a "howl," critics are "foul harpies of slander,"
public opinion is "unreasoning clamor," regulation is "meddling," any
inconvenient law is a "blue" law. As rebate giver he is sustained by the
assurance that "in Rome you must do as the Romans do." As disburser
of corruption funds he learns that he is but "asserting the higher law
which great enterprises have the right to command." Blessed phrases
these! What a lint for dressing wounds to self-respect! Often the reminiscent criminaloid, upon comparing his misdeeds with what his clans-
men stood ready to justify him in doing, is fain to exclaim with Lord
Clive, "By God, sir, at this moment I stand amazed at my own moderation!" When the revealing flash comes and the storm breaks, his difficulty
in getting the public's point of view is really pathetic. Indeed, he may
persist to the end in regarding himself as a martyr to "politics" or "yellow
journalism" or the "unctuous rectitude" of personal foes or "class envy"
in the guise of a moral wave.

*The criminaloid flourishes until the growth of morality overtakes the
growth of opportunities to prey.* It is of little use to bring law abreast
of the time if morality lags. In a swiftly changing society the law inevi-

tably tarries behind need, but public opinion tarries behind need even more. Where, as with us, the statute has little force of its own, the backwardness of public opinion nullifies the work of the legislator. Every added relation among men makes new chances for the sons of Belial. Wider interdependencies breed new treacheries. Fresh opportunities for illicit gain are continually appearing, and these are eagerly seized by the unscrupulous. The years between the advent of these new sins and the general recognition of their heinousness are few or many according to the alertness of the social mind. By the time they have been branded, the onward movement of society has created a fresh lot of opportunities, which are, in their turn, exploited with impunity. It is in this gap that the criminaloid disports himself. The narrowing of this gap depends chiefly on the faithfulness of the vedettes that guard the march of humanity. If the editor, writer, educator, clergyman, or public man is zealous to reconnoiter and instant to cry aloud the dangers that present themselves in our tumultuous social advance, a regulative opinion quickly forms and the new sins soon become odious.

Now, it is the concern of the criminaloids to delay this growth of conscience by silencing the alert vedettes. To intimidate the molders of opinion so as to confine the editor to the "news," the preacher to the "simple Gospel," the public man to the "party issues," the judge to his precedents, the teacher to his textbooks, and the writer to the classic themes—such are the tactics of the criminaloids. Let them but have their way, and the prophet's message, the sage's lesson, the scholar's quest, and the poet's dream would be sacrificed to the God of Things As They Were.

2

CRIMINALS OF THE UPPERWORLD

Albert Morris

One of the most difficult tasks of the criminologist is to define what he means by a criminal. No clean line can be drawn that will separate criminals from noncriminals nor mark off nicely the varying degrees of criminality. For sociological purposes, the legal concept of the criminal is unsuitable. Technical offenders who break laws that require no criminal intent or that have little moral significance are not apt to have the criminal nature that demands our interest. The criminologist would like to leave these pseudocriminals aside and consider only "real" criminals. Not all of these are of equal importance. Occasionally men of previously good behavior are overwhelmed by a crisis too great for them to conquer. It may never recur and they may never relapse. The defect may be chiefly within themselves (the psychoneurotic offender) or in their environment (unusual provocation). These men may lack steadiness, but they have not the criminal habit.

Among the real criminals, then, it is the habitual offenders who are

Reprinted from Albert Morris, *Criminology* (New York: Longmans, Green and Co., 1935), pp. 152–158.

truly important. Many of these may be thought of as delinquents grown older and more experienced, for men who have lived upright lives for twenty years are not likely to change their habits overnight. The causes of their criminality are written in the history of the forces that played through them during their childhood and youth. Their lives are the normal products of a faulty past. As naturally as other men have become salesmen or lawyers these men have become criminals. They are not even aware that their viewpoint differs from that of their fellows until the contrast is brought sharply to their attention. So far as they can see, all men are playing the same game in one guise or another. The criminal life has indeed become a habit, accepted as a matter of course. There is no more need to justify it than there is to justify the career of any artisan. . . .

It may be convenient to think of habitual criminals in two main groups: those of the upperworld and those of the underworld. The phrase "criminals of the upperworld" is suggested to define that numerous but never clearly identified group of criminals whose social position, intelligence, and criminal technique permit them to move among their fellow citizens virtually immune to recognition and prosecution as criminals. Between them and their upright fellow citizens there is no chasm, only a broad gray zone that shades insensibly into the black and the white on either side of it. In this shadowland are noncriminals whose ethical standards are more or less debatable and among these many near-criminals who, although keeping within the law, operate in a manner that would suffer by comparison with the open law-breaking of pickpockets or prowlers. Some idea of the range and importance of the activities of the criminals and near-criminals of the upperworld may be gained from the following samples which are illustrative rather than exhaustive:

1. Usurers, such as pawnbrokers and loan sharks, charging interest illegally at rates varying from 250 to 5000 per cent a year on loans totaling well over a billion dollars a year. The business of legitimate small-loan associations which charge high but legal rates of interest are not included in these figures.[1]

2. Operators of "bucket shops," who take their customers' money for the purchase of securities but who frequently do not buy them at all. When the market reaches strategic points they notify their customers that they have been sold out.[2]

3. High-pressure stockbrokers who sell good stocks by telephone or through slick salesmen to people living at a distance and then shift their customers' holdings with or without their consent to worthless stocks on which the brokers receive high commissions.[3]

4. Bankers who peg prices to maintain them at unwarranted levels until securities can be unloaded upon a gullible public.

5. Speculating manufacturers who lift the price of their stocks by postponing legitimate operating expenses so that their net earnings may appear high and insiders may sell stocks advantageously. Later, when the addition of postponed and current expenses apparently depresses earnings, they may repurchase their stocks at bargain prices.

6. Operators who pyramid stocks through holding companies to the point where the paper value of the securities issued is many times the actual value of the basic property.

7. Investment bankers who organize investment trusts to buy securities for their stockholders and who then proceed to play both sides of the market with excessive and unstipulated profits to themselves and with loss or ruin to the stockholders of the investment trusts for whom they have bought the speculative stocks which they, as investment bankers, were marketing. John Flynn reports as one sample of these operations the instance of a banking house that received $200,000 for reorganizing a corporation but made an estimated $15,000,000 out of its operations incident thereto.[4]

8. Directors who use inside information to make profits at the expense of the stockholders in whose interests they are presumed to be working. Flynn cites an instance illustrative of this practice: A board chairman persuaded his codirectors to go into the market and buy the stocks of another company in order to effect a merger. Empowered by his board to name a purchasing committee, he delayed a few days until he could purchase 60,000 shares for his personal account. When the committee then began its purchasing with a resulting rise in the price of the stock, the chairman sold his own shares to his own company at a profit of $165,000. When a stockholder who learned of the operation complained to the board of directors, they considered the matter and reported that no wrong had been done.[5]

9. Investment bankers who sell bonds advertised as backed by first mortgages on property worth twice their value when they know that the real value of the property does not exceed the mortgage.

10. Manufacturers, as noted by Stuart Chase, who take advantage of a virtual monopoly control over natural resources, processes, or inventions to gouge consumers to the limit of their willingness to pay.[6]

11. Manufacturers who sell goods such as cosmetics, toilet articles, preserves, patent medicines (some of them useless, adulterated, or harmful) at many times their value through clever but misleading high-pressure advertising.

12. Grafters in business, such as purchasing agents who must be well paid before they will place orders with concerns desirous of making sales through them or employees who pad expense accounts.

13. Grafters in political offices who seek and receive pay for doing a thousand and one legitimate and illegitimate favors.

14. Corporations that exploit the people of small, unstable nations in which they do business.

15. Employers who exploit the labor of women and children in industry contrary to law.

16. Theater managers who wink at the admission of children to certain motion-picture performances forbidden to them by law.

17. Working girls who add to their earnings by part-time prostitution.

18. Storekeepers and managers of amusement resorts who sell goods or services illegally on the side: for example, narcotics, opportunities for prostitution, or gambling.

19. Contractors and builders who substitute materials inferior to those called for in their specifications in order to increase their margin of profit.

20. Law enforcement officials who break laws in order to enforce others: for example, the common use of the so-called "third degree" as a means of securing evidence or confessions.

21. Organized bodies active in depriving citizens of their political rights as guaranteed, for example, under Amendments 5, 14, and 15 of the Constitution of the United States.

22. Government officials who deliberately use untruthful, misleading, and fraudulent propaganda to stir the people to a particular course of action: for example, the manufacturing of false evidence against a nation to induce citizens to desire to declare war against it. Such activities are analogous to the sale of fur coats, oil stock, or patent medicines by the use of clever but false and misleading claims.

23. Governments that with deliberate malice aforethought disregard international law when it is expedient for them to do so.[7] Probably no great nation has been altogether free from actions of this sort. The seizure and appropriation of neutral vessels with cargoes consigned to neutral ports, the seizure and search of neutral citizens, and the forceful taking of territory from peaceful nations are examples in point. The remark of Premier Asquith that "We are not going to allow our efforts to be strangled in a network of judicial niceties. . . . Under existing circumstances there is no form of economic pressure to which we do not consider ourselves entitled to resort"[8] expresses precisely the attitude, if not the words, of many individual criminals of the underworld who have not been able to get what they want by legitimate means and who finally have been pushed into a tight corner by their illegitimate activities.

These are but a few examples of the criminals of the upperworld.[9] In many instances, the complexity and privacy of their dealings makes a fair identification of them difficult. It is not always easy to evaluate their motives and their methods. This is especially true if our general ethical notions are befogged or dulled by the near universality of sharp, if not illegal, business practices. Yet it needs to be emphasized that the criminals of the upperworld are genuine, not metaphorical, criminals. They may not be recognized as such because we have fallen into the unjustifiable habit of limiting that appellation to the obstreperous, socially inferior denizens of the underworld; the day laborers in the field of crime.

Unlike the criminals of the underworld, the permissive criminals of the upperworld have never been marked off and dramatized as a distinct group upon which public disapproval could be focused. They have never been rounded up by the police nor gathered together in a prison where they could be examined, crushed into some semblance of uniformity, and talked about as a special type of human being. Instead, they have been scattered among us as friends and fellow members in clubs and churches. They have contributed to organizations for the treatment of juvenile delinquents and have served in legislatures passing laws to check crime.

They differ from their upright brethren only in being ethically less sensitive at certain points, due possibly to nature and their persistent closeness to their own particular type of crime. It is doubtful if they look upon themselves as criminals. Their attitude is not likely to be self-critical and they may accept quite naïvely the happy opinion that others hold about them. Failure to be caught and brought to account keeps many of them from being jolted out of their complacency. Their conduct becomes apparent in its true light only when a crisis reveals the details of their methods.

Possibly there are among the tolerated acts many that ought not to have been placed on the statute books as crimes. Passing a law is not always the wisest way to prevent undesirable conduct. Some acts are not easily controlled by the machinery of law enforcement. Is it possible, also, that we have been inveigled by idealists to write into the statutes an ethical code in some respects higher than that by which we care to live? Is it a guilty public conscience that prevents the rigid enforcement of laws, lest our own movements be uncomfortably restricted? Ought we to limit the criminal law to the control of antisocial acts of a crude physical sort and use different methods to control other socially undesirable activities? There seems to be little likelihood of a successful encounter with upperworld crime until issues of this sort are squarely faced.

Obviously, as the facts now stand before us, the criminals of the upperworld are real, numerous, and near at hand. It is likely that they are more costly in an economic sense than those of the underworld. They may well turn out to be more of a menace to society in every way than their less pleasant counterparts, the underprivileged criminal class. Certainly the matter of upperworld crime deserves serious study as an authentic part of the crime problem. Possibly little can be done with it short of fundamental changes in general social attitudes, as, for one example, a new economic perspective in which the competitive struggle for wealth will be secondary and will seem less desirable than a cooperative struggle for human welfare.

Notes

1. See Arthur M. Murphy, "Small-Loan Usury," in Ernest D. MacDougall, ed., *Crime for Profit* (Boston: Stratford Co., 1933), pp. 205–226.
2. See David H. Jackson, "What Are Financial Rackets?" in MacDougall, *op. cit.*, pp. 73–96.
3. *Ibid.*
4. John T. Flynn, "Financial Racketeering," in MacDougall, *op. cit.*, pp. 1–12.
5. *Ibid.*
6. Stuart Chase, *A New Deal* (New York: Macmillan, 1932), chap. 1.
7. Harry Elmer Barnes, "Mercenary Crime and International Relations," in Mac-Dougall, *op. cit.*, pp. 296–324.
8. Quoted in *ibid.*, p. 321.
9. See also John T. Flynn, *Investment Trusts Gone Wrong!* (New York: New Republic, 1930), and *Graft in Business* (New York: Vanguard, 1931); Stuart Chase and F. J. Schlink, *Your Money's Worth* (New York: Macmillan, 1928); Arthur J. Cramp, ed., *Nostrums and Quackery* (Chicago: American Medical Association, 1911); Dennis Tilden Lynch, *Criminals and Politicians* (New York: Macmillan, 1932); Francis Perkins, "The Cost of a Five-Dollar Dress," *Survey Graphic*, 22 (February, 1933), pp. 75–78; *Time* (January 30, 1933), p. 45, and (April 17, 1933), p. 34.

3

WHITE-COLLAR CRIMINALITY

Edwin H. Sutherland

This paper is concerned with crime in relation to business. The economists are well acquainted with business methods but not accustomed to consider them from the point of view of crime; many sociologists are well acquainted with crime but not accustomed to consider it as expressed in business. This paper is an attempt to integrate these two bodies of knowledge. More accurately stated, it is a comparison of crime in the upper, or white-collar, class, which is composed of respectable, or at least respected, business and professional men; and crime in the lower class, which is composed of persons of low socioeconomic status. This comparison is made for the purpose of developing the theories of criminal behavior, not for the purpose of muckraking or of reforming anything except criminology.

The criminal statistics show unequivocally that crime, *as popularly conceived and officially measured,* has a high incidence in the lower class and a low incidence in the upper class; less than 2 per cent of the persons committed to prisons in a year belong to the upper class. These statistics

Reprinted from *American Sociological Review*, 5 (February, 1940), pp. 1–12.

refer to criminals handled by the police, the criminal and juvenile courts, and the prisons, and to such crimes as murder, assault, burglary, robbery, larceny, sex offenses, and drunkenness; it does not include traffic violations.

The criminologists have used the case histories and criminal statistics derived from these agencies of criminal justice as their principal data. From them, they have derived general theories of criminal behavior. These theories are that, since crime is concentrated in the lower class, it is caused by poverty or by personal and social characteristics believed to be associated statistically with poverty, including feeblemindedness, psychopathic deviations, slum neighborhoods, and "deteriorated" families. This statement, of course, does not do justice to the qualifications and variations in the conventional theories of criminal behavior, but it presents correctly their central tendency.

The thesis of this paper is that the conception and explanations of crime which have just been described are misleading and incorrect, that crime is, in fact, not closely correlated with poverty or with the psychopathic and sociopathic conditions associated with poverty, and that an adequate explanation of criminal behavior must proceed along quite different lines. The conventional explanations are invalid principally because they are derived from biased samples. The samples are biased in that they have not included vast areas of criminal behavior of persons not in the lower class. One of these neglected areas is the criminal behavior of business and professional men, which will be analyzed in this paper.

The "robber barons" of the last half of the nineteenth century were white-collar criminals, as practically everyone now agrees. Their attitudes are illustrated by these statements: Colonel Vanderbilt asked, "You don't suppose you can run a railroad in accordance with the statutes, do you?" A. B. Stickney, a railroad president, said to sixteen other railroad presidents in the home of J. P. Morgan in 1890, "I have the utmost respect for you gentlemen, individually; but as railroad presidents I wouldn't trust you with my watch out of my sight." Charles Francis Adams said, "The difficulty in railroad management . . . lies in the covetousness, want of good faith, and low moral tone of railway managers, in the complete absence of any high standard of commercial honesty."

The present-day white-collar criminals, who are more suave and deceptive than the "robber barons," are represented by Krueger, Stavisky, Whitney, Mitchell, Foshay, Insull, the Van Sweringens, Musica-Coster, Fall, Sinclair, the many other merchant princes and captains of finance and industry, and by a host of lesser followers. Their criminality has been demonstrated again and again in the investigations of land offices, railways, insurance, munitions, banking, public utilities, stock exchanges, the oil industry, real estate, reorganization committees, receiverships, bankruptcies, and politics. Individual cases of such criminality are reported frequently, and in many periods more important crime news may be found on the financial pages of newspapers than on the front pages. White-collar criminality is found in every occupation, as can be discovered readily in casual conversation with a representative of an occupation by asking him, "What crooked practices are found in your occupation?"

White-collar criminality in business is expressed most frequently in the form of misrepresentation in financial statements of corporations, manipulation in the stock exchange, commercial bribery, bribery of public officials directly or indirectly in order to secure favorable contracts and legislation, misrepresentation in advertising and salesmanship, embezzlement and misapplication of funds, short weights and measures and misgrading of commodities, tax frauds, misapplication of funds in receiverships and bankruptcies. These are what Al Capone called "the legitimate rackets." These and many others are found in abundance in the business world.

In the medical profession, which is here used as an example because it is probably less criminalistic than some other professions, are found illegal sale of alcohol and narcotics, abortion, illegal services to underworld criminals, fraudulent reports and testimony in accident cases, extreme cases of unnecessary treatment, fake specialists, restriction of competition, and fee splitting. Fee splitting is a violation of a specific law in many states and a violation of the conditions of admission to the practice of medicine in all. The physician who participates in fee splitting tends to send his patients to the surgeon who will give him the largest fee rather than to the surgeon who will do the best work. It has been reported that two-thirds of the surgeons in New York City split fees and that more than one-half of the physicians in a central western city who answered a questionnaire on this point favored fee splitting.

These varied types of white-collar crimes in business and the professions consist principally of violation of delegated or implied trust, and many of them can be reduced to two categories: (1) misrepresentation of asset values and (2) duplicity in the manipulation of power. The first is approximately the same as fraud or swindling; the second is similar to the double-cross. The latter is illustrated by the corporation director who, acting on inside information, purchases land which the corporation will need and sells it at a fantastic profit to his corporation. The principle of this duplicity is that the offender holds two antagonistic positions, one of which is a position of trust that is violated, generally by misapplication of funds, in the interest of the other position. A football coach, permitted to referee a game in which his own team is playing, would illustrate this antagonism of positions. Such situations cannot be completely avoided in a complicated business structure, but many concerns make a practice of assuming such antagonistic functions and regularly violating the trust thus delegated to them. When compelled by law to make a separation of their functions, they make a nominal separation and continue by subterfuge to maintain the two positions.

An accurate statistical comparison of the crimes of the two social classes is not available. The most extensive evidence regarding the nature and prevalence of white-collar criminality is found in the reports of the larger investigations to which reference was made. Because of its scattered character, that evidence is assumed rather than summarized here. A few statements will be presented as illustrations rather than as proof of the prevalence of this criminality.

The Federal Trade Commission in 1920 reported that commercial bribery was a prevalent and common practice in many industries. In certain chain stores, the net shortage in weights was sufficient to pay 3.4 per cent on the investment in those commodities. Of the cans of ether sold to the Army in 1923 to 1925, 70 per cent were rejected because of impurities. In Indiana, during the summer of 1934, 40 per cent of the ice-cream samples tested in a routine manner by the Division of Public Health were in violation of law. The Comptroller of the Currency in 1908 reported that violations of law were found in 75 per cent of the banks examined in a three-month period. Lie detector tests of all employees in several Chicago banks, supported in almost all cases by confessions, showed that 20 per cent of them had stolen bank property. A public accountant estimated, in the period prior to the Securities and Exchange Commission, that 80 per cent of the financial statements of corporations were misleading. James M. Beck said, "Diogenes would have been hard put to it to find an honest man in the Wall Street which I knew as a corporation lawyer" (in 1916).

White-collar criminality in politics, which is generally recognized as fairly prevalent, has been used by some as a rough gauge by which to measure white-collar criminality in business. James A. Farley said, "The standards of conduct are as high among officeholders and politicians as they are in commercial life," and Cermak, while mayor of Chicago, said, "There is less graft in politics than in business." John Flynn wrote, "The average politician is the merest amateur in the gentle art of graft compared with his brother in the field of business." And Walter Lippmann wrote, "Poor as they are, the standards of public life are so much more social than those of business that financiers who enter politics regard themselves as philanthropists."

These statements obviously do not give a precise measurement of the relative criminality of the white-collar class, but they are adequate evidence that crime is not so highly concentrated in the lower class as the usual statistics indicate. Also, these statements obviously do not mean that every business and professional man is a criminal, just as the usual theories do not mean that every man in the lower class is a criminal. On the other hand, the preceding statements refer in many cases to the leading corporations in America and are not restricted to the disreputable business and professional men who are called quacks, ambulance chasers, bucket-shop operators, dead-beats, and fly-by-night swindlers.*

The financial cost of white-collar crime is probably several times as great as the financial cost of all the crimes which are customarily regarded as the "crime problem." An officer of a chain grocery store in one year embezzled $600,000, which was six times as much as the annual losses from five hundred burglaries and robberies of the stores in that chain. Public enemies numbered one to six secured $130,000 by burglary and robbery in 1938, while the sum stolen by Krueger is estimated as $250,-000,000, or nearly two thousand times as much. The *New York Times* in 1931 reported four cases of embezzlement in the United States with a loss of more than a million dollars each and a combined loss of $9 million. Although a million-dollar burglar or robber is practically unheard of, these million-dollar embezzlers are small-fry among white-collar criminals. The estimated loss to investors in one investment trust from 1929 to 1935 was $580,000,000, due primarily to the fact that 75 per cent of the values in the portfolio were in securities of affiliated companies, although it advertised the importance of diversification in investments and its expert services in selecting safe securities. In Chicago, the claim was made six years ago that householders had lost $54,000,000 in two years during the administration of a city sealer who granted immunity from inspection to stores which provided Christmas baskets for his constituents.

The financial loss from white-collar crime, great as it is, is less important than the damage to social relations. White-collar crimes violate trust and therefore create distrust, which lowers social morale and produces social disorganization on a large scale. Other crimes produce relatively little effect on social institutions or social organization.

White-collar crime is real crime. It is not ordinarily called crime, and calling it by this name does not make it worse, just as refraining from calling it crime does not make it better than it otherwise would be. It is called crime here in order to bring it within the scope of criminology, which is justified because it is in violation of the criminal law. The crucial question in this analysis is the criterion of violation of the criminal law.

---

* Perhaps it should be repeated that "white-collar" (upper) and "lower" classes merely designate persons of high- and low-socioeconomic status. Income and amount of money involved in the crime are not the sole criteria. Many persons of "low" socioeconomic status are "white-collar" criminals in the sense that they are well dressed, well educated, and have high incomes; but "white-collar" as used in this paper means "respected," "socially accepted and approved," "looked up to." Some people in this class may not be well dressed or well educated or have high incomes, although the "upper" classes usually exceed the "lower" classes in these respects, as well as in social status.

Conviction in the criminal court, which is sometimes suggested as the criterion, is not adequate because a large proportion of those who commit crimes are not convicted in criminal courts. This criterion, therefore, needs to be supplemented. When it is supplemented, the criterion of the crimes of one class must be kept consistent in general terms with the criterion of the crimes of the other class. The definition should not be the spirit of the law for white-collar crimes and the letter of the law for other crimes, or in other respects be more liberal for one class than for the other. Since this discussion is concerned with the conventional theories of the criminologists, the criterion of white-collar crime must be justified in terms of the procedures of those criminologists in dealing with other crimes. The criterion of white-collar crimes, as here proposed, supplements convictions in the criminal courts in four respects, in each of which the extension is justified because the criminologists who present the conventional theories of criminal behavior make the same extension in principle.

First, other agencies than the criminal court must be included, for the criminal court is not the only agency which makes official decisions regarding violations of the criminal law. In many states, the juvenile court, dealing largely with offenses of the children of the poor, is not under the criminal jurisdiction. The criminologists have made much use of case histories and statistics of juvenile delinquents in constructing their theories of criminal behavior. This justifies the inclusion of agencies other than the criminal court that deal with white-collar offenses. The most important of these agencies are the administrative boards, bureaus, or commissions; and much of their work, although certainly not all, consists of cases that are in violation of the criminal law. The Federal Trade Commission recently ordered several automobile companies to stop advertising their interest rate on installment purchases as 6 per cent, since it was actually 11½ per cent. Also it filed complaint against *Good Housekeeping*, one of the Hearst publications, charging that its seals led the public to believe that all products bearing those seals had been tested in their laboratories, which was contrary to fact. Each of these involves a charge of dishonesty, which might have been tried in a criminal court as fraud. A large proportion of the cases before these boards should be included in the data of the criminologists. Failure to do so is a principal reason for the bias in their samples and the errors in their generalizations.

Second, for both classes, behavior that would have a reasonable expectancy of conviction if tried in a criminal court or substitute agency should be defined as criminal. In this respect, convictability rather than actual conviction should be the criterion of criminality. The criminologists would not hesitate to accept as data a verified case history of a person who was a criminal but who had never been convicted. Similarly, it is justifiable to include white-collar criminals who have not been convicted, provided reliable evidence is available. Evidence regarding such cases appears in many civil suits, such as stockholders' suits and patent-infringement suits. These cases might have been referred to the criminal court but they were referred to the civil court because the injured party was more interested in securing damages than in seeing punishment inflicted. This also happens in embezzlement cases, regarding which surety companies have much evidence. In a short consecutive series of embezzlements known to a surety company, 90 per cent were not prosecuted because prosecution would interfere with restitution or salvage. The evidence in cases of embezzlement is generally conclusive and would probably have been sufficient to justify conviction in all cases in this series.

Third, behavior should be defined as criminal if conviction is avoided merely because of pressure which is brought to bear on the court or substitute agency. Gangsters and racketeers have been relatively immune in many cities because of their pressure on prospective witnesses and public officials; professional thieves, such as pickpockets and confidence men who do not use strong-arm methods, are even more frequently immune. The conventional criminologists do not hesitate to include the life histories of such criminals as data, because they understand the generic relation of the pressures to the failure to convict. Similarly, white-collar criminals are relatively immune because of the class bias of the courts and the power of their class to influence the implementation and administration of the law. This class bias affects not merely present-day courts, but also, to a much greater degree, affected the earlier courts which established the precedents and rules of procedure of the present-day courts. Consequently, it is justifiable to interpret the actual or potential failures of conviction in the light of known facts regarding the pressures brought to bear on the agencies which deal with offenders.

Fourth, persons who are accessory to a crime should be included among white-collar criminals as they are among other criminals. When the Federal Bureau of Investigation deals with a case of kidnapping, it is not content with catching the offenders who carried away the victim; they may catch and the court may convict twenty-five other persons who assisted by secreting the victim, negotiating the ransom, or putting the ransom money into circulation. On the other hand, the prosecution of white-collar criminals frequently stops with one offender. Political graft almost always involves collusion between politicians and businessmen, but prosecutions are generally limited to the politicians. Judge Manton was found guilty of accepting $664,000 in bribes, but the six or eight important commercial concerns that paid the bribes have not been prosecuted. Pendergast, the late boss of Kansas City, was convicted for failure to report as a part of his income $315,000 received in bribes from insurance companies, but the insurance companies which paid the bribes have not been prosecuted. In an investigation of an embezzlement by the president of a bank, at least a dozen other violations of law which were related to this embezzlement and which involved most of the other officers of the bank and the officers of the clearing house were discovered, but none of the others was prosecuted.

This analysis of the criterion of white-collar criminality results in the conclusion that a description of white-collar criminality in general terms will be also a description of the criminality of the lower class. The respects in which the crimes of the two classes differ are the incidentals rather than the essentials of criminality. They differ principally in the implementation of the criminal laws that apply to them. The crimes of the lower class are handled by policemen, prosecutors, and judges with penal sanctions in the form of fines, imprisonment, and death. The crimes of the upper class either result in no official action at all, or result in suits for damages in civil courts, or are handled by inspectors and by administrative boards or commissions with penal sanctions in the form of warnings, orders to cease and desist, occasionally the loss of a license, and only in extreme cases by fines or prison sentences. Thus, the white-collar criminals are segregated administratively from other criminals and, largely as a consequence of this, are not regarded as real criminals by themselves, the general public, or the criminologists.

This difference in the implementation of the criminal law is due principally to the difference in the social position of the two types of offenders. Judge Woodward, when imposing sentence upon the officials of the H. O. Stone and Company, bankrupt real estate firm in Chicago, who had been convicted in 1933 of the use of the mails to defraud, said to them, "You are men of affairs, of experience, of refinement and culture, of excellent reputation and standing in the business and social world." That statement might be used as a general characterization of white-collar criminals, for they are oriented basically to legitimate and respectable careers. Because of their social status they have a loud voice in determining what goes into the statutes and how the criminal law as it affects themselves is implemented and administered. This may be illustrated from the Pure Food and Drug Law. Between 1879 and 1906, 140 pure food and drug bills were presented in Congress and all failed because of the importance of the persons who would be affected. It took a highly dramatic performance by Dr. Wiley in 1906 to induce Congress to enact the law. That law, however, did not create a new crime, just as the federal Lindbergh kidnapping law did not create a new crime; it merely provided a more efficient implementation of a principle which had been formulated previously in state laws. When an amendment to this law, which would bring within the scope of its agents fraudulent statements made over the radio or in the press, was presented to Congress, publishers and advertisers organized support and sent a lobby to Washington which successfully fought the amendment principally under the slogans of "freedom of the press" and "dangers of bureaucracy." This proposed amendment also would not have created a new crime, for the state laws already prohibited fraudulent statements over the radio or in the press; it would have implemented the law so it could have been enforced. Finally, the administration has not been able to enforce the law as it has desired because of the pressures by the offenders against the law, sometimes brought to bear through the head of the Department of Agriculture, sometimes through congressmen who threaten cuts in the appropriation, and sometimes by others. The statement of Daniel Drew, a pious old fraud, describes the criminal law with some accuracy: "Law is like a cobweb; it's made for flies and the smaller kinds of insects, so to speak, but lets the big bumblebees break through. When technicalities of the law stood in my way, I have always been able to brush them aside easy as anything."

The preceding analysis should be regarded neither as an assertion that all efforts to influence legislation and its administration are reprehensible nor as a particularistic interpretation of the criminal law. It means only that the upper class has greater influence in molding the criminal law and its administration to its own interests than does the lower class. The privileged position of white-collar criminals before the law results to a slight extent from bribery and political pressures, but principally from the respect in which they are held and without special effort on their part. The most powerful group in medieval society secured relative immunity by "benefit of clergy," and now our most powerful groups secure relative immunity by "benefit of business or profession."

In contrast with the power of the white-collar criminals is the weakness of their victims. Consumers, investors, and stockholders are unorganized, lack technical knowledge, and cannot protect themselves. Daniel Drew, after taking a large sum of money by sharp practice from Vanderbilt in the Erie deal, concluded that it was a mistake to take money from a powerful man on the same level as himself and declared that in the future he would confine his efforts to outsiders, scattered all over the country, who wouldn't be able to organize and fight back. White-collar criminality flourishes at points where powerful business and professional men come in contact with persons who are weak. In this respect, it is similar to stealing candy from a baby. Many of the crimes of the lower class, on the other hand, are committed against persons of wealth and power in the form of burglary and robbery. Because of this difference in the comparative power of the victims, the white-collar criminals enjoy relative immunity.

Embezzlement is an interesting exception to white-collar criminality in this respect. Embezzlement is usually theft from an employer by an employee, and the employee is less capable of manipulating social and legal forces in his own interest than is the employer. As might have been expected, the laws regarding embezzlement were formulated long before laws for the protection of investors and consumers.

The theory that criminal behavior in general is due either to poverty or to the psychopathic and sociopathic conditions associated with poverty can now be shown to be invalid for three reasons. First, the generalization is based on a biased sample which omits almost entirely the behavior of white-collar criminals. The criminologists have restricted their data, for reasons of convenience and ignorance rather than of principle, largely to cases dealt with in criminal courts and juvenile courts, and these agencies are used principally for criminals from the lower economic strata. Consequently, their data are grossly biased from the point of view of the economic status of criminals and their generalization that criminality is closely associated with poverty is not justified.

Second, the generalization that criminality is closely associated with poverty obviously does not apply to white-collar criminals. With a small number of exceptions, they are not in poverty, were not reared in slums or badly deteriorated families, and are not feebleminded or psychopathic. They were seldom problem children in their earlier years and did not appear in juvenile courts or child-guidance clinics. The proposition, derived from the data used by the conventional criminologists, that "the criminal of today was the problem child of yesterday" is seldom true of white-collar criminals. The idea that the causes of criminality are to be found almost exclusively in childhood is similarly fallacious. Even if poverty were extended to include the economic stresses which afflict business in a period of depression, it is not closely correlated with white-collar criminality. Probably at no time within the last fifty years have white-collar crimes in the field of investments and of corporate management been so extensive as during the boom period of the twenties.

Third, the conventional theories do not even explain lower-class criminality. The sociopathic and psychopathic factors which have been emphasized doubtless have something to do with crime causation, but these factors have not been related to a general process that is found both in white-collar criminality and lower-class criminality; therefore, they do not explain the criminality of either class. They may explain the manner or method of crime—why lower-class criminals commit burglary or robbery rather than false pretenses.

In view of these defects in the conventional theories, a hypothesis is needed that will explain both white-collar criminality and lower-class criminality. For reasons of economy, simplicity, and logic, the hypothesis should apply to both classes, for this will make possible the analysis of causal factors freed from the encumbrances of the administrative devices which have led criminologists astray. Shaw and McKay and others, working exclusively in the field of lower-class crime, have found the conventional theories inadequate to account for variations within the data of lower-class crime and from that point of view have been working toward an explanation of crime in terms of a more general social process. Such efforts will be greatly aided by the procedure which has been described.

The hypothesis which is here suggested as a substitute for the conventional theories is that white-collar criminality, just as other systematic criminality, is learned; that it is learned in direct or indirect association with those who already practice the behavior; and that those who learn this criminal behavior are segregated from frequent and intimate contacts with law-abiding behavior. Whether a person becomes a criminal or not is determined largely by the comparative frequency and intimacy of his contacts with the two types of behavior. This may be called the "process of differential association." It is a genetic explanation both of white-collar criminals and lower-class criminality. Those who become white-collar criminals generally start their careers in good neighborhoods and good homes, graduate from colleges with some idealism, and, with little selection on their part, get into particular business situations in which criminality is practically a folkway, becoming inducted into that system of behavior just as into any other folkway. The lower-class criminals generally start their careers in deteriorated neighborhoods and families, find delinquents at hand from whom they acquire the attitudes toward, and the techniques of, crime through association with delinquents and through partial segregation from law-abiding people. The essentials of the process are the same for the two classes of criminals. This is not entirely a process of assimilation, for inventions are frequently made, perhaps more frequently in white-collar crime than in lower-class crime. The inventive geniuses for the lower-class criminals are generally professional criminals, while the inventive geniuses for many kinds of white-collar crime are generally lawyers.

A second general process is social disorganization in the community. Differential association culminates in crime because the community is not organized solidly against that behavior. The law is pressing in one direction and other forces are pressing in the opposite direction. In business, the "rules of the game" conflict with the legal rules. A businessman who wants to obey the law is driven by his competitors to adopt their methods. This is well illustrated by the persistence of commercial bribery in spite of the strenuous efforts of business organizations to eliminate it. Groups and individuals are individuated; they are more concerned with their specialized group or individual interests than with the larger welfare. Consequently, it is not possible for the community to present a solid front in opposition to crime. The better business bureaus and crime commissions, composed of businessmen and professional men, attack burglary, robbery, and cheap swindles but overlook the crimes of their own members. The forces which impinge on the lower class are similarly in conflict. Social disorganization affects the two classes in similar ways.

I have presented a brief and general description of white-collar criminality on a framework of argument regarding theories of criminal behavior. That argument, stripped of the description, may be stated in the following propositions:

1. White-collar criminality is real criminality, being in all cases in violation of the criminal law.

2. White-collar criminality differs from lower-class criminality principally in an implementation of the criminal law, which segregates white-collar criminals administratively from other criminals.

3. The theories of the criminologists that crime is due to poverty or to psychopathic and sociopathic conditions statistically associated with poverty are invalid because, first, they are derived from samples which are grossly biased with respect to socioeconomic status; second, they do not apply to the white-collar criminals; and third, they do not even explain the criminality of the lower class, since the factors are not related to a general process characteristic of all criminality.

4. A theory of criminal behavior which will explain both white-collar criminality and lower-class criminality is needed.

5. A hypothesis of this nature is suggested in terms of differential association and social disorganization.

CORPORATE AND BUSINESS WHITE-COLLAR CRIME

Ready access to the records of administrative agencies and federal regulatory boards undoubtedly conditioned Sutherland's concentration upon corporate violations to epitomize his newly minted concept of white-collar crime. "Crime of Corporations," the first paper in Part II, was read before the Toynbee Club, a group of sociology students and faculty members at DePauw University, during the spring of 1948. In an informal manner, Sutherland spelled out for his audience the ingredients that were to be arrayed more formally and formidably in his classic monograph, *White Collar Crime*. The major drawback in the paper remains its inability to differentiate between the corporations and their management personnel. It was the absence of relevant material going to the heart of his concept that forced Sutherland to "humanize" or "anthropomorphize" the corporations and which seems to have led him into taking rather too literally the personifications that he himself had created.

Corporations are, of course, legal entities, and they may be subjected to criminal prosecutions, though a corporation obviously cannot be imprisoned. For the purpose of criminological analysis, however, corporations cannot readily be considered persons, except by recourse to the type of extrapolatory fiction that once brought about the judicial punishment of inanimate objects. Sutherland attempted to resolve this dilemma by maintaining, not without some acerbity, that the crimes of corporations are the crimes of their executives and managers, an assertion that contains some truth, some inaccuracy, and a good deal of uncertainty. The sweeping allegation that "the ideal businessman and the large corporation are very much like the professional thief" requires a good deal more refinement than a summary of corporate violations, a listing of presumed attitudes of corporate executives, or a comparison of these to selected characteristics of professional thieves. Nonetheless, Sutherland's prose makes a strong impact—his spare, staccato style and his forceful insistence that acts which cause criminally harmful consequences should be viewed as criminal acts.

Violations of wartime regulations, particularly those within the ken of the Office of Price Administration, provide material for the examination of white-collar crime conducted by Marshall B. Clinard, presently a professor of sociology at the University of Wisconsin. Such violations took place in an atmosphere marked by notable ambivalence. On the one hand, there was an overriding patriotic *esprit de corps* and commitment to the objectives of World War II. On the other hand, in some commercial enterprises and civilian activities there was virtually ubiquitous flaunting of government regulations designed to serve the war effort and maintain the economy.

Quite notable in Clinard's presentation is the careful documentation of public opinion on wartime regulations, a documentation drawn from government and private surveys. Besides its substantive contribution, the Clinard article illustrates the insights possible from academic views and expertise employed in a government enterprise, redounding to the benefit of both scholarship and the public service.

Clinard's work is noteworthy as well for its intellectual kinship with Sutherland's earlier contributions, as a deliberate effort is made to address the subject of wartime regulations so that cumulative and complementary material is forthcoming. Clinard, for example, measures his data against Sutherland's theory of differential association, finding "several limitations" in Sutherland's position. For Clinard, "there can be no single explanation of the OPA violations," although he suggests that intensive examination of the "life organizations of the violators" could yield fruitful conclusions; and he recommends, in particular, concentration on the "different integration of the several roles which the individual plays in society."

Clinard's theme reappears in the paper that follows, Robert E. Lane's, "Why Businessmen Violate the Law." Lane, a professor of political science at Yale University, concentrates upon the structure of a business firm and its industry-wide position as these items relate to white-collar crime, but he also feels compelled, as Clinard did, to call special attention to the "more personal characteristics" of managers of business firms, although he grants that materials regarding such characteristics are "not readily accessible."

In an attempt to interpret management attitudes from an analysis of violation patterns, Lane notes that there was "no evidence of a consistently 'antiregulation' or 'antigovernment' or 'antiauthority' policy on the part of any firm or its management." The contradiction between Lane's conclusions and Sutherland's statement regarding the "professional-thief" nature of corporate crime may stem from the different spheres being described: Sutherland's dealing primarily with the country's largest corporations and Lane's, a population of smaller New England manufacturers. Lane's list of ways to reduce corporate violations clearly indicates that, however uncontaminated his research findings, his general predilections are quite dissimilar to Sutherland's. Lane, for instance, notes that "ambiguous laws lead to a higher rate of violation"; Sutherland, it will be remembered, was more inclined to find the laws quite clear-cut and the violations pre-eminently deliberate. Terms such as "ambiguous" and "explicit" or "clear" are basically value judgments, of course, and the discrepant conclusions of the authors indicate more than anything else the keen and critical eye with which writings on so sensitive a subject as white-collar crime must be read.

The 1961 antitrust violations in the heavy electrical equipment industry are described in detail in the fourth paper in this part, which concentrates on the behavior and views of the perpetrators. The 1961 antitrust cases represent the most widely publicized and carefully studied corporate offenses in the history of the United States. The antitrust cases, in fact, are often referred to in other readings in this volume to buttress or to rebut points regarding white-collar crime, though several authors take pains to point out that the 1961 price-fixing schemes should not be taken to represent what are said to be the wider range of more subtle and more complex forms of corporate white-collar crime.

The reading on violations by General Electric, Westinghouse, and other manufacturers attempts to abstract from congressional hearings, interviews, and other reports those items most directly related to prior studies of white-collar crime. Its review of Sutherland's ideas in terms of the 1961 cases finds many of the classical views on white-collar crime strikingly on target, while others are said to be notably awry, though both the unique nature of the particular case and the passage of time since Sutherland first wrote must be noted. The conclusion of the article is in the traditional equivocating style as it asks for more work of a similar nature before it will venture very far theoretically; in essence, its author takes his stand with Huntington Cairns that "the history of social theory is too largely a record of generalizations wrung from insufficient facts."

Avoidance of the term "crime" is perhaps the first thing that strikes the reader of Raymond C. Baumhart's paper, "How Ethical Are Businessmen?" Father Baumhart, a Jesuit priest who conducted the survey upon which the article is based while a graduate student at the Harvard Business School, is painstakingly fair as he balances the moral merits against the sins of management as these are gleaned from questionnaire responses. It needs emphasis, perhaps, that his respondents, as subscribers to the *Harvard Business Review,* may represent the more ethical elements of the business world and that, being written replies to a mail questionnaire, the more flagrant kinds of violations are perhaps underplayed. The heart of the paper lies in Father Baumhart's conclusion that sound ethics, when practiced in the business world, are a function of rational expediency—in the long run, his respondents conclude, "sound ethics is good business." (It would be interesting, however, to determine how well "sound ethics" would resist perversion when they were no longer believed to be "good business.") Certainly, the sensitivity of the corporate executives to industrial climate and to the values of their superiors, clearly illuminated in Father Baumhart's study, fits neatly into Sutherland's emphasis upon learning through interaction as a key to criminal violations, be they in the lower class or in the business world.

The final paper in this part, Alan M. Dershowitz' survey and evaluation of different approaches to the control of corporate crime, provides a substantial analytical framework for consideration of alternative social policies and their likely consequences. The author, at present a professor at the Harvard Law School, prepared the article as a student note during his senior year in the Yale Law School. Motives of perpetrators and subsequent implications of white-collar crimes for the corporation, its stockholders, and the general society are dissected as Dershowitz concentrates on "acquisitive corporate crime"—acts engaged in for the immediate purpose of increasing corporate, as distinguished from personal, wealth.

The Dershowitz reading presents in its clearest form a theme that often is taken to distinguish white-collar from other forms of crime, a theme that provides white-collar crime with what may be its most intriguing and perplexing attribute: its presumed responsiveness to social control measures. Penologists may argue that robbers are not likely to be seriously deterred by rearrangements of penalties for robbery, and knowledgeable persons appear to agree that most murders, usually committed in fits of passion or anger, are beyond the reach of deterrent sanctions. White-collar crime, however, is believed to be a kind of human activity inordinately sensitive to the suasion of criminal law, and its practitioners and those in danger of so acting are presumed to be especially susceptible to the threat of criminal retaliation. It is on the basis of this framework that criminologists sometimes find themselves in a position that on cursory examination appears to be more emotional than scientific—that of advocating the elimination of imprisonment and long sentences for most traditional offenders, while favoring imposition of the derogated penalties for white-collar violators.

4

CRIME OF CORPORATIONS

Edwin H. Sutherland

About twenty years ago I began to study violations of law by businessmen and have continued the study intermittently to the present day. This study was begun for the purpose of improving the general explanations of criminal behavior. The theories of crime which were then current and which are still current emphasized social and personal pathologies as the causes of crime. The social pathologies included, especially, poverty and the social conditions related to poverty, such as poor housing, lack of organized recreational facilities, the ignorance of parents, and family disorganization. The personal pathology emphasized in the earlier period was feeblemindedness; the early theory asserted that feeblemindedness is inherited and is the cause of both poverty and crime. At about the time I started the study of business crimes, the personal pathology which was used to explain crime was shifting from defective intelligence to defective emotions, as represented by such concepts as frustration, the inferiority complex, and the Oedipus complex.

Reprinted from Albert Cohen, Alfred Lindesmith, and Karl Schuessler (eds.), *The Sutherland Papers* (Bloomington: Indiana University Press, 1956), pp. 78–96.

These theories that crime is due to social and personal pathologies had considerable support from the fact that a very large proportion of the persons arrested, convicted, and committed to prisons belong to the lower economic class.

In contrast to those theories, my theory was that criminal behavior is learned just as any other behavior is learned and that personal and social pathologies play no essential part in the causation of crime. I believed that this thesis could be substantiated by a study of the violation of law by businessmen. Businessmen are generally not poor, are not feebleminded, do not lack organized recreational facilities, and do not suffer from the other social and personal pathologies. If it can be shown that businessmen, without these pathologies, commit many crimes, then such pathologies cannot be used as the explanation of the crimes of other classes. The criminologists who have stated the theories of crimes get their data from personal interviews with criminals in the criminal courts, jails, and prisons, or from criminal statistics based on the facts regarding such criminals. But when businessmen commit crimes, their cases go generally before courts under equity or civil jurisdictions or before quasi-judicial commissions, seldom before the criminal courts. Consequently, the criminologists do not come into contact with these businessmen and have not included their violations of law within general theories of criminal behavior.

I have used the term "white-collar criminal" to refer to a person in the upper socioeconomic class who violates the laws designed to regulate his occupation. The term "white collar" is used in the sense in which it was used by President Sloan of General Motors, who wrote a book entitled *The Autobiography of a White Collar Worker*. The term is used more generally to refer to the wage-earning class that wears good clothes at work, such as clerks in stores.

I wish to report specifically on a part of my study of white-collar crimes. I selected the seventy largest industrial and commercial corporations in the United States, not including public utilities and petroleum corporations. I have attempted to collect all the records of violations of law by each of these corporations, so far as these violations have been decided officially by courts and commissions. I have included the laws regarding restraint of trade; misrepresentation in advertising; infringement of patents, copyrights, and trademarks; rebates; unfair labor practices, as prohibited by the National Labor Relations Law; financial fraud; violations of war regulations; and a small miscellaneous group of other laws. The records include the life careers of the corporations, which average about forty-five years, and the subsidiaries as well as the main corporations. In this search, I have been limited by the available records found in a university library, and this is far from complete. I am sure that the number of crimes I shall report on is far smaller than the number actually decided by courts and commissions against these corporations.

This tabulation of the crimes of the seventy largest corporations in the United States gives a total of 980 adverse decisions. Every one of the seventy corporations has a decision against it, and the average number of decisions is 14.0. Of these seventy corporations, 98 per cent are recidivists; that is, they have two or more adverse decisions. Several states have enacted habitual criminal laws, which define an habitual criminal as a person who has been convicted four times of felonies. If we use this number and do not limit the convictions to felonies, 90 per cent of the seventy largest corporations in the United States are habitual criminals. Sixty of the corporations have decisions against them for restraint of trade, fifty-four for infringements, forty-four for unfair labor practices, twenty-seven for misrepresentation in advertising, twenty-six for rebates, and forty-three for miscellaneous offenses.

These decisions have been concentrated in the period since 1932. Approximately 60 per cent of them were made in the ten-year period subsequent to 1932, and only 40 per cent in the forty-year period prior to 1932. One possible explanation of this concentration is that the large corporations are committing more crimes than they did previously. My own belief is that the prosecution of large corporations has been more vigorous during the later period and that the corporations have not appreciably increased in criminality.

Of the seventy large corporations, thirty were either illegal in their origin or began illegal activities immediately after their origin, and 8 additional corporations should probably be added to this thirty. Thus, approximately half of the seventy corporations were either illegitimate in birth, or were infant and juvenile delinquents, as well as adult criminals.

All of the 980 adverse decisions were decisions that these corporations violated laws. Only 159 of these 980 decisions were made by criminal courts, whereas 425 were made by courts under civil or equity jurisdiction and 361 by commissions. The most important question regarding white-collar crime is whether it is really crime. That is a difficult and somewhat technical question, and I shall not attempt to deal with it here since I have published another paper on that question. The general conclusion stated in that paper is that the violations of law which were attested by decisions of equity and civil courts and by administrative commissions are, with very few exceptions, crimes.

The statistics which I have presented are rather dry and may not mean much to the average student who is not a specialist in this field, but the prevalence of white-collar crimes by large corporations can be illustrated more concretely. If you consider the life of a person, you find that from the cradle to the grave he has been using articles which were sold or distributed in violation of the law. The professional criminals use the word "hot" to refer to an article which has been recently stolen. For the purpose of simplicity of statement, I wish to use this word to refer to articles manufactured by corporations, but I shall expand the meaning to include any official record without restricting it to recent times and shall refer to a class of articles rather than articles manufactured by a particular concern. Using the word in this sense, we can say that a baby is assisted into this world with the aid of "hot" surgical instruments, rubbed with "hot" olive oil, wrapped in a "hot" blanket, weighed on "hot" scales. The father, hearing the good news, runs a "hot" flag up on his flag pole, goes to the golf course and knocks a "hot" golf ball around the course. The baby grows up surrounded by such articles and is finally laid to rest in a "hot" casket under a "hot" tombstone.

I now wish to describe in more detail violations of some of the specific laws and shall take first misrepresentation in advertising. Although the Pure Food and Drug Law contains a provision prohibiting misrepresentation on the labels of foods and drugs, the administrators of that law have not published regular reports including the names of the corporations that have been found to be in violation of the law. I shall therefore restrict the discussion to the misrepresentations in advertisements which have been decided on by the Federal Trade Commission.

This is one of the less important white-collar crimes in comparison with the others. Decisions have been made in ninety-seven cases against twenty-six of seventy corporations. No decisions were made against forty-four of the seventy large corporations under this law. Of these forty-four corporations against which no decisions were made, twenty-seven may be classed as nonadvertising corporations. That is, they do not advertise for purposes of their sales, although they may advertise for general goodwill or for the goodwill of the newspapers and journals. They sell their products to expert buyers, who cannot be influenced by advertising. It would be a waste of money for U.S. Steel to distribute pamphlets among the expert buyers of its products, claiming that its products were made from the finest ores or with Bessemer steel imported from England or to show a picture of a movie star in a Pullman saying, "I always select railroads which use rails made by U.S. Steel, because they are better rails" or a picture of a baseball manager saying, "I feel that my players are safer if they ride the trains on rails made by U.S. Steel, because these rails are safer." If these large corporations which do not advertise for sales purposes are eliminated, approximately 60 per cent of the large corporations which do advertise for sales purposes have decisions against them for misrepresentation in advertising.

These misrepresentations in advertising are not, in most cases, mere technical violations. The Federal Trade Commission each year makes a survey of several hundred thousand advertisements in periodicals and over the radios. From these they select about 50,000 which are questionable, and from these they pick out about 1,500 as patently false, making adverse decisions against about 1,000 of these each year. Also, in their selection, they tend to concentrate on certain products in one year and other products in other years. About 1941, they concentrated on false advertisements of vitamins and issued desist orders against about twenty-five firms on this one product. The advertisements of vitamins at that time claimed with practically no qualifications that vitamins would restore vigor, aid digestion, eliminate sterility, prevent miscarriage, increase sex vigor, decrease blood pressure, reduce neuritis, reduce insomnia, stop falling hair, cure hay fever and asthma, cure alcoholism, prevent tooth decay, eliminate pimples, make chickens lay more eggs, and keep the dog in good health.

Misrepresentations fall into three principal classes: First, some advertisements are designed to sell products which are physically dangerous, with the dangers denied, minimized, or unmentioned. Most of these advertisements are in the drug and cosmetic businesses. Only two of the seventy large corporations have decisions against them for advertisements of this nature.

Second, some advertisements exaggerate the values of the products, and this is equivalent to giving short weights. An extreme case of advertisements of this nature was a case decided against two hoodlums in Chicago about 1930. They sold a bottle of medicine at a price of $10 to a blind man with the claim that this would cure his blindness. When analyzed, the medicine was found to consist of two aspirins dissolved in Lake Michigan water. The hoodlums were convicted and sentenced to six months' imprisonment. The advertisements by large corporations are frequently of this class, except that they are not so extreme and are not followed by convictions in criminal courts and imprisonment. Garments advertised and sold as silk or wool are almost entirely cotton. Alligator shoes not made from alligator hides, walnut furniture not made from walnut lumber, turtle-oil facial cream not made from turtle-oil, Oriental rugs not made in the Orient, Hudson seal furs not made from the skins of seals are further instances of such misrepresentation. Caskets advertised as rustproof are not rustproof, garments as mothproof when they are not mothproof, garden hose as three-ply when it is only two-ply, and radios as "all-wave reception" that do not receive all waves. Electric pads are advertised with switches for high, medium, and low heat, when in fact they have only two degrees of heat. Storage eggs are sold as fresh eggs, old and reconditioned stoves as new stoves, and worn and reconditioned hats as new hats. Facial creams sold as skin foods, corrective of wrinkles, do not feed the skin or correct wrinkles. Some corporations advertise that their tea is made from tender leaves, especially picked for these corporations, when in fact their tea is purchased from lots brought in by importers who sell the same tea to other firms. Cigarettes are advertised as having been made from the finest tobacco, for which the company pays

25 per cent more, but other cigarettes are also made from the "finest tobacco" for which the manufacturers pay 25 per cent more than they do for chewing tobacco.

The third class of misrepresentation overlaps the two preceding and is separated from them principally because certain advertisements do special injury to the competitors rather than to consumers. One mail-order company advertised its furnaces as containing features which no other furnaces contained, when in fact the furnaces of competitors contained the same features. Consumers Research Service, which claimed to make impartial and unbiased appraisals of automobiles, was found to be receiving payments from an automobile company for reporting that their cars were superior.

I wish to describe a few of the important cases of misrepresentation in advertising. A prominent automobile manufacturer originated the 6 per cent installment purchase plan in 1935. This plan as advertised stated that the interest rate on unpaid balances on cars purchased on the installment plan was only 6 per cent. The Federal Trade Commission, after an investigation, reported that the interest rate was actually in excess of 11 per cent and that the exaggeration in the interest rate was nearly 100 per cent. Before the commission had ordered the pioneer firm to desist from this misrepresentation, practically all the other large automobile companies adopted the same method of taking money under false pretenses. Again, in 1936, all the important automobile companies were ordered on two counts to desist from misrepresentation in advertising their cars. First, they quoted a price which did not include necessary parts and accessories, the price for the car as actually equipped being 10 per cent higher than the advertised price. In addition, they added handling charges independent of transportation costs, which further increased the price required. Second, they advertised a picture of a car which was not the model actually named and priced. Again, in 1941, three of the four principal manufacturers of automobile tires were ordered to desist from misrepresentation in their advertisements of special sales prices on the Fourth of July and on Labor Day. These companies advertised prices which were reductions of 20 to 50 per cent from the regular prices. When the Federal Trade Commission investigated, it found that the 20 per cent reduction was actually only an 8 per cent reduction and the 50 per cent reduction only an 18 per cent reduction. In addition, one tire company was found to have engaged in misrepresentation in two respects. First, it advertised that with its tires a car would stop 25 per cent quicker. It did not say 25 per cent quicker than what, but the implication was 25 per cent quicker than with tires of other manufacturers; this was not true. Second, it made claims for the greater safety of its tires on the basis of the fact that these tires were used in the Indianapolis Speedway races, whereas in fact the Speedway tires had been especially constructed, so that there was no assurance that the company's tires for regular passenger cars were safer than other tires.

When the Federal Bureau of Investigation hunts kidnappers, it tries to find everyone who is in any way accessory to the kidnapping. The Federal Trade Commission, similarly, has attempted to some degree to bring into the picture those who are accessory to misrepresentation in advertising. They have, for instance, issued desist orders to many of the advertising agencies that prepare the advertising campaigns for the manufacturers. Though these desist orders have included many small and unimportant advertising agencies, they have included also the largest and most prominent agencies.

Also, practically all the newspapers and popular journals have participated in dissemination of false advertisements. These include publications which range from the Gannett publications at one extreme to the *Journal of the American Medical Association* at the other. Although the *Journal of the American Medical Association* claims that it does not carry advertisements which have not been checked and found to be true, it has for years carried advertisements of Philip Morris cigarettes. In earlier years, the Philip Morris Company had claimed that these cigarettes cured irritated throats and in later years claimed that they produced less irritation in the throat than other cigarettes. As proof of their truth, these advertisements cited the opinions and experiments of physicians many, if not all, of whom had received payment for their statements. Competing tobacco companies employed other physicians, who performed experiments and gave testimony which conflicted with the testimony in the *Journal of the American Medical Association*. The Philip Morris Company made a grant of $10,000 to St. Louis University to test these propositions. The medical school insisted on complete freedom in its methods of testing and in making its report. The report was that no accurate method of testing throat irritation or of testing the effect of the substances in question had been devised and that conflicting claims of experimenters were all bunk. The Philip Morris Company gave no publicity to that report, but their advertisements continued to appear in the *Journal of the American Medical Association*.

I do not want to take the time to go into similar detail in regard to other types of violations of law, but I shall describe a few incidents involving violations of the National Labor Relations Law. This law was enacted first in 1933 and in more developed form in 1935. It stated that collective bargaining had proved to be a desirable policy and prohibited employers from interfering with the efforts of employees to organize unions for purposes of collective bargaining. A violation of this law was declared to be an unfair labor practice. Decisions have been made against forty-three of the seventy large corporations, or 60 per cent, with a total of 149 decisions. Of these forty-three corporations, 72 per cent are recidivists, or repeaters; thirty-nine used interference, restraint, and coercion; thirty-three discriminated against union members; thirty-four organized company unions; thirteen used labor spies; and five used violence. Violence has been confined largely to the steel and automobile industries. One steel corporation from 1933 to 1937 purchased 143 gas guns, while the police department of Chicago purchased in the same years only thirteen; the steel corporation also purchased 6,714 gas shells and grenades, while the Chicago police department purchased only 757. The corporations customarily argue that they purchase this military equipment merely to protect themselves against the violence of the unions. Doubtless the equipment is used for protective purposes, but it is also used on some occasions for aggression. I wish to report one decision of the National Labor Relations Board concerning the Ford Motor Company. Henry Ford is reported to have said in 1937, "We'll never recognize the United Automobile Workers Union or any other union." The Ford Corporation organized a service department, under the supervision of Harry Bennett, an expugilist, and staffed it with 600 members equipped with guns and blackjacks. Frank Murphy, at the time Governor of Michigan and previously mayor of Detroit, said, regarding this service department, "Henry Ford employs some of the worst gangsters in our city."

In 1937 the United Automobile Workers Union was attempting to organize the employees in the River Rouge plant of the Ford Motor Company. A public announcement was made that the organizers would distribute literature at this plant at a specified time. Reporters and others gathered in advance. When a reporter asked a guard what they were going to do when the organizers arrived, the guard replied, "We are going to throw them to hell out of here." The organizers arrived, went with their literature up onto an overhead pass into one of the entrances. There they were informed that they were trespassing on private property. According to many witnesses they turned quietly and started away. As they were leaving, they were attacked by the service staff. They were beaten, knocked down, and kicked. Witnesses described this as a "terrific beating" and as "unbelievably brutal." The beating not only occurred on the overhead pass but was continued into the public highway. One man's back was broken and another's skull fractured. The cameras of reporters, who were taking pictures of the affray, were seized by the guards and the films destroyed. A reporter who was taking a picture from the highway was observed by a guard, who shouted, "Smash that camera!" The reporter jumped into the automobile of another reporter, and they were chased by the guards at a speed of 80 miles an hour through the streets of Detroit until they could secure refuge in a police station. According to prearranged plans, women organizers arrived later to distribute literature. As they alighted from the streetcar at the entrance to the plant, they were attacked by the guards and pushed back into the cars. One woman was knocked down and kicked. While these assaults were being committed, city policemen were present but did not interfere; the director of the service department was also present.

I wish next to give a few illustrations of embezzlement and violation of trust by officers of corporations. Seiberling organized the Goodyear Rubber Company and was its manager for many years. Because of financial difficulties in the corporation, he lost control of it in 1921. His successors found that Seiberling was short nearly $4,000,000 in his account with the company; that is, he had embezzled that amount from the company. The suits which were brought resulted in a settlement by which Seiberling agreed to reimburse the company. He not only did this but also secured credit from Ohio financiers and started the Seiberling Rubber Company, which has been quite successful.

President Sloan, Mr. Raskob, and other officers of General Motors developed a plan to pay bonuses to the officers and directors of General Motors. Under this plan, President Sloan secured a total payment from the corporation of $20,000,000 between 1923 and 1928. When suits were started in later years, these excessive payments prior to 1930 were not included in the suits because of the statute of limitations. The court held, however, that these officers had appropriated by fraudulent methods of calculating their bonuses approximately $4,000,000 and ordered them to repay this amount to the corporation.

George Washington Hill and other officers of the American Tobacco Company were criticized and sued for appropriating corporate funds for their enormous salaries and bonuses. One of these suits was to be tried before Judge Manton in the federal court in New York City. Shortly before the trial, Judge Manton suggested to the attorney for the American Tobacco Company that he needed to borrow $250,000. The attorney mentioned this to the assistant to the president of the American Tobacco Company, who mentioned it to Lord and Thomas, the advertising firm for the company, and Lord and Thomas lent Judge Manton the $250,000. Judge Manton decided the case in favor of the American Tobacco Company. Probably his decision was correct, but he was convicted of receiving a bribe, the attorney for the company was disbarred from practice in federal courts, and the assistant to the president, who made the arrangements, was promoted immediately after the decision to the position of vice president, where he was entitled to a bonus. In another suit, the American Tobacco Company paid from its own treasury $260,000 to the complainant, $320,000 to its law firm, and made other payments to bring the total for fixing this case to approximately a million dollars. A court later ordered the officers, against whom the suit was brought, to reimburse the corporation for these payments.

Finally, I wish to discuss the violation of the antitrust laws. Restraint of trade was prohibited by the Sherman Antitrust Act of 1890 and by several subsequent laws, as well as by the laws of most of the states. Decisions that such laws were violated have been made against sixty of the seventy large corporations in 307 cases. Three motion-picture corporations stand at the top of the list for restraint of trade with twenty-two, twenty-one, and twenty-one decisions, respectively. Thus, 86 per cent of the seventy corporations have decisions against them for restraint of trade, and 73 per cent of the corporations with such decisions are recidivists. Although no decisions have been made against the other ten corporations, other evidence indicates that probably every one of them has, in fact, violated these laws. These decisions tend to corroborate the statement made by Walter Lippmann: "Competition has survived only where men have been unable to abolish it." Not law but expediency and practicability have determined the limits of restraint of trade. Big Business does not like competition, and it makes careful arrangements to reduce it and even eliminate it. In certain industries, the negotiations among large corporations to avoid competition are very similar to international diplomacy, except that they are more successful.

For competition these businessmen have substituted private collectivism. They meet together and determine what the prices shall be and how much shall be produced; they also regulate other aspects of the economic process. This is best illustrated by the trade associations, although it is not limited to them. These trade associations not only fix prices and limit production, but also they have set up systems of courts with penalties for violation of their regulations. Their system of justice applies both to their own members, in which case they have a semblance of democracy, and also to nonmembers, in which case they resemble dictatorship and racketeering. Among ninety-two trade associations investigated in 1935 to 1939, twenty-eight had facilities for investigating or snooping on their members, eleven had provisions for fining those who violated regulations, and eighteen had provisions for boycotting the offenders.

Although businessmen often complain that the antitrust law is so vague that they cannot determine whether they are violating the law or not, a very large proportion of the decisions against these seventy corporations are for making agreements to have uniform prices; that is, not to compete as to prices. This practice is clearly in violation of the antitrust law, and no one at all acquainted with its provisions and with the decisions made under it could have the least doubt that such behavior is illegal. Also, many of the agreements limit production. Businessmen have insisted for at least seventy-five years on limiting production in order to keep prices from falling. Though many people have regarded as ridiculous the agricultural policy of killing little pigs, it is in principle the policy which industrial corporations have been using for many generations, long before it was ever applied in agriculture.

What significance do these violations of the antitrust law have? The economic system, as described by the classical economists, was a system of free competition and *laissez faire*, or free enterprise, as we call it today. Free competition was the regulator of the economic system. The laws of supply and demand, operating under free competition, determined prices, profits, the flow of capital, the distribution of labor, and other economic phenomena. When profits in an industry were high, other businessmen rushed into that industry in the hope of securing similar profits. This resulted in an increase in the supply of commodities, which produced a reduction in prices, and this in turn reduced profits. Thus, the excessive profits were eliminated, the prices were reduced, and the public had a larger supply of the commodity. Through this regulation by free competition, according to the classical economists, Divine Providence produced the greatest welfare of the entire society. Free competition was, to be sure, a harsh regulator. Cut-throat practices were general, and in the achievement of the welfare of the total society weaker establishments were often ruined.

Because free competition regulated the economic system, governmental regulation was unnecessary. The economic system of the classical economists developed primarily because business revolted against the governmental regulations of the feudal period, which were not adapted to the changing conditions of the eighteenth century. Government kept out of business after this system was established, except as it enforced contracts, protected the public against larceny and fraud, and enforced the principles of free competition by the common-law prohibition of restraint of trade.

During the last century this economic and political system has changed. The changes have resulted principally from the efforts of businessmen. If the word "subversive" refers to efforts to make fundamental changes in a social system, the business leaders are the most subversive influence in the United States. These business leaders have acted as individuals or in small groups, seeking preferential advantages for themselves. The primary loyalty of the businessman has been to profits, and he has willingly sacrificed the general and abstract principles of free competition and free enterprise in circumstances that promised a pecuniary advantage. Moreover, he has been in a position of power and has been able to secure these preferential advantages. Although businessmen had no intention of modifying the economic and political system, they have produced this result. The restriction of the principle of free competition has been demonstrated by the practically universal policy of restraint of trade among large corporations.

The restriction of free enterprise has also come principally from businessmen. Free enterprise means, of course, freedom from governmental regulation and governmental interference. Although businessmen have been vociferous as to the virtues of free enterprise and have, in general, insisted that government keep its hands out of and off business, business-men above all others have put pressure on the government to interfere in business. They have not done this *en masse*, but as individuals or as small groups endeavoring to secure advantages for themselves. These efforts of businessmen to expand the governmental regulations of business are nu-merous and have a wide range. One of the best illustrations is the early and continued pressure of business concerns to secure tariffs to protect them from foreign competition. Many statutes have been enacted as the result of pressure from particular business interests to protect one indus-try against competition from another, as illustrated by the tax on oleo-margarine. Another illustration is the fair trade laws of the federal and state governments, which prohibit retail dealers from cutting prices on trademarked articles. The federal fair trade law was enacted in 1937. The bill was presented by Senator Tydings, as a rider to a District of Columbia appropriations bill, where it could not be discussed on its merits. The bill was prepared by the law partner of the Senator, and this law partner was the attorney for the National Association of Retail Druggists. The bill was supported by many national associations of manufacturers and deal-ers, who were opposed to the competitive principle and to free enterprise. The bill was opposed by the Department of Justice and the Federal Trade Commission, which have been attempting to preserve the principle of free competition and free enterprise.

In fact, the interests of businessmen have changed, to a considerable extent, from efficiency in production to efficiency in public manipulation, including manipulation of the government for the attainment of prefer-ential advantages. This attention to governmental favors has tended to produce two results: First, it has tended to pauperize business in the sense in which charity tends to pauperize poor people; second, it has tended to corrupt government. But the most significant result of the violations of the antitrust laws by large business concerns is that these have made our system of free competition and free enterprise unworkable. We no longer have competition as a regulator of economic processes; we have not sub-stituted efficient governmental regulation. We cannot go back to compe-tition. We must go forward to some new system—perhaps communism, perhaps cooperativism, perhaps much more complete governmental regu-lation than we now have. I don't know what lies ahead of us and am not particularly concerned, but I do know that what was a fairly efficient sys-tem has been destroyed by the illegal behavior of big business.

Furthermore, the businessmen have practically destroyed our system of patents by the same procedures. The system of patents was authorized in our Constitution to promote the development of science and the arts. The patent system has become one of the principal methods of promoting monopoly. Not one patent in a hundred pays even the costs of registration. Patents are important for business establishments primarily because they can be used to eliminate or regulate competitors. This is illustrated by the variation in the extent to which corporations apply for patents and bring suits for infringement of patents. In industries such as steel, very few patents are secured and very few patent-infringement suits initiated, because establishments in this country are protected from competition by the heavy capital investment. On the other hand, in industries such as the chemical industry and the manufacture of electrical equipment, new competitors can start with a very small investment. The large companies protect themselves against competition by taking out patents on every possible modification of procedure, bringing suits on every possible pretext, and granting licenses to use patents only with a highly regimented and bureaucratic control. The patent is important principally because it is a weapon for fighting competitors. This can be seen in the practice of some of the small concerns, where widespread monopoly is not threatened. The Miniature Golf Corporation secured a patent on its vacant-lot recreation and filed scores of suits against anyone who used this method without a paid license from them. The Good Humor Corporation engaged in patent litigation for more than a decade with the Popsicle Company and other manufacturers of ice-cream bars to determine which firm had invented this contribution to science and the arts. Similarly, the Maiden-form Brassiere Company and the Snug-Fit Foundations, Inc., were before the courts for many years regarding their patented designs, each charging the other with infringement.

The general conclusion from this study of the seventy large corporations is that the ideal businessman and the large corporation *are* very much like the professional thief:

First, their violations of law are frequent and continued. As stated previously, 97 per cent of the large corporations are recidivists.

Second, illegal behavior by the corporations is much more prevalent than the prosecutions indicate. In other words, only a fraction of the violations of law by a particular corporation result in prosecution, and only a fraction of the corporations which violate the law are prosecuted. In general, a few corporations are prosecuted for behavior which is industry-wide.

Third, the businessman who violates laws regulating business does not lose status among his business associates. I have mentioned President Sloan of General Motors and Seiberling (previously of the Goodyear Rubber Company), and many others could be mentioned who have appropriated the funds of their own corporations fraudulently and who have not lost status in their own corporations or in the eyes of other businessmen. Leonor F. Loree, chairman of the Kansas City Southern, knowing that his company was about to purchase stock of another railway, went into the market privately and secretly purchased shares of this stock in advance of his corporation, and then, when the price of the stock increased, sold it at the higher price, making a profit of $150,000. This profit, of course, was made at the expense of the corporation of which he was chairman, and he could make the profit because as an officer he knew the plans of the corporation. The courts, however, determined that this profit was fraudulent and ordered Mr. Loree to reimburse the corporation for the violation of his trust. Shortly after this decision became generally known, Mr. Loree was elected president of the New York Chamber of Commerce, perhaps in admiration of his cleverness.

Fourth, businessmen feel and express contempt for legislators, bureaucrats, courts, "snoopers," and other governmental officials and for the law, as such. In this respect, also, they are akin to the professional thieves, who feel and express contempt for police, prosecutors, and judges. Both professional thieves and corporations feel contempt for government because government interferes with their behavior.

Businessmen, being like professional thieves in these four respects, are participants in organized crime. Their violations of law are not identical and haphazard, but they have definite policies of restraint of trade, of unfair labor practices, of fraud and misrepresentation.

Businessmen differ from professional thieves principally in their greater interest in status and respectability. They think of themselves as honest men, not as criminals, whereas professional thieves, when they speak honestly, admit they are thieves. The businessman does regard himself as a lawbreaker, but he thinks the laws are wrong or at least that they should not restrict him, although they may well restrict others. He does not think of himself as a criminal, because he does not conform to the popular stereotype of the criminal. This popular stereotype is always taken from the lower socioeconomic class.

I have attempted to demonstrate that businessmen violate the law with great frequency, using what may be called the methods of organized crime. I have attempted in another place to demonstrate that these violations of law are really crimes. If these conclusions are correct, it is very clear that the criminal behavior of businessmen cannot be explained by poverty, in the usual sense, or by bad housing or lack of recreational facilities or feeblemindedness or emotional instability. Business leaders are capable, emotionally balanced, and in no sense pathological. We have no reason to think that General Motors has an inferiority complex or that the Aluminum Company of America has a frustration-aggression complex or that U.S. Steel has an Oedipus complex or that the Armour Company has a death wish or that the DuPonts desire to return to the womb. The assumption that an offender must have some such pathological distortion of the intellect or the emotions seems to me absurd, and if it is absurd regarding the crimes of businessmen, it is equally absurd regarding the crimes of persons in the lower economic class.

5

CRIMINOLOGICAL THEORIES OF VIOLATIONS
OF WARTIME REGULATIONS

Marshall B. Clinard

Within recent years there have been a number of papers which have attempted to reformulate criminological theory so as to include not only violations of the customary criminal law but violations of the white-collar type, where the measures taken are generally either civil or administrative in character.[1] White-collar crime has not been integrated into criminological theory in part because its scientific implications have not as yet been fully recognized. This is indicated by the fact that practically no research is now being done in this field. There is also an element of doubt upon the part of some as to whether such behavior actually is criminal. Moreover, there is possibly some hesitancy of otherwise scientific writers to examine the behavior of business concerns since this involves certain values of the economic system which are partially in the mores of our day and should not be questioned.

This paper is a description of violations of the price and rationing regulations issued by the Office of Price Administration.[2] The interest is primarily in the violations by wholesaler and manufacturing concerns and

Reprinted from *American Sociological Review*, 11 (June, 1946), pp. 258–270.

retailers, not those by consumers, or persons stealing or counterfeiting ration currency.

Since the establishment of the OPA in February, 1942, nearly 600 price and rent regulations and almost twenty ration orders have been issued. The prices of over 8,000,000 articles are regulated by this agency. Many of these regulations and orders act as controls over the behavior of almost every consumer in the United States, and almost every person engaged in business activity is governed by one or more of the specific trade regulations. This means that the regulations exercised control over 130,000,000 people, including the owners of several million rental dwellings and 2,000,000 business establishments, of which 380,000 are preretail establishments (wholesale and manufacturing), and the balance retail, including 600,000 food stores and 250,000 gas stations.

These new controls over business were the most drastic ever issued in this country, even though businessmen have long been under some regulation and have been subject to government reports. Moreover, in a nation which has long been characterized by widespread disrespect for law, one had to contend with such factors as previous business practices which were legal before the enactment of the OPA, a shortage of supplies and poor distribution, a bitter attack on the OPA by special interests, hostility of businessmen toward wartime regulations which they often tended to regard as New Deal measures, and discussions among themselves and in trade journals which might tend to reinforce this hostility. One also had to contend with the reluctance of certain legislative groups to give sufficient financial support to the agency for enforcement.

The public has overwhelmingly supported these controls, as shown by all surveys that have been made, the proportion favoring price control ranging from 80 to 97 per cent.[3] Other evidence that public opinion has been in favor of the OPA is the fact that the courts in 1944, for example, decided 96 per cent of all litigation, both civil and criminal, in favor of the OPA. Further indication of public support is indicated by the active assistance of volunteer price panel members and assistants who at a single time have numbered as many as 200,000. Even businessmen support the government price-control program, as was indicated in a 1945 survey of 434 wholesalers in fifteen cities where only one out of four thought the government was doing a poor job in controlling prices in general, and one out of three thought that it was doing a poor job in their own type of business.

The majority of these regulations and controls have been in effect for over three years and during this time have received extensive explanation, wide publicity, and wide newspaper coverage of prosecutions. Appeals have been made for the price-control program based not only on the intellectual reasons for the existence of the regulations as inflationary controls, but also frequent appeals to patriotism as a basis for compliance, which ordinarily cannot be used to enforce law in peacetime. Members of most concerns involved had a member of the immediate family in the armed service. Studies of profits of concerns and their own statements on opinion surveys indicate the majority of them made either equal profits or actually greater profits than they made before the war and that many of the concerns involved in OPA violations were in excellent financial condition. On one national opinion survey, approximately one-half of the food wholesalers reported they were making satisfactory profits. Examining the push and pull of these two sets of factors, however, one would anticipate that the positive-factors might sufficiently counterbalance the negative factors so that one might not have expected quite the extensive violations of these wartime laws as actually occurred.

There has been much discussion as to whether these violations actually constitute crimes, since in only a small number of cases is the issue of willfulness raised and in even fewer cases is a criminal sanction sought. Sutherland has correctly indicated that the essential nature of a crime is not willfulness or even that a penalty has been imposed, but rather that the unlawful act is punishable.[4] The crucial issue is the existence of a violation which may be followed by some sort of penalty. Hall, similarly, has advanced the thesis that the distinction between crimes and torts, and between the customary use of the term "penal" as opposed to "nonpenal," is artificial and not logical theoretically.[5]

Following this reasoning, for criminological purposes, nearly all violations of OPA regulations constitute criminal acts. Violations of the Emergency Price Control Act are defined by Congress as socially injurious and a violation of law. If, in the administrator's judgment, there is unlawful behavior he may institute court action or settle the claim. Whether the violation is handled by civil or criminal measures is the agency's decision. The only specific limitation is that the criminal sanction can be employed only in cases where the violation was willful. There is, moreover, no implication that the criminal sanction will be employed in all willful cases, thus leaving the use of alternative measures entirely to the agency. In Canada, on the other hand, where formal action is deemed necessary in the event of a price or rationing violation, all offenses are dealt with by criminal prosecution rather than by civil action, with the exception of a few cases where the license was canceled. Moreover, five states and some seventy-five municipalities in the United States have enacted black-market statutes and ordinances making violations of the OPA's law a misdemeanor punishable by fine or imprisonment.

An examination of cases, including rationing cases under the Second War Powers Act, would show that in thousands of cases involving almost identical violations sometimes administrative measures have been used, at other times civil, and occasionally criminal prosecution. Cases involving evasive violation where there is definite willfulness, such as falsification of records and inventories in rationing cases, are handled sometimes with an injunction suit, with a suspension order proceeding, and at other times with criminal prosecution. In certain cases, it is felt that the purposes of enforcement would be better accomplished if an injunction were used, even if the violators' actions were willful. Experience has shown that it would be impossible to use the criminal sanction in all cases where it might be used, since criminal cases require considerable preparation, and the capacity of the Justice Department and the federal courts to handle a large number of cases is limited.

A study of rationing-suspension order cases under the Second War Powers Act, which are entirely administrative in character, would show that many of these cases, largely gasoline, involved violations which were both extensive and evasive. All rationing-suspension order proceedings involve wrongful diversion of strategic supplies. It is not necessary for the OPA to prove willfulness, but proof of willfulness may affect the length of the suspension order. Of particular interest in this connection is the Supreme Court decision in the *Steuart Oil Company* case which upheld the validity of the suspension order.[6] The company maintained that it was a penalty and that the OPA did not have authority to use such penal action. It was the contention of the OPA that it was not a penalty, but withdrawal of an allocation. The Supreme Court said that the suspension order was remedial but conceded that it was an injury to the person suspended. From the point of view of criminology, however, it seems that the suspension of a business for periods ranging up to the duration of the war is a penalty regardless of the legal interpretation.

Another OPA sanction—the injunction—is used in cases where there has been a violation or to prevent future violations. It has been the major sanction, and many of the most serious cases have been handled with an injunction simply because it is quickly and more easily obtained. It is particularly useful where there is a failure to keep records, which is in many instances a way of avoiding the detection of such violations as side payments. In fact, several courts have objected to the use of injunctions to hide willful violations that might be punished by other measures. It is also of interest that characteristically both a treble damage and an injunction suit for past violations are used, the treble damage suit being definitely penal in nature.[7] The court has held that an injunction does not follow in all cases where a violation is shown. Thus, in the *Hecht* decision,[8] where the defendant had made every effort to comply with every regulation even though there were extensive violations, the Supreme Court stated that the court did not have to grant an injunction as it would not accomplish any further purpose. Injunctions have been and continue to be granted, however, in cases where willfulness is not raised.

Two other sanctions that the OPA has available for price violations are the license suspension and treble damage suits. The former is considered suitable for serious cases and is used only after at least two violations have occurred over a period of time. A formal license warning notice must be issued after the first violation and there must be another violation before this sanction can be instituted. The treble damage actions are of three types: the administrator's own, for violations in the course of trade or business; the administrator's consumer suit, where the administrator sues to recover for a violation at the retail level; and the suit where the consumer himself sues for treble damages. The first two suits are considered penalties, whereas the latter suit is considered largely as a remedial action, particularly if the recovery is only for the single amount of the overcharge. The penal nature of the treble damage action is recognized by the fact that no money paid to the United States Treasury as the result of a treble damage settlement or suit brought by the OPA can be deducted as a business expense under the Internal Revenue statutes. In the case of all treble damage suits, Congress has differentiated between violations which were not willful and negligent and those which were willful or negligent. If the defendant is able to establish the former contention only the single amount of the overcharge can be awarded. The defendants have not been very successful in establishing this so-called "Chandler defense," since the courts usually do not consider it if the OPA later shows that there were side payments, falsification of records, tie-in sales, and other violations demonstrating willfulness, or if there was an absence of proper records, failure to instruct employees, and other similar violations.

While it has already been indicated that the question of willfulness is not essential in order to judge violations of price and rationing regulations as crimes, it might be well to point out the extent to which violations are intentional. Since most regulations have been in existence for several years and have been accompanied by wide publicity both in newspapers and trade journals, it appears unlikely that many businessmen, after the initial period of price control, could be ignorant of the provisions of the regulations. Estimates by a group of wholesalers in 1945 show that one-third believe most violations to be deliberate. More specifically, 10 per cent felt that everyone violates deliberately, 14 per cent estimated over three-fourths, and another 11 per cent felt that more than half of all violations were deliberate. Perhaps an even more empiric index is the extent of evasive violations such as falsification of records, including those in connection with side payments. When a violation is evasive, there can be no question but that it was intentional and that the person was familiar with the provisions of the regulation, as well as the nature of the investigations, at least enough to try to cover it up. Of the group of food wholesalers interviewed in 1945, more than one out of five thought this to be a frequent practice. Moreover, 57 per cent of the wholesalers interviewed in this same survey stated that enforcement efforts are effective in securing compliance, which would indicate awareness that many of the actions described here are intentional violations of the law.

Even when violations of government regulations are intentional, many businessmen, while they may regard themselves as law violators, do not consider that they have committed crimes and, therefore, could not possibly be treated as criminals.[9] Some representative statements of this view are the following by food wholesalers.

> "I sure wouldn't think any man should go to jail for a price violation." (*Grocery dealer in St. Louis*)

> "I don't think jail is good. That's for hoodlums and gangsters." (*Grocery dealer in Chicago*)

> "It would be a terrible thing to go to jail, pretty hard for a man's family, too. Jail is for racketeers. That is just another day for them but very different for a legitimate businessman." (*Fruit and vegetable dealer in Los Angeles*)

While this attitude was by no means unanimous among businessmen, as shall be indicated shortly, this view is general enough to make it obvious that among many of the business group the mores are not involved in such violations. Such laws are *malum in prohibita*, and the force of public opinion has as yet not been sufficiently developed to make such laws *malum in se*. In fact, the great extension of modern criminal law has come in those fields where there is no unanimity that such behavior is criminal either on the part of the general public or the important classes or groups involved.[10] Actually, the injury to society is far greater in many of these crimes, which may involve several hundred thousand dollars, and the example of disobedience of law is far more flagrant than in the case of most ordinary crimes. Perhaps, as Fuller has suggested, enforcement of the law and education as to its purpose will bring about greater consensus in society that crimes committed by businessmen are as much crimes as those of the lower socioeconomic class.[11]

In connection with the criminal prosecution of business violators, against whom the OPA probably brought more cases than other agencies, the attitude of the courts is most important. While the opinions of the courts are undoubtedly the reflection, in part, of public opinion in general or the opinion of certain social classes, at the same time the attitude of the community toward certain laws, particularly new laws, is influenced by the attitudes of its judges.

Most OPA criminal cases were generally well selected before being turned over to the Department of Justice for prosecution, as is indicated by the fact that convictions were secured in over 94 per cent of the cases in 1944. Yet the sentences imposed on OPA violators after conviction were in general extremely mild. For example, during the year

1944, of 3,486 persons who were convicted of violations of the price and rationing regulations, only 27 per cent received imprisonment or imprisonment and fine. Of the total convicted, 46 per cent received only a fine, and 28 per cent were placed on probation. During the fiscal year ending June 30, 1944, only 470 persons were received in federal prisons for price and rationing violations. Of the total group, ninety-seven received a sentence of a year and a day or more. Only eighty, or 17 per cent, were sentenced for price violations, of whom one-fourth received sentences of a year and a day or more. One reason for the light sentences was the attitude toward offenses of this type, but still another reason was the fact that the offenders seldom had a criminal past or other circumstances which would warrant a severe sentence. As the judges on occasion stated from the bench, they "would not make criminals of reputable businessmen."

The length of some of the sentences imposed on businessmen who had willfully violated the OPA regulations and in so doing made large sums of money were almost trivial compared with the sentences given offenders who violated ordinary criminal laws pertaining to property offenses. Of course, because of their reputation, a short sentence may be as effective with businessmen as a long sentence with lower-class criminals. Likewise, a large fine may be more difficult for an ordinary criminal to pay than for a businessman, and the former might conceivably prefer a short imprisonment to such a large fine.

While this method of dealing lightly with violators who had no previous record may be in line with advanced criminological theory, it raises certain questions, also from the view of society in general, that the penalty of imprisonment which was the most feared by businessmen according to their own statements was so seldom invoked as a deterrent for others. A survey of wholesalers' opinions revealed that they considered imprisonment a far more effective penalty than any other OPA action, including fines.[12] In fact, some 65 per cent made this statement. Some of the comments are illustrative of this view. About jail sentences they had this to say:

"Jail is the only way: nobody wants to go to jail."

"Everybody gets panicky at the thought of a jail sentence."

"A jail sentence is dishonorable, it jeopardizes the reputation."

"It [jail] spoils the offender's reputation and frightens the other fellow."

With regard to fines and other money penalties businessmen[13] had this to say:

"They don't hurt anybody."

"They're never missed."

"People are making enough money nowadays to pay a fine easily. It just comes out of the profits like a tax."

"The violators violate again, so they must not care about paying a fine."

Total violations of OPA regulations by business concerns, both retail and preretail, have undoubtedly been a large figure. Violations of this type uncovered during 1944 alone numbered 338,029. This figure represents violations by approximately 11 per cent of the business firms of the United States.[14] The number of food dealers found in violation was 197,799, including 62,382 meat and dairy dealers. Apparel concerns found in violation were 17,848.

The estimates of about one out of ten business concerns in violation is undoubtedly too low because not all concerns were investigated. Of those investigated, approximately 57 per cent were found in violation, which, if applied to the total concerns, would be approximately 1,100,000 violations. On the other hand, this figure may be too high because the fields of business selected for investigation by the OPA are likely to be those in which there is more evidence of violations than in the case of other business fields[15] and there may also be some duplication of business concerns in the above figures.

During 1944 there were actions in 322,131 cases of violation. Warnings or other informal adjustments, including dismissals, were issued in 271,874 cases, or 84 per cent of the total cases. In the remaining 16 per cent of the cases, administrative action was used in 26,763, and court proceedings were instituted in 28,902 cases. Of these 55,666 cases, representing some 3 per cent of all business establishments, there were 10,504 (or 19 per cent) settlements and 2,745 (or 5 per cent) suits in treble damage cases against manufacturers and wholesalers; 6,171 (or 11 per cent) settlements and 1,373 (or 2 per cent) suits in treble damage cases against retailers; 10,088 (or 18 per cent) rationing-suspension order proceedings; 13,074 (or 23 per cent) injunction suits; and 145 (or 0.3 per cent) license-suspension suits for price violation. There were 2,223 (or 4 per cent) suits brought by the OPA under local legislation, and criminal prosecution was begun by the Department of Justice against 3,934 defendants, or 7 per cent. In 1914, $21,000,000 was collected in treble damages and fines.

The extensive volume of these cases can well be illustrated by comparing the number of enforcement cases of the OPA with those of other federal agencies. Without doubt, the OPA has brought more actions, including more court actions, against violations by businessmen than all other federal regulatory agencies, with exception of the Bureau of Internal Revenue, in the past ten years.[16] In fact, approximately one-half of all civil cases in the federal courts during 1945 were for violations of the price, rationing, and rent regulations, and nearly one-sixth of all criminal cases were for such violations. The Securities and Exchange Commission during the ten-year period 1934 to 1944 annually brought court action in only an average of eighty-five cases, fifty-one being civil actions and thirty-four (232 defendants) being criminal prosecutions by the Department of Justice. The Federal Trade Commission in 1944 dealt with about 900 violations of which less than 5 per cent involved court proceedings. The Food and Drug Administration annually brings action against some 3,500 concerns, filing injunctions in about thirty-five cases and using criminal prosecution in 380 cases, 91 per cent of the convictions resulting in fines only. In view of the limited enforcement staffs of these agencies, these figures probably do not show the extent of the actual violations. The OPA has a much larger enforcement staff, consisting of over 3,000 investigators and 600 attorneys in addition to volunteer assistance; and while inadequate to investigate several million business concerns, it has had a staff much larger than any agency other than the Bureau of Internal Revenue. The large number of court actions brought by the OPA was also a reflection of a stronger policy in dealing with business violators, a policy that was in part made possible by the fact that it was a wartime measure.

Analysis of several thousand price violations indicates that they may be classified into a number of different types[17] in much the same fashion as violations of the customary criminal law can be classified. Because of the extent of these wartime controls there is latitude for considerable variation in types of violation. The absence of previous experience with wartime regulatory measures restricting the economic life of the entire population indicates that patterns of violation have developed in a relatively short period of time. The majority of violations of price regulations are by the seller rather than the buyer. This is so because under the provisions of the Price Act a buyer for ultimate consumption may not ordinarily be a violator and from the further fact that the initiation of a price violation ordinarily originates with the seller. Violations by a seller fall into three main types: (1) direct violations in the form of straight overceiling charges, including overceiling purchases in the course of trade or business when such practices are forbidden; (2) indirect overceiling sales, involving the use of evasive practices to cover up the violation and to hamper detection of a violation; and (3) violations of record keeping and reporting requirements. Price violations by the buyer, in those regulations where such behavior is prohibited, are derivative in the sense that the seller ordinarily initiates the transaction. Even assuming the purchaser to be a willing buyer, if he pays a price above ceiling he must pass on the overcharge, provided he is not the ultimate consumer and does not wish to sell at a loss.

It is unnecessary here to give examples of the first type of price violation. Examples of the second, or evasive, type of price violation are numerous. One practice is to secure cash payments in addition to those which appear to have been made in the regular transaction at ceiling price. These "cash-on-the-side" payments are not recorded or reported and are oftentimes difficult to ascertain unless the buyer "talks." The invoice is made out at the correct ceiling price and from all that appears on the buyer's records no price violation took place. Often charges are made for goods which are not actually delivered. Often side payments are treated as a loan, which the seller in fact never repays to the buyer. In other instances it has been disclosed that side payments are received and covered up by the seller's placing one of his employees on the payroll of the buyer to draw a salary for services which are actually not rendered. There have also been instances wherein sellers have refused to supply certain commodities to purchasers unless they agree to buy stock in corporations in which the sellers are interested. The stock, of course, is worth only a small fraction of the price paid. Those buyers who become stockholders are plentifully supplied with wanted commodities at what appear to be ceiling prices. Still other side payments are in the form of patronage dividends. Extra charges also consist of gifts, tips, bets, bribes, kickbacks, and fictitious quantity estimates. Occasionally, charges are made for delivery or other services not formerly performed or previously performed free, charges made for fictitious legal or brokerage services, and pyramiding of mark-ups through dummy jobbing concerns.

A further evasive method devised to violate price ceilings is through the use of "tying" agreements. This practice consists of making the purchase of an unwanted commodity the condition of purchasing a desired commodity. The seller will refuse to deliver the desired commodity unless a purchase is made of a product for which there is little or no demand or upon which his margin of profit is high. Tie-in sales may be direct in their nature in that the purchaser is specifically given to understand that he cannot purchase the wanted commodity without purchasing the less desirable product, or they may be indirect in those instances where word is passed out to the purchasers that it is desirable that they order and purchase products other than those wanted.

Still another type of evasive practice is that involving quantity or quality violations. In such cases, there may be a short weight of the commodity. Other cases may involve grading violations, such as upgrading, failure to grade, or improper labeling of the commodity. In some instances there is reduction in size or inferior composition or construction, such as the use of substitute materials of inferior grade, blending with less expensive grades of materials, reduction in amount of materials used, and decrease in length of guarantee periods.

The third type of price violation, record keeping and reporting violations, does not in and of itself directly affect prices charged or received and is, therefore, classified as nonsubstantive. This type may be further broken down into those which involve failure to comply with records and reports requirements and those where there is neglect or intentional refusal to comply in order to cover up substantive violations. The purpose of these requirements is to aid the public and the OPA in enforcing price ceilings. Violations of these requirements permit the seller to evade detection of his substantive violations and hamper the public and the OPA in their enforcement activity, since it is often difficult, if not impossible, to tell what the seller's maximum prices are unless proper records are kept. Investigations indicated that the records of many businessmen have not been adequately kept even in peacetime. It was largely for this reason, as well as because of the prevalence of evasive violations, that base period pricing methods such as the General Maximum Price Regulation (GMPR) were very difficult to enforce.

There are indications from both studies[18] as well as reports in trade journals that nearly all types of these violations were frequent, although there were considerable variations from industry to industry. A national survey of wholesalers' opinions in 1945 as to the frequency of various types of violations indicates that the most frequent violation, in their opinions, involves tie-in sales; second in importance was selling above ceiling; third was falsification of records, including side payments; and fourth was quality deterioration. The frequency of tie-in sales, exceeding even selling above ceiling, is probably indicative of enforcement activities which drove under cover the more open violations. Evasive violations are more difficult to detect. Of the wholesalers interviewed, 38 per cent contended that tie-in sales were frequent, 27 per cent thought that selling above the ceiling and quality deterioration were frequent, and 22 per cent felt that falsification of records, including side payments, was frequent. Many wholesalers, however, contended that tie-in sales and quality deterioration were more or less accepted practices in the trade during peacetime.

Actually, a large proportion of OPA violations are various types of fraud, as they constitute devices for obtaining money fraudulently by misrepresentation. Certainly the delivery of goods in which the quantity or quality is not the same as the invoice specifies is fraud. Even if the OPA statute were not in existence, in many cases where lack of good faith in the contract action could be shown, there would be the right of recovery under existing state and federal laws.

This wide-scale violation of law requires some systematic explanation. If this behavior is called criminal, as we have contended it is, such an assumption discounts traditional ways of explaining crime on the basis of such factors as heredity, feeblemindedness, poverty, race, immigrant background, and probably psychopathology.[19] Moreover, studies which show that offenders are generally youthful are invalidated by the fact that offenders of this type are generally middle-aged. In fact, it may be assumed that such offenders are likely to be more highly educated and usually married, so that neither the fact of education nor marital status would appear to be important in connection with such criminal behavior.

Assuming that such behavior does require explanation, several theories may be advanced. It is not the intention of this paper to make definitive answers, but rather to suggest several lines along which further research can be carried out. The most obvious approach is situational. The assumption may be made that businessmen are alike as to personality and what makes one individual violate rather than another is the pressure of profits and supplies.[20] Fortunately, there is one study which suggests tentative answers to this question.[21] As the result of interviews with several hundred producers and distributors of consumer goods, it was concluded that sales and profits were not related to price violations. On the other hand, an acute shortage of supplies, irrespective of sales, contributed to price increases.

Another situational approach is the contention that large firms comply with the regulations and small ones do not. It has been suggested that large firms consider their reputations, are aware of their social responsibility, employ so many persons that violations could not be kept secret, are more frequently and thoroughly investigated by the OPA, and have large staffs to become familiar with and explain all regulations. Small firms, on the other hand, are thought to have little reputation to lose, do not keep adequate records and, therefore, could make frequent cash transactions which might involve violations, and are not as frequently investigated by the OPA. However, a survey which sought an answer to this particular problem among Chicago business concerns, while inconclusive, suggests that size of the firm alone does not appear to be an important factor in violation.[22]

A second type of explanation is one which may be termed "differential association." This explanation implies that the person has acquired certain antisocial norms through association with other persons which predispose him to violate the law. Such differential association may be of three types. It may involve persons who have had a previous criminal record or those who have been associated with persons previously engaged in criminal behavior. Other differential association may rather have been confined to acquiring knowledge and experience with unethical or illegal practices of the business world. Sutherland has suggested[23] this as a general explanation of white-collar crime and, more specifically with reference to OPA violations, has stated his opinion that

In general, this seems to me to be fairly well in accord with the theory of differential association; not that the local grocer or the customers of that grocer violate these regulations by associating with gangsters, but that they violate the regulations (1) because they had, prior to enactment of the law, contact with such patterns of behavior and a whole organized set of customs and attitudes in connections with them, and these continue to operate after the law declares the practices to be illegal; (2) because specific stimulations and techniques are acquired from others who are violating the law.[24]

A third type, closely related to the previous one, is the development of sufficient negative attitudes toward the OPA and government regulations which are so reinforced by similar beliefs of other businessmen that the regulations are not considered legal.

The first type of explanation, which traces price and rationing violations to association with previous criminal norms, is rather widely held, particularly among the general public. The idea became widespread due primarily to an unfortunate publicity policy in the early days of the OPA which was intended to awaken the public to the dangers of price and rationing violations. Statements were issued that organized racketeers were engaging in black-market activities and there were a large number of articles in magazines and newspapers, as well as motion-picture shorts, which described such cases. The term "black market" itself became almost synonymous with organized criminal behavior, whereas actually it should be used more correctly to describe any price or rationing violation, whether in legitimate channels such as ordinary business or otherwise. Even businessmen appear to have been influenced by such stories, for in interviews they will occasionally refer to a mysterious black market. Actually, with the exception of one type of activity, there appears to be little evidence of any organized criminal underworld engaging in price and rationing violations. The one exception has been the theft and counterfeiting of ration currency, which has been largely a field of professional criminal activities. Contrary to popular impression, a relatively small percentage of offenders have any previous criminal record, exclusive of traffic violations, although it is possible that many businessmen may have engaged in white-collar criminality for which they were never prosecuted. If we consider price and rationing cases involving criminal prosecution, which probably represents a sample of more flagrant OPA cases, we find that only about one out of ten are reported to have had a criminal record. Of those imprisoned, which may or may not represent the more serious cases, although they are more likely to have been more serious than those who were fined or placed on probation, only about one-third have criminal records. Those prosecuted criminally are chiefly violators of the rationing orders, including dealers who violated the rationing provisions, as well as those who stole or counterfeited the currency. A relatively few persons have been prosecuted for price violations, and the proportion who have a criminal record is even smaller. It is likely that one reason why such a small number of persons have been prosecuted for price violations is the fact that few persons of this type have previous records of criminal behavior and this makes the possibility of conviction difficult.

The fact that businessmen have been associated with others who have engaged in customary business practices of a quasi-legal character appears to have some partial validity in explaining violations. In some businesses, such as gasoline and apparel, it appears to be more important than in others. Such an etiology appears to be typical of certain marginal operators who have come into the business to make a quick fortune.

While it is likely that many cases of violations of price and rationing regulations, where there has been continuous and intimate association with differential norms, can be satisfactorily explained by a theory of differential association, there are several limitations in such a general theory. Without going into great detail, a few major objections may be briefly stated. Such a theory does not adequately explain why some individuals who are familiar with the techniques of violation, as well as frequently associating with persons similarly familiar, do not engage in such practices. It is doubtful whether any businessman can participate in a given line of business for any length of time without acquiring a rather complete knowledge of practices in his trade. Certainly besides talking with competitors and customers, he has ample opportunity to read of techniques of violations in newspapers and trade journals. It is difficult to explain, therefore, the fact that thousands of business concerns, even in those commodities where one expects less group ethics, appear to comply fully with the regulations.

A second criticism of differential association is that the behavior is accounted for in terms of a single role that the person is playing, which in this case is the role of a businessman. The same individual may play a variety of roles, and behavior such as that involved in violating a law may well involve an integration of several different roles. In the case of offenders of the lower socioeconomic classes, there is likely to be more similarity in the behavior of different roles in which the person is engaged. When we are considering offenders of the white-collar class, there is probably less similarity in the several roles. Still another difficulty in differential association as an explanation of behavior is that the theory tends to overemphasize the more recent developments in the individual's personality rather than the importance of early behavior patterns in the formation of personality. These early behavior patterns may well be important enough to counterbalance later association with criminal or antisocial conduct.

Finally, the theory of differential association does not allow sufficiently either for independent invention of a complex technique or the need for acquiring any technique for violations which are extraordinarily simple. The validity of this particular statement should, of course, be ascertained by further detailed study of a number of cases. Certainly many OPA violations involving similar techniques have appeared in isolated areas. In many violations only a single person appears to have been involved. There appears, for example, to be ample evidence that rather complex evasive violations of rent regulations have appeared in relatively isolated areas, and they appear to have been independently devised, since there is ordinarily little association among landlords.

Some suggest the explanation that compliance is determined by whether attitudes of businessmen are in favor of, intermediate, or hostile to price control, the origin of which may be sought in their attitudes toward past profit trends, profit expectations, price expectations, long-range considerations, fairness of the regulations, and certain misconceptions which they may have had about the purposes of price control. A survey of Chicago manufacturers and distributors shows that when attitudes toward price control are cooperative there are less violations, and when they are hostile there are likely to be more violations.[25] The results, however, indicate that attitudes do not appear to be the cause of violations, but rather only one element of a larger situation.

It appears that there can be no single explanation of OPA violations. They are not the result entirely of either supply and demand, profits, or types of businesses. Likewise, violations do not appear to arise to any degree out of contacts with criminal conduct norms or result from negative attitudes toward the OPA. Differential association with deviant norms of the business world explains some cases, but not all; nor does it explain why some engage in such activity, while others do not although they have had extensive differential association. These cases of white-collar crime offer an excellent opportunity for examining the life organization of violators to ascertain what set of factors make up for conformist and nonconformist behavior. Why is it that some businessmen who have been presented with numerous opportunities to violate do not do so, while others with only limited opportunity have readily violated?

Solution of this problem appears to be in the individual's personality pattern. There may be psychogenic characteristics, general reaction patterns, such as disregard for the rights of society in general, or basic attitudes, such as attitudes toward law and the importance of reputation which were developed in the early years of life. These may be a result of the different integration of the several roles which each individual plays in society. As Sellin states, "An important function of etiological research is, therefore, the formulation of generalizations which permit us to differentiate the violator from the conformist, in terms of personality structure or growth process."[26] Besides Sellin, Sutherland[27] and Dunham and Lindesmith[28] have suggested that this is one of the most crucial issues in criminological research. Perhaps before finding an answer to this question, criminology will have to await further understanding of the nature of personality differences. The life histories of violators of wartime regulations offer us an opportunity for some preliminary conclusions as to why persons do not conform to law.

Notes

1. See Edwin H. Sutherland, "White-Collar Criminality," *American Sociological Review*, 5 (February, 1940), pp. 1–12; "Is 'White Collar Crime' Crime?" *American Sociological Review*, 10 (April, 1945), pp. 132–139; and "Crime and Business," *Annals of the American Academy of Political and Social Science*, 217 (September, 1940), pp. 112–118; see also articles by Jerome Hall: "Interrelationships of Criminal Law and Torts," *Columbia Law Review*, 43 (September, 1943), pp. 753–779, 967–1001; "Prolegomena to a Science of Criminal Law," *University of Pennsylvania Law Review*, 89 (March, 1941), pp. 549–580; and "Criminal Attempts—A Study of Foundations of Criminal Liability," *Yale Law Journal*, 49 (March, 1940), pp. 789–840.

2. See further Marshall B. Clinard, *The Black Market: A Study of White Collar Crime* (New York: Holt, 1952).

3. See *Public Opinion on Control of Prices, Wages, Salaries during War and Reconversion* (Chicago: National Opinion Research Center, 1947).

4. Sutherland, "Is 'White Collar Crime' Crime?" *op. cit.*

5. Hall, "Interrelationships of Criminal Law and Torts," *op. cit.*, pp. 999–1000.

6. *Steuart & Brother, Inc.* v. *Bowles*, 322 U.S. 398 (1944).

7. An injunction without treble damage action to recover the amount of the overcharge is analogous to serving a hypothetical injunction on a bank robber as he comes out of a bank with his loot, to cease and desist from further violations but allowing him to retain the stolen money. Many injunctions, which prevent the possibility of future violations, are similar in nature to serving an injunction on a bank robber as he goes into a bank to rob it.

8. *The Hecht Company* v. *Bowles*, 321 U.S. 321 (1944).

9. To reason that because some businessmen do not approve of the law and, therefore, see no reason for obeying it seems little more valid, from the standpoint of protection of society in general, than to state that because some criminals of the lower socioeconomic class do not approve of some criminal laws they can violate them.

10. Richard C. Fuller, "Morals and the Criminal Law," *Journal of Criminal Law and Criminology*, 32 (March–April, 1942), pp. 624–630.

11. *Ibid.*, pp. 629–630.

12. This opinion is further supported by a survey of OPA district enforcement attorneys who reported that where sentences were generally adequate observance of regulations was best, and a converse situation existed where sentences were inadequate.

13. In 1945, approximately 2,500 housewives were asked what the government should do with retailers who intentionally violated price regulations. Slightly over one-third thought they should be fined, 8 per cent would give them a jail sentence, 21 per cent would make them close their stores for a while, and 12 per cent would make them pay up to three times the amount of the overcharge (Office of Price Administration, *Opinion Briefs*, No. 7, April 12, 1945).

14. This includes only cases of the OPA Enforcement Department. Many cases were investigated by price panel volunteers of the Price Department who took actions without referring cases to the Enforcement Department. Rent cases, and practically all consumer cases, are not included in any of the figures. Also not included are the large number of private treble damage suits brought by consumers against dealers nor the majority of prosecutions under local legislation of which there are no accurate records. In New York City alone in 1944 there were 18,875 prosecutions of retailers by the New York Department of Markets, and the sheriff's office in the three-month period during January 15, 1945, prosecuted over 4,000 wholesale dealers.

15. For other estimates of the extent of violations of OPA regulations, see George Katona, *Price Control and Business* (Bloomington, Ind.: Principia Press, 1945), pp. 47–48, 57–58.

16. The estimated annual grand total of all OPA violations, including consumer, rent, retail and preretail, which is approximately 900,000, is equal to the total crimes known to the police, which is also approximately 900,000 (*Uniform Crime Reports*, vol. 15, no. 1).

17. For other classifications of white-collar crime, see Sutherland, "White Collar Criminality," *op. cit.*, p. 2; *Tenth Annual Report of the Securities and Exchange Commission*, pp. 143–146; and *1944 Report of the Federal Trade Commission*, pp. 38–44, 57–59.

18. For example, see Katona, *op. cit.*, and various studies of the Bureau of Labor Statistics.

19. See Sutherland, "White Collar Criminality," *op. cit.*

20. In this regard, a comment by a nonprocessing meat slaughter is interesting: "When I sold to black markets I couldn't sleep at night; since I comply [summer, 1943] I can't sleep at night because I am losing money" (Katona, *op. cit.*, p. 47).

21. Katona, *op. cit.*, p. 141.

22. *Ibid.*, p. 129.

23. Sutherland, "Crime and Business," *op. cit.*, p. 116.

24. Extract from letter to author, August 6, 1943. Reviewing Harry Lever and Joseph Young, *Wartime Racketeers*, Sutherland has suggested that if enforcement of new regulations could be started promptly, the development of many new patterns of violation could be prevented (*American Sociological Review*, 10 [December, 1945], pp. 817–818).

25. Katona, *op. cit.*, p. 170.

26. Thorsten Sellin, *Culture Conflict and Crime* (New York: Social Science Research Council, 1938), p. 40.

27. Edwin H. Sutherland, "The Relation between Personal Traits and Associational Patterns," in Walter Reckless, ed., *The Etiology of Delinquent and Criminal Behavior* (New York: Social Science Research Council, 1943), pp. 131–138.

28. Alfred R. Lindesmith and H. Warren Dunham, "Some Principles of Criminal Typology," *Social Forces*, 19 (March, 1941), pp. 307–314.

6

WHY BUSINESSMEN VIOLATE THE LAW

Robert E. Lane

Recent interest in the problem of illegality in the business community focuses attention on the considerable scope of this phenomenon. Thus, in 1951, the National Labor Relations Board formally ordered 115 firms to cease certain illegal practices and informally adjusted another 796 cases. In the same year, the Federal Trade Commission investigated 869 cases of deceptive practices and found business management guilty of illegal practices in 107; the Wage and Hour and Public Contracts Divisions of the Department of Labor inspected 33,479 establishments and found 56 per cent of them guilty of violations of the law. Of course, these represent only a fraction of the cases of violation, but they insistently raise the question: Why do some businessmen violate these laws while others do not? This paper is an attempt to contribute to the growing evidence and doctrine in this field. It is based upon the following sources of information: (1) interviews with top management in twenty-five New England industrial firms; (2) interviews with seven leaders of govern-

Reprinted from *Journal of Criminal Law, Criminology and Police Science,* 44 (July, 1953), pp. 151–165.

mental regulatory agencies; (3) analysis of the cases reported in Federal Trade Commission Decisions, Decisions and Orders of the National Labor Board, court cases arising from these decisions, and court cases arising from the action of the Wage and Hour and Public Contracts Divisions of the Department of Labor; and (4) a statistical study of the violations of trade practice and labor regulation in the New England shoe industry.

THE ECONOMICS OF VIOLATION

Most businessmen and most responsible government officers, at least from the sample interviewed, believe that businessmen run afoul of the law for economic reasons—they want to "make a fast buck."[1] They are led to transgress because, to be specific, if they adopt an advertising campaign which overstates the facts or if they reclassify their personnel into "management" positions (and so avoid the overtime provisions of the Fair Labor Standards Act) or if they get rid of the union (and the union demands), their profit positions will reflect these acts in a favorable manner. Thus, the manufacturers of bottling crowns may agree, illegally, to fix a scale of prices and standardize their products,[2] a jewelry manufacturer illegally fixes his discount rates so as to attract chain retail outlets without regard to savings in costs to himself,[3] a Southern textile manufacturer fires two employees seeking to establish a union and therefore a union wage scale.[4]

But there are two difficulties with this simple economic explanation. In the first place, it probably doesn't cover some of the cases where management-union relations are involved. Thus, an important life insurance company finds itself involved with the National Labor Relations Board because one of its supervisors fired a man who had testified previously before the board—Why? Not because of economic reasons, but because he had made the supervisor "look silly" in public.[5] The other objection to the economic motivation argument is that it really doesn't explain much. Two films with similar opportunities for breaking the law may show different records: One violates the law, another does not. Why? The simple explanation based on economic motivation does not tell us.

Pushing the economic argument further, however, perhaps "need" rather than "opportunity for gain" is the criterion, perhaps if one firm is in a more desperate situation than the other it will be more likely to violate the law. Or it may be that a firm which will abide by the law when it is prosperous, will violate the law when it is necessitous.[6]

To support this point of view, take the case of a small tool-making organization in Chicago in the immediate postwar period. In 1947, when this firm employed twenty-five men and enjoyed relative prosperity, the

International Association of Machinists organized the firm and, in an election, won the contractual right to represent the employees in collective bargaining. By 1949, however, the number of employees had fallen to twelve and the firm was in a serious position. It was at this point that the president of the firm decided to terminate his relationship with the union and, illegally, refused to bargain collectively with them. Although he later explained that this was because he doubted whether the union really represented the men, his letter to the union explaining his position gave other reasons. The union wage scale, he said, is "responsible for placing our industry in a noncompetitive and embarrassing position. . . . During the period of the time in question, our company sustained very substantial losses. . . . It is for these reasons that we were obliged to terminate our contract and withdrew recognition from the union."[7]

Table 1. Growth and Decline of Labor Relations and Trade Practices Violators and Nonviolators in the Shoe Industry over a 10- to 15-Year Period (1936–1950)*

	Declined	No change	Grew
Labor relations violators	26%	31%	42%
Misrepresentation cases	50	38	12
Nonviolators	31	31	38

*Only those for whom there are data over a 10-year period are here recorded.

Is a weak or declining financial position a common cause for violation? In order to find out the relationships between the fortunes of a firm and violation of the law, a study of the 275 shoe-manufacturing firms in New England was made and the records of violators of labor relations laws and trade practices laws analyzed. Since data on the financial position of these firms were difficult to obtain, reported number of employees was used to indicate growth and decline. The record is as indicated in Tables 1 and 2.[8]

By concentrating on the time period immediately before and after the violation a more precise analysis is possible:

Table 2. Relation of Growth and Decline of Firms to Violation of Labor Relations and Trade Practices (Misrepresentation) Laws

	Year of violation and preceding year			Year subsequent to violation and following year		
	De-clined	No change	In-creased	De-clined	No change	In-creased
Labor relations violators	7%	73%	20%	25%	50%	25%
Misrepresentation cases	25	75	0	33	67	0

These data reveal several new aspects of the problem. For one thing, it seems apparent that violation of the trade practices laws is more closely associated with economic decline than is violation of the labor relations laws. Violation of these trade practices laws is associated with decline before the event, thus suggesting a causal relationship, and declines after the violation, thus suggesting that apprehension and conviction are in some way punishing to a firm. On the other hand, the complex of events which caused the Chicago tool firm to break the law seems not to have been prevalent in the New England shoe industry; here economic condition was more or less irrelevant to the question of lawbreaking.

Comparing the figures for trade practice violation and labor relations violation suggests that the two laws do not appear in the same light to industrialists busy in the processes of making the nation's goods. For one thing, the labor relations laws are more recent than the trade practice laws and most of the violations (63 per cent) occurred during the first three and a half years of the National Labor Relations Act. Thus, it might be said that violation of recent laws is less related to the prosperity of the firms than violation of the older established (and accepted) laws of the land. But there is another factor. The trade practices acts prohibit false advertising, misleading statements, price fixing, illegal discounts, and related activities. These activities, however, seem closer to the normally accepted ideas of "immoral" or "criminal" behavior and their prohibition corresponds more to the businessman's concept of right and wrong. Therefore, in addition to the recentness of the law, there is a question of the closeness of the law to the moral judgments of the businessmen who must live within it.

There are other pieces of evidence which tend to support the idea that the more profitable firms do not violate some laws as easily and quickly as the less profitable firms. An analysis of the incidence of violation of the Fair Labor Standards Act (1938) shows that there is a higher proportion of violations in those industries suffering relative hard times. This seems also to be true of price-control legislation, for during the war "compliance with price-control regulations seemed to be more satisfactory among firms with rising profits than among those with declining profits."[9]

AMBIGUITY, IGNORANCE, AND
DIFFICULTY OF COMPLIANCE

In one sense, it is quite unfair to management to consider a large number of the recorded cases as willful violations of the law. In all those instances culminating in "leading cases," no one knows the law until the court has spoken. While these cases may indicate a propensity to probe the law's farthest limits, this is quite different from deliberate infraction of a known law. Following this line of reasoning, the officers of the Cement Institute can hardly be thought guilty of illegal motives when they administered their basing-point system, since the system had a history of several decades during which it was regarded as legal.[10] Nor can the management of the Mt. Clemens Pottery Company be considered guilty of illegal design for not paying overtime on the basis of portal to portal rates, since, until the court spoke, their employees were not thought to be on the job until they were, in fact, working for the company.[11]

But setting aside questions of ambiguous law (and all laws are ambiguous at their margins), may there not be many cases where management runs afoul of the law simply because they are not aware of its stated provisions? Can management be expected to keep posted on the variety of national and state laws affecting their operations? Some businessmen interviewed thought that this was a serious matter, and among the executives of the smaller companies a few expressed regret over the amount of time necessary to preserve a law-abiding record. The agencies themselves show a recognition of this problem of unintentional violation, the Federal Trade Commission stating:

> It is manifestly difficult to draft a statement of policy on a broad base which does not afford an evasive device to the willful violator while seeking to avoid unduly harsh treatment of the unintentional or casual violator.[12]

Even more specific is the Wages and Hours and Public Contracts Divisions statement:

> The divisions knew that violators generally may be placed in three groups—those who willfully violate; those who are in violation because of ignorance of the law; and those who inadvertently misapply provisions of the law, thus committing technical violations.[13]

On the other hand, most of the businessmen interviewed felt that, with the help of their lawyers and the loose-leaf services, they were unlikely to be caught off-guard by unfamiliar legislation. Speaking of violators of the price-control laws during the war, one observer says, "It appears unlikely that, after the initial period, many businessmen are ignorant of the provisions" of the law.[14] There are no data on this question of "knowledge of the law among violators," but we will attempt to get at it indirectly.

The hypothesis that ignorance and improper technical advice is a primary cause of violation is often supported by the belief that the smaller firms violate the law out of proportion to their numbers in the business population, partly, at least, because of poor legal counsel. A majority of the administrators polled expressed this point of view, and it is common among businessmen. But, if we examine the data of the 275 shoe manufacturers in New England (Table 3), this does not seem to be true, at least in this instance.

Table 3. Per Cent of Violations of Labor Relations and Trade Practices Legislation in New England Shoe Industry by Size (1933–1949)

Size groups (no. of employees)	Per cent of size group who violated NLRA and LMRA	Per cent of size group who violated trade practice laws (misrepresentation)
Under 100	10.9	0
101 – 500	14.0	5.9
501 –1,000	30.0	15.0
Over 1,000	11.1	33.3

Since there can be little doubt that large companies hire more and better counsel and are better informed on the law, these data should go far toward supporting those managers who claimed that "ignorance" of the law was not a legitimate excuse.[15]

Could one, then, reverse the principle—larger companies with superior legal resources violate more, proportionately, than smaller companies? No, this is not possible either, as Table 4 and Figure 1, showing the relationship of size to wage and hour violations, will quickly prove.

There is, in fact, no clear relationship between size (and therefore legal services) and violation; each industry and each regulatory measure has a pattern of its own.[16]

If, as seems likely, management only very rarely violates the law because of ignorance of the relevant provisions, perhaps it is possible that management sometimes finds it genuinely difficult to comply with the known law. Does the law require the impossible? Of the twenty-five manufacturers consulted, none believed that he was handicapped by inadequate records, personnel, or facilities in complying with labor relations

Table 4. Per Cent of Inspected Establishments in Three Industries in Substantial Violation of Fair Labor Standards Act and Public Contracts Act by Size of Establishment (1948)

Number of employees	Per cent of inspected establishments in substantial violation		
	Textile and related products	Leather and leather goods	Metals and metal products
4– 7	42	42	52
8– 19	31	38	43
20– 49	34	32	37
50– 99	25	34	33
100–199	28	38	29
200–499	26	42	27
500 or more	35	30	22

legislation. These laws were opposed on other grounds. One, the smallest (thirty-five employees) felt that he was handicapped in obeying the wages and hours laws because he did not have the necessary records. None of the others felt that this was a burden. Although a number felt that trade practices regulation created hazards for them, only two felt that they were handicapped in complying because of lack of data or cost records. Of course, it is expensive to maintain such records, but often, as it turns out, these records have multiple uses and are only partly chargeable to government regulation.

On the basis of the above considerations, we may say that although ambiguous provisions of the law and factually contested situations often lead to "violation" (in a technical sense) ignorance of the law and incapacity to respond seem, in most cases, to be relatively unimportant causes of violation.

Figure 1. Relation of Rate of Violation of Wage and Hour Laws (1948) to Size of Establishment in Metal, Shoe, and Textile Industries

Per cent of inspected establishments in substantial violation of wages and hours laws 1948

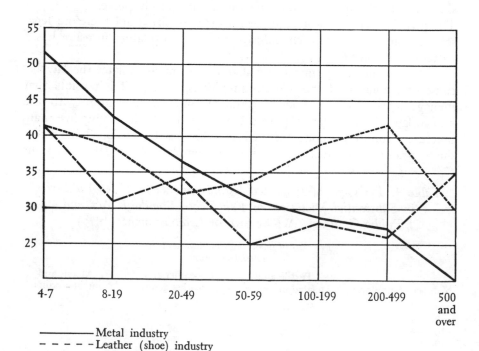

Metal industry
Leather (shoe) industry
Textile industry

VIOLATORS AND THEIR ASSOCIATES

Edwin H. Sutherland, a few years prior to his death, reformulated his theory of criminal behavior in order to explain violations of the law by business management. Central among his ideas is the doctrine of "differential association,"[17] a doctrine which holds that men who associate with those who favor violation (or at least are indifferent to it) more than with those who oppose any violation of law, are more likely themselves to be violators. It is based on the common view that men pick up most of their opinions and orientations from their associates, and it has much evidence to support it in the criminological literature. Note, however, that there are two parts to the doctrine: (1) positive association with men contemptuous of the law and (2) isolation from those who uphold legality, even if the laws in question are distasteful.

But what kind of evidence of business friendship groups and their opinions on legality is available? Not much; the evidence must be circumstantial.

One approach might be to examine the policies of different firms in the same "interest groups," on the grounds that common association of directors and ranking officers might create a common pattern.[18] One clue to the rate of violation of the labor relations laws is given by the proportions between representation cases and unfair labor practice cases, the fewer unfair labor practice cases per representation case, the more law-abiding the management. An analysis of the violation rates in the Mellon interest group, the du Pont interest group, the Cleveland interest group, and two firms associated with the Avery family (U.S. Gypsum and Montgomery Ward) shows that there is little common policy among the firms in each group. It doesn't appear that any common association (or even control) has an influence on attitudes toward the law. Incidentally, however, it is notable that the incidence of violation in the firms of these big business interests is markedly lower than the general rates for all business.

An analysis of the rates of violation of labor relations laws in the shoe industry gives some support to the differential association hypothesis. This may be found in the fact that in some shoe-manufacturing communities none of the shoe firms violates, whereas in other shoe-manufacturing communities almost half of the firms get into trouble with the law. There may be several reasons for this, but it seems fairly conclusive that one of the reasons is the difference in attitude toward the law, the government, and the morality of illegality. Table 5 shows how these rates of violation vary in eight New England communities. It would be interesting, in this respect, to examine in more detail the special ideological environment of a businessman operating in the "rugged individualist" city of Auburn,

Maine. It seems probable that a manager who lunched and played golf with other business managers of Auburn, Maine, would feel differently and behave differently from the manager who was surrounded by the businessmen of Brockton, Massachusetts. This point of view was supported indirectly by the managers interviewed, who generally agreed that they followed community patterns of behavior, in terms of wage scales, vacations, union recognition, and so forth.

Table 5. Per Cent of Firms Violating Labor Relations Laws in Selected Communities

Place	Number of shoe firms	Number of violating firms	Per cent of violating
Haverhill, Mass.	28	2	7.0
Lynn, Mass.	27	1	3.7
Brockton, Mass.	17	0	0.0
Boston, Mass.	16	0	0.0
Manchester, N.H.	10	3	30.0
Auburn, Me.	9	4	44.4
Lowell, Mass.	8	3	37.5
Cambridge, Mass.	5	2	40.0

But the idea of differential association has two parts to it: association with men whose attitudes encourage violation and isolation from men whose attitudes discourage violation. Is there any evidence of such isolation? How could this be proved?

There is evidence of such isolation and, although it is not conclusive, it is worth looking at. In the first place, there is the question of reading matter, which ranges in attitude from temperate periodicals, such as *The Harvard Business Review* and *Fortune,* to some trade journals that serve to keep alive government-business hostility beyond the point of usefulness. It is possible for men to immerse themselves in a section of the press so hostile to government that violation of the law must seem most appropriate. By the same token, they may isolate themselves from journals which preserve a balance between criticism and neutral reporting. These choices, furthermore, extend to selection of luncheon clubs, radio programs, daily papers, and other vehicles for attitudes and ideas.

The problem of isolation from divergent points of views is much more serious in small towns than in large cities with their cosmopolitan press, diversified social life, and greater tolerance for heterodoxy. Big-city business management does, as a matter of fact, seem to accept restrictions of the law somewhat more readily than small-town management. This is not only a commonsense proposition, borne out by impressionistic observation of management in the twenty-five interviews, but it is also supported by our study of the shoe industry, as indicated by Table 6. Again, it must be true that there are many factors at work, but on the whole the results seem to confirm the differential association hypothesis.

THE PERSONAL EXPERIENCES AND
PERSONALITY OF VIOLATORS

Even when we have accounted for the financial needs of a firm and for the ambiguity or difficult requirements of the law, possible management ignorance with respect to the law, and social pressures, there still remains the personality and personal experiences of the individual managers. It is impossible and wrong to make of this matter a wholly fatalistic process whereby the situation of the firm, the incidence of the law, and the degree of social pressure combine to eliminate the power of decision among the firm's managers. We must include these more personal characteristics too, even though they are not readily accessible.

One of the defects of the fatalistic interpretation of business violation is that it impersonalizes business leadership. While in the larger corporations there may be a tendency toward impersonalization through frequent group consultation, the use of legal counsel, guidance of cost accountants, reliance on market reports, and so forth, the marginal figures of Ford, Girdler, Rand, Avery, Weir, and others suggest that, within the margin and without benefit of publicity, temperament and psychic factors are still important determinants of business policy. Among smaller firms this is even more certainly true.

Among the variety of personal characteristics and experiences two may be considered here as representative of the wide range of factors of this kind: (1) previous experience with regulation and (2) personal attitudes toward authority as expressed in the law. To take first the matter of previous experience with regulation, how may this affect business responses to new and additional measures?

One approach is to find out whether the experience of violation and conviction leads to further violation or leads to a more law-abiding pattern of behavior. Unlike the crime records, the records of business violation show that recidivism is infrequent; violation and apprehension is not the preface to future violation, it is likely to be the end of the matter.

Table 6. Violators of Labor Relations and Fair Trade Laws
by Size of Town

Size town	Number of shoe firms	Number of violators (labor relations)	Per cent of violators (labor relations)	Number of violators (trade practice)	Per cent of violators (trade practice)
Under 5,000	20	0	0	2	10.0
5,000– 10,000	34	8	23.6	3	8.5
10,000– 25,000	46	9	26.5	2	4.3
25,000–100,000	87	10	11.5	2	2.3
Over 100,000	76	8	10.4	2	2.6

Thus, out of 200 violators of the National Labor Relations Act between December, 1935, and August 21, 1947, only thirteen, or 6.5 per cent, were repeaters.[19] This pattern is also true of violators of the trade practice laws: There were 188 orders and stipulations in 1948 to 1949, but only four punitive orders indicating serious second offenders.[20]

Another method of showing the effect of previous regulation on the rate of violation is to examine the effect of some of the newer regulatory measures in industries that have always been under close public supervision. If it is true that experience of regulation teaches management how to keep within the law, what to expect, what kind of legal counsel to hire, and, perhaps, what to do to minimize the impact of the regulation, we should expect these regulated industries to have lower rates of violation under the newer measures. In fact, this does seem to be the situation, at least with respect to the wages and hours laws. While 7 per cent of all inspected establishments were in "serious" violation of the Fair Labor Standards Act in the fiscal year 1948, the averages of certain industries accustomed to other forms of government regulation were: alcoholic beverages, 2 per cent; heat, light, power, water, 2 per cent; drugs and medicines, 3 per cent.[21]

But men do not react solely on the basis of what they "know" from such experiences to be true. They also respond to their inward feelings, which sometimes transcend and override their knowledge. Among these feelings, the emotional responses to authority have been singled out for much discussion by psychologists and their associates, so that it begins to appear that this is a central feature of individual adjustment to society. At least for the discussion of men's responses to governmental regulation, attitudes toward authority might seem to be among the most important of all phases of emotional life.

For obvious reasons, this line of analysis cannot be pursued in any detail—it would require psychoanalytic case studies for satisfactory study —but a few fragments of information will suggest caution before we go out on this particular limb. One such piece of evidence comes from a study made of the violation pattern of seventy large corporations, where it was found that there was great consistency of behavior toward specific laws over long periods of time when the managing personnel changed several times over. It seemed to be the position of the firm, rather than any emotional qualities of its management, which led it to violate. The obverse of this situation was shown in the fact that there was no tendency to react against a wide range of laws, no evident general antiregulation animus, at any one time.[22]

This is evidently a general pattern. In our sample of 275 New England shoe manufacturers, there were forty-five violations of the labor laws, involving thirty-five firms, and twenty violations of the trade practice laws, involving fourteen firms. In addition, there were two firms engaged in court cases under the wages and hours laws. In no instance did a firm violate more than one law. There was no evidence of a consistently "anti-regulation" or "antigovernment" or "antiauthority" policy on the part of any firm or its management.

But caution along these lines does not mean rejection of the thesis. We know that men tolerate restrictive governmental authority in different degrees and express this difference in their decisions and behavior. When, for example, the National Labor Relations Board says of a firm, "the respondent, under the active personal leadership of its president, . . . frustrated its employees' organizational efforts by a campaign of willful unfair labor practices"[23] we infer that this firm is guided by a man who has invested much emotional energy into a joint attack upon unions and the law. Something other than economic forces and social pressure is here at work.

REDUCING THE RATE OF VIOLATION

It is one thing to suggest the causes of violation; it is something else again to discover the cures. Nevertheless, it is curious, considering the talent and resources available both to the business community and the national government, that so little has been done to discover and promote such cures. Compared to the attention given to industrial relations, business-government relations have almost been ignored. This state of affairs is reflected in the limited nature of suggestions for reducing the rate of violation and minimizing business-government friction offered by businessmen and administrators.

When questioned on the most appropriate means of reducing friction and violation of the law, twenty-five managers interviewed on this problem suggested, in order of frequency, the following policies:

1. Stop the drift to socialism and the restriction of freedom.
2. Economize, cut the government payroll, balance the budget.
3. Increase governmental efficiency, pass Hoover recommendations, eliminate waste.
4. Increase government familiarity with business processes.
5. Cut controls to absolute minimum (allowing trade practice, or sweatshop, or antitrust controls only—or none).
6. Reduce uncertainty by stabilizing rules and regulations.
7. Recruit a better grade of government personnel and reduce turnover.
8. Increase morality and honesty in government-business relations.

Regrettably, these suggestions were rarely supported with specific data or an indication of how they might have reduced the rate of violations in the business community had they been applied earlier.

The seven highly placed administrators consulted on this general problem naturally turned toward other kinds of solutions. The principal suggestions might be summarized as follows:

1. The development of a more sympathetic attitude toward business problems on the part of administrators.

2. Enlargement of the educational program of government, attempting to convey information not only on the provisions of the law, but the reasons it was enacted and the goals it seeks to establish.

3. Establishment of greater consultative relationships with business, particularly with the key men in each industrial area.

4. Critical re-examination of administrative procedures to reduce duplication and unnecessary paper work.

5. Sympathetic liaison with the professions allied to business management—law, public relations, personnel, etc.

Both of these sets of "solutions" offer a useful agenda for consideration and discussion, but much remains to be done. In connection with this agenda, the preceding analysis of the causes of violation seems to indicate a more particular focus on certain kinds of situations and circumstances. These may be briefly outlined as follows:

1. While it is generally (but not universally) true that "economic" gain is necessary for violation to take place, marginal and declining firms are more likely to violate the law than prosperous firms. Any help the government can extend to these firms will, therefore, probably reduce the rate of violation.

2. Ambiguous laws lead to a higher rate of violation. In spite of occasional business opposition, therefore, it is desirable for responsible administrators to have authority to issue legally binding interpretations of the laws they administer, providing these are subject to adequate court review. Furthermore, administrators should weigh more heavily the effects of uncertainty in calculating whether or not to "stick their necks out."

3. Although it is rare that businessmen violate a law because they do not know of its provisions, the government could do much to improve the channels of information between management and the regulatory agencies. There is no reason that these should be monopolized by third parties or by the legal profession.

4. Since violation is a product, in part, of social pressure and community attitudes, government and business should jointly seek to build respect for law—even distasteful law enforced by a repugnant administration. Government cannot do this alone; business cannot do this without

a record of fair dealing by the government. It is a task for both elements of society. Further study would quickly reveal the communities where this is most urgent.

5. Government should approach each manager as a unique individual with a unique set of experiences, a personality different from all others, confronted by a problem which looms large, even though he be one of thousands in an official's lifetime. Only thus can the personal and individual nature of business decisions be understood and personal inclinations to violate be met and headed off by responsible government.

More could be said of a specific nature: Better business bureaus and local chambers of commerce could do much to stop violation at its source; governmental cease-and-desist orders could often be recast so as to give more attention to what is proscribed and less to proving guilt; trade journals could reconsider the effects of hostile expressions which may build circulation, but create a trade sentiment which breeds friction and violation; the impact of new laws could be lessened by a "dry-run" period of education and experimentation; and so forth. But, these suggestions, like those of the business community and those of the administrators, need further study and research.

What is clear from all this, however, is the need for both business and government to re-examine their relationship and to attempt to re-create a mutual respect which will facilitate their partnership in a democratic society.

Notes

1. An exceptionally good statement of this position was contained in a letter to the author from Corwin Edwards, director of the Bureau of Industrial Economics of the Federal Trade Commission: "I think the economic explanation of violations of law is the principal one. Inadequate enforcement certainly carries a heavy responsibility, but by decreasing the risk it strengthens the economic incentive to violate. Though there are some cases where the law is difficult to obey, these seem to me to be relatively few as compared to those in which it is merely more profitable not to obey."

2. *Crown Manufacturers Assn. of America*, 45 F.T.C. 89 (1948).

3. *Kreisler Mnfg. Corp.*, 45 F.T.C. 136 (1948).

4. *Sellers Mnfg. Co. & Textile Workers Union of America, C.I.O.*, 92 NLRB 279 (1950).

5. *John Hancock Mutual Life Insur. Co. & Samuel Kohen*, 92 NLRB 122 (1950).

6. Violations of price control and rationing seems to be less related to financial need than to the opportunity to make more than "ordinary" profits. See Marshall B. Clinard, *The Black Market: A Study of White Collar Crime* (New York: Holt, 1952), pp. 313–326.

7. *Toolcraft Corp. & Die & Toolmakers Lodge 113, Intl. Assn. of Machinists*, 92 NLRB 655 (1950).

8. The data on growth and decline of shoe firms are taken from the roughly annual *Directory of New England Manufacturers* (Boston: George D. Hall Co., 1936–

1950). Data included information on (1) twenty-four violators of labor relations regulations; (2) ten violators of misrepresentation provisions of the trade practices laws; and (3) a control group of eighteen firms, selected at random, which violated neither law.

Since the National Labor Relations Act was most likely to be violated where there were union men in the shop, inquiry was made to ascertain the extent of unionism in the New England shoe industry. There were forty-seven nonviolating firms petitioning for elections during this period (1935–1950) and most other firms included a few union men. Thus the presence of union men was not a highly selective factors.

9. George Katona, *Prince Control and Business* (Bloomington, Ind.: Principia Press, 1946), p. 241.

10. See *F.T.C.* v. *Cement Institute*, 333 U.S. 683 (1948).

11. See *Anderson* v. *Mt. Clemens Pottery Co.*, 328 U.S. 680 (1946).

12. *Annual Report*, 1948, p. 116.

13. *Ibid.*, pp. 28–29.

14. Marshall B. Clinard, "Criminological Theories of Wartime Regulations," *American Sociological Review*, 11 (June, 1946), p. 262.

15. In interpreting these data, one caution should be considered. The large firm with more foremen is exposed to more opportunities for discriminatory firing under the labor relations law, misclassification under the wages and hours law, or other violations of labor laws. Similarly, if a firm has many products it is exposed to more possibilities for violating the fair competition laws. The force of this consideration is weakened, however, by (1) violations under some laws in some industries apparently decrease with size, and (2) analysis of the actual cases shows that they are relatively rarely the product of low-level decisions.

16. See Katona, *op. cit.*, p. 165; Clinard, *The Black Market*, *op. cit.*, p. 325. This discussion of ignorance, size, and violation, although inconclusive, opens up a wide and fertile field for inquiry. What organization of information is necessary to keep a firm within the law? What size firm can best support such technical advice and counsel? What can government do for the small businessman and how effective is the present effort? Do the trade associations perform valuable services in this area or, as some managers informed the author, do they merely repeat each other and the special looseleaf services (Prentice-Hall, Commerce Clearing House, etc.)? Information along these lines might assist enforcement procedures in a manner that policing could not approach.

17. Edwin H. Sutherland, *White Collar Crime* (New York: Dryden Press, 1949), p. 234.

18. The sources of information on "interest groups" were Temporary National Economic Committee, *The Distribution of Ownership in the 200 Largest Non-Financial Corporations* (Washington, D.C.: Government Printing Office, 1940), pp. 1514ff; and National Resources Committee, *The Structure of the American Economy, Part I, Basic Characteristics* (Washington, D.C.: Government Printing Office, 1939), p. 158.

19. Calculated from a random sample taken from National Labor Relations Board, *Table of Cases Decided*, vol. 1–74 (December 7, 1939, through August 21, 1947).

20. *Federal Trade Commission Decisions*, vol. 45 (July 1, 1948, to June 30, 1949).

21. Wage and Hour and Public Contracts Divisions, *Annual Report*, 1948, Table E, pp. 162–165.

22. Sutherland, *op. cit.*, p. 264.

23. *Salant & Salant, Inc. and Amalgamated Clothing Workers of America, CIO*, 92 NLRB 345 (1950).

7

THE HEAVY ELECTRICAL EQUIPMENT
ANTITRUST CASES OF 1961

Gilbert Geis

An inadvertent bit of humor by a defense attorney provided one of the major criminological motifs for "the most serious violations of the antitrust laws since the time of their passage at the turn of the century."[1] The defendants, including several vice presidents of the General Electric Corporation and the Westinghouse Electric Corporation—the two largest companies in the heavy electrical equipment industry—stood somberly in a federal courtroom in Philadelphia on February 6, 1961. They were aptly described by a newspaper reporter as "middle-class men in Ivy League suits—typical businessmen in appearance, men who would never be taken for lawbreakers." Several were deacons or vestrymen of their churches. One was president of his local chamber of commerce; another, a hospital board member; another, chief fund raiser for the Community Chest; another, a bank director; another, director of the taxpayer's association; another, organizer of the local Little League.

The attorney for a General Electric executive attacked the government's demand for a jail sentence for his client, calling it "cold-blooded."

Reprinted from Marshall B. Clinard and Richard Quinney (eds.), *Criminal Behavior Systems* (New York: Holt, Rinehart and Winston, 1967), pp. 139–150. Copyright © 1967 by Holt, Rinehart and Winston, Inc.

The lawyer insisted that government prosecutors did not understand what it would do to his client, "this fine man," to be put "behind bars" with "common criminals who have been convicted of embezzlement and other serious crimes."[2]

The difficulty of defense counsel in considering antitrust violations "serious crimes," crimes at least equivalent to embezzling, indicates in part why the 1961 prosecutions provide such fascinating material for criminological study. Edwin H. Sutherland, who originated the term "white-collar crime" to categorize offenders such as antitrust violators, had lamented that his pioneering work was handicapped by the absence of adequate case histories of corporate offenders. "No first-hand research from this point of view has ever been reported."[3] Sutherland noted, and, lacking such data, he proceeded to employ prosaic stories of derelictions by rather unimportant persons in small enterprises upon which to build an interpretative and theoretical structure for white-collar crime.

To explain corporate offenses and offenders, Sutherland had to rely primarily upon the criminal biographies of various large companies, as these were disclosed in the annals of trial courts and administrative agencies. In the absence of information about human offenders, the legal fiction of corporate humanity, a kind of economic anthropomorphism, found its way into criminological literature. Factual gaps were filled by shrewd guesses, definitional and semantic strategies, and a good deal of extrapolation. It was as if an attempt were being made to explain murder by reference only to the listed rap sheet offenses of a murderer and the life stories and identification data of several lesser offenders.[4]

Sutherland was writing, of course, before the antitrust violations in the heavy electrical equipment industry became part of the public record. Though much of the data regarding them is tantalizingly incomplete and unresponsive to fine points of criminological concern, the antitrust offenses nonetheless represent extraordinary case studies of white-collar crime, that designation which, according to Sutherland, applies to behavior by "a person of high socioeconomic status who violates the laws designed to regulate his occupational activities"[5] and "principally refers to business managers and executives."[6] In particular, the antitrust cases provide the researcher with a mass of raw data against which to test and to refine earlier hunches and hypotheses regarding white-collar crime.

FACTS OF THE ANTITRUST VIOLATIONS

The most notable characteristic of the 1961 antitrust conspiracy was its willful and blatant nature. These were not complex acts only doubtfully in violation of a highly complicated statute. They were flagrant, criminal offenses, patently in contradiction to the letter and the spirit of the Sherman Antitrust Act of 1890, which forbade price-fixing arrangements as restraints upon free trade.[7]

The details of the conspiracy must be drawn together from diverse second-hand sources, because grand jury hearings upon which the criminal indictments were based were not made public. The decision to keep the records closed was reached on the ground that the traditional secrecy of grand jury proceedings took precedence over public interest in obtaining information about the conspiracy and over the interest of different purchasers in acquiring background data upon which to base civil suits against the offending corporations for allegedly fraudulent sales.[8]

The federal government had initiated the grand jury probes in mid-1959, apparently after receiving complaints from officials of the Tennessee Valley Authority concerning identical bids they were getting from manufacturers of highly technical electrical equipment, even though the bids were submitted in sealed envelopes.[9] Four grand juries were ultimately convened and subpoenaed 196 persons, some of whom obviously revealed the intimate details of the price-fixing procedures. A package of twenty indictments was handed down, involving forty-five individual defendants and twenty-nine corporations. Almost all of the corporate defendants pleaded guilty; the company officials tended to enter pleas of *nolo contendere* (no contest) which, in this case, might reasonably be taken to indicate that they did not see much likelihood of escaping conviction.

The pleas negated the necessity for a public trial and for public knowledge of the precise machinations involved in the offenses. At the sentencing hearing, fines amounting to $1,924,500 were levied against the defendants, $1,787,000 falling upon the corporations and $137,000 upon different individuals. The major fines were set against General Electric ($437,500) and Westinghouse ($372,500). Much more eye-catching were the jail terms of thirty days imposed upon seven defendants, four of whom were vice presidents; two, division managers; and one, a sales manager.

The defendants sentenced to jail were handled essentially the same as other offenders with similar dispositions. They were handcuffed in pairs in the back seat of an automobile on their way to the Montgomery County Jail in Norristown, Pennsylvania, fingerprinted on entry, and dressed in the standard blue denim uniforms. During their stay, they were described as "model prisoners," and several were transferred to the prison farm. The remainder, working an eight-hour day for 30 cents, earned recognition from the warden as "the most intelligent prisoners" he had had during the year on a project concerned with organizing prison records. None of the seven men had visitors during the Wednesday and Saturday periods reserved for visiting; all indicated a desire not to be seen by their families or friends.

Good behavior earned the men a five-day reduction in their sentence.

Toward the end of the year, the remaining defendants, who had been placed on probation, were released from that status, despite the strong protests of government officials. The judge, the same man who had imposed the original sentences, explained his action by noting that he "didn't think that this was the type of offense that probation lent itself readily to or was designed for." Supervision was seen as meaningless for men with such clean past records and such little likelihood of recidivism, particularly since the probation office was already "clogged to the gunwales"[10] with cases.

The major economic consequences to the corporations arose from civil suits for treble damages filed against them as provided in the antitrust laws. The original fines were, of course, negligible: For General Electric, a half-million dollar loss was no more unsettling than a $3 parking fine would be to a man with an income of $175,000 a year. Throughout the early stages of negotiations over the damage suits, General Electric maintained that it would resist such actions on grounds which are noteworthy as an indication of the source and the content of the rationale that underlay the self-justification of individual participants in the price-fixing conspiracy:

> We believe that the purchasers of electrical apparatus have received fair value by any reasonable standard. The prices which they have paid during the past years were appropriate to value received and reasonable as compared with the general trends of prices in the economy, the price trends for materials, salaries, and wages. The foresight of the electrical utilities and the design and manufacturing skills of companies such as General Electric have kept electricity one of today's greatest bargains.[11]

By 1962, General Electric was granting that settlements totaling between $45 and $50 million would have to be arranged to satisfy claimants. Municipalities and other purchasers of heavy electrical equipment were taking the period of lowest prices, when they assumed the price-rigging was least effective, using these prices as "legitimate," and calculating higher payments as products of the price conspiracy. The initial General Electric estimate soon proved untenable. A mid-1964 calculation showed that 90 per cent of some 1,800 claims had been settled for a total of $160 million, but General Electric could derive some solace from the fact that most of these payments would be tax-deductible.

TECHNIQUES OF THE CONSPIRACY

The modus operandi for the antitrust violators shows clearly the awareness of the participants that their behavior was such that it had better be carried on as secretly as possible. Some comparison might be made between the antitrust offenses and other forms of fraud occurring in lower economic classes. It was one of Sutherland's most telling contentions that neither the method by which a crime is committed nor the manner in which it is handled by public agencies alters the essential criminal nature of the act and the criminal status of the perpetrator.[12] Selling faucet water on a street corner to a blind man who is led to believe that the product is specially prepared to relieve his ailment is seen as no different from selling a $50 million turbine to a city which is laboring under the misapprehension that it is purchasing the product at the best price possible from closed competitive bidding. The same may be said in regard to methods of treatment. Tuberculosis, for example, remains tuberculosis and its victim a tubercular whether the condition is treated in a sanitarium or whether it is ignored, overlooked, or even condoned by public authorities. So too with crime. As Miss Stein might have said: A crime is a crime is a crime.

Like most reasonably adept and optimistic criminals, the antitrust violators had hoped to escape apprehension. "I didn't expect to get caught and I went to great lengths to conceal my activities so that I wouldn't get caught," one of them said.[13] Another went into some detail concerning the techniques of concealment:

> It was considered discreet to not be too obvious and to minimize telephone calls, to use plain envelopes if mailing material to each other, not to be seen together on traveling, and so forth . . . not leave wastepaper, of which there was a lot, strewn around a room when leaving.

The plans themselves, while there were some slight variations over time and in terms of different participants, were essentially similar. The offenders hid behind a camouflage of fictitious names and conspiratorial codes. The attendance roster for the meetings was known as the "Christmas card list" and the gatherings, interestingly enough, as "choir practice."[14] The offenders used public telephones for much of their communication, and they either met at trade association conventions, where their relationship would appear reasonable, or at sites selected for their anonymity. It is quite noteworthy, in this respect, that while some of the men filed false travel claims, so as to mislead their superiors regarding the city they had visited, they never asked for expense money to places more distant than those they had actually gone to—on the theory, apparently, that whatever else was occurring, it would not do to cheat the company.

At the meetings, negotiations centered about the establishment of a "reasonable" division of the market for the various products. Generally, participating companies were allocated essentially that part of the market which they had previously garnered. If Company A, for instance, had under competitive conditions secured 20 per cent of the available business, then agreement might be reached that it would be given the opportunity to submit the lowest bid on 20 per cent of the new contracts. A low price would be established, and the remainder of the companies would bid at approximately equivalent, though higher, levels. It sometimes happened, however, that because of things such as company reputation or available servicing arrangements, the final contract was awarded to a firm which had not submitted the lowest bid. For this, among other reasons, debate among the conspirators was often acrimonious about the proper division of spoils, about alleged failures to observe previous agreements, and about other intramural matters. Sometimes, depending upon the contract, the conspirators would draw lots to determine who would submit the lowest bid; at other times, the appropriate arrangement would be determined under a rotating system conspiratorially referred to as the "phase of the moon."

EXPLANATIONS OF THE CONSPIRACY

Attempts to understand the reasons for and the general significance of the price-fixing conspiracy have been numerous. They include re-examination of the antitrust laws,[15] as well as denunciations of the corporate ethos and the general pattern of American life and American values.[16] A not inconsiderable number of the defendants took the line that their behavior, while technically criminal, had really served a worthwhile purpose by "stabilizing prices" (a much-favored phrase of the conspirators). This altruistic interpretation almost invariably was combined with an attempted distinction among illegal, criminal, and immoral acts, with the offender's expressing the view that what he had done might have been designated by the statutes as criminal, but either he was unaware of such a designation or he thought it unreasonable that acts with admirable consequences should be considered criminal. The testimony of a Westinghouse executive during hearings by the Senate Subcommittee on Antitrust and Monopoly clearly illustrates this point of view:

> *Committee attorney:* Did you know that these meetings with competitors were illegal?
>
> *Witness:* Illegal? Yes, but not criminal. I didn't find that out until I read the indictment. . . . I assumed that criminal action meant damaging someone, and we did not do that. . . . I thought that we were more or less working on a survival basis in order to try to make enough to keep our plant and our employees.

This theme was repeated in essentially similar language by a number of witnesses. "It is against the law," an official of the Ingersoll-Rand Corporation granted, but he added: "I do not know that it is against public welfare because I am not certain that the consumer was actually injured by this operation." A Carrier Corporation executive testified that he was "reasonably in doubt" that the price-fixing meetings violated the antitrust law. "Certainly, we were in a gray area. I think the degree of violation, if you can speak of it that way, is what was in doubt." Some of these views are gathered together in a statement by a former sales manager of the I-T-E Circuit Breaker Company:

> One faces a decision, I guess, at such times, about how far to go with company instructions, and since the spirit of such meetings only appeared to be correcting a horrible price level situation, that there was not an attempt to actually damage customers, charge excessive prices, there was no personal gain in it for me, the company did not seem actually to be defrauding, corporate statements can evidence the fact that there have been poor profits during all these years. . . . So I guess morally it did not seem quite so bad as might be inferred by the definition of the activity itself.

For the most part, personal explanations for the acts were sought in the structure of corporate pressures rather than in the avarice or lack of law-abiding character of the men involved. The defendants almost invariably testified that they came new to a job, found price fixing an established way of life, and simply entered into it as they did into other aspects of their job. This explanatory scheme fit into a pattern that Senator Philip A. Hart of Michigan, during the subcommittee hearings, labeled "imbued fraud."[17]

There was considerable agreement concerning the manner in which the men initially became involved in price fixing. "My first actual experience was back in the 1930s," a General Electric official said. "I was taken there by my boss . . . to sit down and price a job." An Ingersoll-Rand executive said, "[My superior] took me to a meeting to introduce me to some of our competitors . . . and at that meeting pricing of condensers was discussed with the competitors." Essentially the same comment is repeated by witness after witness. A General Electric officer said, "Every direct supervisor that I had directed me to meet with competition. . . . It had become so common and gone on for so many years that I think we lost sight of the fact that it was illegal." Price fixing, whether or not recognized as illegal by the offenders, was clearly an integral part of their jobs. "Meeting with competitors was just one of the many facets of responsibility that was delegated to me," one witness testified, while an Allis-Chalmers executive responded to the question, "Why did you go to the meetings?" with the observation: "I thought it was part of my duty to do so."

What might have happened to the men if, for reasons of conscience or perhaps through a fear of the possible consequences, they had objected to the "duty" to participate in price-fixing schemes? This point was raised only by the General Electric employees, perhaps because they alone had some actual evidence upon which to base their speculations. In 1946, General Electric had first issued a directive, number 20.5, which spelled out the company's policy against price fixing in terms stronger than those found in the antitrust laws. A considerable number of the executives believed, in the words of one, that the directive was only for "public consumption," and not to be taken seriously. One man, however, refused to engage in price fixing after he had initialed the document forbidding it. A witness explained to the Senate subcommittee what followed:

> [My superior] told me, "This fellow is a fine fellow, he is capable in every respect except he was not broad enough for his job, that he was so religious that he thought, in spite of what his superiors said, he thought having signed that, that he should not do any of this and he is getting us in trouble with competition.

The man who succeeded the troublesome official, one of the defendants in the Philadelphia hearing, said that he had been told that he "would be expected to do otherwise" and that this "was why I was offered that promotion to Philadelphia because this man would not do it." At the same time, however, the General Electric witnesses specified clearly that it was not their job with the company that would be in jeopardy if they failed to price-fix, but rather the particular assignment they had. "If I didn't do it, I felt that somebody else would," said one, with an obvious note of self-justification. "I would be removed and somebody else would do it."

Westinghouse and General Electric differed considerably in their reactions to the exposure of the offenses, with Westinghouse electing to retain in its employ persons involved in the conspiracy, and General Electric deciding to dismiss the employees who had been before the court. The reasoning of the companies throws light both on the case and on the relationship between antitrust offenses and the more traditionally viewed forms of criminal behavior.

Westinghouse put forward four justifications for its retention decision. First, it declared, the men involved had not sought personal aggrandizement—"While their actions cannot in any way be condoned, these men did not act for personal gain, but in the belief, misguided though it may have been, that they were furthering the company's interest"; second, "the punishment incurred by them already was harsh" and "no further penalties would serve any useful purpose"; third, "each of these individuals is in every sense a reputable citizen, a respected and valuable member of the community and of high moral character"; and fourth, there was virtually no likelihood that the individuals would repeat their offense.[18]

General Electric's punitive line toward its employees was justified on the ground that the men had violated not only federal law but also a basic company policy and that they therefore deserved severe punishment. The company's action met with something less than whole-hearted acclaim; rather, it was often interpreted as an attempt to scapegoat particular individuals for what was essentially the responsibility of the corporate enterprise and its top executives. "I do not understand the holier-than-thou attitude in GE when your directions came from very high at the top," Senator Kefauver said during his committee's hearings; while Senator John A. Carroll of Colorado expressed his view through a leading question: "Do you think you were thrown to the wolves to ease the public relations situation . . . that has developed since these indictments?" he asked a discharged General Electric employee. The witness thought that he had.

Perhaps most striking is the fact that though many offenders quite clearly stressed the likely consequences for them if they failed to conform to price-fixing expectations, not one hinted at the benefits he might expect, the personal and professional rewards, from participation in the criminal conspiracy. It remained for the sentencing judge and two top General Electric executives to deliver the harshest denunciations of the personal motives and qualities of the conspirators to be put forth during the case.

The statement of Judge J. Cullen Ganey, read prior to imposing sentence, received widespread attention. In it, he sharply criticized the corporations as the major culprits, but he also pictured the defendants in a light other than that they chose to shed upon themselves:

> They were torn between conscience and an approved corporate policy, with the rewarding objective of promotion, comfortable security, and large salaries. They were the organization, or company, man; the conformist who goes along with his superiors and finds balm for his conscience in additional comforts and security of his place in the corporate set-up.[19]

The repeated emphasis on "comfort" and "security" constitutes the basic element of Ganey's view of the motivations of the offenders. Stress on passive acquiescence occurs in remarks by two General Electric executives viewing the derelictions of their subordinates. Robert Paxton, the retired company president, called antitrust agreements "monkey business" and denounced in vitriolic terms one of his former superiors who, when Paxton first joined General Electric, had put him to work attempting to secure a bid on a contract that had already been prearranged by a price-fixing agreement. Ralph Cordiner, the president and board chairman of General Electric, thought that the antitrust offenses were motivated by drives for easily acquired power. Cordiner's statement is noteworthy for its dismissal of the explanations of the offenders as "rationalizations":

One reason for the offenses was a desire to be "Mr. Transformer" or "Mr.

Switchgear"* . . . and to have influence over a larger segment of the industry. . . . The second was that it was an indolent, lazy way to do business. When you get all through with the rationalizations, you have to come back to one or the other of these conclusions.

There were other explanations as well. One truculent offender, the sixty-eight-year-old president of a smaller company who had been spared a jail sentence only because of his age and the illness of his wife, categorically denied the illegality of his behavior. "We did not fix prices," he said. "I can't agree with you. I am telling you that all we did was recover costs." Some persons blamed the system of decentralization in the larger companies, which, they said, placed a heavy burden to produce profit on each of the relatively autonomous divisions, particularly when bonuses— "incentive compensation"—were at stake; others maintained that the "dog-eat-dog" business conditions in the heavy electrical equipment industry were responsible for the violations. Perhaps the simplest explanation came from a General Electric executive. "I think," he said, "the boys could resist everything but temptation."

PORTRAIT OF AN OFFENDER

The highest-paid executive to be given a jail sentence was a General Electric vice president, earning $135,000 a year—about $2,600 every week. The details of his career and his participation in the conspiracy provide additional insight into the operations of white-collar crime and white-collar criminals.

The General Electric vice president was one of the disproportionate number of Southerners involved in the antitrust violations. He had been born in Atlanta and was forty-six years old at the time he was sentenced to jail. He had graduated with a degree in electrical engineering from Georgia Tech and received an honorary doctorate degree from Siena College in 1958; he was married and the father of three children. He had served in the Navy during World War II, rising to the rank of lieutenant commander; he was a director of the Schenectady Boy's Club, on the board of trustees of Miss Hall's School, and, not without some irony, he was a member of Governor Rockefeller's Temporary State Committee on Economic Expansion.

Almost immediately after his sentencing, he issued a statement to the press, noting that he was to serve a jail term "for conduct which has been interpreted as being in conflict with the complex antitrust laws." He

* Earlier, a witness had quoted his superior as saying: "I have the industry under my thumb. They will do just about as I ask them." This man, the witness said, "was known as Mr. Switchgear in the industry."

commented that "General Electric, Schenectady, and its people have undergone many ordeals together and we have not only survived them, but have come out stronger, more vigorous, more alive than ever. We shall again." Then he voiced his appreciation for "the letters and calls from people all over the country, the community, the shops, and the offices . . . expressing confidence and support."[20]

The vice president was neither so sentimental about his company nor so certain about the complexity of the antitrust regulations when he appeared before the Kefauver committee five months later. "I don't get mad, Senator," he said at one point, referring to his behavior during a meeting with competitors; but he took another line when he attempted to explain why he was no longer associated with General Electric:

> When I got out of being a guest of the government for thirty days. I had found out that we were not to be paid while we were there [A matter of some $11,000 for the jail term], and I got, frankly, madder than hell.

Previously, he had been mentioned as a possible president of General Electric, described by the then president, as "an exceptionally eager and promising individual." Employed by the company shortly after graduation from college, he had risen dramatically through the managerial ranks, and passed that point, described by a higher executive, "where the man, if his work has been sufficiently promising, has an opportunity to step across the barrier out of his function into the field of general management." In 1946, he had his first contact with price fixing, being introduced to competitors by his superior and told that he "should be the one to contact them as far as power transformers were concerned in the future."

The meetings that he attended ran a rather erratic course, with numerous squabbles between the participants. Continual efforts had to be made to keep knowledge of the meetings from "the manufacturing people, the engineers, and especially the lawyers," but this was achieved, the witness tried to convince the Kefauver committee, because commercial transactions remained unquestioned by managerial personnel so long as they showed a reasonable profit. The price-fixing meetings continued from 1946 until 1949. At that time, a federal investigation of licensing and cross-patent activities in the transformer industry sent the conspirators scurrying. "The iron curtain was completely down" for a year, and sales people at General Electric were forbidden to attend gatherings of the National Electrical Manufacturers' Association, where they had traditionally connived with competitors.

Meetings resumed, however, when the witness' superior, described by him as "a great communicator, a great philosopher, and, frankly, a great believer in stabilities of prices," decided that "the market was getting in chaotic condition" and that they "had better go out and see what could be done about it." He was told to keep knowledge of the meetings from Robert Paxton, "an Adam Smith advocate" and then the plant works manager, because Paxton "don't understand these things."

Promoted to general manager in 1954, the witness was called to New York by the president of General Electric and told specifically, possibly in part because he had a reputation of being "a bad boy," to comply with the company policy and with the antitrust laws and to see that his subordinates did so too. This instruction lasted as long as it took him to get from New York back to Massachusetts, where his superior there told him, "Now, keep on doing the way that you have been doing but just . . . be sensible about it and use your head on the subject." The price-fixing meetings therefore continued unabated, particularly as market conditions were aggravated by overproduction which had taken place during the Korean War. In the late 1950s, foreign competition entered the picture, and lower bids from abroad often forced the American firms to give up on particular price-fixing attempts.

In 1957, the witness was promoted to vice president, and again brought to New York for a lecture from the company president on the evils of price fixing. This time, his "air cover gone"—he now had to report directly to top management—he decided to abandon altogether his involvement in price fixing. He returned to his plant and issued stringent orders to his subordinates that they were no longer to attend meetings with competitors. Not surprisingly, since he himself had rarely obeyed such injunctions, neither did the sales persons in his division.

The witness was interrogated closely about his moral feelings regarding criminal behavior. He fumbled most of the questions, avoiding answering them directly, but ultimately coming to the point of saying that the consequences visited upon him represented the major reason for a reevaluation of his actions. He would not behave in the same manner again because of what "I have been through and what I have done to my family." He was also vexed with the treatment he had received from the newspapers: "They have never laid off a second. They have used some terms which I don't think are necessarily—they don't use the term 'price fixing.' It is always 'price rigging' or trying to make it as sensational as possible."[21] The taint of a jail sentence, he said, had the effect of making people "start looking at the moral values a little bit." Senator Hart drew the following conclusions from the witness's comments:

> *Hart*:   This was what I was wondering about, whether absent the introduction of this element of fear, there would have been any re-examination of the moral implications.
>
> *Witness*:   I wonder, Senator. That is a pretty tough one to answer.
>
> *Hart*:   If I understand you correctly, you have already answered it. . . . After the fear, there came the moral re-evaluation.

All things said, the former General Electric vice president viewed his situation philosophically. Regarding his resignation from the company, it was "the way the ball has bounced." He hoped that he would have "the opportunity to continue in American industry and do a job," and he wished some of the other men who had been dismissed a lot of good luck. "I want to leave the company with no bitterness and to go out and see if I can't start a new venture along the right lines." Eight days later, he accepted a job as assistant to the president in charge of product research in a large corporation located outside of Philadelphia. Slightly more than a month after that, he was named president of the company, at a salary reported to be somewhat less than the $74,000 yearly received by his predecessor.

A SUMMING-UP

The antitrust violations in the heavy electrical industry permit a re-evaluation of many of the earlier speculations about white-collar crime. The price-fixing behavior, flagrant in nature, was clearly in violation of the criminal provisions of the Sherman Antitrust Act of 1890 which had been aimed at furthering "industrial liberty." Rather, the price-fixing arrangements represented attempts at "corporate socialism," and in the words of Senator Kefauver to a subcommittee witness:

> It makes a complete mockery not only of how we have always lived and what we have believed in and have laws to protect, but what you were doing was to make a complete mockery of the carefully worded laws of the government of the United States, ordinances of the cities, rules of the REA's [Rural Electrification Administration], with reference to sealed secret bids in order to get competition.

The facts of the antitrust conspiracy would seem clearly to resolve in the affirmative any debate concerning the criminal nature and the relevance for criminological study of such forms of white-collar behavior,[22] though warnings regarding an indefinite and unwarranted extension of the designation "crime" to all acts abhorrent to academic criminologists must remain in force. Many of Sutherland's ideas concerning the behavior of corporate offenders also receive substantiation. His stress on learning and associational patterns as important elements in the genesis of the violations receives strong support;[23] so too does his emphasis on national trade conventions as the sites of corporate criminal conspiracies.[24]

Others of Sutherland's views appear to require overhaul. His belief, for example, that "those who are responsible for the system of criminal justice are afraid to antagonize businessmen"[25] seems less than totally true in terms of the electrical industry prosecutions. Sutherland's thesis that "the customary pleas of the executives of the corporation . . . that they were ignorant of and not responsible for the action of the special department . . . is akin to the alibi of the ordinary criminal and need not be taken seriously"[26] also seems to be a rather injudicious blanket condemnation. The accuracy of the statement for the antitrust conspiracy must remain moot, but it would seem important that traditional safeguards concerning guilty knowledge as a basic ingredient in criminal responsibility be accorded great respect. Nor, in terms of antitrust data, does Sutherland appear altogether correct in his view that "the public agencies of communication, which continually define ordinary violations of the criminal code in a very critical manner, do not make similar definitions of white-collar crime."[27]

Various analytical schemes and theoretical statements in criminology and related fields provide some insight into elements of the price-fixing conspiracy. Galbraith's caustic observation regarding the traditional academic view of corporate price-fixing arrangements represents a worthwhile point of departure:

> Restraints on competition and the free movement of prices, the principal source of uncertainty to business firms, have been principally deplored by university professors on lifelong appointments. Such security of tenure is deemed essential for fruitful and unremitting thought.[28]

It seems apparent, looking at the antitrust offenses in this light, that the attractiveness of a secure market arrangement represented a major ingredient drawing corporate officers to the price-fixing violations. The elimination of competition meant the avoidance of uncertainty, the formalization and predictability of outcome, the minimization of risks. It is, of course, this incentive which accounts for much of human activity, be it deviant or "normal," and this tendency that Weber found pronounced in bureaucracies in their move from vital but erratic beginnings to more staid and more comfortable middle and old age.[29]

For the conspirators there had necessarily to be a conjunction of factors before they could participate in the violations. First, of course, they had to perceive that there would be gains accruing from their behavior. Such gains might be personal and professional, in terms of corporate advancement toward prestige and power; they might be vocational, in terms of a more expedient and secure method of carrying out assigned tasks. The offenders also apparently had to be able to neutralize or rationalize their behavior in a manner keeping with their image of themselves as law-abiding, decent, and respectable persons.[30] The ebb and flow of the price-fixing conspiracy also clearly indicates the relationship, often overlooked in explanations of criminal behavior, between extrinsic conditions and illegal acts. When the market behaved in a manner the executives thought satisfactory or when enforcement agencies seemed particularly threatening, the conspiracy desisted. When market conditions deteriorated, while corporate pressures for achieving attractive profit-and-loss statements remained constant, and enforcement activity abated, the price-fixing agreements flourished.

More than anything else, however, a plunge into the elaborate documentation of the antitrust cases of 1961 and an attempt to relate them to other segments of criminological work points up the considerable need for more and better monographic field studies of law violators and of systems of criminal behavior, followed by attempts to establish theoretical guidelines and to review and refine current interpretative viewpoints. There have probably been no more than a dozen, if that many, full-length studies of types of criminal (not delinquent) behavior in the past decade. The need for such work seems overriding, and the 1961 antitrust cases represent but one of a number of instances, whether in the field of white-collar crime, organized crime, sex offenses, personal or property crimes, or similar areas of concern, where we are still faced with a less than adequate supply of basic and comparative material upon which to base valid and useful theoretical statements.

Notes

1. Judge J. Cullen Ganey, in *Application of the State of California*, 195 F. Supp. 39 (E.D. Pa. 1961).
2. *The New York Times* (February 7, 1961).
3. Edwin H. Sutherland, *White Collar Crime* (New York: Dryden Press, 1949), p. 240. Note: "Private enterprise remains extraordinarily private. . . . We know more about the motives, habits, and most intimate arcana of primitive peoples in New Guinea . . . than we do of the denizens of executive suites in Unilever House, Citroen, or General Electric (at least until a recent Congressional investigation)." Roy Lewis and Rosemary Stewart, *The Managers* (New York: New American Library, 1961), pp. 111–112.
4. For an elaboration of this point, see Gilbert Geis, "Toward a Delineation of White-Collar Offenses," *Sociological Inquiry*, 32 (Spring, 1962), 160–171.
5. Edwin H. Sutherland in Vernon C. Branham and Samuel B. Kutash, *Encyclopedia of Criminology* (New York: Philosophical Library, 1949), p. 511.
6. Sutherland, *White Collar Crime, op. cit.*, p. 9, fn. 7.
7. *United States Statutes*, 26 (1890), p. 209; *United States Code*, 15 (1958), 1, 2. See also William L. Letwin, "Congress and the Sherman Antitrust Law, 1887–1890," *University of Chicago Law Review*, 23 (Winter, 1956), pp. 221–258; and Paul E. Hadlick, *Criminal Prosecutions under the Sherman Anti-Trust Act* (Washington, D.C.: Ransdell, 1939).
8. Note, "Release of the Grand Jury Minutes in the National Deposition Program of the Electrical Equipment Cases," *University of Pennsylvania Law Review*, 112 (June, 1964), pp. 1133–1145.
9. John Herling, *The Great Price Conspiracy* (Washington, D.C.: Robert B. Luce, 1962), pp. 1–12; John G. Fuller, *The Gentleman Conspirators* (New York: Grove Press, 1962), pp. 7–11. See also Myron W. Watkins, "Electrical Equipment Antitrust Cases—Their Implications for Government and Business," *University of Chicago Law Review*, 29 (August, 1961), pp. 97–110.

10. Telephone interview with Judge Ganey, Philadelphia, August 31, 1964; *The New York Times* (December 20, 1961).

11. *The New York Times* (February 7, 1961).

12. Edwin H. Sutherland, "White-Collar Criminality," *American Sociological Review*, 5 (February, 1940), pp. 1–12.

13. U.S. Senate, Subcommittee on Antitrust and Monopoly, Committee on the Judiciary, 87th Cong., 2d Sess. 1961, "Administered Prices," *Hearings*, pts. 27 and 28. Unless otherwise indicated, subsequent data and quotations are taken from these documents. Space considerations dictate omission of citation to precise pages.

14. The quotation is from an excellent article by Richard Austin Smith, "The Incredible Electrical Conspiracy," *Fortune*, 63 (April, 1961), pp. 132–137, and 63 (May, 1961), pp. 161–164ff.

15. See Leland Hazard, "Are Big Businessmen Crooks?" *The Atlantic*, 208 (November, 1961), pp. 57–61.

16. See Anthony Lewis, *The New York Times* (February 12, 1961).

17. *Hearings*, pt. 27, p. 16773. Analysis of the relationship between occupational norms and legal violations could represent a fruitful line of inquiry. See Earl R. Quinney, "The Study of White Collar Crime: Toward a Reorientation in Theory and Research," *Journal of Criminal Law, Criminology, and Police Science*, 55 (June, 1964), pp. 208–214.

18. Sharon, Pa., *Herald* (February 6, 1961).

19. *The New York Times* (February 7, 1961).

20. Schenectady, N.Y., *Union-Star* (February 10, 1961).

21. *Hearings*, pt. 27, p. 17076. A contrary view is expressed in Alan J. Dershowitz, "Increasing Community Control over Corporate Crime—A Problem in the Law of Sanctions," *Yale Law Journal*, 71 (December, 1961), footnoted material pp. 287–289. It has been pointed out that *Time* (February 17, 1961, pp. 64ff) reported the conspiracy in its business section, whereas it normally presents crime news under a special heading of its own. Donald R. Taft and Ralph W. England, Jr., *Criminology*, 4th ed. (New York: Macmillan, 1964), p. 203.

22. See Edwin H. Sutherland, "Is 'White Collar Crime' Crime?" *American Sociological Review*, 10 (April, 1945), pp. 132–139. Note: "It may be hoped that the Philadelphia electric cases have helped to dispel this misapprehension. . . . It should now be clear that a deliberate or conscious violation of the antitrust laws . . . is a serious offense against society which is as criminal as any other act that injures many in order to profit a few. Conspiracy to violate the antitrust laws is economic racketeering. Those who are apprehended in such acts are, and will be treated as, criminals." Lee Loevinger, "Recent Developments in Antitrust Enforcement," *Antitrust Section, American Bar Association*, 18 (1961), p. 102.

23. Sutherland, *White Collar Crime, op. cit.*, pp. 234–257.

24. *Ibid.*, p. 70.

25. *Ibid.*, p. 10.

26. *Ibid.*, p. 54.

27. *Ibid.*, p. 247.

28. John Kenneth Galbraith, *The Affluent Society* (Boston: Houghton Mifflin, 1958), p. 84. See also Richard Hofstadter, "Antitrust in America," *Commentary*, 38 (August, 1964), pp. 47–53.

29. Max Weber, *The Theory of Social and Economic Organization*, trans. by A. M. Henderson and Talcott Parsons (New York: Oxford University Press, 1947), pp. 367–373.

30. See Donald R. Cressey, *Other People's Money: The Social Psychology of Embezzlement* (New York: The Free Press, 1953); Gresham M. Sykes and David Matza, "Techniques of Neutralization: A Theory of Delinquency," *American Sociological Review*, 22 (December, 1957), pp. 664–670.

8

HOW ETHICAL ARE BUSINESSMEN?

Raymond C. Baumhart

What Would You Do If—

As a director of a large corporation, you learned at a board meeting of an impending merger with a smaller company? Suppose this company has had an unprofitable year and its stock is selling at a price so low that you are certain it will rise when news of the merger becomes public knowledge. Would you buy some stock? Or tell a friend? Or tell your broker?

As president of a company in a highly competitive industry, you learned that a competitor had made an important scientific discovery which would give him a substantial advantage over you? If you had an opportunity to hire one of his employees who knew the details of the discovery, would you do it?

What Do You Think About—

An executive earning $10,000 a year who has been padding his expense account by about $500 a year?

Reprinted from *Harvard Business Review*, 39 (July–August, 1961), pp. 6–19, 156–176.

An executive's owning stock in a company with which his own company regularly does business?

The idea that management should act in the interest of shareholders alone?

These problems were posed as part of a lengthy questionnaire on business ethics completed by some 1,700 *Harvard Business Review* executive readers—34 per cent of the 5,000 cross section polled. This high rate of return and the hundreds of thoughtful essays written by these anonymous administrators on the margins of their questionnaires and on separate letterheads paint a picture of executives' deep concern over business behavior.

During the past decade, much has been written about ethics in business. Most of the books and articles are based on the experiences of one man or on *a priori* reasoning. Few authors have approached business ethics empirically, surveying the ideas, problems, and attitudes of a large number of businessmen. This study employs such an empirical approach.

We hoped that in the process of securing and reporting the data, we would prompt top management to re-examine fruitfully its thinking and practices. In addition, we wished to give scholars the businessman's point of view; that is, what he regards as ethical problems and unethical behavior—though, of course, this is not meant to imply that ethics is a matter of statistics or that a majority response constitutes an ethical answer.

BUSINESS RESPONSIBILITY?

Polybius, the Greek historian, summarized a nation's decline in a single sentence: "At Carthage, nothing which results in profit is regarded as disgraceful."[1] Modern critics have leveled this same charge at business in the United States, and we wondered if executives still adhere to this Carthaginian creed. To find out, we asked respondents to comment on a recent statement by a student of business:

> The businessman exists for only one purpose, to create and deliver value satisfactions at a profit to himself. . . . If what is offered can be sold at a profit (not even necessarily a long-term profit), then it is legitimate. . . . The cultural, spiritual, social, and moral consequences of his actions are none of his occupational concern.[2]

From top to bottom of the corporate ladder, a convincing 94 per cent says: "We disagree!" As one personnel director sees it: "This man lives in a vacuum, ignoring the society that gave him his opportunity, his responsibility to make it better rather than worse as a result of his existence." In twentieth-century America, it seems, some things which result in profit are regarded as disgraceful—even by professional profit makers.

In fact, our respondents indicate that they regard untempered profit maximization as immoral, agreeing with the thesis advanced recently by Robert N. Anthony. Five out of every six executives in our survey reacted affirmatively to this paraphrase of his view:

> For corporation executives to act in the interest of shareholders alone, and not also in the interest of employees and consumers, is unethical.[3]

Further, the answers of our executive panel reveal attitudes far different from those of the legendary rugged individualist. For example, only one executive in five agrees with the traditional dictum: "Let the buyer beware." But don't conclude that the "ethical" attitude revealed by these answers stems solely from a desire to do what is right because it is right. This conclusion would ignore the belief of our respondents that "sound ethics is good business in the long run." Only one respondent in a hundred disagrees with this statement!

Apparently management does believe that shady or ruthless operations might make money for a time but that a corporation cannot mistreat the public for long and still survive. Once stung, the public has a long memory....

Are executives as socially responsible as these findings suggest? We wonder, especially in light of the fact that 15 per cent of our panel agree with the statement that "whatever is good business is good ethics." This response prompts us to exercise caution in praising our panel's posture of social awareness. To say that "whatever is good business is good ethics" makes economic efficiency the norm of ethical behavior; in other words, the economic consequences of a business transaction determine whether it is right or wrong. This . . . sounds pretty much like that Carthaginian creed that nothing resulting in profit is disgraceful. The small size of this group doesn't alter the fact of its existence.

However, looking at the sum of our information about the social consciousness of the executives responding, we gain the overall impression that most businessmen have a definite awareness of their social responsibilities. They view the corporation as being more than a money-making producer of goods and services. Their level of ethical ideals appears to be high. There is even substantial agreement among them that a few specific practices are absolutely wrong; for example, 88 per cent regard providing a "call girl" as always unethical* and 86 per cent say they regard padding

---

* That some of these practices are especially controversial is attested to by the fact that we received a number of letters from purchasing agents protesting our connecting pur-

expense accounts as always unethical. Clearly, these executives see a business enterprise as a society of human beings, a society with obligations not only to the people who provide capital, but also to employees, customers, suppliers, government, and even, at times, competitors.

I'M ETHICAL, BUT IS HE?

Although our respondents profess a lofty level of ethical aspiration for themselves, they reveal a lower opinion of the practices of the "average" businessman. It is commonly observed that there is sometimes a discrepancy between what a man says he thinks or does, and what he *actually* thinks or does. Such a discrepancy is very likely to be present in answers to questions which require ethical choices. Replies to such queries often correspond more closely to the image which the respondent would like others to have of him than to a realistic picture of himself. It is human to try to picture oneself in the most favorable way.

We wanted to take this tendency into account in our study, and so we asked some of our case situation questions in two different ways. One half of our panel was asked: "What would you do?" The other half: "What would the average executive do?" These questions and their replies are shown in Chart 1. The differences in the answers of the two groups are striking.

Such differences certainly need closer scrutiny. Could they have been due to a flaw in our sampling? Apparently not. Our panel was split on a random basis. On checking, the two halves of our sample match demographically; in fact, the two halves of our sample are so very much alike in their opinions that the replies to the twenty-five questions which all executives were asked are, statistically, virtually identical. Hence, the differences in the replies of the two groups must clearly signal that our respondents did recognize the ethical content in the questions and reacted accordingly.

Actual business practice, then, is probably closer to what respondents say "the average executive would do" than it is to what they say "I would do." On this basis, the number of executives who apparently condone expense account padding and would use privy knowledge for personal financial gain is hardly reassuring.

chasing agents with "call girls" in the questionnaire and requesting that we refrain from publishing our findings. The question was included for methodological reasons, with no evidence in the questionnaire itself that we believed this to be a prevalent practice by purchasing agents or that we were singling them out for attention. As was originally intended, the findings are reported above by Father Baumhart without explicit reference to purchasing agents; but, in the light of public editorializing about our asking the question, we feel that we must take some notice of it, if only to avoid the appearance of yielding to pressure tactics on the part of an important segment of American business. (The editors, *Harvard Business Review*.)

Chart 1. I'm More Ethical than He

CASE 1 Imagine that you are a member of the board of directors of a large corporation. At a board meeting you learn of an impending merger with a smaller company which has had an unprofitable year, and whose stock is presently selling at a price so low that you are certain it will rise when news of the merger becomes public knowledge.

	What I Would Do	What the Average Executive Would Do
Buy some for self?	42%	61%
Tell a good friend?	14%	46%
Tell broker?	2%	11%
Do nothing?	56%	29%

CASE 2 As president of a company manufacturing consumer goods, you are considering new ideas for increasing sales. Your marketing department has presented two programs, each of which would achieve the desired increase in sales. One program employs an advertising theme portraying ownership of your product as a symbol of the purchaser's superiority, while the other program uses an advertising theme emphasizing the quality of your product.

	What I Would Do	What the Average Executive Would Do
Emphasize product quality	66%	50%
Emphasize purchaser superiority	11%	33%
No reason to make a choice here	23%	17%

CASE 3 An executive earning $10,000 a year has been padding his expense account by about $500 a year.

	What I Think of This	What the Average Executive Thinks of This
Acceptable if other executives in the company do the same thing	6%	27%
Acceptable if the executive's superior knows about it and says nothing	11%	28%
Unacceptable regardless of the circumstances	86%	60%

CASE 4 Imagine that you are the president of a company in a highly competitive industry. You learn that a competitor has made an important scientific discovery which will give him an advantage that will substantially reduce, but not eliminate, the profits of your company for about a year. If there were some hope of hiring one of the competitor's employees who knew the details of the discovery, would you try to hire him?

	What I Would Do	What the Average Executive Would Do
Probably would hire him	48%	70%
Probably would not hire him	52%	30%

NOTE: The figures for Cases 1 and 3 do not add to 100% since some respondents gave more than one answer to the case problem.

CYNICISM

The possibility that general business behavior is quite different from the personal ethical attitudes reported by our respondents is increased by their cynicism about typical executive behavior. This cynicism is illustrated by our panel's reaction to this observation by a friendly critic of business, who said, "The American business executive tends to ignore the great ethical laws as they apply immediately to his work. He is preoccupied chiefly with gain."[4]

Almost half of our panel agree. This same cynicism is underscored in replies to a later question about adoption of industry-wide ethical practices codes. Four of every seven executives believe that businessmen "would violate a code of ethics whenever they thought they could avoid detection."

If our respondents possess the high ethic described earlier and at the same time are cynical about the ethics of other executives, then undoubtedly they do not identify themselves with the "average" executive. Would such a lack of identification be true of doctors, lawyers, or professors? And does it not suggest that management still has a distance to go before it can truly be called a profession?

Coupled with this cynicism is the clear suggestion in our data that some executives have a "double ethic." This double ethic consists of applying one standard to friends and another standard to strangers. Some examples:

Many executives who would tell a friend secret news of a forthcoming merger would not tell their broker.

Essay answers about practices of pricing, hiring, and rebidding on contracts reveal the existence of an ethic which has a special niche for friends.

Favoring friends can be an expression of gratitude, which is praiseworthy, unless the gratitude is displayed at the expense of justice.

ETHICAL INFLUENCES

This cynicism, this double ethic, ... must certainly be considered when trying to predict a man's behavior in a touchy situation, especially if he believes that most others would behave unethically if they were in his position. Which is going to influence him more—his ethic, or the behavior of others?

We asked one random half of our respondents to rank five factors according to the influence they exert on an executive to make ethical decisions. The five factors were company policy, industry climate, behavior of superiors, behavior of equals, and personal code of behavior. We asked the other random half of our respondents to rank five similar factors according to the influence they exert for unethical decisions. The rather remarkable results can be found in Table 1 and Table 2.

What can we learn from the rankings? Here is one line of interpretation:

If an executive acts *ethically* (Table 1), this is attributable to his own set of values and his ability to resist pressure and temptation, with some credit due to his superiors and company policy.

If an executive acts *unethically* (Table 2), it is largely because of his superiors and the climate of industry ethics.

A wag might say that this sounds like the legendary playwright who blamed all his failures on inept casts and stupid audiences, and accepted the praise for his successful shows as his rightful due. On the other hand, a friend of business might say that it is a hopeful sign that many executives indicate they follow their own consciences in making decisions.

NOT HIS KEEPER

It is obvious that those around a man influence his behavior. But to what extent does this influence operate? Are executives "other-directed" rather than "inner-directed," as David Riesman suggested in *The Lonely Crowd*? Do executives look mainly to the company for their standards— are they the "organization men" described by William H. Whyte, Jr.? Or, more simply, what do our data say about the following item from the *Wall Street Journal*, commenting on the recent antitrust decisions in the electrical industry: "The simplest, if not the complete, answer [to why high-ranking executives had knowingly done wrong] goes back to the organization man"?[5]

Close examination of our data reveals a tendency in every age group,

Table 1. What Influences an Executive to Make Ethical Decisions?

Possible influence	Importance as an ethical influence (average rank)
A man's personal code of behavior	1.5
The behavior of a man's superiors in the company	2.8
Formal company policy	2.8
Ethical climate of the industry	3.8
The behavior of a man's equals in the company	4.0

NOTE: The average rankings given are derived from a ranking of each item in the 5 groups (1, 2, 3, 4, or 5), with most influential = 1, and least influential = 5.

company milieu, and management level for a man to accept the values of his superiors. This tendency, stemming from a respect for the talents of the superior as well as for his authoritative position, should be acknowledged by every administrator as a part of his power for good or evil. The larger the number of his subordinates, the greater is his power in this matter. And it is also natural for men to expect responsible action from someone with so much power.

Thus, Judge J. Cullen Ganey, in his statement on the electrical industry antitrust cases, despite the absence of probative evidence, felt compelled to say that "the real blame is to be laid at the doorstep of the corporate defendants and those who guide and direct their policy." And the public has been reluctant to accept the idea that the electrical equipment companies' top managements are blameless, for the public holds these men in a position analogous to the parents of a twenty-one-year-old who has done serious wrong. Though the parents be liked and respected, they must endure the common opinion that they should somehow have prevented the son's mistake. . . .

Have the troubles of the electrical industry introduced bias into the answers given to our questions? Undoubtedly. A pilot study preparatory to the present survey was completed before Judge Ganey's January decision, and we can compare results from the two studies. There is a noteworthy difference in the ranks assigned in the question discussed above. In the pilot study, formal company policy was ranked as the second most important factor influencing ethical behavior; superiors were ranked as the third. In the present study, these two factors have changed places, presumably because of the ineffectuality of policy directives used by the defendant companies. Also, from the time of the pilot study to the present one, there has been a slight increase in the percentage of men who say that unfair pricing or price collusion is the source of a personal role conflict.

Also of interest is our finding that financial need is ranked as least important of the five factors influencing unethical behavior. We doubt that money is unimportant to our respondents. A partial answer undoubt-

Table 2. What Influences an Executive to Make Unethical Decisions?

Possible influence	Importance as an unethical influence (average rank)
The behavior of a man's superiors in the company	1.9
Ethical climate of the industry	2.6
The behavior of a man's equals in the company	3.1
Lack of company policy	3.3
Personal financial needs	4.1

NOTE: The average rankings given are derived from a ranking of each item in the 5 groups (1, 2, 3, 4, or 5), with most influential = 1, and least influential = 5.

edly lies in the fact that some 86 per cent of the executives responding have five-figure incomes. At least the pressures of starvation are not at the door. What is important is to note that bad example, pressure from superiors, or equals, and industry environment are seen by our respondents as more closely related to dishonest behavior than is the need for money.

We asked John J. Brennan, Jr., Vice-President and Treasurer of Electronics Corporation of America, how he interpreted our findings. Here are the remarks he made in reply:

> The pattern and level of corporate ethical standards are determined pre-dominantly by the code of behavior formulated and promulgated by top management. The rest of the organization, almost perforce, will follow these ethical operating precepts and examples; but in the absence of such norms, the same organization will be motivated by individual, and possibly inconsistent, codes of behavior.
>
> The executive whose concepts of ethics are vague, and whose principles of ethics are ill-defined—and possibly even vascillating and inconsistent—is in constant danger of yielding to expediency and even pursuing unethical practices; or, worse, providing an undesirable environment wherein his subordinates can make such decisions based solely on their own personal ethical principles, with no frame of ethical reference from the top.
>
> Of course, a well-defined personal code, however high in standards, does not of itself ensure ethical conduct; courage is always necessary in order to assert what one knows to be right.

A Nestor of the business world once said that the best advice he could give to a young man embarking on a business career was: Find a good boss. Our data suggest a corollary: *If you want to act ethically, find an ethical boss. . . .*

The importance of this is underlined by looking at the differences in rankings that one's fellow executives have in influencing a man's behavior. These peers are said to have little influence for *ethical* behavior, but are relatively important in influencing *unethical* conduct. In other words, an executive's fellows are more likely to drag him down than to lift him up. . . .

CHAPTER AND VERSE

Every industry develops its own way of doing things, its generally accepted practices. Since industry climate is an important influence on unethical behavior, how does this influence manifest itself in specific practices that are generally accepted in the industry?

To find out, we asked:

In every industry, there are some generally accepted business practices.

In your industry, are there any such practices which you regard as un-ethical?

Taking away those who "don't know," we have the startling finding that four out of five executives giving an opinion affirm the presence in their industry of *practices which are generally accepted and are also un-ethical.* . . . More than half of our respondents were willing to tell us the "one practice in their industry they would most like to see eliminated." We have analyzed and grouped the replies, and Table 3 contains chapter and verse of the unethical practices that our executives want erased in their own industries. Perhaps seeing some of their answers will give a sense of their sincerity and good will in reporting these practices.

"Seeking preferential treatment through lavish entertainment." (*In-surance executive*)

"Kickback to purchasing department employees." (*Manager, con-sumer services company*)

"The idea that industry should have a few women employees on the payroll for entertainment of prospective customers." (*Personnel director, Western manufacturing firm*)

"Payoffs to government officials." (*Financial counsel*)

"Price rigging between supplier and contractor." (*Secretary, construc-tion firm*)

"Accounts of similar size, purchasing ability, and credit rating are charged prices varying as much as 25 per cent (by our competitors). So far, we have not deviated from our policy of charging the same price to everybody." (*President of small company*)

"Occasional exchanges of price information prior to contract bidding." (*President, consumer services company*)

"The payment or large gifts to employees of other companies, cus-tomers, or competitors for 'favors' or information." (*Vice president, com-pany making industrial products*) . . .

Table 3. Unethical Practices Executives Want to Eliminate

Practice	Per cent of executives specifying this practice
Gifts, gratuities, bribes, and "call girls"	23
Price discrimination, unfair pricing	18
Dishonest advertising	14
Miscellaneous unfair competitive practices	10
Cheating customers, unfair credit practices, overselling	9
Price collusion by competitors	8
Dishonesty in making or keeping a contract	7
Unfairness to employees, prejudice in hiring	6
Others	5

Ambiguous advertising intended to mislead consumers." (*Research and design expert*)

"Mutual fixing of rates of interest to be charged a borrower at two or more banks." (*Young financier*)

"Underbidding with the intention of substituting inferior workmanship or materials." (*Vice president, manufacturing company*)

"Selling a 'tremendous bill of goods' of which the buyer knows too little." (*President, consulting firm*)

"Loaning customer more than he needs or more than is prudent for him to borrow." (*Manager, Midwestern bank*) . . .

DRAWING THE LINE

Of course, to decide exactly where to draw the line on many of these issues is not easy. For example, the majority of executives regard gift giving as an "unwise practice." Similarly, the majority think that "a company should have a written policy about gifts." But only 27 per cent of these same executives are willing to stipulate a $100 maximum value for gifts. Presumably, the other 73 per cent are of the opinion that there are situations where gifts of greater value are appropriate and acceptable.

With respect to gift giving, as well as to owning stock in a company which does business with one's own company, most respondents . . . refuse to say that the practice is *always* unethical. The broad principle is clear: An executive must be loyal to his company. But not every gift promotes disloyalty or results in the recipient's favoring one supplier over another. Nor does every executive who owns stock in a company which does business with his own face a conflict of interest.

These are complex problems; often they involve, simultaneously, several ethical principles. The details of each particular case determine the application of the various principles and, consequently, make the difference between an ethical and an unethical practice. At the same time, this inability or unwillingness to draw immediate and fast lines raises two serious questions: (1) How do executives react to having to make decisions with strong ethical content? (2) Do executives need better guidelines to help them make the correct decision in such situations?

ROLE CONFLICT

The first of these questions relates to what a social scientist calls "role conflict." A role conflict confronts an executive when he is required to fill simultaneously two roles (patterns of behavior) which present inconsistent or contradictory expectations. For example, the behavior expected of an executive as an "economic man" often differs from what is expected of him as an "ethical man." To investigate such situations, we posed the following question: "Probably there have been times when you have experienced a conflict between what was expected of you as an efficient, profit-conscious businessman and what was expected of you as an ethical person. Please describe the situation which has been for you the source of deepest concern because of such a conflict."

Nearly half of our respondents generously spent the time necessary to supply us with an essay answer. Surprisingly, one out of every four executives reporting says that he has experienced no such conflict!

It is difficult to believe that these men never experienced a situation in business where cheating, lying just a little, or using a minor shady practice could have brought them some advantage. . . . Perhaps some respondents believed they were being asked to reveal a conflict in which they had acted unethically and replied "no such conflict" because, in the situation, they had acted ethically.

But it is hard to escape the conclusion that many executives who answered "no such conflict" have a deficient notion of ethics or lack an awareness of the social implications of business decisions. One professor of business administration, commenting on these answers, said that they reminded him of some executives who identify as ethical problems only those situations involving large sums of money. He has now overcome his surprise at such statements as, "Our company has no ethical problems. The last one we had was five years ago when the treasurer absconded with $50,000."

SPECIFIC SITUATIONS

What kinds of conflicts were mentioned by the remaining 75 per cent? They cover a wide range and make fascinating reading. Firing and layoffs were reported by 102 executives as being the problems over which they had experienced the deepest concern.

In the words of one training supervisor: "When it is necessary to reduce the work force, the decision of separating the older, less efficient employees or the younger employees with greater technical skills and vigor is a real tough problem."

An eastern plant manager sees a similar problem in a broader context: "No provision in our society for providing useful work for well-meaning, moral, hard-working individuals who just can't make the grade in the occupation they have chosen and must be dismissed for efficiency reasons. This is a most serious problem for me, and I have fired many persons for this reason."

The president of a small company has the same problem, but a different solution: "Discharge of ethical, but incompetent, employees. I can't do it." . . .

The product supervisor in a large manufacturing company is especially aware of one facet of the layoff problem: "Treatment of clerical-level, salaried employees during periods of economic recession. This group seems always to take the brunt of any work force reductions."

Finally, a southern personnel director thoughtfully observes: "It has always concerned me that the industry's regular (periodic) reductions in work force should always bear so heavily on the 'little people'—particularly when adversity has not always been equally shared by stockholders and top management."

The final quotation deserves some reflection on our part. No doubt most discharges and layoffs are ethical, and probably the conflicts cited by some of the 102 are waged between their head and their heart, rather than between economic efficiency and ethical behavior. But justice can, at times, demand that the brunt of a recession be borne by stockholders and executives, rather than by the little people. Perhaps we should recall here that 73 per cent of our respondents agree that "for corporation executives to act in the interest of shareholders alone, and not also in the interest of employees and consumers, is unethical." But it will take a secure and courageous administrator, indeed, to stand up and suggest reducing prices and dividends instead of reducing the number of wage earners.

COMMUNICATIONS

One in ten of our respondents has experienced deepest concern over a problem in honest communication—of telling the whole truth. Some examples:

A vice president, industrial manufacturing, is disturbed by "requests by customers for false billings to avoid taxes or help in their depreciation schedules." . . .

A securities salesman finds that "my customers often approach me with an idea that would be profitable to me, but which I feel is unwise for them. At times, my best advice will cost me a sale and perhaps a customer."

COLLUSION AND GIFTS

Opportunities for collusion and other sharp practices in pricing are the next most frequently mentioned conflict—seventy-nine executives. For instance:

The president of a small southern company mentions "the use of extreme pressure by competition to force me to collude with them to fix prices."

A sales manager is annoyed by "price differentials extended to 'price buyers,' but not to loyal customers—a rotten practice."

The treasurer of a small retailing firm puts a perennial problem in the form of a question: "What is a fair profit at retail level for installment purchases?"

Gifts, entertainment, and kickbacks compose the fourth most prevalent conflict category, fifty-six men.

A top executive in one of our giant corporations deplores "attending industry 'junkets' in the name of promoting the welfare of the industry, which are actually only 'binges' at the expense of neglected stockholders for whom we are trustees and managers."

A Western sales manager is bothered by "the excessive entertainment which some buyers seem to feel it is our duty to supply. I feel a buyer who can be bought for entertainment is not a moral person fundamentally, and I don't trust him." . . .

PRESSURE

A number of executives, forty to be exact, though they cite different kinds of conflicts, stress an important theme in their essays: Pressure from superiors played a part in the situation in which they had experienced the deepest concern. For example:

A controller resents "repeatedly having to act contrary to my sense of justice in order to 'please.' In upper-middle management, apparently, one's own ethical will must be subordinated to that of interests 'at the top'—not only to advance, but even to be retained." . . .

The sales manager of a very large corporation phrases his views most bluntly: "The constant everyday pressure from top management to obtain profitable business; unwritten, but well understood, is the phrase 'at any cost.' To do this requires every conceivable dirty trick."

But many men voice more than these generalized anxieties and cite specific practices toward which they are being pushed—and which they do not like.

A high-salaried manager is worried because "my management has, in effect, required that I go along with certain antitrust violations involving restraint of trade."

Another executive says: "As controller, I prepared a P&L statement which showed a loss. An executive vice president tried to force me to falsify the statement to show a profit in order to present it to a bank for a line of credit. I refused and was fired on the spot."

A young engineer testifies that he was "asked to present 'edited' results of a reliability study; I refused and nearly got fired. I refused to defraud the customer, so they had others do it." . . .

Of course, the task of top management is to get results. And to do so every executive must apply some sort of pressure or sanction to subordinates in order to obtain excellent work. A good boss ought to have the ability to "stretch" his men. But it is important that he not "overstretch" them, physically, psychologically, or ethically. . . . Impossible demands, say our respondents, especially if accompanied by an implied "produce or get out" attitude, can quickly result in unethical behavior. One certainly wonders if the lonely subordinate, faced with demands like these, does not occasionally dream about a union for middle management, complete with seniority and grievance procedures.

A common retort—and defense—of top management on this issue maintains that "it is only fair that pressure be kept on subordinates. After all, stockholders and competitors keep the pressure on top management all the time." Yet few *top* executives in our survey specifically mention such pressures. Perhaps "pressure" is part of a self-induced image of how a president or vice president *should* act. This reporter doubts that widely disparate and anonymous stockholders exercise specific pressure on top management comparable to the pressure that top executives bring to bear on their subordinates. As for the pressure of competition, few industries operate under conditions of absolutely free competition. Perhaps, the very fact that executives blame competitive pressure for widespread unethical behavior is a good sign that cutthroat competition exists in an industry and ought to be modified. . . .[6]

WHAT OF THE FUTURE?

Anyone who is pessimistic about business ethics in the United States would qualify his views after reading a sample of our completed questionnaires. They contain many heartening examples of courageous decisions made for ethical reasons. For example:

A sales manager refused to give a "payoff required to secure distribution of a consumer product in a grocery chain. Have been tempted but have not gone along with this 'under-the-counter' dealing. Our sales are hurt as a result."

The president of a company engaged in mass communication faced the choice of "giving up a valued client of long standing and great profitability and having to resort to laying-off hard-to-replace employees; or yielding to the client's demand to do something I didn't believe in. I chose the former course."

With men like these holding some of the reins of industry, surely there is reason for hope. Of course, the continuing good influence of organizations like better business bureaus and the Federal Trade Commission affords additional reason for optimism.

Someone has defined a leader as a man who raises his own standards above the ordinary and is willing to let other people judge him by these raised standards. Here are several signs that ethical leadership is present in business today:

1. The forthright speech delivered recently by Henry Ford II not only reproved the actions of some of his acquaintances, but also promised that the Ford Motor Company would maintain the highest standards of business integrity.

2. The Gillette Company, in its 1960 annual report, introduced a section specifying company practice with respect to gift taking and conflicts of interest. Perhaps shareholders in other firms would like to see this idea adopted and even extended.

3. The Association of National Advertisers and the American Association of Advertising Agencies recently invited all advertising media to criticize advertisements considered offensive and have developed a procedure for evaluating the criticisms.

This survey provides useful empirical knowledge about the problems and views of executives concerning business ethics. Some of the findings are not complimentary to businessmen. They are reported, not to chastise, but to reveal specific areas for improvement.

Only the candor of our respondents made this report possible. Presumably, they chose to reveal these business shortcomings in the hope of remedying them. . . .

It is noteworthy that, in our responses, there were no major differences of opinion among the various levels of management. The same is true of analysis by industry, business activity, and income levels.

Further, the desire for *change* permeates executive belief from the top to the bottom of the corporate structure. But this change will not come about, say executives, merely by hoping for it, instituting half-measures, or issuing platitudes. The time has come for courageous top-management leadership to implement executives' desires to raise the level of business ethics.

Notes

1. *The Histories of Polybius,* trans. by W. E. Paton (New York: Putnam, 1923), vol. 3, p. 393.

2. Theodore Levitt, in *Advertising Age* (October 6, 1958), p. 89.

3. Robert N. Anthony, "The Trouble with Profit Maximization," *Harvard Business Review,* 38 (November–December, 1960), p. 126.

4. Louis Finkelstein, "The Businessman's Moral Failure," *Fortune,* 58 (September, 1958), p. 116.

5. John Bridge, "Antitrust and the Organization Man," *Wall Street Journal* (January 10, 1961), p. 10.

6. A long discussion of the feasibility of ethical codes, problems of self-enforcement, and the role of religion in business has been omitted at this point.

9

INCREASING COMMUNITY CONTROL OVER CORPORATE CRIME: A PROBLEM IN THE LAW OF SANCTIONS

Alan M. Dershowitz

When individuals employ the corporate form in an illegal fashion, the community, acting through its various official agencies, may respond in a variety of ways. It may punish, it may enjoin future illegality, and it may require compensation of the injured. The edict implementing the community response may run directly against the corporate form, and it may run directly against the individuals. In each case, the responsible agency should select a response or a set of responses that will most justly and efficiently maximize formalized community values. This article attempts to construct an analytical framework against which available and proposed community responses to the illegal employment of the corporate form may be evaluated.

The construction of such a framework cannot begin until the concept "corporation" is defined. The corporation is a legal form embodying a complex of relationships. At this level, it has much in common with such other abstract legal forms as marriage, property, and contract. Because "corporation" is a term on a very high level of abstraction, it frequently

Reprinted by permission of the Yale Law Journal Company and Fred B. Rothman & Company from the *Yale Law Journal*, 71 (September, 1961), pp. 289–306.

tends to conceal the real actors in a given situation.[1] Many would agree with the following abstract proposition: When corporation X is found guilty of price fixing it should be fined $Y. Reduced to a more meaningful level of analysis, however, such a proposition inevitably conceals a complex of relationships. Corporation X, for example, may be owned by 10,000 shareholders who annually hire officers A, B, and C to operate the business for a fixed salary plus a specified share of the profits. If these officers, without the knowledge of the shareholders, conspire with agents of "competing" corporations to fix prices over a five-year period, and if at the end of this five-year period, the officers retire from their positions; and if corporation X is subsequently found guilty of price fixing, the impact of the fine of $Y would be distributed among the "innocent" stockholders. This example illustrates how differently the equities in a given situation may appear when described at different levels of abstraction. Many who would agree that the "corporation" should be fined, might well be troubled by the punishment of the stockholders. To be sure, facile equation of the corporate form with the policy makers and stockholders may produce little distortion when the small, closely held corporation is considered. But such an equation is apt to be highly misleading when applied to the more complex "endocratic" corporation.[2]

Individuals may engage in self-serving criminal behavior with differing effects upon the corporate form. An individual may commit a crime which benefits himself at the expense of the corporation (e.g., embezzling corporate funds); he may commit a crime which benefits himself without affecting the corporation (e.g., overstating business expenses on the income tax form); or he may commit a crime which benefits himself and also benefits the corporation (e.g., increasing both corporate profits and his own commission by doing corporate business in violation of Sunday closing laws). Some crimes may, of course, fit into any of these categories, their classification depending on surrounding circumstances. A conspiracy to fix prices, for example, may be engaged in by a sales executive in order to eliminate or reduce the psychological and physical strain of active competition, even though he knows that the conspiracy will result in lower profits to the corporation; in such a case the interests of the individual would be "out of harmony" with the interests of the corporation. A price-fixing conspiracy may similarly be engaged in, but without discernible effect upon the corporation, if the prices were fixed accurately to reflect competitive prices; in such a case, the interests of the individual would be "in neutral harmony" with the interests of the corporation. Finally, a price-fixing conspiracy could be engaged in by an individual whose compensation was in some way geared to corporate profits for the specific purpose of increasing such profits by preventing competitive forces from bringing down prices; in such a case, the interests of the individual would be in "active harmony" with the interests of the corporation. This article will concern itself only with the case of the individual who illegally employs the endocratic corporate form for the *immediate* purpose of increasing corporate, as distinguished from personal, wealth; such conduct shall henceforth be referred to as "acquisitive corporate crime."

A PROPOSED HYPOTHESIS

A hypothesis concerning the rate of acquisitive crime among endocratic corporations will now be proposed. This hypothesis does not presume to account for all the variables reflected in a decision to engage in illegal conduct; it simply purports to serve as a conceptual framework against which the administration of sanctions may be evaluated.

The rate of acquisitive corporate crime engaged in on behalf of any endocratic corporation will (1) vary directly with the expectation of net gain to that corporation from the crime and (2) vary inversely with the certainty and severity of the impact with which the criminal sanction personally falls upon those who formulate corporate policy.

hypothesis

This hypothesis assumes that in many instances the immediate goals of policy makers who engage in corporate crime is the enrichment of the corporate treasury. This assumption is not meant to minimize the selfish personal motives of such individuals. For corporate policy formulators generally have direct and important personal interests—both financial and social—in an increase in the profits of the corporation. Greater dividends, salaries, incentive compensation, bonuses, promotions, security, and prestige—all of which may flow from increased profits—are frequently the ultimate conscious motives behind the decision to employ the corporate form in an illegal fashion. But the immediate goal of these formulators, the method chosen to secure these ultimate ends, is an increase of *corporate* profits. To the extent that the enhancement of one's corporate status motivates the conduct of corporate personnel, so an increase or decrease in the expectation of enhancing corporate profits should affect the rate of acquisitive corporate crime.

It is additionally assumed that the corporate form, the conduit which initially receives the bounty of the acquisitive crime for ultimate distribution to the policy formulators and others, does not make decisions. Decisions are made for it and through it by a variety of persons at a variety of levels both within and without the corporate hierarchy. These policy formulators presumably can be coerced into refraining from employing the corporate form in an illegal fashion if the personal ends which they seek to achieve by such illegality—increased wealth, security, prestige—are jeopardized by the real threat of punishment. . . .

PRESENTLY IMPOSED SANCTIONS

In order to measure the effectiveness of available sanctions against the profit-diminution variable of the hypothesis, it must be determined in what ways and to what extent the law of corporate criminal liability presently affects the expectation of net gain to the endocratic corporation whose policy formulators are contemplating a course of acquisitive corporate crime. One general type of corporate crime which is frequently acquisitive—violation of antitrust laws—has been selected for detailed analysis in order to make this determination. Since antitrust violations are relatively widespread and since the sanctions imposed are relatively severe, a high degree of generalization and extrapolation may be made from any findings and conclusions concerning the effectiveness of available antitrust sanctions.

The antitrust conviction of an endocratic corporation is presently followed by a number of results designed, in part, to diminish the profits which accrued to the corporation from the criminal conduct. Conviction of certain antitrust violations may also be followed by a variety of *equitable* decrees designed to prevent future misconduct and to restore pre-existing conditions. Such decrees, however, are not designed to diminish profits and do so, if at all, only incidentally.[3] Moreover, divestiture, the equitable remedy most likely to have any profit diminishing effect, is a radical device for restructuring an industry and has been invoked too infrequently to warrant consideration as a significant profit diminishing sanction.

The two principal profit-diminishing sanctions imposed upon the convicted corporation are (1) the *criminal fine*, which is the sanction most frequently imposed upon the endocratic corporation convicted of antitrust violation and which may deprive the corporation of at least some of its illegal profits and (2) the private *treble damage suit*, which is facilitated by criminal conviction and which may deprive the corporation of residual illegal profits.

These profit-diminishing sanctions are closely interrelated, because a criminal conviction or a plea of guilty, as opposed to a plea of *nolo contendere*, may facilitate victory in a subsequent treble damage suit because of its admissibility as evidence of violation. If an indicted corporation can enter a plea of *nolo* (thereby minimizing the possibility of a future treble damage suit) by subjecting itself only to a nominal fine, it is likely that such a plea will be entered almost as a matter of course. If, on the other hand, the corporation can enter such a plea only by subjecting itself to the possibility of a crippling fine, it is likely that the corporation will risk litigation rather than plead *nolo*—even though the litigation might result in a conviction admissible in subsequent damage actions.

It may be argued that the relationship between the fine and the treble damage suit has been attenuated by the *General Electric* case in which Judge Ganey refused to accept pleas of *nolo contendere* without the consent of the government.[4] But there are no indications that this exercise of discretion by one federal judge portends a new general policy in the federal courts. The *General Electric* case was extraordinary in a number of respects, and it is unlikely that many courts will see fit to depart from their long uninterrupted history of uncritically accepting the plea of *nolo contendere* in almost any case in which it is offered.[5] The significance of the private damage suit thus still remains substantially dependent upon the severity of the criminal fine.

The Criminal Fine. The criminal fine as presently administered against the endocratic corporation guilty of acquisitive crime is totally ineffective as a profit-diminishing sanction.[6] Its ineffectiveness is primarily attributable to the exceedingly low maximum penalties permitted by governing statutes; these statutes were generally enacted about the turn of the century, and the maximum fines then established have, in many cases, remained unchanged despite an enormous growth in corporate earnings. The Sherman Antitrust Act—the basic antitrust statute—reflected this condition for nearly two-thirds of a century. From its inception in 1890, the statute provided a maximum fine of $5,000, and actual fines imposed under this statute probably averaged less than $2,500. Notwithstanding the fact that the fines levied on industrial giants such as Socony Oil, General Motors, and DuPont were relatively minute (on at least one occasion apparently amounting to as little as *one ten-millionth of the net profits aggregated* during the period covered by indictment), efforts to increase the maximum penalties were fruitless until 1955 when the maximum was raised to $50,000. Even this figure, however, is less than adequate when one realizes that the Justice Department seeks criminal remedies only in "flagrant" cases where the amount of profits involved is likely to be a substantial multiple of the $50,000 maximum or the $13,000 average fine imposed under the amended statute. The recent *General Electric* case provides a vivid example. Although the government called this "the largest of all criminal antitrust cases" and the indictment covered almost $7 billion of fixed prices, the average fine imposed upon each corporate defendant on each count amounted to $16,550, and the maximum fine of $50,000 was imposed, but only once out of the 159 sentences. The criminal fine as presently administered against the endocratic corporation guilty of acquisitive crime is thus little more than "a reasonable license fee" for engaging in such conduct and may be practically ignored in an analysis of the profit-diminishing effect of present sanctions.[7]

The Treble Damage Suit. The private treble damage suit, despite its potential value, achieves only sporadic effectiveness as a profit-diminishing sanction because of the infrequency with which it is successfully employed. Until 1940, a half-century of private antitrust litigation yielded only 175 reported cases, with judgment for plaintiff in all but thirteen cases. Since that time both the quantity of litigation and the percentage of plaintiff success has increased, but not enough to establish the private damage suit as a generally effective profit-diminishing sanction. Between 1952 and 1959—a period of vigorous government antitrust enforcement—only twenty out of the 144 litigated cases (14 per cent) resulted in judgment for the plaintiff. It has been estimated that in addition to the litigated cases, plaintiffs received some settlement in about 25 per cent of filed cases. But the most startling conclusion is that when these figures are weighted and added, the result is that in the overwhelming majority of all cases in which the government convinced a court that a violation of the antitrust laws had been committed, the convicted corporation paid nothing to private claimants in the form of damages or settlement. Thus, although in any given case the profit-diminishing effect of the private damage suit may be substantial (even crippling to a small corporation), its uncertainty and haphazard employment make it unsatisfactory as a general method of substantially reducing expectation of net gain to the endocratic corporation contemplating acquisitive crime.

In terms of the hypothesis therefore the "motive" for engaging in acquisitive corporate crime is not substantially reduced by the present imposition of available sanctions upon the endocratic corporation. Policy formulators contemplating a course of acquisitive corporate crime will not abandon their proposed course for fear of a four- or five-figure fine's being imposed upon the corporation. And although the possibility of being subjected to a series of crippling treble damage suits may indeed diminish the expectation of corporate net gain, the infrequency of such recovery and the relative ease with which such recovery can be frustrated by a plea of *nolo*, almost assures the policy formulators that the corporation, even if it is ultimately convicted, will generally retain a substantial portion of its illegal profits. The policy formulators, therefore, will probably carry their contemplated illegal policies into fruition, unless some coercive force is employed against them to prevent this.

Criminal Sanctions against Policy Formulators. The direct coercion variable of the initial hypothesis postulates that the "rate of acquisitive corporate crime engaged in on behalf of any endocratic corporation will . . . vary inversely with the certainty and severity of the impact with which the criminal sanction personally falls upon those who formulate policy." The history of antitrust enforcement indicates, however, that severe criminal sanctions have rarely been imposed directly upon the formulators of endocratic corporate policy. During the first five decades of the antitrust laws, 252 criminal prosecutions were conducted.[8] Twenty-four such prosecutions resulted in jail sentences, thirteen of which were imposed upon trade union leaders. Of the eleven cases involving businessmen, ten concerned actual racketeering such as threats, intimidations and violence. In the one remaining case, the jail sentence was suspended and not actually served. Since 1940, twenty businessmen have served, or are now serving, jail sentences for violation of the antitrust laws. These sentences range from thirty to ninety days each. Analysis reveals that these sentenced businessmen are of two major types: They are either the principal officers of small closely held corporations or they are relatively minor executives of large endocratic corporations. The explanation for this enforcement picture is evident. In the case of the small closely held corporation, where, in effect, the "principal officer" is frequently indistinguishable from the corporation, the government has little difficulty pinpointing the actual formulators and agents of the criminal policy. In the endocratic corporation, however, although few doubt that many acquisitive crime decisions are in some way formulated, or at least ratified, by the top-management officials, it is difficult if not impossible to pinpoint guilt above the level of those who carry out the necessary overt acts. Thus, although imprisonment, regardless of duration, is probably the most effective practical deterrent that can be imposed upon the formulators of endocratic corporate policy, the present system almost dictates its misdirection.[9] In the small closely held corporation, where any economic sanction which is imposed upon the "corporation" is felt directly by the policy formulators, direct criminal sanctions against these formulators are least needed. In the large endocratic corporation, where most economic sanctions imposed upon the corporation are distributed in infinitesimal doses to the policy formulators and, accordingly, where direct criminal sanctions against these formulators are most needed, the law has yet to develop an effective method of pinpointing criminal responsibility in the corporate hierarchy.

When measured in terms of the initial hypothesis of this article, therefore, the present system of deterring the endocratic corporation from engaging in acquisitive crime is unsatisfactory. Because of the presently insubstantial nature of the criminal fine and the uncertain impact of the private damage suit, the endocratic corporation contemplating acquisitive crime presently has a high expectation of net gain. Likewise, because of the difficulty of pinpointing guilt above the level of overt actors, the real formulators of endocratic corporate policy have little cause to fear criminal penalties. These phenomena help to explain why, in the area in which effective criminal sanctions *should* achieve the highest degree of overall deterrence, they are essentially ineffective as evidenced by the startling rate of acquisitive-crime recidivism among endocratic corporations.

CAN THE PRESENT SYSTEM OF SANCTIONS
BE EFFECTIVELY MODIFIED?

The efficiency of the present system might be increased by introducing a variety of repairs at key points in the sanctioning process. For example, the severity of the corporate criminal fine might be increased, private damage suits facilitated, or the sanctions imposed upon the formulators of endocratic corporate policy strengthened. But an analysis of these repairs will reveal that the present system is so inherently misdirected that any modification short of drastic revision will achieve only a modicum of success.

The Criminal Fine. An increase in the present level of criminal fines would directly reduce the expectation of net gain to the corporation by its very application and would indirectly reduce this expectation by facilitating the private damage suit by raising the "price" of pleading *nolo contendere*. But the criminal fine is inherently unsuited to the role of forcing an endocratic corporation convicted of acquisitive crime to disgorge its illegal profits. The fine has traditionally been employed to inflict economic punishment, not to extract illegal profits. When a thief, for example, is convicted, the criminal fine is not employed to deprive him of his bounty. Rather, *after* the state has summarily taken away the convicted thief's bounty, the fine (or jail sentence or execution) is imposed as a punishment, to place the thief in a worse position than the one he occupied prior to the theft. As presently administered against the endocratic corporation, the criminal fine—like a sales tax—deprives the criminal corporation of a small portion of its bounty, but permits it to retain the "lion's share." The state's portion could, of course, be increased. But any attempt to raise the maximum will inevitably meet organized opposition from industrial leaders who claim that such an increase "would work a hardship on the small businessman who may violate the antitrust laws." The fear that a vindictive judge could wipe out a small incorporated proprietor simply by exercising his generally unreviewable discretion is one which, if valid, could be overcome. A *percentage fine* could be introduced, whereby the maximum fine which could be imposed upon any corporation would be based upon the economic size of that corporation calculated from a fine base keyed, for example, to the defendant corporation's taxable income or total capital. Such a system would be a substantial improvement over the present one, and it would multiply the effectiveness of the criminal fine as a profit diminishing sanction. But it would extract all the illegal profits only sporadically since any relationship between the fine and the illegal profits would remain fortuitous.

The Treble Damage Suit. The private treble damage suit could also be strengthened as a profit-diminishing sanction. Plaintiff's obligation to introduce evidence of violation could be lightened by curtailing or eliminating the use of the *nolo* plea in criminal cases. But this remedy might multiply the present amount of protracted government antitrust litigation and might, in fact, reduce the number of government prosecutions because of the high cost of terminating defended cases. Plaintiff recovery could probably be increased if defenses such as "passing on," *pari delicto* ["in equal fault"] and "unclean hands" were entirely abolished or if plaintiff's burden of proving with "certainty" a "direct and proximate" causal relationship between violation and damages were further eased. But retention of these bars to recovery is considered essential if the private treble damage suit is to retain its compensatory character, for a lowering of these bars would increase windfall recovery to nondeserving plaintiffs and would convert the treble suit to a privately administered criminal fine. Furthermore since every dollar of proved damages automatically results in treble "compensation," judges and juries are apt to continue insisting upon a clear relationship between violation and damages and upon a showing that the plaintiff was the terminal loss bearer. It has been suggested, therefore, that the present system of "treble or nothing" should be modified, so that the court or jury, in its discretion, could award as compensation any sum between actual and treble damages. Such a modification would probably increase the probability of some recovery in actions filed, but at the expense of decreasing the magnitude of recovery in any given case; this, in turn, by decreasing plaintiff incentive would tend to reduce the number of actions filed.

Two conflicting forces are thus apparently tugging at some of these suggestions. One force pulls in the direction of increasing the impact of the damage suit as a method of deterring acquisitive corporate crime by neutralizing illegal profits, while the other force simultaneously pulls in the direction restricting the civil plaintiff to just compensation for his losses. This "tug of war" is a reflection of the confusion inherent in the mechanism of the private damage suit.

The private treble damage suit is an awkward combination of compensation and reward, and because it is instituted by a wronged private party, it is totally misoriented in relation to profit disgorgement. Instead of posing relevant inquiries in terms of the *defendant* corporation's right to *retain* its illegal bounty, the treble damage suit poses the inquiries in terms of the validity or invalidity of particular *plaintiffs'* claims against a portion of this bounty. Such bars to recovery as the defenses of "passing on," *pari delicto*, and "unclean hands" and the tests of "reasonable certainty" and "direct and proximate result" each, in effect, pose the following question in varying forms:

Assuming that there is a good reason for denying to defendant the bounty of its crime, is there not also a good reason for denying to this particular plaintiff a portion of this bounty?

If the question is answered in the affirmative, the defendant retains his bounty regardless of how inequitable such retention is. This question is a perfectly natural and proper one to ask in a compensatory proceeding between two private parties. And any effort to eliminate this question without radically changing the nature of the proceeding or the respective parties is bound therefore to meet with failure. But such a question is entirely irrelevant to a system whose initial goal is the total disgorgement of illegal profits. This inherent misorientation of the private damage suit as a profit-neutralizing device renders it an imprecise means by which to deter acquisitive crime in the endocratic corporation.

Criminal Sanctions against Policy Formulators.   To strengthen the sanctions upon the formulators of endocratic corporate policy, the government could more frequently seek and the judges could more frequently impose upon convicted corporate officials jail sentences longer in duration than the present effective maximum of thirty to ninety days. These modifications might have some appreciable deterrent impact upon the incidence of acquisitive corporate crime, but they could not cope with the major difficulty inherent within the present system. The major difficulty is not the leniency with which available sanctions are imposed upon convicted corporate officials; it is *the inability to convict* true policy formulators at the highest echelons of endocratic corporate life. This is partially attributable to the ease with which oral communications may be kept secret and the difficulty the state has in proving that which only the participants know—who in the chain of command formulated, as distinguished from implemented, the policy. The problem of isolating true formulators is even more difficult if what corporate sociologists call the "rule of anticipated reactions"[10] is indeed true. One writer has declared that, in the absence of any overt communication,

> The subordinate may, and is expected to, ask himself "how would my superior wish me to behave under these circumstances?" Under such circumstances, authority is implemented by a subsequent review of completed action, rather than a prior command. Further, the more obedient the subordinate, the less tangible will be the evidence of authority. For authority will need to be exercised only to reverse an incorrect decision.[11]

The difficulty of proving the existence and operation of such authority is a basic and inherent problem within the present system, and this problem would be alleviated but slightly by imposing more frequent or more severe penalties upon those whom the system is capable of convicting—the policy implementors.

PROPOSALS

It is submitted that the present inherently ineffective complex of sanctions should be replaced by a system which would (1) enable the government to recover from the convicted corporation all profits illegally earned in much the same way it recovers stolen goods; (2) oblige the government to return to any injured party compensation for any damages that he can prove resulted proximately from the crime; and if necessary, (3) impose an affirmative duty on corporate executives to exercise reasonable care in preventing acquisitive crime within the area of corporate business under their control. As will be demonstrated, the proposed system should prove superior to present sanctions in terms of both criteria implicit in the initial hypothesis of this article: the certainty with which the guilty corporation is deprived of its illegal profits, and the certainty and severity with which personal penalties are imposed directly upon the formulators of corporate policy.

Attachment of Illegal Profits. Acquisitive corporate crime, like acquisitive personal crime, will persist if the criminal is permitted to retain the fruits of his illegal activity. The criminal law, therefore, generally does not tolerate such retention. The corporation which has been convicted of acquisitive crime, however, *may retain all to which some other party*, either the government or an injured plaintiff, *can not show worthier claim.* If acquisitive corporate crime is to be deterred, the corporation, like any other acquisitive criminal, should, in all cases, be deprived of all the fruits of its illegal activity. This result could be approximated in the following manner:

The government should be empowered to institute a criminal proceeding against any corporation which it has reason to believe has engaged in acquisitive corporate crime and to institute (as part of the same trial or, with permission of the court, as a wholly separate action) *a civil attachment* proceeding to recover all profits which it could prove, by a preponderance of the evidence, accrued to the corporation from conduct proved illegal beyond a reasonable doubt. The government would bear the burden of going forward with evidence that during the years covered by the indictment a certain amount of profit ($X) was earned by the corporation in transactions related to the conduct that was allegedly illegal. The defendant corporation would then bear the burden of going forward with evidence that some or all of that profit ($Y) would have been earned even without the allegedly illegal conduct, and therefore such profit ($Y) was not earned as the proximate result of criminal activity. If the government sustained its burden of proving that a certain amount of profit ($X) was earned from the illegal conduct, and if the corporation sustained its burden of proving that certain profits ($Y) would have resulted without the illegal conduct, then, upon a finding of guilty against the corporation, the government would receive a judgment for the amount (if any) by which the former figure exceeded the latter ($X − $Y)—the amount of profit that would not have been earned but for the illegal conduct. The defendant corporation would, of course, be permitted to deduct from this figure the amount of any judgments which were previously obtained against it by a private party as a result of the same violation.

This proposal should not be more difficult to administer than present antitrust sanctions. It allows the government to combine in one proceeding an essentially criminal cause of action with an essentially civil remedy. The successful combination of these elements has a long history under the French *partie civil* system,[12] and there is no reason to believe that presence of a jury under American law would make the practice less successful. The method of securing a criminal conviction would not be altered by the proposed system; only the results of conviction would differ. The corporation could be forced to disgorge all its illegal profits as a direct and immediate result of criminal conviction, whereas under present remedies even the partial diminution of such profits is guided by no uniform policy and may be obtained, if at all, only after many proceedings and over long periods of time. Enforcement under the proposed system would not be dependent upon the willingness or ability of a private party to file suit, upon whether the losses were passed on to disorganized or inarticulate consumers, or upon whether any particular plaintiff deserved to recover; and enforcement could not be prevented by a "gentleman's agreement" between large industries not to sue "their fellow private corporations for treble damages unless pressed to do so by stockholders." Total attachment of illegal corporate profits would depend solely upon the ability of the government to show that certain profits were derived from illegal activity.

The government should be held to have satisfied its burden of going forward when it has introduced evidence of the profit resulting from illegal transactions, as calculated from the revenue from relevant transactions and the costs connected with such transactions (as derived from corporate records). This evidence should prove to be less difficult to obtain than the evidence presently required of plaintiffs in private damage actions. The government would not be obliged to speculate on the impact on profits of market conditions and other factors. It would only have to show that there were criminal transactions, and that certain cost-revenue differentials resulted from those transactions. The defendant corporation, with its superior familiarity with the relevant records, would have to bear the burden of demonstrating what other factors might have contributed to the profits and how much profit—if any—would have been earned even without the illegal conduct. Ideally, the government judgment would thus closely approximate the net profits realized by the corporation from its illegal conduct.

Compensation. Compensation of injured parties should be as important a goal as the attachment of illegal profits. But compensation and attachment are separate ends, best pursued by separate machinery. Under the proposed system, the private treble damage suit, which has unsuccessfully attempted to combine compensation and attachment, would be abolished. The single damage suit would be retained; and prior to the filing of the government action, any allegedly damaged plaintiff could sue for compensation. Any damages awarded in such private suits would be provable by the offending corporation in mitigation of the damages awarded in a subsequent government action. But no private suits could be commenced after the government action was filed, and those already pending would be stayed. If the government prevailed in its action and the defendant corporation's illegal profits were attached, any person (or corporation) who, under present law, would have had a damage remedy against the defendant corporation could seek compensation by filing an action against the government, provided such suits were filed within a specified period of time following the government judgment. If, at the end of the period of limitations, the face amount of the total claims did not exceed the attached profits, the government could, in its discretion, settle all claims which it felt were justified and litigate all claims which it felt were too remote or otherwise spurious. If the government were left with a residue, it would retain it as *bona vacantia* ["vacant, unclaimed, or stray goods"] in the same way it presently retains unclaimed stolen goods. If, however, the face amount of claims exceeded the attached profits, the government could not enter into any settlement without the consent of the defendant corporation. Whenever the amount of the claims exceeded the amount of the attached profits the defendant corporation would be permitted to defend, in the name of the government, against any claim which it felt was spurious. But if all the attached profits were distributed as the result of settlements approved by the defendant corporation and judgments in contested actions, claimants remaining uncompensated would be permitted to sue the defendant corporation directly. Any allegedly damaged plaintiff, whether claiming against the government or suing the defendant corporation, would have the burden of proving a "direct and proximate" causal relationship between the violation and the damages. And all the defenses traditionally available to defendants in compensatory proceedings would be retained since this proceeding would be exclusively compensatory in nature. Any claim once filed against the government and terminated either by settlement or by litigation would be *res judicata* in favor of the defendant corporation; and likewise any claim previously filed against the corporation and so terminated would be *res judicata* in favor of the government.

This proposal would facilitate *bona fide* compensation. When the attached profits exceeded or equalled the alleged damages, the government would probably be motivated to settle most well-founded claims with the least possible litigation. A claim form could be prepared, and as experience was acquired, standards for testing the *bona fides* of claimants could be developed. Hopefully, the government would be motivated by a desire to see equity done and, in addition to satisfying all *bona fide* active claimants, it would seek out and compensate those terminal loss bearers—the ultimate consumers—to whom the present system practically forecloses recovery.

It may be argued that it would be unfair to require the *defendant* corporation to compensate residual claimants after the government has attached all its illegal profits. Such an argument would be premised upon the existence of an equation between illegal profits earned and damage caused. There is, however, no necessary relationship between the two. A corporation may, in an attempt at acquisitive crime, cause damage without increasing profits or cause damage in excess of increased profits. The proposed system of government administration does not claim to be an exclusive compensatory device, as is the case with some foreign systems.[13] Rather, it provides a device whereby the government attaches illegal profits and compensates as many claimants as it can out of such profits. The corporation still has the obligation of "repairing" any residual damage that it caused.

Direct Coercion. The real threat of total attachment of illegal profits may go a long way toward eliminating the need for imposing prison sentences upon corporate policy formulators in order to deter acquisitive corporate crime. It has been assumed throughout this article that such formulators, realizing that an increase in corporate profits will inure to their personal benefits, have not been motivated to take positive action directed at preventing lower-level corporate personnel from engaging in acquisitive criminal activity, and that in many cases they themselves have formulated or ratified such activity. If the effective operation of an attachment system made it clear to such formulators that nothing could be gained for the corporation from the illegal conduct of its personnel, they would probably not be motivated to formulate or ratify such conduct. Indeed, the inconvenience of a trial and the possibility that collectable damages would exceed illegal profits might motivate them to take positive prophylactic action in order to reduce the incidence of illegal corporate conduct.

If the motive for permitting acquisitive corporate crime could be thus eliminated, the high social cost of imprisonment may not have to be incurred in order to deter such crime. For the theory of deterrence, based as it is upon an hedonistic calculus, assumes the existence of a substantial motive for committing a given act which must be countervailed by the certain knowledge that the pleasure sought to be obtained from the act will quickly be followed by pain sufficient to neutralize the motive. If the motive is eliminated, therefore, the imposition of a deterrent force may not be necessary.

But if attachment worked imperfectly there might still be a sufficient motive for a corporate policy maker to permit or encourage acquisitive corporate crime. It may thus be necessary, even with the proposed attachment scheme, to provide for a method of imposing prison sentences upon the formulators of corporate criminal policy.

The present law, however, is incapable of sorting out and identifying policy *formulators* as distinguished from policy *implementors* in cases involving the endocratic corporation. Seventy years of enforcement history under the antitrust laws provide adequate general testimony to this weakness; and the *General Electric* case presents specific testimony. In the *General Electric* case, which involved billions of dollars worth of sales over an extended period of time, the policy formulators took the position that "the action of these few individuals [the convicted implementors] were not in conformance with company policy, but a deliberate violation of [company] policy and of the expected high standards of our corporate way of life."[14] The government, to be sure, was "unable to uncover probative evidence which could secure a conviction beyond a reasonable doubt of those in the highest echelons of the corporations."[15] But many observers feel that some of the high-echelon corporate officers were or should have been cognizant of the source from which substantial percentages of total corporate profits were derived. It is apparent that the present criminal process, which developed as a reaction to individual delinquency, has not yet reached a level of sophistication which enables it effectively to sort out the various components in the complex of legal relationships known as the corporation. If the *Wall Street Journal* was correct when it concluded that "The violations [in the recent General Electric case] were known and condoned at the high echelons of the companies or else the top officials were not acquainted with important aspects of their business,"[16] then the criminal law should reflect society's unwillingness to tolerate either situation.

The community could probably increase the efficiency of the criminal process by imposing upon every corporate executive an affirmative duty to exercise reasonable care to discover and prevent acquisitive corporate crime within the area of business actually under his effective control, and by making failure to fulfill this duty a misdemeanor, punishable by a short prison term. The elements of such a crime would be (1) the commission of an acquisitive corporate crime; (2) in an area of the corporate business sufficiently under the defendant's actual control so that by the exercise of reasonable care he could have discovered and prevented the crime in question. The prosecution would, of course, have the burden of proving these elements beyond a reasonable doubt.

Proof of the first element could be facilitated by permitting the introduction into evidence of the corporate conviction. Proof of the second element could be adduced from the testimony of corporate personnel and outside observers as to the actual scope of authority and control capable of being exercised by defendant, as well as from relevant corporate charts, documents, and memoranda. The defendant could secure an acquittal by casting doubt upon any of the necessary elements; and evidence of the exercise of reasonable care, if believed, would certainly cast doubt upon the second element.

The prosecution could thus secure conviction of a corporate executive without proving actual formulation, ratification, or awareness; all it would have to prove, in effect, was that by the exercise of reasonable care the defendant could have discovered and prevented the crime. Executives would thus be motivated to take all reasonable prophylactic action to reduce the incidence of acquisitive crime within the area of their business responsibility and control.

It may be argued that such a scheme introduces into a criminal proceeding the concept of vicarious liability, hitherto reserved exclusively for civil proceedings. The scheme, however, introduces no such element. A may be said to be vicariously liable for the acts of B only if B's act, without anything more, results automatically in A's liability; A stands in the shoes of B, and nothing that A does or fails to do can affect his liability if it is truly vicarious. The Soviet Criminal Code, for example, condemns to exile in Siberia the members of the family of a soldier who flees abroad if they did *not* know of his plan (if they did know but failed to report it the penalty is more severe).[17] This indeed is vicarious liability; it focuses exclusively upon the act of B and does not permit A to introduce as a defense his own diligence or lack of control over the acts of B. The American law of conspiracy imposes vicarious liability upon conspirator A for the criminal acts of conspirator B committed in furtherance of the conspiracy; for once the status of conspirator has attached, the law becomes unconcerned with A's knowledge, diligence, or control. And in the civil context, respondeat superior imposes vicarious liability; for the negligent act of employee B automatically imposes liability upon employer A without regard to A's diligence, control, or knowledge.

But the scheme proposed here is of a different nature; it imposes an affirmative duty upon A to act with reasonable care to prevent those criminal acts of B over which A exercises actual control. A is being punished for his own failure to exercise such care; he is not being punished for the criminal act of B. Although B's act is necessary, it is not a sufficient condition for A's liability. The prosecution must establish a variety of elements focused exclusively upon A before conviction may be secured.

The criminal law frequently punishes "acts of omission" or failure to perform a prescribed duty if public necessity so demands. But such omissions or failures should be punished by imprisonment only if the public necessity outweighs the undesirability and high social cost of incarcerating offenders who are generally negligent rather than malicious. Hence, the scheme providing for imprisonment of executives who fail to perform the prescribed duty should not be adopted unless it is certain that the proposed method for attaching all illegal profits cannot, by itself, sufficiently curtail acquisitive corporate crime.

CONCLUSION

The mode of analysis embodied in this article suggests a potential for increasing community control over acquisitive corporate behavior.

The analysis implicit in this article is meant primarily to erect a conceptual framework against which to evaluate the sanctions employed in combatting *any* type of acquisitive endocratic corporate crime. If an individual, for example, violates a Sunday closing law by keeping corporate premises open and thereby earns $10,000 additional profits for the corporation, a fine levied against the corporation cannot be expected to deter such activity unless the fine approaches $10,000; and even if it were so high it would probably not deter the individual who, by violating the law, could increase profits by $50,000. But an attachment of illegal corporate profits and personal sanctions against the individual might effect the desired deterrence. This analysis would likewise hold true, for example, for illegal use of the mails, overweight transportation hauls, false or misleading advertising, violations of pure food and drug laws, Robinson-Patman violations, numerous S.E.C. violations, workman's eight-hour laws, closing-time laws, blue sky laws, illegal sale of liquor, or usury, permitting gambling on corporate premises.[18]

Each of the proposed applications of the analysis is separately oriented toward the accomplishment of its particular goal. The first—*attachment*—poses the relevant inquiries in terms of the convicted corporation's right to retain illegal profits. The second—*compensation*—poses the relevant inquiries in terms of the *bona fides* of the allegedly damaged plaintiff's claim. And the third—*direct coercion*—poses the relevant inquiries in terms of where in the corporate hierarchy such coercion will have the greatest deterrent and prophylactic effect.

It remains to be seen whether the proposals for decreasing the rate of acquisitive corporate crime can be made applicable to the control of other kinds of behavior (both criminal and noncriminal) engaged in by individuals on behalf of such diverse groups as unions, partnerships, syndicates, political parties, families, religious bodies, conspiracies, gangs, and governmental units.

Notes

1. See Bayless Manning, "Corporate Power and Individual Freedom," *Northwestern University Law Review*, 55 (March–April, 1960), p. 42. (The extensive footnote documentation for this article has been abbreviated to conserve space.)

2. The endocratic corporation is defined as the "large, publicly held corporation, whose stock is scattered in small fractions among thousands of stockholders." Eugene V. Rostow, "To Whom and for What Ends Is Corporate Management Responsible?" in Edward S. Mason, ed., *The Corporation in Modern Society* (Cambridge: Harvard University Press, 1959), p. 303.

3. See Alan D. Neale, *The Antitrust Laws of the United States of America* (Cambridge: Cambridge University Press, 1960), pp. 393–394.

4. The *General Electric* case was an all-out "do or die" effort by the Justice Department to reverse a trend of government failures to secure antitrust convictions. The government, therefore, made two unprecedented moves in order to convince the judge that this was not an ordinary case and that the usual procedure of accepting *nolo* pleas as a matter of course should be temporarily suspended. The head of the antitrust division personally appeared to argue in opposition to the acceptance of *nolo* pleas, and he came armed with a personal letter from the Attorney General of the United States setting forth the view that the future efficacy of criminal sanctions in the antitrust field would suffer immeasurably if *nolo* pleas were accepted in this blatant and unusual case. Only then did the judge indicate his decision to reject the *nolo* pleas.

5. See Victor H. Kramer, "Criminal Prosecutions for Violations of the Sherman Act: In Search of a Policy," *Georgetown Law Journal*, 48 (Spring, 1960), p. 535; and Paul E. Hadlick, *Criminal Prosecutions under the Sherman Anti-Trust Act* (Washington, D.C.: Ransdell, 1939), pp. 131–139.

6. Before the profit-dissipating effect of the present level of criminal fines can be evaluated, it must be determined whether or not *any* criminal fine, regardless of its severity, can be effectively directed against the endocratic corporation. Glanville Williams echoes the views of many commentators when he unhesitatingly replies that it cannot. "[S]uch a fine . . . is recouped by charges against the public at large." (Glanville Williams, *Criminal Law: The General Part* [London: William Stevens, 1953], p. 685).

7. Some commentators who admit the ineffectiveness of the criminal fine as a profit-diminishing solution still call for its retention (see, for example, Williams, *op. cit.*, p. 684; Edwin H. Sutherland, *White Collar Crime* [New York: Dryden Press, 1949], p. 43; Neale, *op. cit.*, pp. 394, 396; Kramer, *op. cit.*, p. 531), arguing that the *moral opprobrium* of society increases when a corporation is stigmatized by the imposition of a *criminal* penalty. "Moral opprobrium," however, is a conclusionary phrase, which indicates that a variety of consequences will probably follow a given stigmatizing event. When employed in relation to a human being, it may have meaning in terms of his desirability as a neighbor, an employer, an employee, or one in whom to place one's trust. When employed in relation to an endocratic corporation, "moral opprobrium" is supposed to have meaning in terms of what advertising executives denominate the "corporate image." It is apparently felt that a "tarnished" corporate image may result from criminal conviction and that this may have a variety of undesirable consequences, such as the loss of present or future customers, stockholders and employees, or a public clamor for closer government regulation. But the public must have some awareness of a given event before it can consider it opprobrious, and it is doubtful whether the general public is at all aware of the existence of corporate criminal liability. In the first place, the abstract image of the endocratic corporation as a criminal may be difficult for the average individual to conceive. In addition to this natural irreconcilability of the "corporate image" and the "criminal image," public awareness suffers from the de-emphasis of corporate crime by the media of community. This is partially understood by the fact that a substantial amount of acquisitive crime is engaged in by the mass media themselves; as one commentator says, "Public opinion in regard to

pickpockets would not be well organized if most of the information regarding this crime came to the public directly from the pickpockets themselves" (Sutherland, *op. cit.*, p. 50). The nature and extent of the newspaper coverage in the *General Electric* case—a case which probably received more publicity than any corporate crime in recent history—was revealing. Newspaper surveys were conducted at two key points in the case (see *New Republic* [February 20, 1961] p. 7; and *New Republic* [March 13, 1961]). It was observed that because of the "negligible and emasculated reporting of this issue by the bulk of the nation's press [the] reaction of the American public to the largest antitrust suit in our history has generally been that of mute acquiescence" (*New Republic* [March 13, 1961], p. 30).

8. Baltimore Sun (February 8, 1961); all the cases are collected in staff report to the Monopoly Subcommittee, House Committee on Small Business, "United States versus Economic Concentration and Monopoly," 79th Cong., 2d Sess. (1946), p. 257.

9. Governmental inability and unwillingness to obtain criminal convictions against individuals as well as corporations in cases of acquisitive corporate crime may be largely responsible for the ineffectiveness of available criminal sanctions. There is some evidence that the present system of imposing criminal penalties upon the "corporation" and individuals in the same proceeding has had a debilitating effect upon the imposition of direct criminal sanctions against the policy formulators.

10. Herbert A. Simon, *Administrative Behavior*, 2d ed. (New York: Macmillan, 1957), pp. 129–130.

11. *Ibid.*

12. C. J. Hamson, "Protection of the Accused—English and French Legal Methods," *Criminal Law Review* (May, 1955), pp. 272–282; Stephen Schafer, *Restitution to Victims of Crime* (London: William Stevens, 1960), pp. 21–24.

13. Schafer, *ibid.*, pp. 104–108.

14. *The New York Times* (February 8, 1961).

15. *The New York Times* (February 7, 1961).

16. *Wall Street Journal* (February 8, 1961).

17. Soviet Criminal Code, Article 58(i)(c) (1948).

18. All but the first sentence of the paragraph has been incorporated into the text from a footnote.

COMMERCIAL AND PROFESSIONAL WHITE-COLLAR CRIME

Black-market dealings in meat, illegal dispensing of prescriptions, ambulance chasing, fee-splitting and unnecessary surgery, embezzlement, tax evasion, violation of rent-control ceilings, and imposition of illegal working conditions upon household help constitute the offenses dealt with in the following section. Looked at together, they have little in common, except that their perpetrators rarely regard themselves as criminals or as persons deserving severe social censure and criminal or administrative sanctions.

It is this element of self-definition on the part of white-collar offenders that triggers the notable interchange of remarks between Frank E. Hartung, professor of sociology at Wayne State University, and Ernest W. Burgess (1886–1966), at the time a professor of sociology at the University of Chicago, following Hartung's presentation of his findings regarding violations of wartime regulations in the wholesale meat industry in Detroit. Burgess argues that a crucial distinction exists between offenses which arouse strong public disapproval and those kinds of acts which are regarded by most persons with only mild disfavor, if indeed they are viewed with any disfavor at all. It is worth observing how Burgess uses Edward A. Ross' writings, pre-

155

sented as the first reading in this volume, for purposes quite at odds with those of Ross, who attempted to flagellate the social conscience into taking a more severe stand against the newer forms of offenses, such as those classified as white-collar crime. Burgess, ignoring the thrust of the Ross polemic, relies upon it merely to support his observation that the newer types of offenses arouse little public anger and indignation.

Hartung's counterarguments are often telling, but he is led into quibbling with Burgess over whether half of the adults in the United States did or did not participate in the black market, whether the wartime regulations did or did not have public support, and whether sentencing procedures tend or tend not to favor the white-collar offender. These are, of course, matters of some factual import, but they are quite peripheral to the core of the dispute, which centers about the question of whether violators, and especially white-collar offenders, who do not regard themselves as criminals and who are not so regarded by the general public should be considered criminals by persons involved in the study and discussion of criminal behavior.

The jousting between Hartung and Burgess, since it joins many fundamental issues involved in white-collar crime, should be recognized for the semantic bout that it is. In terms of logic, both are correct; in terms of fact, both seem to be dealing with irrelevant matters. Hartung cares to call criminals those persons who violate the law; Burgess prefers to restrict the term to those persons who are socially condemned and who regard themselves as criminals. Both writers seemingly are caught in a definitional labyrinth of Sutherland's creation in which the ground rules are that whether or not an act is *really* criminal constitutes an essential component of the analytical enterprise.

The interchange of views between Hartung and Burgess provides a backdrop for the remaining pieces in this section. Vilhelm Aubert, a professor of sociology at the University of Oslo, expands with considerable insight upon the necessity to ask the right questions rather than to debate about definitions. He wants to know why it is that certain acts are proscribed by a legislative body, while other acts, seemingly of equivalent social consequence, are ignored. Aubert argues that "[t]he terminology one accepts in the present controversy [about the proper definition of white-collar crime] will depend upon how much one wants to get rid of these white-collar activities," a viewpoint that is more interesting than persuasive. While reformist zeal may, of course, condition acceptance or rejection of various definitions of a subject matter, other elements are at least equally apt to play into definitional choice, matters such as logic and analytical utility. It is, in fact, noteworthy how often writers in the present volume feel obliged when they are disputing Sutherland's use of the term "white-collar crime" to stress that they nonetheless are strongly dedicated to the eradication of the practices embraced within Sutherland's definition.

The study of rent-control violations in Honolulu by Harry V. Ball, presently director of the Juvenile Control Institute at the University of Hawaii, pays close attention to the relationship between statutory law and the behavior of persons affected by the law. The reading offers support for the view that deprivation suffered as a consequence of a legal enactment influences violation; as the author reports, "the tendency to perceive one's treatment under the law to be unfair and thus be tempted to violate the law appeared directly related to the law's severity." In his conclusion, Ball pays editorial tribute to the large majority of conforming landlords in Honolulu; by indirection, he may lead readers to wonder why it was that these law-abiding persons did not come to define the law in the same manner as their violating compatriots. This issue is, of course, beyond the purview of Ball's study, but it is one that in its generic form has persistently challenged students of criminal behavior.

The reading by Edmond Cahn (1906-1964), former professor of law at New York University, is notable for its manner of dismissing out of hand the assiduously cultivated propaganda of the United States Internal Revenue Service that virtually all American citizens pay their taxes with scrupulous honesty. The Service appears to have concluded that such a position, whether accurate or fictitious, offers that element of encouragement necessary for the equivocating taxpayer faced with only a tax form and a call of conscience.

It is their concentration upon the rationalizations of violators that unites Cahn's philosophical discussion of the moral base for tax conformity and Donald R. Cressey's inquiry into embezzlement by persons in positions of financial trust. Cressey, a professor of sociology at the University of California, Santa Barbara, proceeds by a technique known as "analytical induction" to attempt to determine those characteristics applicable to all embezzlers in his sample. The method of analytical induction has been criticized as producing exceedingly general descriptive statements which cannot be employed for purposes of prediction, statements which, therefore, fail to meet standards of scientific adequacy.

Sutherland, as we have noted, had reservations about grouping embezzlement with other kinds of white-collar crime, particularly since it represents an offense committed against the corporation or business enterprise by an employee and one that thus might more reasonably be said to resemble employee theft or shoplifting rather than antitrust violations or entrepreneurial offenses. Cressey shares this definitional stricture. His volume, *Other People's Money,* also makes particular note of the fact that Sutherland's theory of differential association, with its concentration on the learning of criminal behavior, fails to account adequately for the fact that embezzlers knew the techniques of fraud they practiced and that they required not association with others but rather acceptance by themselves of the legitimacy of defalcation as a means of acquiring funds to resolve a "nonshareable" problem.

Rationalizations and matters of self-image are related to the broader question of occupational orientation in the sixth article in this part by Richard

Quinney, a member of the sociology department at New York University, as he examines prescription violations among retail pharmacists. Deviant behavior, Quinney maintains, is a function of social structure, and he demonstrates that pharmacists attuned to the "business" role are wont to violate regulations to a much greater extent than those oriented to a "professional" role.

The final reading in this part examines deviations from acceptable professional standards among lawyers. The article by Kenneth J. Reichstein, of the department of sociology at Temple University in Philadelphia, concentrates upon ambulance chasing, a form of conduct that may lead to disbarment of lawyers, but one that only rarely is officially defined as a crime. Reichstein's chapter raises interesting questions about the validity (or the necessity) of differentiating those kinds of behavior officially labeled as crimes and separating them from deviant conduct which may result in administrative recriminations more severe than the consequences of criminal prosecution. For a lawyer to be disbarred, for example, is likely to be more disabling than for him to be fined or imprisoned. Certainly, violations among doctors in regard to fee-splitting, ghost surgery, and unnecessary operations appear notably unresponsive to criminal sanctions, with no record of a single prosecution for what are believed to be common practices. It is now known, of course, how many practitioners refrain from such behavior out of fear of criminal retaliation or professional censure. The paucity of research on professional violations whets the appetite for penetrating studies, though it also clearly indicates the considerable obstacles in the way of gaining accurate information regarding occupations given to self-protection and to group solidarity in the face of what are perceived to be external threats or untoward outgroup interference.

10

WHITE-COLLAR OFFENSES IN THE WHOLESALE MEAT INDUSTRY IN DETROIT

Frank E. Hartung

This article is a tentative and partial statement of some of the theoretical considerations presented by a study of white-collar crime. It deals with violations of Office of Price Administration regulations in the Detroit wholesale meat industry and is part of a larger study of law and social differentiation. The points briefly to be considered are (1) the objective basis on which white-collar offenses are to be considered as criminal, (2) whether an act committed without deliberate intention is to be regarded as criminal, (3) the significance of white-collar offenses for current criminological theories, and (4) a characteristic of these offenses which distinguishes them from usual crimes and which has special significance for the community.

A white-collar offense is defined as a violation of law regulating business, which is committed for a firm by the firm or its agents in the conduct of its business.[1] Thus Nickel, the $60-a-week clerk who embezzled about one million dollars from the Mergenthaler Linotype Company for his personal use, is not a white-collar criminal as here defined. But Richard

Reprinted from *American Journal of Sociology*, 56 (July, 1950), pp. 25–34.

Whitney, who embezzled a like amount from a children's trust fund in order to carry out certain operations for his Wall Street firm, does meet the terms of the definition.

A question about this type of offense is whether it is "really" criminal. The problem is that of the application of criteria to behavior. There is a widely held view that white-collar offenses are criminal. In this view two criteria are stipulated for a criminal act: (1) An act must have been proscribed (or in some cases prescribed) by a duly constituted legislative body and (2) the legislative body must have declared such an act to be punishable, with the sanctions specified. In jurisprudence the "pure-theory-of-law" school and some other writers have explicitly accepted these criteria.[2] In criminology, Sutherland and Clinard have shown that white-collar offenses meet these two criteria and are therefore to be considered as criminal.[3] In his recent book, Sutherland applied these criteria to the behavior of seventy large corporations. Clinard was concerned with violations of wartime statutes and regulations as exemplified by violations of OPA laws and rules.

Specifically, the Emergency Price Control Act of 1942, as amended, and the Second War Powers Act, as amended, stated it to be the purpose of the acts in the interest of national security to stabilize prices; to prevent abnormal increases in prices; to prevent profiteering, manipulation, or other disruptive practices resulting from abnormal market conditions or scarcity caused by, or contributing to, the national emergency; to protect persons with relatively fixed incomes against undue impairment of their standard of living; to prevent hardships to business, schools, and universities; to prevent a postwar collapse of values; and to permit certain voluntary practices by the government and business to accomplish these purposes. Certain agencies were specifically stated to have the duty of working for these objectives. As for the penalties established, they need not be discussed here, beyond stating that they involved damages, fines, imprisonment, and partial or complete suspension of the right to do business.

These two statutes which regulated business meet the test of the criteria of formally defined proscribed and prescribed acts and of punishability. The agencies charged with the enforcement and administration of this type of regulatory law need not, of course, be concerned primarily with the application of allowable criminal sanctions. Indeed, with hardly any exception save that of the pre-Taft–Hartley National Labor Relations Board, federal agencies appear to have been more concerned with obtaining compliance with the law than with punishing violations. For whatever reasons, these agencies have not defined themselves as being white-collar police departments charged with law enforcement. The various OPA administrators, charged with the responsibility of discharging the provisions of the laws creating OPA, perhaps fortunately did not have a criminological viewpoint in their work. It was also evident to this writer, from extended discussions with OPA enforcement attorneys over more than a year, that most of these attorneys defined their positions as administrative, law enforcement in any police sense of the term being secondary in their eyes. Nevertheless, violations of the two laws named above and of the regulations to which they give rise, since they had the full force and effect of law, can legally, logically, and technically be classified as criminal acts. They are so regarded in this paper. And, just as in the case of other statutes and other offenses, the repeal, abrogation, or expiration of these laws and regulations removed what were formerly violations of them from the classification of criminal. They may be just as irritating, immoral, or abominable today as they were in June, 1946, but they are no longer criminal. We cannot properly be concerned in criminology with what *should* be criminal, but only with what *is* criminal.

The formal definition of crime implies that the distinction between civil and criminal sanctions does not, in fact, distinguish between two different types of sanctions. The distinction between civil and criminal sanctions seems to be less meaningful, at least in the case of the laws here considered, than that between misdemeanor and felony. A brief consideration of "willfulness" in reference to OPA sanctions and of the indecision of Congress as to which violations should or should not be criminal will serve to make this lack of distinction a little more evident.

It is beyond the limitations of this paper to consider the congressional debates, hearings, and bills which resulted in the creation of OPA. It may be noted, however, that Congress was in grave doubt as to the distinction that should be made between "civil" and "criminal." The Emergency Price Control Act as passed in the House in 1942 provided criminal penalties for the violation of *any* of the provisions of the prohibitory section (sec. 4) and also for making statements or entries which were false in any material respect in any document or report required under the record-keeping sections (secs. 2 and 202). It was not until the act came out of the conference committee that criminal prosecutions were limited to "willful" violations, with prosecutions subject to the control and supervision of the United States Attorney General. This is, it seems, an indication of the artificial distinction between "civil" and "criminal."

It is generally believed that willfulness, or criminal intent, is necessary to the commission of a criminal act. This is, however, by no means a universal criterion.[4] In enforcement of the OPA statutes and regulations, it was not always necessary to establish willfulness in the so-called "civil" sanctions. An interesting innovation came with the "Chandler defense" amendment in 1944 to the treble damage sanction. If a defendant in such action could show both that his overceiling violation was not willful and that he took reasonable precautions to avoid violation, he was subject to the payment of damages of only $25.00 or the amount of the overcharge, whichever was the greater. This is in contrast to the situation prior to the amendment, when the damages were $50.00 or three times the amount of the overcharge, whichever was the larger. The effect of this amendment was to make the amount of damages dependent upon willfulness, whereas, previous to this, no such requirement was necessary for a valid civil liability.[5] If this is the beginning of a "criminal" test in a civil action, it indicates a point at which the distinction between these two allegedly different types of rules disappears.

It was recognized both in the law and in the enforcement policy of OPA that the unintentional violations were just as inflationary in effect as the willful ones. Effective enforcement required that nonwillful violations had to be curbed just as much as willful ones, a recognition of the principle that the social consequences of behavior are largely independent of the individual's motivation. Enforcement action in the case of unintentional and open violations of OPA regulations relied largely upon the use of the injunction. The purpose of the injunction was simply to prevent violations of "any rule, regulation, order, or subpoena" issued upon authority of the two above laws.

The most common use of the injunction without the use of other sanctions in the preretail meat industry in Detroit was in connection with the open violation of the general provisions of Maximum Price Regulation 574. This regulation established overriding ceiling prices for live cattle and calves purchased for slaughter. It also established maximum amounts which slaughterers could pay for all cattle slaughtered during an accounting period. In addition, it allowed the administrator to establish the maximum percentage of "choice" and "good" cattle which a slaughterer could slaughter or deliver for meat during an accounting period. This regulation was important as a measure to control the price which the ultimate consumer paid for his beef; to prevent a disproportionate disappearance of the lower grades of beef through upgrading of the lower to the higher grades; and to prevent the smaller slaughterers from being driven out of business by the integrated large packers, who also process their kill. The small slaughterers account for only about 15 per cent of wholesale cattle slaughter, but are extremely important in local operations. OPA believed that enforcement of MPR 574 was largely successful in accomplishing these objectives.

About twenty-five instances of violation of MPR 574 were proceeded against in the Detroit district OPA office. All save one were open violations, in that the record-keeping and report-filing requirements were met. The source of the cattle, the prices paid, and the descriptions required were all properly recorded. The exceptional case, an attempt at evasive violation of MPR 574 through the hidden ownership of a farm and the clandestine slaughter of uninspected cattle thereon, was proceeded against criminally, all defendants being found guilty after a jury trial and sentenced to fines and prison terms.

One may question whether an open violation, unintentional in motivation, which could readily be discerned by an inspection of purchase invoices should be considered criminal. In answer to this, the declared purposes of the Second War Powers Act should be recalled. The object of MPR 574 was to implement this law so far as the price of beef and the distribution of beef were concerned. Since these violations resulted in a serious and substantial diversion of rationed meats, their effect upon the rationing program resulted in as much harm to the public welfare and to civilian food planning and were as damaging to the war effort as if they had been intentional. Indeed, in ration-suspension proceedings, which involved a much more serious sanction than the injunction, it was held that a failure to observe the rules relating to food processing, rationing, and distribution was demonstrative of incapacity to serve as a trustee of scarce, rationed commodities, since the trust involved heavy community responsibilities. In addition, these violators obtained through their illegal acts a distinct competitive advantage over those slaughterers who observed the law.

It is concluded, on the basis of the above discussion, that those acts in which there is an absence of intention to violate are nevertheless criminal acts if they meet the tests of formally defined social injury and of the possibility of legal sanctions.

The Emergency Price Control Act and the Second War Powers Act provided a variety of sanctions in the case of violations. Specifically, they are: License Warning Notice, injunction, criminal contempt, monetary damages, suspension of dealing in rationed commodities, suspension of license to deal in controlled commodities, fine or imprisonment, and both fine and imprisonment.

The types of violations were: open overceiling sales or purchases, evasive overceiling sales or purchases, and violations in reporting or recording. The last type was not a substantive violation but was often indicative of evasive violations and was usually so considered in investigations. Table 1 is a summary of the violations committed and formal sanctions imposed in the Detroit wholesale meat industry for the period December, 1942, through June 30, 1946, as indicated by an exhaustive search of OPA records. It includes only those cases in which a formal sanction was applied. Consequently, it excludes a number of serious cases still in litigation at the time this study was completed, as well as those which were dropped or dismissed.

Several interesting facts are revealed in Table 1 and the data on which the table is based. For one thing, these offenses tend to resemble more usual criminal offenses in several ways: They range from systematic to technical violations; there are both single offenders and repeated offenders. Table 1 shows that eighty-three different firms and 132 personal (not corporate) defendants had 122 cases charged against them in which they committed 195 offenses, for which 233 sanctions were imposed by the courts and by OPA. The 122 cases do not by any means tell the whole story of offenses committed. This is because one case usually included a number of separate offenses. In court proceedings, the number of counts was as high as nineteen, each count representing one violation. If all these counts had been totaled, the number of offenses would have been in excess of 1,000. The category "Violations: total," therefore, is only the total of three types of offenses—open, evasive, and record keeping. It can be stated without qualification that all evasive violations were willful, in that the perpetrators of them knew that they were offending and took pains to avoid detection. It cannot be said that all open violations were inadvertent, because there is good evidence to show that a number of them

Table 1. Summary of Violations and Sanctions in the Detroit Wholesale Meat Industry (December, 1942, through June 30, 1946)

Number of cases	122
Number of concerns	83
Number of personal defendants	132
Persons having previous criminal records[a]	2
Violations	
(1) Open overceiling	65
(2) Evasive overceiling	58
(3) Record keeping	72
Total[b]	195
Damages paid: total	$132,811.71
Range of damages[c]	$40.00–$6,000.00
Fines paid: total	$97,500.00
Range of fines[c]	$100.00–$15,000.00
Sanctions imposed	
(1) License warning notice	45
(2) Injunction	63
(3) Damages	58
(4) Prison only	3
(5) Prison and fine	12
(6) Fine only	22
(7) Suspended sentence	6
(8) Probation	8
(9) Suspension order[d]	16
Total	233
Prison terms: total months	105–177
Range of prison terms[c]	3 mo.–1 yr.

[a] As indicated by a check of Detroit police department and Federal Bureau of Investigation records.
[b] Not the actual number of offenses but the total of the three types of violations, tallying one complaint for an injunction or one criminal information as one case, regardless of the number of counts alleged.
[c] Exact limits not given, so as to avoid possible identification.
[d] Estimated total days of partial or total suspension of business: 2,129.

were as studied and deliberate as were the evasive ones. Open violations did not result in criminal prosecution. In sixteen cases of suspension-order proceedings, however, violations led to the imposition of this serious sanction. Suspension of the right to deal in certain commodities, for a stipulated period, was often at least as serious as a fine.

On the other hand, open violations and violations in record keeping were sometimes wholly inadvertent and technical. Violations in record keeping were always diligently investigated because they might have been indicative of evasive violations.

A second significant item in Table 1 is that only two of the 132 personal defendants had a previous criminal record. Neither of these two men, however, could in any way have been regarded as a gangster or a racketeer; neither of the convictions was for activities related to the meat industry, and both had been committed outside Michigan some years previously. The violations in the Detroit wholesale meat industry were committed by persons more or less well established in the different levels of the industry, from slaughterers to processors to wholesalers and to peddlers. It is this fact which, to a greater extent than any other, leads to the conclusion that the established businessman or firm was the black marketeer. The importance of this for a general theory of criminality is great. Without going into a detailed discussion, the following may be indicated. There is the problem of accounting for the commission of offenses by persons who have not previously offended, so far as is known.[6] If these cases are criminal and typical of OPA violations—and it is the position of this writer that they are—it becomes necessary to incorporate the description and analysis of these offenses and offenders into the field of criminology. From this it follows that a perhaps drastic modification of now accepted criminological generalizations and theories becomes necessary. This is indicated because the current generalizations are based upon a biased sample of offenders. There is no available information on white-collar offenders as far as the usual "factors" are concerned: broken home, childhood experiences, race, nativity or nationality background, amount of formal education, occupational training and experience, physical characteristics *à la* Hooton and Sheldon, and the like. Imagine what a cry of outraged ego would have electrified Congress if, upon establishing an evasive overcharge, the OPA had inquired into the businessman's love life to ascertain if he were frustrated or had investigated at what grade he had quit school or had measured his cephalic index and his mesomorphy or had tried to obtain any of the usual items that comprise the subject matter of current empirical studies of offenders. To restate Sutherland, the study of white-collar crime will not so much reform the criminal as it will the criminologists. It should be stated specifically that current criminological theory fails to account for the offenders whose acts have been studied in this paper. "Factors" in crime, such as broken home, race and nativity, amount of formal education, and the like, seem to be practically meaningless as far as these offenders are concerned. Shaw's approach, excellent as it is so far as institutionalized crime is concerned, is of little use here. Perhaps the two approaches of most promise are those of Sutherland and Taft.[7] The violations studied in this paper are systematic in Sutherland's meaning of that term. It is not clear, however, just how adequately "differential association" plus "opportunity" will account for them. In regarding crime as a product of American culture, Taft's approach faces the problem of accounting for the fact not only that a high proportion of businessmen and firms did not violate OPA regulations, but also that many deliberately refused to do so when they thought it was safe. At any rate, the approaches of Sutherland and Taft are infinitely to be preferred to the psychoanalytic. The latter viewpoint is of no help here, at least as it is expounded by Aichhorn, Alexander, Abrahamsen, Healy, and Lindner, because it insists that antisocial behavior—whatever that may be!—is the criterion of crime. (One would like to see the concept of infantile sexuality applied to the company which falsified its records.)

We may now consider another point, namely, a special characteristic of OPA violations which is not found in the usual criminal offenses and which makes them of peculiar significance both to the community at large and to a theory of criminality in particular. Summarily stated, an OPA violation in its very nature not merely involved one offense (by one individual or concern in the conduct of its business affairs) but began a progressive chain of offenses which did not stop until the ultimate consumer paid the amount involved in all the offenses of the given chain.

Table 2 illustrates this feature of white-collar offenses. This table is a partial census made by this writer, through a search of Detroit district office OPA records, of the sources of supply of a firm we shall call "Company 219." This firm was involved in three OPA cases, with the following total of sanctions imposed on it: two injunctions, $12,000 in fines, twenty-four months' imprisonment and nine years' probation. Table 2 refers to only one of three cases of Company 219. We were able to establish, through a search of Detroit OPA records, that at least four Detroit retail outlets were involved in OPA actions as a consequence of selling at over-ceiling prices the poultry which they had bought from Company 219 at prices in excess of their legal purchase prices. This poultry had been purchased by the company in the deals listed in Table 2. This table shows the following in round numbers where the data were obtainable from OPA records: the weight of live pounds of poultry purchased, the amount of the ceiling price, the amount of the illegal side-money paid by the company and received by the sources, and the action taken against the sources by OPA. These actions are summarized in the right-hand column.

It may be stated almost categorically that any preretail or wholesale firm engaged in price-ceiling violations set into operation a series or chain of price violations which eventually resulted in the ultimate consumer's paying more for his goods than he should have had to under the law. If, at any stage in the process of putting goods into the possession of the ultimate consumer, a price violation occurred, this violation was passed on to the succeeding stages. If the violation were committed by the primary wholesaler or processor, all the succeeding secondary wholesalers and the retail outlet were progressively involved. If the violation were by a secondary wholesaler, all the stages after him were involved. One may make an analogy here with a pebble dropped into a pond, which sets up a series of successive waves. No wholesaler could commit a violation "by himself," so to speak, but must inevitably have directly involved other firms in his violation. The retailers who paid above the ceiling legally allowed them in the course of trade or business were thereby violating

Table 2. Summary of Violations Committed by, and Sanctions Imposed on, Sources of Supply of One Criminal Violator

Sources	Pounds of Poultry	Ceiling price	Illegal side-money	Action taken by OPA
1	41,000	$14,000.00	$2,200.00	Charged as co-conspirator, but not co-defendant
2	20,000	7,000.00	700.00	?
3	33,000	?	1,700.00	Treble damages of $5,100.00; License Warning Notice
4	52,000	?	3,600.00	One year and one day in prison; $3,000.00 fine; six months in prison; $150.00 fine (two defendants)
5	25,000	?	1,100.00	Treble damages of $3,300.00; License Warning Notice
6	22,000	?	500.00	Double damages of $1,000.00; License Warning Notice
7	10,000	?	300.00	Treble damages of $900.00; injunction
8	3,200	?	300.00	Double damages of $600.00; License Warning Notice
9	?	20,000.00	2,000.00	Charged as co-conspirator but not co-defendant
10	?	?	?	?
11	?	?	?	?
12	?	?	?	?
13	11,500	?	300.00	Statute of limitations
14	12,500	?	300.00	Statute of limitations
15	2,000	?	50.00	Statute of limitations (apparently non-willful)
16	23,000	?	750.00	Treble damages of $2,250.00; License Warning Notice
17*	70,000	?	2,100.00	Treble damage suit; judgment of $6,300.00 collected
Total	325,200		15,900.00	$22,600.00 damages and fines; 2 prison terms, 1 injunction, 5 License Warning notices, 2 charges of conspiracy

* Does not include seven other larger shipments of source 17.

OPA regulations. Let it not be assumed that they all absorbed this excess price and sold to the ultimate consumer at their legal ceiling price—thereby breaking even or perhaps losing money. The chain of violations was completed by their overcharges to their customers. As a matter of fact, in its enforcement program, the OPA often "worked" this chain of violations from the middle to both ends and from one end to the other. The retail customers of a violating wholesaler were investigated. The wholesale suppliers of violating retailers were investigated. It was possible to establish the existence of these chains by following through OPA investigations, as we did in the case of Company 219.

This chain effect was by no means unique to the wholesale meat industry in Detroit. Not only the meat industry nationally, but also the entire business community subject to OPA control in which there are two or more steps in the handling of goods before the ultimate purchaser obtained them would show this characteristic. We found this to be the case not only in wholesale meat but also in fish, poultry, eggs and dairy products, produce, groceries, and sugar. The investigation of all these categories, save meat, has been partial but still intensive enough to establish an empirical basis for the above generalization. It may be remarked, incidentally, that each industry, apparently spontaneously, developed techniques, particularly in evasive violations, which were peculiar to it and designed for its "needs." In addition, it may be indicated that the necessary involvement of others and the setting into operation of a chain of violations are not unique to OPA violations. This would be true of certain other laws regulating business. OPA violations, in their chain effect, are similar to the bribing of policemen and the operation of organized vice, in that neither of these types of activities can be carried through by the initiator of the illegal deeds but must necessarily involve other persons. This writer is not presently attempting a theory of either criminality in general or of white-collar crime in particular but is merely throwing the problem open for discussion, so to speak. Perhaps part of the answer is to be found in a typological approach to offenses and offenders.[8]

In summary, we may make the following points: (1) Violations of OPA regulations in the preretail meat industry are criminal acts, in that they meet the criteria of formally defined, proscribed and prescribed acts and of punishability. (2) The distinction between civil and criminal sanctions is held not to distinguish between two different types of sanctions. (3) Willfulness or deliberate intent to violate is not essential to making a white-collar offense a criminal act. (4) At least in the industry considered in this paper, the commission of an offense almost always necessarily involved the commission of another similar offense by a different party.

COMMENT

Ernest W. Burgess

The theory of white-collar crime implicit in this paper is that little or no distinction should be made between different violations or violators of all laws or regulations which have the sanction of a penalty. It is a legalistic and not a sociological position to regard these as one and the same.

Many years ago Edward A. Ross made a distinction between crimes recognized by law for generations and disapproved by the mores and what he called "criminaloids," which are new offenses as the result of recent legislation or of regulations by governmental agencies, carrying with them a penalty for violation. If all persons violating traffic regulations, health ordinances, etc., are to be considered criminals, then the numbers of criminals in the population undoubtedly greatly outnumber those who have never committed an act that is against the law or the regulations of some governmental agencies.

The point, then, is not to consider all violators of statutes, ordinances, and regulations as a homogeneous group. The differences are far greater than the resemblances between the automobilist who exceeds the speed limit, the OPA violator, and the burglar. Legally, they all violate a law or a regulation and are subject to a penalty. Sociologically, they are different, and it is the differences that are significant. OPA violations in the Detroit wholesale meat industry are unsatisfactory evidence of crime in any but the technical, legal sense of the word. The following are outstanding differences between these violations and offenses generally recognized as criminal by the community.

1. There is no evidence presented that OPA violators conceived themselves as criminal or were so considered by the public. In fact, for only two out of 122 is a previous criminal record reported.

2. The Emergency Price Control Act and the Second War Powers Act were suddenly imposed upon businessmen, defining many business transactions as offenses which had previously been legal.

3. No concerted organized effective attempt was made by civic leaders, churches, schools, the press, and governmental agencies to apply social condemnation to violations by businessmen and to purchases by consumers. Consequently, these acts were not stigmatized by the public as falling in the same category as murder, burglary, robbery, forgery, and rape.

4. Large sections of the population, comprising perhaps over half the adults, participated in black-market purchases during the war.

5. Few cases of violation (only 6.4 per cent) drew prison sentences,

and these were very light as compared with non-white-collar "crimes," averaging only from three months to one year.

The attempt to make little or no distinction between white-collar crime and other offenses promises confusion rather than clarification in criminology. It is important to distinguish between offenses which carry with them strong public disapproval and those violations of regulations (or recently enacted statutes) in which large sections of the public are willing accomplices.

REJOINDER

Frank E. Hartung

The opponents of the concept of white-collar crime are in disagreement as to why it should be opposed. Paul W. Tappan is opposed to the concept because, he says, its proponents are sociological and not legalistic. Professor Burgess objects because "it is a legalistic and not a sociological position."

Professor Burgess makes the point that all violators of all statutes carrying a penalty are not a homogeneous group. With this I agree, particularly as in a footnote to the reading I specifically referred to a typological approach to offenses and offenders. However, why should not traffic-ordinance violators be considered as criminal, since upon conviction, they are subject to fine or imprisonment or perhaps both? In its "Offense Classifications" *Uniform Crime Reports* has four classifications for traffic offenses. More important, though, and quite fundamental is Professor Burgess' rejection of the proposition that all who are found guilty of violating criminal laws are to be considered criminals. He says that the violations referred to in the reading are "unsatisfactory evidence of crime in any but the technical legal sense of the word." On what other but a "technical legal" basis should one be adjudged criminal? Professor Burgess argues as if violations of the mores should be considered criminal; presumably this is why he alleges that the present article is not sociological. It is anomalous that today a sociologist should defend an informal definition of crime. The ludicrous position taken by the psychoanalysts on "infant criminality" is an example of where the informal definition leads one. In psychoanalysis the newly born infant is said to be criminal because of his antisocial conduct: Antisocial behavior is criminal; the infant defecates in public and has no respect whatever for the rights and wishes of others; this is antisocial, and, therefore, the infant is criminal!

It is high time for sociologists—for everyone—to discard the "antisocial" and "mores" approach to crime. Anyway, it is against the mores to violate the law.

Let me now briefly consider Professor Burgess' numbered comments.

1. Although it is not included in the present article, I have considerable evidence that OPA violators and the public both considered OPA violations to be criminal. I hope to publish some of this material soon, based upon extensive interviews with both violating and nonviolating meat wholesalers and an areal sample of more than 600 Detroit adults.[9]

2. Not all OPA "controls" were so sudden as many people suppose. The two statutes and the regulations discussed in this article incorporated numerous laws which had been enacted as long ago as 1906 and which were supported by the vast majority of the packing industry. The law against selling uninspected meat is an old one; so, too, is the local law against selling contaminated meat. The new and sudden provisions in OPA were rationing and ceiling prices.

3. A number of public opinion studies made during and just after the war showed that the public defined OPA violations as being criminal.

4. To assert that "perhaps over half the adults participated in black-market purchases" is simply romanticism.

5. Many people will doubtless find it reasonable to believe that an "outstanding difference" between white-collar and non-white-collar crimes is that the former result in fewer and lighter prison terms. (Is not Professor Burgess saying here that white-collar crimes are *really* crimes?) However, because of the complete absence of any comparative studies I myself will be very wary of accepting this assertion as true. It is estimated that only about 3 per cent of the major crimes committed in this country result in prison terms. And, of course, not all these sentences are for the legally allowable maximum term.

If the proposition is true that the concept of white-collar crime promises confusion in criminology, as Professor Burgess claims, it is only because it calls into question the doubtful generalizations based upon the older and biased samples of the criminal population. In my opinion, Sutherland's analysis of white-collar crime is the most significant advance in criminology since Goring's *The English Convict* and Healy's *The Individual Delinquent*. It has definite implications for sociological theory in general and for urban sociology in particular.

CONCLUDING COMMENT

Ernest W. Burgess

A criminal is a person who regards himself as a criminal and is so regarded by society. He is the product of the criminal-making process. Professor Hartung gives no evidence that the so-called "white-collar" criminal that he studied could be included under this definition. Under his definition of criminals the great majority of adults are criminals. But that is only because he employs a legalistic and not a sociological definition of the criminal. My point that half the adult population participated in black-market transactions is one not of "romanticism" but of fact.

Notes

1. See Edwin H. Sutherland, *White Collar Crime* (New York: Dryden Press, 1949), p. 9.

2. See, for example, Hans Kelsen, *General Theory of Law and State* (Cambridge: Harvard University Press, 1945); William Ebenstein, *The Pure Theory of Law* (Madison, Wis.: University of Wisconsin Press, 1945); Jerome Hall, "Prolegomena to a Science of Criminal Law," *University of Pennsylvania Law Review*, 89 (March, 1941), pp. 549–580.

3. Sutherland, *op. cit.*; Marshall B. Clinard, "Criminological Theories of Violation of Wartime Regulations," *American Sociological Review*, 11 (June, 1946), pp. 258–270.

4. See Livingston Hall, "Statutory Law of Crimes, 1887–1936," *Harvard Law Review*, 50 (February, 1937), pp. 616–657. Hall shows that in many states one may be committed to prison without the protection of either or both of the rules of criminal intent and the presumption of innocence, for a number of offenses.

5. *Bowles v. Rack*, 55 F. Supp. 865 (1944).

6. Violations of local ordinances and state laws are not included in this study. These cases number in the hundreds over a period of a few years. One large packer, for example, has been found guilty about thirty times in three years of violating Michigan pure-food laws!

7. Edwin H. Sutherland, "A Theory of Criminology," *Principles of Criminology*, 4th ed. (Philadelphia: Lippincott 1939), chap. 1; Donald R. Taft, "Crime as a Product of American Culture," in *Criminology* (New York: Macmillan, 1942), chap. 15.

8. See Alfred R. Lindesmith and H. Warren Dunham, "Some Principles of Criminal Typology," *Social Forces*, 19 (March, 1941), pp. 307–314.

9. See Frank E. Hartung, *Law and Social Differentiation* (Ann Arbor, Mich.: University of Michigan Microfilms, 1949), chap. 6.

11

WHITE-COLLAR CRIME AND SOCIAL STRUCTURE

Vilhelm Aubert

One sign of maturity in a research field is the constant and conscious utilization of specific empirical findings to throw light on general theoretical problems. As long as this takes place only as a caprice of occasional deviants, a science has not reached the stage where research becomes genuinely cumulative. The study of crime is in this respect a pertinent example of missed opportunities. The numerous studies in the etiology of criminal and delinquent behavior have, by and large, constituted an applied field, where research might instead also have been oriented toward basic social theory or at least toward theories of the middle range.

One main obstacle to the development of a fruitful theoretical orientation is to be found in the tendency to treat criminal behavior, on the one hand, and the system of legal sanctions, on the other, as two separate problems. In our opinion, crime and punishment are most fruitfully handled as two aspects of a group process or two links in a specific type of social interaction.

It is frequently impossible to discover the sociopsychological origins

Reprinted from *American Journal of Sociology*, 58 (November, 1952), pp. 263–271.

and functions of criminal behavior without insight into the social processes behind the enactment of the corresponding parts of the criminal legislation. The social norms and mores that gave impetus to the enactment and the groups that uphold these norms are important to know for purposes, also, of tracing the criminal recruitment mechanisms. The nature of the norms thus legally sanctioned may, for instance, to some extent determine whether the criminals tend to be rebels, psychopaths, or rational profit seekers.

The interdependence of the origin and function of social norms and the origin of deviations is seen very clearly in societies which make political activities criminal. Unless we know fairly well the location and scope of the groups supporting the legislation, the function it serves in those groups, and the social norms it is based upon, we shall not succeed in explaining and predicting offenses. As we shall see later, this type of interdependence is apparent in the study of white-collar crimes. In the study of more "orthodox" or "classical" crimes it has, however, been largely ignored, in spite of occasional programmatic pleas for an interaction approach.[1]

There are some fairly obvious reasons why the origin and functions of deviant behavior—criminal or not—have been the main focus of scientific attention, to the neglect of the complementary phenomenon of norm-conformity and pressure to conform. It seems somehow to be "natural" to ask why the deviants become deviants and not why the conforming majority conform and support definitions of specific types of behavior and attitudes as deviations and prosecute them as such. Merton made the parallel observation concerning the sociology of knowledge that it seems more "natural" to search for a causal explanation of scientific and other intellectual "errors" than to inquire into the whys and wherefores of "truth." But, he proceeds, the "Copernican revolution" in the sociology of knowledge came when the scientists began to ask for explanations not only of the mistakes, but also of the true, plausible, or valid knowledge.[2] A similar revolution is much needed in the study of criminology and criminal law.

It is, by the way, likely that its close relationship to law explains why criminology in this respect has remained a more obedient servant of society's conventions than many other fields of social science. There is an understandable resistance on the part of lawmakers, judges, and lawyers to become the object of scientific studies, as the criminals are. And this resistance becomes effective by virtue of the close association between them and the criminologists.

There are other factors which may help us to understand the strong scientific attraction inherent in deviant behavior. In contrast to conformity, deviant behavior is dramatic and often highly entertaining. In Gestalt terminology, deviation is the "figure" against the "ground" of conformity. There can be little doubt that much scientific effort in sociology has been drawn to the outstanding and dramatic—although theoretically isolated—events, at the expense of the dull trivialities which frequently may provide us with better keys to the understanding of general problems.

The recent concern among social scientists with white-collar crime tends to bring long-neglected relationships between criminal behavior, criminal law, penal sanctions, and social structure into focus. The unexpected and somehow deviant nature of many recent laws defining white-collar crimes has made it natural to ask for an explanation of the norms themselves and not only of their infringements. As soon as this happens, new theoretical vistas are immediately opened.

Although white-collar crime today in itself is a very important practical problem, its research importance does not lie within the specific field itself. What is theoretically important is that white-collar crime seems to be one of those phenomena which are particularly sensitive to—and therefore highly symptomatic of—more pervasive and generalizable features of the social structure. That is why the field merits even more attention than it is given today.

Although the selection of white-collar crime as a field of research is a real achievement, the discussion has had an unfortunate slant. Not the least responsible for this is the pioneer in the study of white-collar crime, the late E. H. Sutherland. His formulation of the problem, "Is white-collar crime a crime?"[3] has given rise to futile terminological disputes, which are apt to become clouded by class identifications and ideological convictions.

The discussion some years ago between Hartung and Burgess demonstrates some dangers inherent in this way of phrasing the problem.[4] Hartung seemed to interpret the question of whether white-collar crimes are crimes or not as a research problem and gave an affirmative answer as if it were a significant result of his studies. Although the material presented by Hartung is of considerable interest, the conclusion seems less significant, since the problem mentioned is largely a matter of definition. Burgess on the other hand rejects Hartung's (and Sutherland's) answer on the basis of a theory about differences in causation, the implication being that there exists a specific "criminal-making process" common to all traditional crimes but not white-collar crimes, providing these former crimes with a uniform explanation. In view of the evidence, this seems hardly less dogmatic than the opposite view.

When Burgess suggests that "a criminal is a person who regards himself as a criminal and is so regarded by society," he is suggesting a subtle and in some ways significant criterion. It has the disadvantage, however, that only very careful attitude studies can reveal if it applies or not in a concrete case. For this end, a unifying concept of those who fulfill the criterion is much needed. But if it were to be taken for granted without further research that all traditional crimes fulfill the criterion while none of the white-collar crimes do, it is merely a way to dispose of a complicated empirical problem in the guise of mere conceptual clarification and definition.

Sutherland defined white-collar crime as "a crime committed by a person of respectability and high social status in the course of his occupation."[5] As a prototype of white-collar crimes, he focused special attention on crimes committed by businessmen in the course of their business activities. Hartung uses a somewhat narrower definition: "A white-collar offense is defined as a violation of law regulating business, which is committed for a firm by the firm or its agents in the conduct of its business." Cressey seems implicitly to be using a wider concept—in accordance with Sutherland's explicit definition—a concept broad enough to include also embezzlement.[6] In the following, we shall primarily have in mind white-collar crimes in the more narrow sense, those crimes which all the cited writers would accept as such.

The following characteristics of white-collar crimes are claimed to be established by the research done on these problems, primarily Sutherland's.

As far as the "law in books" is concerned, white-collar crimes have much in common with most "traditional" crimes. Statutes define a penal sanction against them. According to Norwegian law, these may be quite severe; for price violation they may amount to as much as three years' imprisonment. It is maintained that the situation is similar according to American law, although the evidence is not equally clear.

The "law in action" is, however, in this field characterized by slow, inefficient, and highly differential implementation. And, it is maintained, more so than in other areas of the criminal law. Sometimes the lack of efficient implementation is foreshadowed already in the "law in books" by the setting up of special types of enforcement machinery or the failing to solve obvious enforcement problems. Frequently, however, there is a real gap between the two levels of the law.

White-collar crimes are numerous and, as it follows from the definition, committed by people of high social status, which usually also means high income.

A trivial conclusion to be drawn from this is that low socioeconomic status and associated factors cannot be considered crucial in the explanation of crime in general; that is, if white-collar crimes were to be considered crimes. It is, moreover, possible that the acknowledged existence of white-collar crimes may tend to draw some of the attention away from these factors in other areas of criminal behavior also. The same may happen to theories that explain crimes in terms of personality disorganization, low intelligence, physical type, or the like, although such theories are not meant to cover white-collar crime.

There is usually no clear-cut opposition between the white-collar criminals and the general public, who are themselves often violating the same laws on a modest scale. The public has customarily a condoning, indifferent, or ambivalent attitude. It must be admitted that this conclusion is based to a large extent upon impressionistic observation rather than systematic surveys, although some surveys exist.

It has been established in some studies that the white-collar criminal finds support for his behavior in group norms, thus tending to break down further the view that violations of laws are rooted in man's raw nature, in his unrestrained biological impulses. We must agree with Merton's statement that "certain phases of social structure generate the circumstances in which infringement of social codes constitutes a 'normal response.'"[7] It is nothing new in criminology that crimes are frequently committed by persons who give each other social (and other) support in groups in pursuance of criminal careers.[8] But what distinguishes the white-collar criminal in this respect is that his group often has an elaborate and widely accepted ideological rationalization for the offenses and is a group of great social significance outside the sphere of criminal activity—usually a group with considerable economic and political power.

This brief survey does not give a definite answer to the question: "Is white-collar crime a crime?" The definition of an activity as "crime" is always, apart from its scientific merits, a "persuasive definition."[9] It contains an element of propaganda. The terminology one accepts in the present controversy will depend upon how much one wants to get rid of these white-collar activities. Disregarding that, for the moment, we have seen that white-collar crimes have at least one characteristic in common with all the conventional crimes: They are forbidden by law, and the law stipulates a penal sanction against infringements. But with respect to the other characteristics mentioned (respectively, differential and inefficient implementation; status of violators; tolerance of public; and social support of offenders), they seem to differ somewhat from many other types of law violations. It should be noted, however, that some of these differences are only differences in degree and emphasis. Furthermore, the crimes which fall outside the white-collar category are not as homogeneous as some writers seem to believe, which makes comparisons even more difficult.

For purposes of theoretical analysis, it is of prime importance to develop and apply concepts which preserve and emphasize the ambiguous nature of the white-collar crimes and not to "solve" the problem by classifying them as either "crimes" or "not crimes." Their controversial nature is exactly what makes them so interesting from a sociological point of view and what gives us a clue to important norm conflicts, clashing group interests, and maybe incipient social change. One main benefit to be derived from the study of white-collar crimes springs from the opportunity which the ambivalence in the citizen, in the businessman, and among lawyers, judges, and even criminologists offers as a barometer of structural conflicts and change-potential in the larger social system of which they and the white-collar crimes are parts.

The laws against white-collar crime are usually not in obvious and apparent harmony with the mores. They are largely an outcome of the increased complexity of modern industrial society, a complexity which requires legal control of activities with long-range and often very indirectly damaging effects. Price regulation, intending to curb inflation, is a pertinent example. An illegal price will frequently create no immediate reaction and invoke no sanctions from the mores in the community. A tie-in with the mores can only be established through public acceptance of relatively complicated means-end hypotheses from modern economic science. As long as these hypotheses have not become integrated parts of the individual's moral system, there will be a gap between the letter of the law and the requirements of the informal norms of the daily interaction between the members of society.

There can be small doubt that this gap exists in many modern societies. And in some areas, in relation to some groups, there is not only a gap but a conflict between the laws and the mores or ideologies which one traditionally accepted. In such cases, ambivalence may arise in the attitudes toward white-collar crimes, originating in a loyalty divided between the laws and the traditional beliefs. These ambivalent attitudes, their detailed structures and functions, are the most fruitful stating point for empirical research on white-collar crime in its relation to social structure.

With detailed surveys of these attitudes in hand, research should be further oriented toward the actual external cross pressures that operate in this area of opinion formation. What is, more specifically, the content of the partly conflicting group norms? How can we locate the opinion leaders ("norm speakers") and followers ("norm receivers") within the relevant groups? How can we give an adequate description of an individual's position as a member of more than one group, as illustrated by his conflicting roles as a law-abiding member of the nation and as a loyal member of the business community? How does group membership affect the perception of specific white-collar crimes and of sanctions against them? Under what conditions of group membership, previous norms, personal interests, etc., do the threat of penal sanctions exert pressure (and how strong a pressure) toward conformity with the legal norms? What are the sanctions that exert pressure toward conformity with conflicting norms?[10]

All these problems, selected at random, have fairly obvious empirical implications. Answers would be highly relevant to current social theory. One basic methodological problem will, of course, be to develop precise and psychologically meaningful criteria of group membership.

Our approach does not lead to any extensive search for the idiosyncratic motivation of individual deviations from legal norms. It is assumed as a working hypothesis that the white-collar criminal is usually no "genuine deviant." He is only apparently so, as long as his group and its norms are unknown. Festinger has recently pointed out the fallacy of attributing deviant behavior or opinions to an individual when his group affiliations are not adequately understood.[11] Here lies a field of the utmost theoretical importance, requiring the most subtle research techniques.

We assume that white-collar crimes are determined by social norms, accepted and enforced by groups and individuals with whom the individual identifies, groups which tend to give social support to the illegal activity. On the other hand, the legal rules and their enforcement are also determined by social norms, accepted and enforced by other kinds of social groups with which the legislators and enforcement agencies identify themselves and with which even the violators often have some measure of identification. The problems of the etiology of crime and of punishment seem then to relate to the same set of basic theoretical concepts. Moreover, it must be assumed that there is a constant process of interaction between the groups involved and some interdependence of the conflicting social norms. The individual's behavior and attitudes, under cross pressure from both, can no more be understood on the basis of the one alone than on the basis of the other alone.

In the light of the preceding, I shall present a few aspects of two studies that have recently been carried out in Oslo. Both of them are concerned with types of behavior which fulfill, or nearly so, Sutherland's definition of white-collar crimes.

In the first study, we made a survey of the attitudes of certain types of businessmen toward the rationing of goods and price regulation and toward their violation. It was already known that the number of such violations was great, as shown by the criminal statistics for postwar years. The general impression of the survey confirmed the statistics, although we made no systematic attempt to discover violations within our probability sample from a few business branches in Oslo. The survey concentrated on perceptions and attitudes only.[12]

The roles and attitudes of our subjects seem to be analyzable in terms of Stouffer's concepts, "universalistic" and "particularistic obligations."[13] The businessman has conflicting roles as a law-abiding citizen and as a member of the business community. The felt universalistic obligation is to obey the law, an obligation which finds some support in the "general sense of justice," but which is not fortified by very strong or efficient sanctions against breach. The felt particularistic obligation implies avoidance only of certain blatant offenses and, on the other hand, resistance to these laws in general. This is an obligation to business colleagues, supported by their ideology and frequently also by profit motives. In general, it seems that the particularistic obligation takes precedence over the universalistic obligation. Subjects do, however, vary considerably in this respect. Our data do not, unfortunately, permit us to explain these variations.

The attitude toward the legal regulations was negative in general. But, on a more specific level, it was frequently admitted that parts of the legal structure were necessary. This ambivalence was even more marked in the attitudes toward violations and violators of the laws. On the one hand, on a general level, these were frequently condemned in principle. Most often, however, the respondents defended and tried to justify many types of specific violation. It was apparent that they perceived at least two general types of violators: "the good established firms" and "the outsiders" (including new firms, small firms, disreputable firms, etc.). Violations by the former category were considered much more harmless than those committed by the "outsiders." It seems that the businessmen in this case have developed norms of their own, more tolerant and therefore partly contrasting with the legal norms.

Here lies a problem of more general importance. Burgess and others pointed out that legal definitions of crimes are inadequate in the study of causation, because the types of behavior legally classified together need not show any uniformity in terms of etiology. The perception of an act as criminal on the part of violators and public is presented as a more suitable criterion. We have found that on the basis of such a criterion it will be necessary to classify some violations of a specific law as criminal and others as not. Detailed studies of attitudes toward specific laws would therefore be necessary in order to make any kind of statement about criminal behavior, if Burgess's criterion were to be accepted.

There was a tendency on the part of our respondents to structure their attitudes in a way which did not correspond to legal definitions. Irrespective of the terminology one accepts, we shall expect different motivation on the part of those who violate the regulations in an "acceptable" way and those who do it with less decorum, as, for example, a free-lance black marketeer. We notice furthermore that some of those who violate the laws in nonacceptable ways engage in behavior which does not possess all the characteristics ascribed to white-collar crimes by Sutherland, in spite of the fact that they meet his explicit definition of white-collar crime.

The results indicate that the concept "white-collar crime" may not be of such general usefulness in building up hypotheses about crime causation as some have believed. Most likely, the main merit of the concept has been to draw attention to new and important data useful in showing the one-sidedness of many previous generalizations about criminal behavior. The concept does, furthermore, take on increased significance if we look at the phenomena discussed from the other side; that is, if we focus on the etiology of criminal law and law enforcement.

Most of the laws and a very significant part of the enforcement machinery that make up the legal background of economic regulation in Norway aim specifically at the business group, which contains at least a large segment of people with high socioeconomic status. It seems justified to interpret the growing number of legally defined crimes in this area as a symptom of a slow change in Norwegian social structure, where two partly competing social hierarchies, each with its own marks of distinction, are existing peacefully side by side. Of these, the labor movement and the government agencies it controls represent the ascendant hierarchy, while the business group and its fringes represent the descendant hierarchy. It seems that the definition of new legal crimes of the white-collar brand has served an important social function by giving the ascendant group a feeling of possessing the economic power corresponding to its political supremacy. We do, on the other hand, find traces of resistance to implementation in the social structure in general and in the enforcement machinery. The result is slowness and inefficiency, which create a feeling of harmlessness among the violators. This may then serve the function of pacifying the businessmen and in that way insure the social peace which Norway has enjoyed after the war.[14]

If the preceding speculations prove to have some basis in reality, it appears that causes and functions of white-collar crime legislation differ significantly in some respects from other types of criminal legislation.

The second study[15] referred to dealt with a type of behavior which can only be characterized as white-collar crime according to a fairly wide interpretation of Sutherland's definition. We investigated a new piece of social legislation, regulating the working conditions of domestic help. Violations of this law are committed by housewives, frequently citizens of relatively high socioeconomic status, in the course of their occupation. Violations are punishable, although a penal sanction presupposes persistence in violation in spite of warnings. It must be admitted that both the position of the violators and the nature of the sanction make this behavior marginal to current discussions about white-collar crimes. Nevertheless, it raises so many of the same problems that it merits some attention in the present context.

Viewed as a study of criminal—or "criminaloid"—behavior and of crime causation, the survey had some peculiar features. It was, in the first place, not based upon any prison population or population identifiable through police or court records. It was entirely a study of "hidden criminality" and it revealed close to 100 per cent "criminality" in the probability sample which was studied. The identification of violations was based upon a fairly intricate interview, eliciting factual information about the respondent's own behavior and (in interviews with housemaids) their employer's behavior. The respondent was usually ignorant of the laws pertaining to her behavior. A procedure like the one we applied seems to be the logical consequence of a strictly legal definition of criminal behavior. It did, however, give a rather frightening demonstration of the technical problems involved in the mapping of criminal behavior in this sense.

As for the correlates, or possible causes, they differed considerably from those which usually predominate in criminological theory. It turned out that the age of the victim was associated with the incidence of violation. The insight into the content of the legal norms on the part of the potential violators was another factor of some importance. The size of the family also seemed to have something to do with violations. The factor, however, which seemed most significantly (negatively) associated with violation was the clarity and scope of the contract upon which the work relationship was based.

The aforementioned factors differentiated our respondents. If we want to understand why there are so many "crimes" in the whole group, the newness of the law is significant and its reformative nature likewise. The relative isolation of the victims and the uncontrollability of the illegal behavior probably also have a great deal to do with the high incidence of violations.

If those variables that are mentioned here are significant causally, it goes once more to show that specific types of law violations need specific types of explanations.[16] Using the legal definition of "crime," there is probably little in common between all the phenomena covered by the concept. And the same seems to be true of white-collar crime. This type can also differ very much in its nature and may need quite different causal explanations. We disregard then such global and rather empty principles as the one that "all criminal behavior is learned."

In the present study, we made an attempt to examine rather carefully the conditions determining the form and content of the criminal clause in the new law. This revealed a striking ambivalence on the part of the legislators to the behavior in question. Most likely this ambivalence reflects the existence of two groups in the legislature, groups which are frequently divided on issues of social legislation. This division corresponds roughly to the one described previously, that is, between the left and the right. The legislators expressed a serious wish to put teeth into the new law by supporting it with penal sanctions. On the other hand, however, it was emphasized that the aim of the law was already achieved and sanctions were therefore unnecessary. Furthermore, it would be impossible to enforce the law through inspection in the homes. The resulting criminal clause was a hybrid. It did stipulate a penal sanction, but at the same time, it was made practically unenforceable.[17]

The function of this social legislation as it was finally formulated seems again to be the avoidance of a serious split on the issue between contrasting ideological factions in the legislature and corresponding groups in the population. Perhaps the mere existence of a criminal clause goes some way to satisfy those who on ideological grounds demand action against employers who misuse their housemaids. Its lack of enforcement, on the other hand, protects the opposite interest group against any immediate serious bother. It looks as if, in the kind of social structure one finds in Norway today, this sort of purely formal criminalization serves primarily to preserve "the groupness of the group," according to Llewellyn the basic "law-job."[18]

Let us now summarize some of the experiences from the two Norwegian studies, in so far as they pertain to the discussion of white-collar crime.

The public's and the violators' perceptions of crimes in general are frequently not congruent with legal definitions, the implication being that we may find important differences in motivation and other causal mechanisms within even very specific legal categories. Consequently, we find differences to an even higher degree within broader concepts such as white-collar crime.

According to the definition that "a criminal is a person who regards himself as a criminal and is so regarded by society" some white-collar offenses are crimes while others are not.

The Burgess' dictum.

But it looks as if at least the large bulk of laws stipulating penalties for white-collar offenses have something in common sociologically. This needs much further study, however. The major variables which account for the defining of such acts as crimes seem to be connected with the concept of multiple social hierarchies or diverse status systems.

Legal definitions of white-collar crime imply a need for the study of hidden criminality, which constitutes the vast majority of these offenses. Out of this arise methodological problems of vast scope, severely limiting the possibility of answering the problem of causation.

In the area of research discussed in this paper, it seems that the most fruitful orientation in the research is a study of the interaction between the legal stimulus and the response of violators and the public. This requires careful study of the legislative process and the machinery of enforcement, as well as the study of individual motives, attitudes, and social situation of offenders.

Finally, the basic concepts involved in such a study should not be of a specifically criminological or legal nature, but belong in a general theory of social psychology.

Notes

1. Thorsten Sellin, *Culture Conflict and Crime* (New York: Social Science Research Council, 1938), chap. 2.

2. Robert K. Merton, "The Sociology of Knowledge," in Robert K. Merton, *Social Theory and Social Structure* (New York: The Free Press, 1950), p. 222.

3. Edwin H. Sutherland, "Is 'White-Collar Crime' Crime?" *American Socio-logical Review*, 10 (April, 1945), 132–139.

4. Frank E. Hartung, "White-Collar Offenses in the Wholesale Meat Industry in Detroit," *American Journal of Sociology*, 56 (July, 1950), pp. 25–30, and Ernest W. Burgess' comment which follows (pp. 31–34).

5. Edwin H. Sutherland, *White Collar Crime* (New York: Dryden Press, 1949), p. 9.

6. Donald R. Cressey, "The Criminal Violation of Financial Trust," *American Sociological Review*, 15 (December, 1950), p. 741.

7. Robert K. Merton, "Social Structure and Anomie," *American Sociological Review*, 3 (Octber, 1938), p. 672.

8. See Muzafer Sherif and Hadley Cantril, *The Psychology of Ego-Involvements* (New York: Wiley, 1947), chap. 10.

9. See Charles L. Stevenson, *Ethics and Language* (New Haven, Conn.: Yale University Press, 1948), pp. 210ff.

10. A theoretical outline of many of the concepts involved in such studies is to be found in Torgny T. Segerstedt, *Social Control as a Sociological Concept* (Uppsala: Lundequistska Bokhandeln, 1948).

11. Leon Festinger, "Informal Communication in Small Groups," in Harold Guetzkow, ed., *Groups, Leadership, and Men* (Pittsburgh, Pa.: Carnegie Press, 1951), p. 32.

12. Full report in Vilhelm Aubert, *Priskontroll og Rasjonering* (Oslo: Institute for Social Research, 1950).

13. Samuel A. Stouffer and Jackson Toby, "Role Conflict and Personality," *American Journal of Sociology*, 56 (March, 1951), pp. 395–406.

14. It will be seen that our interpretation has borrowed something from Thurman Arnold, *The Folklore of Capitalism* and *Symbols of Government* (New Haven, Conn.: Yale University Press, 1937 and 1935, respectively).

15. Full report in Vilhelm Aubert, Torstein Eckhoff, and Knut Sveri, *En Lov i Søkelyset* (Oslo: Institute for Social Research, 1952).

16. For additional evidence from another "unorthodox" kind of crime, see Arnold M. Rose, "The Social Psychology of Desertion from Combat," *American Sociological Review*, 16 (October, 1951), pp. 614–629.

17. The social functions of such statutes have previously been analyzed by Thurman Arnold, *op. cit.*, and Jerome Frank, *Courts on Trial* (Princeton, N.J.: Princeton University Press, 1949).

18. Karl N. Llewellyn, "Law and the Social Sciences, Especially Sociology," *American Sociological Review*, 14 (August, 1949), p. 454.

SOCIAL STRUCTURE AND RENT-CONTROL VIOLATIONS

Harry V. Ball

This study is focused upon the legal controls of residential rents, their differential impressions of fairness upon the landlords, and the relationships between these and violations of rent ceilings in Honolulu in 1952.

Beginning prior to the establishment of Hawaii as a Territory of the United States, the rental housing business in Honolulu operated under what Friedrich has called "the normal law of landlord and tenant."

> Dwellings are let according to the rules of property and contract. The landlord as owner of the dwelling can fix the rent of his property at whatever figure he chooses. If a tenant does not pay his rent, the landlord has such remedies as distress and eviction. Upon the expiration of the lease, the landlord can take possession of the property, refusing to renew the lease for any or no reason. The competition between landlords is supposed to protect the tenant against the charge of extortionate rents.[1]

When the United States became involved in World War II, statutory

Reprinted from *American Journal of Sociology*, 65 (May, 1960), pp. 598–604.

rent control was introduced in Honolulu by local city-county ordinance under the emergency powers granted that government unit by the legislature of Hawaii earlier that year, 1941. The stated intent of this ordinance was to prevent speculative and manipulative practices by landlords, while allowing the landlords a fair return on the value of their property. For the period of wartime martial law in Hawaii, 1942 to 1945, the ordinance was in effect by command of the military governor, after which it continued under its original civil jurisdiction. (At no time between 1941 and 1952 did Honolulu operate directly under the rent control authorized by the federal Congress and established through the Office of Price Administration and its successor agencies.)

When direct control of consumer prices was generally abolished in 1947, modified control of residential rent was retained by the federal Congress. Landlords at that time were thus differentiated from most other kinds of businessmen in the regulation of their businesses. However, the independence of the Honolulu controls permitted variations to be introduced between them and the controls operating in the rest of the nation. Whereas most newly constructed rental housing units were exempted by post-1947 legislation from regulation by statutory-administrative law of the federal government, *all* privately owned housing in Honolulu continued under statutory control even after 1947. As a result, the landlords of all the private rental housing units in the city were under the general legal rule not to charge more than the legally established maximum rent. Any person who willfully violated this rule was subject, upon conviction, to penal sanctions consisting of a fine up to $1,000 or imprisonment up to a period of one year.

The inclusiveness of the Honolulu ordinance did *not* mean, however, that the legal maximum rent of every unit in 1952 had been determined by a single standard, by the application of a single criterion or set of criteria. When the ordinance was initiated in December, 1941, it specified May 27, 1941, as the "freeze" or "fair-rent" date: for all units rented on May 27, 1941, the rent and services in effect on that date were declared to constitute the "maximum-rent" and "minimum-service" standards for each unit, regardless of subsequent changes in ownership, tenancy, or landlord-tenant agreements. For units which had not been rented on the fair-rent date but which had been rented sometime between May 27, 1940, and May 26, 1941, inclusive, the ordinance specified that the ceiling and service standards were to be those which had last existed during that specified year. Thus, the statute embodied the principle that "fair rents" are those rents generally prevailing in a "normal market" and, in effect, it defined the state of the housing market of May 27, 1941, as "normal."

Another provision applied to all units not rented between May 27, 1940, and May 27, 1941, but rented subsequently. The ceilings of this class of rental accommodations were to be determined by the Rent Control Commission upon the basis of the rent and services "generally prevailing for comparable housing accommodations" on the fair-rent date. The power to decide matters of "comparability" was vested entirely in the commission.

The ordinance did provide for raising the legal maximum rent of particular units under these ceilings to compensate for "substantial" increases in taxes or other operating and maintenance costs or "substantial capital improvements or alterations." But there could be no raising of the ceiling on grounds of increased market value, even if the housing accommodation had been sold to a new landlord at a cost much greater than the owner's original investment on the fair-rent date. In short, for housing rented between May 27, 1940, and May 27, 1941, or existing then but only subsequently rented there was no provision in the ordinance for explicit specific application of the concept of a "fair return upon investment" to individual accommodations.

In 1945, the Board of Supervisors intervened in a dispute between the local Rent Control Commission and the Federal Housing Administration and amended the ordinance, directing the commission to accept the rent ceilings on new construction provided by the FHA or other authorized federal agencies. According to the rent-control administrator, these FHA ceilings provided the landlord a gross return of about 16 per cent on the cost of construction and land and were considerably higher than the ceilings then being established by the commission upon the basis of comparability. When, in 1947, the federal Congress exempted most new construction from federal rent control, the board again amended this section to authorize the commission to employ its discretion in accepting or rejecting the bases of the ceilings set by federal agencies.

In this situation, the commission did not attempt to "roll back" the ceilings on new construction which had been established between 1945 and 1947 by the FHA. Rather, it adopted (or retained) as the major determinant of the ceilings on subsequent new construction the federal agency's concept of 1947 of a net return of 6.5 per cent of the total of the original cost of construction plus the assessed value of the land.

In the light of the permanence of this special treatment for newly constructed housing, the rent-control administrator and his investigators tended to give comparable considerations to older housing entering the rental market for the first time since May 27, 1940. It became a prevalent practice to establish ceilings on these older units also upon the basis of a 6.5 per cent net return. However, the net return in this instance was based upon an estimate of the original cost of construction rather than the current or replacement cost. Thus, it did not constitute the clear-cut "return on investment" for the current landlord that the net-return formula represented for landlords of newly constructed accommodations. Rather, it constituted a third class of determinations of legal maximum rent.

Thus, while the general rule that no landlord may charge a rent in excess of the legally established maximum applied to all landlords, a number of subclasses of landlords existed by 1952 on the basis of the methods of determining ceilings. The ordinance, the "law in books," had established two substatuses initially, and then it shifted to one mandatory and one optional status. The operations of the commission and its staff, the "law in action," had established three substatuses. Three classes of landlords were created by the three ceilings, and one individual, of course, could belong in more than one class simultaneously:

1. Landlords with fair-rent–date ceilings. The landlord of a unit constructed prior to 1945 which had been given an initial ceiling prior to 1947 according to the last rent charged between May 27, 1940, and May 27, 1941, or the rent levels generally prevailing for comparable housing accommodations on May 27, 1941.

2. Landlords with fair-return ceilings. The landlord of a unit constructed prior to 1945 which had received its initial ceiling in 1947 or later. The ceiling determination provided for roughly a 6.5 per cent return on the estimated original cost of construction plus the assessed value of the land.

3. Landlords with new-construction ceilings. The landlord of a unit constructed in 1945 or later. For the most part, these ceilings were established to provide a 6.5 per cent return on the cost of construction plus the assessed value of the land. This approximated a net return upon investment formula.

The original expressed intent of the rent-control ordinance was to produce rents which would be fair to both landlords and tenants. But in 1952, new-construction ceilings took considerable account of the general postwar inflation, fair-return ceilings in many instances took some account of this inflation, and fair-rent–date ceilings took account of the inflation only with respect to substantial increases in direct operating costs. Thus, the evidence was substantial that these differential treatments would endow the general norm not to violate ceilings with a different meaning for each subclass of landlords.

Let us turn now to a consideration of the other side of this institutional arrangement—the landlords and that part of their conduct which the legal rules regulated. The best estimates are that in Honolulu in 1952 there were about 36,000 private rental units and about 10,000 landlords. The vast majority of the landlords were small investors, described by Grebler as follows:

He sometimes originated rental housing; more often, rental housing of certain types was built by contractors or operative builders for the purposes of immediate sale to the small investor. The structures have usually been two to four family dwellings, one of which is typically occupied by the owner, who also frequently performs the simple management functions. The motivation of this kind of investor often is to have the net rental income carry his own housing costs. Small, nonprofessional investors have also entered the field of rental housing without this motivation, attracted by the social distinction of real estate ownership and expectations of above average net returns on invested capital or of capital appreciation.[2]

In Honolulu these small investors very frequently held only one or two units for rent.

The large long-run investors among landlords in Honolulu usually tended to be relatively small by Mainland standards and to be more interested in above-average returns than some large Mainland institutions. It was very rare to find a landlord who held more than fifty units, and the large operators often controlled only one apartment building or one collection of single-family units.[3] The large estates in Hawaii had specialized in land leases rather than in housing operations.

A few speculative sponsors had emerged in postwar Honolulu. Most of their operations centered around large apartment houses in the vicinity of Waikiki; many picked up some windfall profits, and virtually all their units had new-construction ceilings. The operative house builder was not yet significant in the rental market of Honolulu in 1952.

Thus, as a group, the individuals who had entered the rental housing business had usually done so for one or more of the following reasons: the social distinctions attached to landlordism, which were particularly significant in Honolulu; expectations of above-average net returns on investment or of above-average capital appreciation; or a belief that it was a safe, inflation-proof provision for retirement and a business which could be operated by relatively inexperienced survivors. Against these expectations, landlords found themselves singled out for price regulation in 1952, restricted to prices which in most instances took little or no account of inflation, and operating far more complicated businesses than anticipated.

Forty-two landlords of units with fair-rent–date ceilings and eight landlords with new-construction ceilings were interviewed to ascertain what factors they believed should be taken into account in establishing "fair rents." The landlords with the new-construction ceilings, especially the speculative sponsors, gave greatest prominence in their replies to the idea of providing a proper margin of profit, although they were consistently vague about the precise meaning of "proper."

On the other hand, the landlords with fair-rent–date ceilings, who were much more typical of Honolulu landlords, viewed the problem as a personal, complex, and relative matter. What stood out in their replies were: (1) the rents other landlords were believed to be getting for "comparable units" (with considerable variation in the criteria for "comparable"); (2) the amount by which the landlord believed other prices and incomes had generally risen or fallen since the rent in question was established; (3) the original expectations of the landlord in terms of purchasing power—what he had specifically hoped to accomplish with his rent income; and (4) the difficulty in renting a unit at a given price. It was in terms of the last three generally, but especially (2) and (3), that these landlords often volunteered information about the unfairness, as they saw it, of rent control.

It could be concluded that this examination of landlordism, with respect to its special motivation as an occupation and the techniques of determining "fair rent," corroborated the findings produced by the analysis of the legal structure. The multiple modes of legal maximum-rent determination did seem to constitute a gradation of restrictions upon the opportunities of landlords to establish what they considered to be "fair rents."

But were these apparent consequences actually demonstrable for individual landlords? Were individual landlords with fair-rent–date ceilings more likely to feel restricted or deprived than individual landlords with new-construction ceilings? The hypothesis was formed that the proportion of landlords who believed their legal maximum rent to be unfair would be greatest for those with fair-rent–date ceilings, intermediate for those with fair-return ceilings, and least for those with new-construction ceilings.

This hypothesis was tested against data collected from a 5 per cent sample of all rental units within the city of Honolulu which were then registered with the Rent Control Commission. A questionnaire had been mailed to the landlords of each of the 1,522 rental accommodations (in the original sample) which had been established by means of a tenant interview as still in the rental market. A total of 1,068 questionnaires, about 70 per cent, were available for this analysis.[4] One item in the questionnaire asked each landlord to state precisely what rent he believed would provide him a fair return. The responses to this question were classified according to (1) the kind of ceiling determination of the unit in question and (2) whether the landlord's own estimate of a fair rent was above or below the legal maximum rent, as indicated by the record for that unit in the commission's files.

The legal maximum rent was evaluated as unfair in 70.4 per cent of the responses under fair-rent–date ceilings, in 53.6 per cent of the responses under fair-return ceilings, and in 40.3 per cent of the responses under new-construction ceilings—differences statistically significant at the .01 level by the chi-square test. The null hypothesis that they had been produced by chance was rejected. The evaluations by the individual landlords of the unfairness of their ceiling rents did vary consistently with the hypothesized relative deprivations involved in the modes of determining maximum rent.

Since the differential treatments under the law did tend to provide the affected individuals with different meanings for the general norm against violating ceilings, did they also tend to produce differing rates of violation of this general norm? Inkeles has pointed out that "the need for a theory of personality is perhaps most evident in the study of those 'rates' which represent the summary or end-product of thousands or millions of individual decisions and acts, yet which are of distinctive size for different societies or cultures. To illustrate . . . suicide and delinquency rates."[5] Our problem here is analogous to his, but one major qualification should be introduced. This is that different dimensions or components of personality, even different theories of personality, have varying relevance to different sets of institutional arrangements and the actions they are intended to induce or inhibit.

Now one may assume that, insofar as a landlord has a concept of a fair rent which exceeded the legal maximum for some accommodation, he is persistently motivated to seek to reduce the discrepancy. Perhaps this is not sufficient in itself to induce a landlord to violate his ceiling. But it would certainly enter the mind of any landlord who, for whatever reasons, "needs" more money, or serve as reason enough for any landlord who simply "wants" his "fair return" or whatever he originally anticipated from his rental business.

There are thus two problems: first, what the relationship was between the individual violations of ceilings and the individual evaluations of their fairness or unfairness, and, second, what the final relationship was between the legal structure, as expressed in the three methods of determining ceilings and the fact of control itself, and the rates of violations of the ceilings.

To answer these questions, data on the violations among the 1,522 units in the housing sample were required. As indicated previously, the legal maximum-rent and minimum-service standards for each of these units had been obtained from the files of the commission. At the same time, at least one adult tenant of each rental unit was interviewed to determine the rent actually paid and the services actually provided. These two sets of data were compared for each accommodation, and each was accordingly categorized as a "violation" or "nonviolation."

Table 1 presents these categories of violation and nonviolation crosstabulated by the landlords' evaluations of the fairness or unfairness of their ceilings for their 1,050 responses. The differences were statistically significant at the .01 level. The most striking finding was that not one fair response was located in the violation category. This is strong evidence for the hypothesis that having a concept of a fair rent in excess of one's legal maximum rent was a prominent component in motivating the landlord to violate his ceiling. And it was previously shown that the frequency of occurrence of this was related to the kind of determination of the ceiling involved. On the other hand, 54.6 per cent of the nonviolations also involved an evaluation of an unfair ceiling. Thus, in 67.5 per cent of the instances of declared unfairness, this, while important, was not sufficient to induce an act of violation.

With respect to the second question, the results of the cross-tabulation of violations by mode of ceiling determination were as expected. The proportion of violations was 29.2 per cent for fair-rent–date ceilings, 14.9 per cent for fair-return ceilings, and only 7.3 per cent for new-construction ceilings. The differences were statistically significant at the .01 level. The legal structure did appear to exert more pressure on some persons than on others to engage in nonconformist rather than conformist behavior.[6] And a substantial contribution to the understanding of the "how" was made by the intervening analyses of the differential perceptions and concomitant motivation.

It has been suggested that the real differences with regard to violations lay in opposition to rent control and that the evaluation of unfairness by many violators may have been merely a postviolation rationalization. In other words, opposition to rent control might indicate the extent to which the violations represented an "acting-out" by individuals strongly hostile to authority in general.

Two analyses were made which tested the significance of opposition to rent control and which may be considered at least a partial test of this idea. In the questionnaire each landlord was asked, "Do you believe rent control is necessary in Honolulu at the present time?" He was asked to indicate his answer: "Yes," "Yes, but with changes in the ordinance (law)," or "No." A few respondents wrote "Don't know," or refused to answer at all.

The violation rate for those landlords who indicated rent control was not necessary was 23.2 per cent; for all others, it was 21.2 per cent. The t-test did not indicate statistical significance, and neither did a chi-square test with four degrees of freedom performed on the entire array of responses respecting the necessity of rent control.

Finally, this hypothesis was tested: If a landlord defined his ceiling

Table 1. *Percentage Distributions of Ceiling Violations and Nonviolations by Landlord Evaluations*

Evaluation of ceiling	Violations	Non-violations	Total
Fair	—	34.0	26.4
Don't Know	—	4.2	3.3
Unfair	92.5	54.6	63.0
No Response	7.5	7.2	7.3
Total	100.0	100.0	100.0
No.	232	818	1,050

to be unfair and was opposed to rent control, he violated his ceiling. For reasons of sample size, this test was limited to units with fair-rent–date ceilings whose landlords had defined the ceilings to be unfair. Of the 179 violation cases in this class, 54.2 per cent of the landlord responses indicated that rent control was not necessary. Of the 321 nonviolation cases, 55.1 per cent so indicated. The difference was not statistically significant, and the null hypothesis was accepted.

In short, opposition to legal rent control, as such, did not appear to play any systematic role in the act of ceiling violation by landlords in Honolulu in 1952. On the other hand, the legal restrictions placed upon previously legitimate methods for achieving still legitimate aspirations, especially that for more money, seems to have been of considerable importance. The persistent anticipation that rent control would soon be eliminated prevented any major movement from rental to other business. And the tendency to perceive one's treatment under the law to be unfair and thus to be tempted to violate the law appeared directly related to the law's severity. It only remains to stress that 77 per cent of the rental units in the city in 1952 were operated in compliance with these legal rules, in spite of widespread opposition to rent control and an overwhelming belief among landlords generally that they were being treated unfairly.

Notes

1. A. A. Friedrich, "Rent Regulation," in *Encyclopedia of the Social Sciences*, vol. 13 (New York: Macmillan, 1933), p. 293.

2. Leo Grebler, *Production of Housing* (New York: Social Science Research Council, 1950), p. 120.

3. For a detailed discussion of the social history of rent control in Honolulu see Harry V. Ball, "A Sociological Study of Rent Control and Rent Control Violations," Ph.D. Dissertation, University of Minnesota, 1956, pp. 534–837.

4. About 66 per cent of the questionnaires were returned by mail. A 10 per cent sample of the nonrespondents was interviewed. Between respondents and nonrespondents few differences were found, and those which were statistically significant were small in magnitude. For detailed comparisons see Ball, *op. cit.*, pp. 70–77.

5. Alex Inkeles, "Personality and Social Structure," in Robert K. Merton, Leonard Broom, and Leonard S. Cottrell, Jr., eds., *Sociology Today: Problems and Prospects* (New York: Basic Books, 1959), p. 251. I have taken, as a matter of strategy, the position that one should not employ a broader theory or number of ideas about personality than is required by the immediate task at hand.

6. Robert K. Merton, *Social Theory and Social Structure* (New York: The Free Press, 1949), pp. 125–126.

13

CHEATING ON TAXES

Edmond Cahn

A federal statute provided that any alien who had more than once been sentenced to more than a year of imprisonment because of conviction of "a crime involving moral turpitude" would be deported from the United States. In February, 1938, Alberto B————, an alien, pleaded guilty to concealing liquor with intent to defraud the government of whiskey taxes, and in May, 1938, he pleaded guilty to conspiring with others to violate the revenue laws. On each charge he was sentenced to imprisonment for a year and a day. B———— claimed he could not be deported because his crimes did not involve "moral turpitude." When this contention failed in the trial court, he appealed to the United States Court of Appeals. There he argued that the court should follow the rule it had established for an earlier case in 1929, during the Prohibition era. In the previous case, the court had held that selling whiskey in violation of the Prohibition laws was not such "moral turpitude" as to justify deportation.

The Court of Appeals held (2-1) that B———— should be deported.

Reprinted from Edmond Cahn, *The Moral Decision* (Bloomington: Indiana University Press, and London: Stevens & Sons Ltd., 1955), pp. 164–175.

Two very distinguished judges (Augustus N. Hand and Robert P. Patterson) considered that B——— had attempted to defraud the government of taxes and that fraud is an unmistakable badge of moral turpitude. In their view, the earlier case did not apply, because what it involved was not "any specific intent to defraud the government but only a general purpose to disregard the prohibition laws." Prohibition had been repealed long before B——— committed his offenses.

Judge Learned Hand, who is justly celebrated as a judicial sage, expressed his dissent. He said "I could wish that it was commonly thought more morally shameful than it is to evade taxes; but it is certainly true that people who in private affairs are altogether right-minded, see nothing more than a venial peccadillo in smuggling, or in escaping excises on liquor. . . . We must try to appraise the moral repugnance of the ordinary man towards the conduct in question; not what an ideal citizen would feel."[1]

B———'s case deserves exceptionally careful rumination. For if the majority and dissenting opinions are taken together, they recapitulate and exemplify in the clearest possible fashion the two maxims which are immanent in any intelligent moral decision. The first: What men ought to do cannot be determined by what they actually do (else, why any laws or moral precepts whatever?). The second: What men ought to do cannot be determined without regard to what they actually do (else, how can laws or moral precepts be made fit for mundane men?).

Now, at the risk of knocking some paint off the paper-mâché figment of the model American citizen, it is necessary to recognize that one of his characteristic practices has always been and still is to cheat the government on taxes whenever he feels it safe to do so. In point of fact, he has exhibited considerable native ingenuity—though probably less than the citizens or subjects of certain other countries—in discovering ways and means to make the cheating reasonably safe for himself. Over and above the various subtle and legally permissible maneuvers which are euphemistically called "tax-avoidance," there is, as Judge Learned Hand acknowledged, a firmly established American custom of tax evasion. In small, medium, and large amounts at each passing hour, this kind of chicane is practiced by citizens of all ranks and of every level of repute. In colonial times, the so-called "best people" were wont to defraud King George of his legitimate revenues long before political grievances came along to cloak their dishonesty with the excuse that they were only doing their patriotic duty; and so it has been generation by generation ever since. (Some who read here may notice—speaking quite privately—how relieved and pleased they are to be told that theirs is a time-honored American custom.)

There is no blinking the history of the subject. Excise taxes, the kind that B——— failed to pay, have met with popular resistance down the centuries. They were the traditional revenue-raising devices of Europe's absolute despots; they were imposed on necessities of life and increased the sufferings of the poor; they fell due very frequently and thus every minute transaction involved an irritant; and since, as a general rule, the excises were levied to implement the sovereign's economic and political program, they were bound to meet resistance whenever the program turned unpopular. Smuggling became a not disreputable part of the folk mores in America and everywhere else. Even a professional smuggler—like Jean Lafitte—was welcomed beside Andrew Jackson at the Battle of New Orleans in the War of 1812. At the other end of the country during the same war, two-thirds of the enemy's army in Canada were sustained by consuming beef smuggled across the Vermont border. Probably the worthy farmer of that state reasoned to himself the way many an American reasons today when he fills out his income tax return; probably he felt that he was under obligation to his family to do the things he did.

Of course, if someone is caught and his cheating is exposed, much public indignation may ensue and eloquent denunciations are heard; but in every such scandal there are many who fulminate so indignantly because they too have cheated and now discover for the first time a feeling of self-righteousness. They may feel self-righteous because someone was caught while they were not or because the dollar amount of his fraud makes theirs seem unimportant, almost minikin. For this also they abhor him, for he seems to tell them mockingly that their former restraint was needless and that they really should have treated themselves more generously.

But this upsurge of popular excitement soon subsides and little remains beyond the tincture of envy in it. Hence, unless the defendant happens to be a notorious gangster, federal judges generally mete out very short sentences for defrauding the government of taxes; they apparently assume, along with most of the American community, that a single embezzlement of private funds equals in heinousness five to ten frauds on the federal revenue. And then, so many tax prosecutions can be compromised by paying money only and so many more are put aside and allowed to lapse, for reasons proper or improper. Finally, there are uncounted frauds that simply never come to light at all. Well and heartily may a perjurious taxpayer say, in the words that Juvenal supplied for the perjured of his time: "The wrath of the gods may be great, but it assuredly is slow; if then they charge themselves with punishing all the guilty, when will they come to me? And besides I may perchance find the god placable; he is wont to forgive things like this. Many commit the same crime and fare differently: One man gets a gibbet, another a crown, as the reward of crime."[2] In American tax prosecutions, there is no fear of anything remotely like the gibbet.

To complete the picture, we must pay tribute to American inventiveness in concocting balms and unguents for abrasions of the taxpayer's conscience. The variety is admirable; there is a specific salve for every type of citizen. For example, if your political party happens to be in office, you recount to yourself the manifold services you are rendering to it and through it to the nation; why not leave taxes to the others? If your party is out of office, you ask why you should exacerbate the follies of the administration by providing funds for imbeciles to squander. If you are conservative, you oppose change by keeping your money where it is. If a progressive, you remind yourself that tomorrow new demands will inevitably be made on your purse. If opulent, you have proved you know how to use your money better than any politician can use it for you. If poor, you need it more than the government does. If married, you must take care of your family; if single, you have no one else to take care of you. And so the theme flows on and on through inexhaustible variations.

Nevertheless, there is an area of exception where none of these excuses will be received. According to the American estimate, nonchalance stops where "professionalism" begins. In this view, what stamped B———'s acts with moral turpitude was not that he had cheated the government but that he had virtually made a business of doing so. He had lost his amateur status and with it his expectation of indulgence. In the popular American judgment, which exhibits on this score an acumen we cannot but admire, everybody slips from time to time because everybody has his share of the impulses, foibles, and flaws that characterize human nature; no one, however, is licensed either to make a livelihood, as a vendor of narcotics does, by trading on the weaknesses of others or, as a bootlegger does, by converting the casual peccadillo of tax fraud into a systematic business. The ordinary man commits retail cheats on the revenue in order to retain what he has; B——— was committing wholesale cheats in order to enrich himself.

For all the record shows, it is conceivable that later on B——— reformed his ways and redeemed his life by coming forward and serving the United States in World War II. The court's decision which affirmed the order for his deportation to Italy was handed down during the historic summer of 1940, at a time when execution of the order would hardly have been feasible. But, whatever may have happened in the intervening years, there is nothing to justify equating the offenses he had committed with the ordinary tax cheating of the average amateur. On this score, Judge Learned Hand appears to have been in error.

We come now to the very pith and marrow of our problem. Why, in point of fact, ought one to practice honesty in paying taxes to the government? Americans are by no means alone in being rather myopic to this duty; nor does the United States as yet suffer from cheating in such major proportions as some other countries. For example, the government of the Soviet Union has never been able, despite all its propaganda and coercion, to keep pilfering and fraud within limits that would be relatively harmless to its economic program; and the regimes of Western Europe find that they have to carry on their various socialized enterprises in a state of chronic fiscal anemia induced or aggravated by popular dishonesty. Taxes, which to the economist and political scientist represent a levy on the gross national production of goods and services, represent to the ordinary citizen something very much less abstract: they mean a taking away of some of his personal goods or some of his personal services. And whether the government collects by demanding part of his harvest in kind or in money equivalent, it is hard to convince him that his moral obligation is not to protect his own but honestly and cooperatively to assist those who are taking from him.

It is so hard, in fact, that only through requiring the major sources of distribution or payment (vendors, employers, corporate disbursing agents, etc.) actually to collect or withhold the tax money from the citizen and remit it to the treasury for his account, has the contemporary federal revenue system maintained any semblance of efficacy. Yet this device too inspires a practice of dishonesty: Innumerable small merchants simply pocket and retain a generous share of the excise taxes they have collected on the treasury's behalf. As a general rule, should one of these small merchants eventually expand the size of his business, he will become more public spirited in this respect because he will begin to maintain systematic inventory and sales records; it does not take long to find that loose, informal procedures which facilitate him in cheating the government may likewise facilitate some of his employees in cheating him.

Now, although the American mores seem to countenance defrauding the government of taxes (except by "professionals"), they assuredly do not countenance what we have written here. We have depicted the perpetration of tax fraud as a general and usual practice in American life; and by doing so we have violated the established mores. According to the mores, the American who cheats his government must be described as an aberrant exception quite unrepresentative of his fellow citizens and of his community. The tradition insists that he is an exception not merely in being caught but also in being dishonest. For if he were not considered abnormal in respect of dishonesty, if cheating on taxes were acknowledged to be frequent and general, if in effect nearly everybody else swindled the government, what possible scruple could remain to deter a single one of us?

The dilemma is particularly difficult to Americans, for having long since surrendered our manners to conformism, we now bid fair to do the same with our morals. Americans have customarily avoided discomfort from tax scandals by simply denying the facts; in the very face of the objective realities, they still reiterate that tax cheating is not a general American phenomenon. But this attitude cannot endure very much longer, because the high tax rates of the present and the progressive socializations of the proximate future will inevitably compel recognition of the distasteful truth. Perhaps, if we understood just why those average Americans who would not think of cheating their neighbors and customers will nevertheless cheat their government, we would fear the truth less. If we understood the workings of their moral processes, we might gain courage enough to put the traditional hypocrisy aside.

Let us begin on an elementary level. Our average American of the honester sort, having picked up a loaf of bread in a grocery store, has laid his coin on the counter in payment. Although he sees that the grocer is occupied with other customers, he feels not the slightest temptation to cheat by taking his coin back. At the door of the shop, there stands a telephone booth. He enters the booth and makes a call by means of the coin-operated instrument. Having completed the conversation, he almost instinctively sticks his finger into the receptacle provided for return of coins on uncompleted connections, finds that the telephone company's mechanism, operating faultily, has returned his payment, takes the coin, puts it in his pocket, and leaves the store with a gratified smile and a quiet conscience.

The three factors that dull his moral perception in regard to the telephone company—they apply with even greater force to the government—are size, impersonality, and compulsion. He can easily project himself into the grocer's shoes: The grocer is a man like himself with rent to pay and a family to feed. But who, except a child at play or a megalomaniac, can imaginatively perform the functions of a telephone company, much less those of a modern government? The sheer size staggers our imagination and forbids us in the name of common sense to look upon the enormous corporation or the still greater government as another, interchangeable self. What, after all, is this overpoweringly huge entity? If, in essence, it is all the stockholders or all the citizens, then how could the loss of a single coin be divided among them with any consequence that would justify consideration? If it is some abstraction apart from these individuals, then what harm has been done to any human interest? Our average American would conclude, if he ever thought about the subject, that only a machine had been outwitted.

Every manager of a large corporation knows the influence of size and impersonality on employees' and customers' behavior, the dissipations of supplies, the incessant peculations, the strange relaxation of ordinary decencies and scruples. What, moreover, is the history of all the armies and navies that the world ever bore but an unrelieved narrative of theft, plunder, and titanic waste? As soon as the owner becomes too large or too impersonal to permit an imaginative interchange with him, even very honest men may act as though they were blind to his rights. And these factors, serious in themselves, are intensified when the entity is an identified source of compulsion—the telephone company with its legalized monopoly coerces one to deal with it alone and slams the gates of individual choice; still worse, the government does not even inquire whether one desires the manifold services for which it sends its imperious bill. How can conscience possibly liken the government to a corner grocer?

We are about to show that it can. But by way of summary let us first note these three basic observations: (1) So many taxpayers will always be disposed to cheat that only the justified fear of detection and imprisonment will insure fair remittances from them and prevent them from shifting their tax obligations to honest men's shoulders. (2) We should not judge what American taxpayers ought to do merely by observing what they actually do. (3) But on the other hand, if we should adopt a rule of moral rigor and completely fail to take into account the things taxpayers do in the way of amateur tax cheating, we should wind up by inflicting Draconic measures on the citizenry, alienating them from their government, and exacerbating the very evils we set out to reduce. For millennia, the civilized world has endeavored to mark off and separate *meum* from *tuum* and has met with very indifferent success. Now appears a mendicant new aspiration that the mass of men accord the same measure of respect to *nostrum*. It is not impossible that ultimately they will learn to do so, at least if the official personnel improve a great deal in quality and intelligence. But, as matters stand, it will be a long time before any Secretary of the Treasury can recommend dismantling the federal penitentiaries.

These observations made, we are at last prepared to state the reasons why men ought to practice honesty in paying taxes. They are reasons furnished by political, social, and individual morals, and taken together, they leave no doubt that defrauding the United States government of taxes is "a crime involving moral turpitude."

The political standard rests on something firmer than patriotic impulse. Patriotism, if exhibited on an appropriate occasion, in a humanistic manner, and for a country whose history and conduct deserve it, is a highly estimable sentiment; yet it does not seem to preclude the coexistence of other sentiments, such as rapacity and greed. Who is more patriotic than the man who risks his life in time of war or who sends his son to fight for the homeland? Nevertheless, we know that such men have not infrequently cheated the government in various ways and have employed their patriotic sacrifices to rationalize their dishonesties. In the political morality of tax payment, there is something far removed from military patriotism, something that stems rather from the status of a free citizen in a free polity. When the American Revolution preached "No taxation without representation," it must have implied that representation gives taxation a claim on political conscience; representation means assumed, voluntary, not impersonal, not imposed from without, but as to each citizen binding upon conscience because essentially autonomous.

Social morality reaches the same conclusion via a different route. It reasons that taxes are the price each of us pays for his participating share in civilized society and for enjoying the immeasurable benefits of community existence. For what are we, what does any one of us have, without the community? If there is any possession a man can be said to enjoy when he is severed from the community, certainly it is not the wages, the property, the sales, the accrual of dividends and interest that bring about liability for taxes. The community fashions his wealth, whatever it may be; he can only assemble and manage it. The community protects whatever he has or hopes to have. He takes the loaf of bread from the community just as he takes it from the corner grocer. Honesty, reciprocity, and social virtue know no distinction between the grocer and the community, except that on occasion they may speak more urgently for the equities of the latter.

Finally, there is the voice of individual honor, which needs no cue from political democracy or social solidarity to speak its part. It appeals to a man's personal pride and self-esteem, regarding them as quite sufficient in themselves to prevent his sliding down the declivity of fraud. The American who heeds this voice does not defraud the government simply because he does not defraud. Unlike the others, he prizes his integrity more than some oblong pieces of officially printed paper.

Notes

1. *United States ex rel B——* v. *Reimer*, 113 F. 2d 429 (1940). Later, in *Jordan* v. *De George*, 341 U.S. 223 (1951) the United States Supreme Court by 6-3 confirmed the view of the majority.

2. A. F. Cole, ed., *The Satires of Juvenal*, no. 13 (New York: Putnam, 1906), p. 3.

14

THE CRIMINAL VIOLATION
OF FINANCIAL TRUST

Donald R. Cressey

The notion that a scientist must seek to formulate generalizations that include all of the cases of the phenomena with which he is concerned has been brought to the attention of sociologists many times.[1] The perfect form of scientific knowledge is assumed to be universal generalizations which permit the discernment of exceptions, thus making possible the perfecting or refinement of generalizations. However, this notion, which is essentially an assumption regarding the proper design for scientific research, has been applied only rarely in criminology and never in an attempt to formulate a sociological theory of trust violation. In fact, while the criminal violation of financial trust poses serious problems for theoretical criminology, textbook writers and other sociologists who have offered theories of criminal causation have for the most part ignored it.[2] As a result, almost all publications on trust violation have been issued by persons or agencies primarily interested in the techniques used or in prevention of the crime, and the vast majority of the explanations given in the literature merely repeat and emphasize popular views. Few of the

Reprinted from *American Sociological Review*, 15 (December, 1950), pp. 738–743.

explanations have been convincing, since little attempt at an integration with an explicit theory has been made.

On the contrary, most of the current explanations are of a multiple-factor type, usually stated in terms of the way the trust violator spends the funds that he has dishonestly obtained. Thus, "gambling," "drink," and "extravagant living" are listed as causes of embezzlement, even if behavior of this kind is not present in a majority of the cases.[3] Such conceptions are, in general, more in the nature of attempts to place blame or to indicate immorality than they are explanations of the behavior. For example, if it is said that a trust violator who has been considered a "pillar of the community" and a trusted and loyal employee actually has been gambling with his own and his company's money, an indication of immorality has been revealed, but his behavior has not been explained. Equally in contrast to the assumption regarding proper scientific methodology are those conceptions that assert that trust violation is caused by an assumed hidden variable, such as "moral weakness" or "tensions"[4] or by weakness in the systems of checks upon the trusted person.[5] The latter "explanation" merely states, in a sense, that trust violation is caused by the existence of institutions whose functioning depends upon varying degrees of trust.[6]

The central problem of this study is that of providing an explanation in keeping with the assumption of proper scientific method and generalization by determining whether a definable sequence of events is always present when trust violation is present and never present when trust violation is absent. A major related problem is that of accounting for the presence in individual cases of the events which make up the sequence which differentiates violators from nonviolators. These two problems are closely related, since the events in the person-situation complex at the time trust violation occurs cannot be completely separated from the prior life experiences of the trust violator. However, only the first problem—that concerned with what Lewin calls "systematic" causation, in contrast to "historical" or "genetic" causation[7]—will be discussed here.

Hypotheses in regard to the first problem, the problem of systematic causation, were formulated progressively. When a hypothesis was formulated, a search for negative cases was conducted, and when such cases were found the hypothesis was reformulated in light of them. The behavior to be explained in this manner was at first defined as embezzlement, and a legal definition of that crime was used.[8] Upon contact with cases, however, it was almost immediately discovered that the term is not used in a consistent manner in the jurisdiction where the research was conducted and that many persons whose behavior was adequately described by the legal definition actually had been sentenced to the penitentiary on some other charge. Consequently, the legal definition was abandoned and in its place two criteria for inclusion of any particular case in the study were established: (1) The person must have accepted a position of trust in good faith. This is similar to the implication of the legal definition that the "felonious intent" in embezzlement must have been formulated *after* the time of taking possession. All legal definitions are in agreement in this respect. (2) The person must have violated the trust. These criteria permit the inclusion of almost all persons convicted for embezzlement and, in addition, a proportion of those convicted for larceny by bailee, forgery, and confidence game.

The main source of direct information in regard to the behavior, now called "the criminal violation of financial trust," was interview material obtained in informal contacts over a period of five months with all prisoners whose behavior met the criteria and who were confined at the Illinois State Penitentiaries at Joliet.[9] In some cases we were able to write verbatim notes during the interviews without disturbing the subject; in other cases it seemed appropriate to make only outline notes; and in some cases no notes could be taken at all. In the last two instances, the content of the interview was written down in the subject's own words as soon as he left the room.

The length and frequency of interviews with individual subjects depended to a large extent upon the subject himself. Those subjects who seemed reluctant to talk were seen more frequently than those with whom a friendly and confidential relationship was established early in the process; but those who could not present the details of their cases and backgrounds, even if they so desired, were not interviewed as frequently as those who were able to do so. That is, "good" subjects were interviewed more often and more extensively than were "poor" subjects— those whose intelligence, educational background, and vocabulary restricted the communication of their experiences. Those who described their behavior fluently became crucial cases, their testimony causing the abandonment of the hypotheses which had guided the research up to the time they were encountered. The new hypotheses were then checked against the less fluent cases.

The initial hypothesis, which was abandoned almost immediately, was that positions of financial trust are violated when the incumbent has learned, in connection with the business or profession in which he is employed, that some forms of trust violations are merely "technical violations" and are not really "illegal" or "wrong," and, on the negative side, that they are not violated if this kind of definition of the behavior has not been learned. This hypothesis was suggested by Sutherland in his writings on white-collar crime.[10] In the interviews, however, many trust violators expressed the idea that they knew the behavior to be illegal and wrong at all times and that they merely "kidded themselves" into thinking that it was not illegal. Others reported that they knew of no one in their business or profession who was carrying on practices similar to theirs and some of them defined their offenses as theft rather than as trust violation.

In view of these negative cases, a second hypothesis, which included some of the "multiple-factor" ideas of gambling and family emergencies, as well as the potential trust violators' attitudes toward them, was formulated. This hypothesis was in part derived from Riemer's statement that the "opportunities" inherent in trust positions form "temptations" if the incumbents develop antisocial attitudes which make possible an abandonment of the folkways of business behavior.[11] The formulation was that positions of trust are violated when the incumbent structures a real or supposed need for extra funds or extended use of property as an "emergency" that cannot be met by legal means and that if such an emergency does not take place trust violation will not occur. This hypothesis proved fruitful, but like the first one it had to be revised when persons were found who claimed that while an emergency had been present at the time they violated the trust, other, perhaps even more extreme, emergencies had been present in earlier periods when they did not violate it. Others reported that there had been no financial emergency in their cases, and a few "explained" their behavior in terms of antagonistic attitudes toward the employer or feelings of being abused, underpaid, or discriminated against in some other way.

The next revision shifted the emphasis from emergency to psychological isolation, stating that persons become trust violators when they conceive of themselves as having incurred financial obligations that are considered as nonsocially sanctionable and which, consequently, must be satisfied by a private or secret means. Negatively, if such nonshareable obligations are not present, trust violation will not occur. This hypothesis had the advantage of calling attention to the fact that not all emergencies, even if they are created by prior "immoral" behavior on the part of the trusted person, are important to trust violation. It had been suggested by LaPiere and Farnsworth, who cite Sutherland as having shown that in cases of white-collar crime the person is frequently confronted "with the alternative of committing a crime or losing something he values above his integrity,"[12] but it was brought into the present study by a suggestion from a prisoner who stated that he believed that no embezzlement would ever occur if the trusted person always told his wife and family about his financial problems, no matter what the consequences. However, when the cases were re-examined in light of this hypothesis it was found that in a few of them there was nothing which could be considered as financial *obligation*; that is, as a debt which had been incurred in the past and for which the person at present felt responsible. Also, in some cases there had been nonsanctionable obligations at a prior time, and these obligations had not been alleviated by means of trust violation. It became increasingly apparent at this point that trust violation could not be attributed to a single event, but that its explanation could be made only in terms of a sequence of events, a process.

Again the hypothesis was reformulated, emphasizing this time not financial *obligations*, which were considered as nonsocially sanctionable and hence as nonshareable, but as nonshareable *problems* of that nature. This hypothesis also pointed up the idea that not only was a nonshareable problem necessary, but also that the person had to possess (1) knowledge or awareness of the fact that the problem could to some extent be solved by means of trust violation and (2) the technical skill necessary for such violation. Negative cases appeared, however, in instances where men reported that what they considered a nonshareable problem had been present for some period of time and that they had known for some time before the violation took place that the problem could be solved by violating their position of trust by using a particular skill. Some stated that they did not violate the trust at the earlier period because the situation was not in sharp enough focus to "break down their ideas of right and wrong."

Such statements suggested the final revision, which took the following form: Trusted persons become trust violators when they conceive of themselves as having a financial problem which is nonshareable, have the knowledge or awareness that this problem can be secretly resolved by violation of the position of financial trust, and are able to apply to their own conduct in that situation verbalizations that enable them to adjust their conceptions of themselves as trusted persons with their conceptions of themselves as users of the entrusted funds or property.

This hypothesis proved to be far superior to the others, and no evidence necessitating its rejection has been found as yet. In all of the cases interviewed the sequence has been found to be present, and when cases were examined with a view to answering the question: "Why did these men not violate their trust at an earlier period?" it was seen that in earlier periods one or more of the events in the sequence had not been present. A search of cases reported in the literature also showed no negative cases, though it should be pointed out that in many of the reports crucial information which would either contradict or affirm the hypothesis is not given. A similar search of about 200 unpublished cases collected by Sutherland in the 1930's, before he had formulated the differential-association theory, likewise showed no negative cases.

The events present in the process cannot be considered in great detail here. However, brief comments about the sequence are in order.

1. Criteria of an objective nature in regard to the degree of "shareability" which specific types of problems have in our culture were not set up, but instead the subject's definition of the situation was used as a datum.[13] Consequently, a list which would exhaust all of the possible problems which could be considered as nonshareable and which might play a part in the etiology of trust violation is not conceivable. For pur-

poses of illustration, however, we may cite one type of problem which is frequently so defined.

This type of problem is that which the trusted person considers to have resulted from the violation of the obligations "ascribed" to his position of trust; that is, those obligations of a nonfinancial nature which are expected of persons in consequence of their incumbency in positions of financial trust. Just as persons in trusted positions have obligations not to violate the trust by taking funds, most of them also have obligations, for example, to maintain an enviable position in the community and to refrain from certain types of gambling and from what may be loosely described as riotous living.[14] When persons incur financial responsibilities as a result of violation of these ascribed obligations, they often consider that they must be kept secret, and meeting them becomes a nonshareable problem.

The concept of the nonshareable problem and consideration of the type of nonshareable problem just discussed help to make understandable the reported high incidence of "wine, women, and wagering" in the behavior of embezzlers and other trust violators, but these modes of behavior are not used as explanatory principles. In fact, it appears that the use of them as explanations of trust violation merely indicates lack of understanding of the problem.[15]

2. A nonshareable problem becomes a stimulus to violation of a position of trust only when the position is perceived as offering a private solution to this specific problem. In addition to having a financial problem which he feels he cannot share with persons who, from a more objective point of view, could help him, the trusted person must have a certain amount of knowledge or information about trust violation in general, and he must be able to apply that general information to his own specific situation. The presence of this event is often indicated by trust violators in their use of the language "it occurred to me" or "it dawned on me" that the entrusted funds could be used for such and such purpose. This "dawning" or "insight" or "perception" that the nonshareable problem can and may be solved by trust violation involves both knowledge of this fact and a "rationalization" of the behavior.

3. The verbalizations ("rationalizations") used by trust violators are reflections of contact with cultural ideologies which adjust for the person's contradictory ideas in regard to criminality on the one hand and in regard to integrity, honesty and morality on the other. Upon the appearance of a nonshareable problem the trusted person applies to his own situation a verbalization which the groups in which he has had membership have applied to others or which he himself has applied to the behavior of others. This is his motivation.[16] The hypothesized reactions of others to "borrowing" (criminal behavior) in order to solve a nonshareable problem, for example, are much different from the hypothesized re-

actions to "stealing" or "embezzling," and the trusted person behaves accordingly. It is because of an ability to hypothesize reactions which will not consistently and severely condemn his criminal behavior that the trusted person takes the role of what *we* have called the "trust violator." *He* often does not think of himself as playing that role, but instead thinks of himself as playing another role, such as that of a special kind of borrower or businessman.

The final hypothesis in its complete form made it possible to account for some of the features of trust violation and for some individual cases of that behavior which could not be accounted for by other hypotheses. However, the fact that it was revised several times probably means that future revision will be necessary if negative cases are found. The location by another investigator of persons who have violated positions of trust which were accepted in good faith, but in whose behavior the sequence was not present, will call for either a new revision of the hypothesis or a redefinition of the behavior included in the scope of the present hypothesis.

Notes

1. George H. Mead, "Scientific Method and the Individual Thinker," in John Dewey et al., *Creative Intelligence* (New York: Holt, 1917), pp. 176–227; A. D. Ritchie, *Scientific Method* (New York: Harcourt, Brace, 1923), pp. 53–83; Florian Znaniecki, "Social Research in Criminology," *Sociology and Social Research*, 12 (April, 1928), pp. 307–322; Florian Znaniecki, *The Method of Sociology* (New York: Farrar & Rinehart, 1934), pp. 232–233; Kurt Lewin, A *Dynamic Theory of Personality* (New York: McGraw-Hill, 1935), pp. 18–24; Alfred R. Lindesmith, *Opiate Addiction* (Bloomington, Ind.: Principia Press, 1947), pp. 12–14; Ralph H. Turner, "Statistical Logic in Social Research," *Sociology and Social Research*, 32 (January–February, 1948), pp. 697–704.

2. Only three sociologists have published detailed accounts of research on the subject: Elizabeth Redden, *Embezzlement: A Study of One Kind of Criminal Behavior, with Prediction Tables Based on Fidelity Insurance Records*, Ph.D. Dissertation, University of Chicago, 1939; Svend Riemer, "Embezzlement: Pathological Basis," *Journal of Criminal Law and Criminology*, 32 (November–December, 1941), pp. 411–423; and Stuart F. Lottier, "Tension Theory of Criminal Behavior," *American Sociological Review*, 7 (December, 1942), pp. 840–848.

3. See, for example, The United States Fidelity and Guaranty Company, *1001 Embezzlers* (Baltimore: Author, 1937), and *1001 Embezzlers Post War* (Baltimore: Author, 1950); J. Edgar Hoover, "National Bank Offenses," *Journal of Criminal Law and Criminology*, 24 (September–October, 1933), pp. 655–663; Virgil Peterson, "Why Honest People Steal," *ibid.*, 38 (July–August, 1947), pp. 94–103.

4. Harwood Koppel, "Other People's Money," *Collier's*, 67 (April 16, 1921), pp. 11–12; Hoover, *op. cit.*; Lottier, *op. cit.*

5. *Cf.*, George E. Bennett, *Fraud: Its Control through Accounts* (New York: Century, 1930), p. 22; Lester A. Pratt, *Bank Frauds, Their Detection and Prevention* (New York: Ronald Press, 1947), pp. 7–10.

6. Hall has pointed out that the economic system in our modern society presupposes business transactions based on a considerable amount of trust (Jerome Hall, *Theft, Law and Society* [Boston: Little, Brown, 1935]).

7. Kurt Lewin, "Some Social and Psychological Differences Between the United

States and Germany," *Character and Personality*, 4 (June, 1936), pp. 265–293. For a discussion of these two types of explanation in criminology, see Edwin H. Sutherland, *Principles of Criminology*, 4th ed. (Philadelphia: Lippincott, 1947), p. 5; and J. F. Brown and D. W. Orr, "The Field-Theoretical Approach to Criminology," *Journal of Criminal Psychopathology*, 3 (October, 1941), pp. 236–252.

8. "The fraudulent appropriation to his own use or benefit of property or money entrusted to him by another, on the part of a clerk, agent, trustee, public officer or other person acting in a fiduciary capacity" (*Black's Law Dictionary* [St. Paul, Minn., West, 1933], p. 633). Almost all studies pertinent to the current research have been studies of embezzlement. But since this term has been used to denote the behavior of all fidelity bond defaulters, the criminal behavior of all persons employed in banks, and the behavior of swindlers as well as embezzlers, it is obvious that the factual conclusions of the studies are not immediately comparable in all respects. The varied usage of the term is due to oversight on the part of some investigators, but it is also due in part to the existence of a variety of legal definitions among the states and foreign countries.

9. Determination of whether or not a particular prisoner's behavior met the criteria was made by examination of documents in his personal file and by preliminary or "screening" interviews. The document most heavily relied upon for this purpose was the "State's Attorney's Report" (the official statement of facts in each case), but other documents, such as reports of the Chicago Crime Commission, letters from former employers and from friends and relatives, and the prisoner's statement upon admission to the institution also were consulted. In the screening interviews the subjects were never asked the question, "Did you accept your position of trust in good faith?" but instead the interviewer waited for the subject to give the information spontaneously. Ordinarily, evidence of acceptance in good faith came out in the first interview in the form of statements such as the following: "I had no idea I was going to do this until the day it happened." Evidence of acceptance in bad faith was presented, for example, as follows: "My case isn't like embezzlement because I knew when I took their money that I was going to use it for myself."

10. Edwin H. Sutherland, *White Collar Crime* (New York: Dryden Press, 1949).

11. Riemer, *op. cit.*

12. Richard T. LaPiere and Paul R. Farnsworth, *Social Psychology* (New York: McGraw-Hill, 1949), p. 344.

13. Evidence of the presence of nonshareable problems was found in the language used by trust violators. None of them, of course, used the word "nonshareable problem," but many of them stated that they were "ashamed" to tell anyone of a certain situation or that they had "too much false pride" to get help from others.

14. Everett C. Hughes has pointed out that in addition to the specifically determining traits, a complex of "auxiliary traits" is expected of incumbents of certain statuses. "Dilemmas and Contradictions of Status" (*American Journal of Sociology*, 50 [March, 1945], pp. 353–359). In law, this type of obligation is called an "obediential obligation" since it is a consequence of a situation or a relationship, not of a contract (*Black's Law Dictionary, op. cit.*, p. 1274).

15. We do not mean to imply that statistical studies of personal and social traits as selective factors in trust violation have no place. A study, for example, showing a precise relationship between the presence of certain personal and social traits and the structuring of a financial problem as nonshareable would be extremely valuable. What we wish to imply is that such studies of selective factors, even if properly carried out, do not solve the problem of etiology. See, for example, Lindesmith, *op. cit.*, pp. 157–158.

16. See, for example, C. Wright Mills, "Situated Actions and Vocabularies of Motive," *American Sociological Review*, 5 (December, 1940), pp. 904–913.

15

OCCUPATIONAL STRUCTURE AND CRIMINAL BEHAVIOR: PRESCRIPTION VIOLATIONS BY RETAIL PHARMACISTS

Richard Quinney

An increasing number of sociologists have become interested in the study of occupations, noticeably neglecting at the same time the criminal behavior which occurs within occupations.[1] On the other hand, sociologists concerned with the study of white-collar crime have not made any systematic attempts to consider the social structure of occupations in their explanations of white-collar crime. The purpose of this study is to demonstrate that an analysis of the occupation should be considered in the attempt to explain violations of laws and regulations which control occupational activities and that such an approach makes it possible to learn more about both the structure of the occupation and the criminal behavior which occurs within the occupation. More specifically, the principal problem of the study is to offer an explanation for a type of criminal behavior which occurs in retail pharmacy in terms of an analysis of the occupation.

Reprinted from *Social Problems*, 11 (Fall, 1963), pp. 179–185.

RESEARCH PROCEDURE

For a study of occupational violation among pharmacists employed in retail establishments—retail pharmacists—it was first necessary to limit the violation to a type that might form a homogeneous unit of behavior and be subject to a common explanation.[2] While violations of the many state and federal statutes and administrative regulations pertaining to retail pharmacy are all regarded legally as misdemeanors and are subject to particular punishments, the behaviors involved are by no means homogeneous. In the attempt to delineate a specific type of behavior that could be explained by a single theory, the various laws and regulations were subjected to a content analysis in terms of basic occupational activity. The laws and regulations (and their accompanying violations) can be classified into three types: regulation of licensure, regulation of the drugstore, and regulation of prescriptions. Although any one type appeared to represent homogeneous behaviors, the most important type of violation in terms of both public welfare and frequency of occurrence is the violation of laws and regulations that control the compounding and dispensing of prescriptions. Prescription violation was therefore selected as the type of behavior for which an explanation would be sought and thus became the dependent variable of the study.

One of the primary aims of the research design was to provide a comparison of prescription violators and nonviolators. These two groups of retail pharmacists were drawn from the population of retail pharmacists within the city limits of Albany, New York. Through the cooperation of the New York State Board of Pharmacy, the names and addresses of the pharmacists, as well as their violation records over a five-year period, were secured. The twenty prescription violators who had been officially detected by state and federal investigators as violating a prescription law or regulation made up the group of prescription violators. The nonviolator group consisted of sixty pharmacists randomly selected from the remaining retail pharmacists who had been investigated but had never been found to violate a prescription law or regulation. The final study group, then, consisted of eighty retail pharmacists, twenty prescription violators and sixty nonviolators.

Data were collected through structured interviews with the retail pharmacists. The interview schedule, designed also for a broader range of problems, obtained information about the pharmacist's background, career in pharmacy, experiences in pharmacy, and attitudes about the occupation.[3] The respondents were not informed that their violation record was known to the researcher, and any idea that the study was partly concerned with violation could not have occurred until the last few minutes of the interview, after the major information had been secured. In addition to the formal interviews, throughout the study there were informal discussions with persons related in various ways to retail pharmacy, including members of the State Board of Pharmacy, instructors in pharmacy, pharmacy, students, physicians, and customers.

OCCUPATIONAL ROLES IN RETAIL PHARMACY

Most of the sociological studies of occupations have either assumed or demonstrated that occupations are characterized by patterned expectations internalized by the incumbents and reflected in their occupational behavior. On the three occasions that retail pharmacy has received sociological attention, it has been observed that the occupation incorporates two different roles, professional and business. Weinlein noted that the professional aspects of retail pharmacy are vitally influenced by the fact that most of the occupational activities take place in a business establishment, the drugstore.[4] In addition to filling prescriptions, he observed, the pharmacist is involved in many activities of a business nature. Likewise, Thorner described retail pharmacy as an occupation which has the characteristics of both a profession and a business.[5] McCormack defined retail pharmacy as a marginal occupation, because it contains the conflicting goals of a profession and a business.[6] These observations were given support in the present research when it was found that 94 per cent of the pharmacists replied in the affirmative to the question, "Do you find that the public expects the pharmacist to be *both* a business man and a professional man?"

From what was known about retail pharmacy, then, it appeared that various aspects of the social and cultural structure of the occupation would have implications for the study of prescription violation, particularly the status of retail pharmacy as both a profession and a business.[7] Thus, the research was guided by the general hypothesis that social strains in the form of divergent occupational role expectations are structured in the occupation of retail pharmacy and that prescription violation may result, depending upon the individual mode of adaptation. Such a conception that crime (or deviant behavior in general) is structured finds supports in Sutherland's idea of "differential social organization," which proposes that in a heterogeneous type of structure alternative and possibly inconsistent standards of conduct are held by the various segments.[8] A similar idea is found in the sociological tradition of functionalism.[9] Both approaches attempt to account for variations in rates of crime between or within social structures. The strategy taken in the present study was to account for variations in rates of criminal behavior within an occupation.

STRUCTURAL STRAIN AND ADAPTATION

To the retail pharmacist, the existence of two different occupational roles can present a personal dilemma in terms of appropriate occupational behavior. The retail pharmacist is faced with the task of performing his occupational activities with definitions that are not always clear, consistent, and compatible. Structural strain is built into retail pharmacy. The pharmacist must, therefore, make some sort of personal adjustment to the situation.[10]

It was hypothesized that retail pharmacists resolve the dilemma of choosing between different occupational roles—professional and business —by adapting to an *occupational role organization*. Occupational role organization refers to the relative orientation of the retail pharmacist to both the professional and business roles.[11]

The degree to which pharmacists were oriented to the business and professional roles was then measured. By asking the respondents to indicate how important they regard certain activities and goals in pharmacy, it was possible to determine the relative orientation of pharmacists to the two roles. The results suggest that pharmacists orient themselves in different ways to the available roles.[12] It was thus possible to construct a typology of occupational role organizations based on these differences in orientation. Some pharmacists are oriented more to the professional role than to the business role (professional pharmacists—16 per cent of the sample), while others are oriented more to the business role (business pharmacists—20 per cent). Other pharmacists are oriented to both roles (professional-business Pharmacists—45 per cent), while a few appear not to be oriented to either of the roles (indifferent pharmacists—19 per cent).[13] Therefore, since there are two possible occupational roles for the retail pharmacist rather than a single, well-defined role, there appears to be a patterned response in orientation to the two different roles. Retail pharmacists resolve the dilemma of choosing between different occupational roles (or, more generally, adjust to role strain) by adapting to an occupational role organization.[14]

PRESCRIPTION VIOLATION

The foregoing analysis provides a point of departure for an investigation of the possible behavioral consequences of structural strain. Prescription violation may be related to the types of occupational role organizations. More specifically, it was hypothesized that prescription violation occurs with greatest frequency among business pharmacists and least among professional pharmacists, with professional-business pharmacists and indifferent pharmacists being intermediate in the frequency of prescription violation.

The hypothesis was tested by cross-tabulating the prescription-violation records and the occupational role organizations of the retail pharmacists. As shown in Table 1, there is a significant association between prescription violation and occupational role organization in the direction predicted. Prescription violation occurred with greatest frequency among the business pharmacists—75 per cent of these pharmacists were violators—and occurred least among professional pharmacists. None of the professional pharmacists was a violator. The professional-business pharmacists and indifferent pharmacists were intermediate in violation: 14 per cent of the professional-business pharmacists and 20 per cent of the indifferent pharmacists were prescription violators. Therefore, in verification of the hypothesis, it was concluded that prescription violation varies according to the types of occupational role organizations in retail pharmacy.

Table 1. *Relationship between Prescription Violation and Occupational Role Organization*

Prescription violation	Occupational role organizations							
	Professional		Professional-Business		Indifferent		Business	
	N	%	N	%	N	%	N	%
Violators	0	0	5	14	3	20	12	75
Nonviolators	13	100	31	86	12	80	4	25
	13	100	36	100	15	100	16	100

$\chi^2 = 28.6$ df $= 3$ P $< .001$

The research findings suggest that pharmacists vary in the degree to which they are affected by the controls of the occupation. Location within the structure of the occupation determines the effectiveness of the controls on the individual pharmacist. Pharmacists with an occupational role organization that includes an orientation to the professional role are bound by a system of occupational controls which includes guides for the compounding and dispensing of prescriptions. Pharmacists who lack the professional orientation and are oriented to the business role are less bound by the occupational controls. They stress the merchandising aspects of pharmacy and are primarily interested in monetary gains. The formal controls (particularly legal controls) are made effective by the operation of informal controls (in terms of role expectations) which come mainly from within the occupation.[15]

The results, thus, indicate that prescription violation is related to the structure of the occupation and is an expression of that structure. Furthermore, from the standpoint of the individual pharmacist, prescription violation is related to orientation to the different roles in the occupation. From a social-psychological position, then, prescription violation is a matter of *differential orientation*. That is, for each pharmacist, orientation to a particular role more than to another provides a perspective in which violation may seem appropriate.[16] Prescription violation is thus explained in terms of the existence of structural strain in the occupation, because of the existence of divergent occupational roles, and in terms of differential orientation of the pharmacists to the roles in the form of adaptations to occupational role organizations.

CONCLUSION

A theory of prescription violation by retail pharmacists was formulated and verified in this study. There are two divergent occupational role expectations in retail pharmacy—professional and business. Pharmacists adjust to this situation of structural strain by orienting themselves in varying degree to the roles, by adopting an occupational role organization. The types of occupational role organizations in turn differ in the extent to which they generate tendencies toward prescription violation. The occupational role organizations which include the professional role orientation restrain the pharmacist from violating, while the occupational role organizations which do not include the professional role orientation do not exercise this restraint on the pharmacist. Therefore, prescription violation occurs with greatest frequency among business pharmacists and least among professional pharmacists, with professional-business pharmacists and indifferent pharmacists being intermediate in frequency of prescription violation. It was thus concluded that prescription violation is related to the structure of the occupation and the differential orientation of retail pharmacists.

In an attempt to explain a homogeneous unit of behavior, this study was limited to only prescription violation by retail pharmacists. It is possible, however, that the theory as developed has implications both for other types of violation in retail pharmacy and for violations which occur in other occupations.

Occupational role strain is a common phenomenon in modern society, due in part to the frequency and rapidity with which changes in occupational role definitions occur and new occupational roles appear.[17] Particularly, it seems evident that the occupational roles of business and profession are by no means unique to retail pharmacy. Numerous observations show that some businesses are in the process of becoming professions, some professions are taking on some of the characteristics of business, and other occupations (similar to retail pharmacy) have already firmly incorporated the business and professional roles. For example, such occupations as dentistry, optometry, chiropody, osteopathy, and even independent general medicine are similar to retail pharmacy in that they possess the characteristics of both a profession and a business. Such occupational careers as real estate agent, accountant, and electrician, while traditionally business-oriented, are now taking on some professional characteristics. Similarly, some of our traditionally professional careers—such as that of the psychologist—are taking on business characteristics as members become private consultants and counselors.

Also, by way of relating occupational role strain to occupational violation, many of these occupations are subject to laws and regulations similar to those of retail pharmacy. The violation of these laws and regulations is similar to prescription violation in that illegal behavior occurs in the course of serving the customer, as in the failure to retain a dental prescription by the dentist, alteration of a prescription for lenses by an optometrist, and the use of a secret method or procedure of treatment in the case of both osteopathy and medicine. It appears likely that the theoretical orientation employed in this study and the research findings of the study are applicable to other occupations and violations.

Finally, the study of prescription violation adds credence to the increasingly popular conception that deviant behavior is a reflection of social structure. A demonstration of this assumption has been accomplished by bringing together a study of the occupation and a study of criminal behavior in the occupation. If white-collar crime is illegal behavior in the course of occupational activity, then it is reasonable to assume that the occupation itself must become the object of study as well as the illegal behavior which occurs within the occupation. White-collar crime reflects the particular structure of the occupation and is a normal response to one's particular location within the occupation. Criminologists might consider the importance of understanding the occupation in the process of formulating theories of criminal behavior; and, on the other hand, sociologists who study occupations might give some attention to understanding the occupation by an investigation of the criminal behavior in the occupation. Both the structure of the occupation and criminal behavior within the occupation can be better understood if they are considered together.

Notes

1. Approaches to the sociological study of occupations are presented in Sigmund Nosow and William H. Form, eds., *Man, Work, and Society: A Reader in the Sociology of Occupations* (New York: Basic Books, 1962).

2. The importance of delineating homogeneous units of criminal behavior for the purpose of explanation is discussed, among other places, in Marshall B. Clinard, *Sociology of Deviant Behavior* (New York: Holt, 1963), pp. 204–216; Donald R. Cressey, "Criminological Research and the Definition of Crimes," *American Journal of Sociology*, 56 (May, 1951), pp. 546–551; and Alfred R. Lindesmith and H. Warren

Dunham, "Some Principles of Criminal Typology," *Social Forces*, 19 (March, 1951), pp. 307–314. For application of this approach see Marshall B. Clinard and Andrew L. Wade, "Toward the Delineation of Vandalism as a Subtype of Juvenile Delinquency," *Journal of Criminal Law, Criminology, and Police Science*, 48 (January–February, 1958), pp. 493–499; and Donald R. Cressey, *Other People's Money: The Social Psychology of Embezzlement* (New York: The Free Press, 1953). The suggestion that homogeneous units be delimited within white collar crime has been made in Vilhelm Aubert, "White Collar Crime and Social Structure," *American Journal of Sociology*, 58 (November, 1952), pp. 263–271; and Gilbert Geis, "Toward a Delineation of White-Collar Offenses," *Sociological Inquiry*, 32 (Spring, 1962), pp. 160–171.

3. For the larger study see the writers *Retail Pharmacy as a Marginal Occupation: A Study of Prescription Violation*, Ph.D. Dissertation, University of Wisconsin, 1962.

4. Anthony Weinlein, *Pharmacy as a Profession with Special Reference to the State of Wisconsin*, MA Thesis, University of Chicago, 1943.

5. Isador Thorner, "Pharmacy: The Functional Significance of an Institutional Pattern," *Social Forces*, 20 (March, 1942), pp. 321–328.

6. Thelma H. McCormack, "The Druggists' Dilemma: Problems of a Marginal Occupation," *American Journal of Sociology*, 61 (January, 1956), pp. 308–315.

7. Discussions of profession and business as two separate occupational institutions are found in Talcott Parsons, "The Professions and Social Structure" and "The Motivation of Economic Activities," in Talcott Parsons, *Essays in Sociological Theory* (New York: The Free Press, 1949), pp. 185–217; and Theodore Caplow, *The Sociology of Work* (Minneapolis: University of Minnesota Press, 1954), pp. 100–123. Accounts of the historical development of retail pharmacy which document the existence of both professional and business roles may be found in Richard A. Deno, Thomas D. Rowe, and Donald C. Brodie, *The Profession of Pharmacy* (Philadelphia: Lippincott, 1959); and Edward Kremers and George Urdang, *History of Pharmacy* (Philadelphia: Lippincott, 1951).

8. Sutherland discussed "differential social organization" or "differential group organization" in "Development of the Theory," in Albert K. Cohen, Alfred R. Lindesmith, and Karl F. Schuessler, eds., *The Sutherland Papers* (Bloomington, Ind.: Indiana University Press, 1956), pp. 13–29; and Edwin H. Sutherland and Donald R. Cressey, *Principles of Criminology*, 6th ed. (Philadelphia: Lippincott, 1960), pp. 79–80. This aspect of Sutherland's theory has been pointed out by Donald R. Cressey in "Epidemiology and Individual Conduct: A Case from Criminology," *Pacific Sociological Review*, 3 (Fall, 1960), pp. 38–58.

9. Robert K. Merton, "Social Structure and Anomie," *American Sociological Review*, 3 (October, 1938), pp. 672–682; and Talcott Parsons, *The Social System* (New York: The Free Press, 1951), pp. 249–325.

10. The idea of structural strain is found in Parsons, *The Social System*, ibid. The concept has been recently employed in Neil J. Smelser, *Theory of Collective Behavior* (New York: The Free Press, 1963). Discussions of adjustment to structure role strain (and role conflict) are found in Leonard S. Cottrell, Jr., "The Adjustment of the Individual to His Age and Sex Roles," *American Sociological Review*, 7 (October, 1942), pp. 617–630; J. W. Getzels and E. G. Guba, "Role, Role Conflict, and Effectiveness: An Empirical Study," *American Sociological Review*, 19 (February, 1954), pp. 164–175; William J. Goode, "A Theory of Role Strain," *American Sociological Review*, 25 (August, 1960), pp. 483–496; Neal Gross, Ward S. Mason, and Alexander W. McEachern, *Explorations in Role Analysis* (New York: Wiley, 1958), chaps. 16–17; Samuel A. Stouffer, "An Analysis of Conflicting Social Norms," *American Sociological Review*, 14 (December, 1949), pp. 707–717; Jackson Toby, "Some Variables in Role Conflict," *Social Forces*, 30 (March, 1952), pp. 323–327; Walter I. Wardwell, "The Reduction of Strain in a Marginal Social Role," *American Journal of Sociology*, 61 (July, 1955), pp. 16–25; and Donald M. Wolfe and J. Diedrick Snoek, "A Study of Tensions and Adjustment under Role Conflict," *Journal of Social Issues*, 18 (July, 1962), pp. 102–121.

11. See Ronald G. Corwin, "The Professional Employee: A Study of Conflict in Nursing Roles," *American Journal of Sociology*, 66 (May, 1961), pp. 605–615.

12. After pertinent materials in the sociology of occupations and retail pharmacy were studied, several items were selected through their construct validity to measure professional and business role orientation.

13. It should be noted that this distribution is skewed slightly in the direction of business pharmacists. The reasons for this are that the number of prescription violators in the study sample overrepresents the proportion of violators in the population of retail pharmacists; and, as it will be shown, the group of prescription violators contains a disproportionate number of business pharmacists. Thus, an entirely random sample of retail pharmacists would contain a few more professionally oriented pharmacists.

14. An occupational role organization may be regarded as the integration of the individual's total occupational role system. See Goode, *op. cit.*, pp. 485–487. Each type of occupational role organization represents a particular method for "ego's manipulation of his role structure" in an attempt to reduce role strain.

15. This interpretation finds support in Howard S. Becker and James W. Carper, "The Elements of Identification with an Occupation," *American Sociological Review*, 21 (June, 1956), pp. 341–348; Caplow, *op. cit.*, pp. 113–121; Edward Gross, *Work and Society* (New York: Crowell, 1958), pp. 134–139; Oswald Hall, "The Informal Organization of the Medical Profession," *Canadian Journal of Economic and Political Science*, 12 (February, 1946), pp. 30–44; Louis Kriesberg, "Occupational Controls among Steel Distributors," *American Journal of Sociology*, 61 (November, 1955), pp. 203–212; and Tamotsu Shibutani, *Society and Personality* (Englewood Cliffs, N.J.: Prentice-Hall, 1961), esp. pp. 60, 91–94, 276–278.

16. This is essentially the same as Glaser's concept of "differential identification" (Daniel Glaser, "Criminality Theories and Behavioral Images," *American Journal of Sociology*, 61 [March, 1956], pp. 433–445).

17. See Walter I. Wardwell, "A Marginal Professional Role: The Chiropractor," *Social Forces*, 30 (March, 1952), pp. 339–348.

16

AMBULANCE CHASING: A CASE STUDY OF DEVIATION AND CONTROL WITHIN THE LEGAL PROFESSION

Kenneth J. Reichstein

Today, a large proportion of the lawsuits filed in courts throughout the country are personal injury suits. They are the result of the high rates of costly accidents to persons and property that are a significant by-product of mass methods of production and transportation common to a modern industrial society. These suits are a form of institutionalized conflict to determine both the responsibility for and the amount of damages.

The plaintiff's side of the conflict consists of the injured claimant and his lawyer. Their relationship is based upon a contingent-fee arrangement, closely tying the lawyer's interest to the client's. This arrangement differs from that common to other areas of law, where the fee is roughly proportional to the amount of time and energy expended on the case. Since the latter method is prohibitive for most personal injury victims, who have limited financial resources, the contingent fee is a means for surmounting this economic barrier. The fee is contingent upon the amount of damages the lawyer can obtain for his client (customarily one-third), either through an out-of-court settlement or an in-court award. Thus, it contains an element of risk for the lawyer, because he can lose the case and receive

Reprinted from *Social Problems*, 13 (Summer, 1965), pp. 6–17.

nothing for his efforts. Moreover, the lawyer may have to wait several years before the case is decided to get his share, during which time he may have to advance his client legal, medical, and living expenses. In spite of these drawbacks, personal injury cases are very much sought after by lawyers since the amounts involved are considerable.

The lawyers who take personal injury cases from the plaintiff's side (and most get to handle them only from this side) are generally small-firm lawyers and solo practitioners. The elite of this group are skilled trial lawyers who have accumulated considerable knowledge of anatomy and physiology necessary for their work. They belong to an organization known as the National Association of Claimants' Compensation Attorneys (NACCA) which conducts training programs for its members and generally acts to further their interests. Nevertheless, the reputation of the personal injury (plaintiffs) segment of the profession is one of the poorest, since it is based upon impressions of "ambulance chasing" and other illicit practices which purportedly stem from the use of the contingent fee.

On the defense side of the conflict, there are insurance companies, self-insured railroads, and their counsel. Although the defendant on record in the case is an individual or corporation charged with negligence, the actual defense is most frequently an insurance company which will have to pay any damages awarded. Because they are the ones that are financially accountable, insurance companies maintain claims departments to protect their interests and include clauses in their form contracts with clients, giving the company control of the legal defense. This prerogative enables them to channel their cases to law firms specializing in personal injury defense work. These firms are generally larger in size than firms on the plaintiff's side.

During the process itself, the plaintiff's side strives to get as large an award as possible, within the limits set by the extent of the accident, while the insurance company tries either to disclaim liability or to hold down the amount of liability. In the early stages, insurance claims adjustors and plaintiff's attorneys negotiate informally to settle the case out of court. But at the same time, each side obtains evidence to build a legal argument in the event the case has to go to trial. The parties investigate the scene of the accident, take depositions from witnesses, and analyze medical reports of examinations of the injured. Considerable effort goes into the preparation and conduct of a personal injury trial, yet parties may decide to settle at any point in the process.

THE STRUCTURE, FUNCTIONS, AND DYSFUNCTIONS OF AMBULANCE CHASING

Within this background description of personal injury practice, "ambulance chasing" refers to the activity of plaintiffs' lawyers who earnestly seek after or solicit the legal business of injured parties apparently qualified to claim compensation for their injuries. The object of the solicitation process is to sign the injured party to a contingent-fee contract that will entitle the lawyer to a fixed percentage of any amount paid to the injured party in return for legal representation. For several decades, it has been a recurrent form of professionally unethical conduct throughout the country, despite numerous attempts on the part of bar associations and grand juries to stamp it out.[1] To be sure, other types of legal business are also solicited, yet personal injury solicitation is considered to be very widespread, perhaps because the contingent-fee arrangement converts these cases into highly valued commodities. Thus, one court declared that almost all serious personal injury cases are chased and that estimates of the number in which a "chaser" contacts the injured party run as high as 95 percent.[2]

The above definition of ambulance chasing notwithstanding, the phrase is an ambiguous term, because there is no one set pattern of personal injury solicitation. First, the subject doing the "chasing" is not clearly defined. The actual chaser, or runner, is frequently a layman rather than a lawyer. Lawyers in rural areas may resort to patrolling highways and country roads looking for accident victims, but such activity is not likely to be performed by urban lawyers who are generally officed in the downtown business section of a city where the courts are located. Then again, the size and complexity of the soliciting organization range from the lone lawyer-chaser, to the attorney or law firm that keeps an investigator-chaser on its payroll, to the independent chaser-entrepreneur maintaining a substantial communications network with persons having contact with accident victims who feed tips to the chaser. Another highly organized solicitation system is the one set up by railroad unions. The union appoints as regional counsel lawyers who agree to pay the expenses of the union's legal aid department in return for receiving the cases of railroad workers injured in their area. These cases are solicited by union members designated by the union. In addition, the lawyer's payment to a layman for forwarding a case will vary from a ten dollar bill or a few bottles of liquor given as a gratuity to a policeman or a doctor, to $100 a case or a share of the lawyer's fee demanded by a professional chaser peddling contingent-fee contracts already signed by an accident victim. Finally, soliciting lawyers may engage in another illicit practice in order to get personal injury clients: They may agree to pay an injured party's medical and legal expenses to induce the prospective client to retain them.

The conduct mentioned above, all subsumed under the term "ambulance chasing," is formally prohibited either by the Canons of Ethics of the legal profession or by statutory or common law. The governing rules fall into two overlapping categories: rules against advertising and solicitation, and rules against stirring up litigation. Rules against advertising and solicitation are core professional norms which serve to differentiate the professions, with their claim to higher ethical standards, from the business world. By adopting these norms, the professions try to deemphasize monetary success valued by the business world and to incorporate what they consider higher values, such as service, competency, and integrity.[3] Thus, Canon 27 of the Chicago Bar Association explicitly states: "The most worthy and effective advertisement possible . . . is the establishment of a well-merited reputation for professional capacity and fidelity to trust." Since advertising and solicitation imply that the layman has the capacity to evaluate skills which took professionals years to learn, prohibiting them enables the professions to control their fields on the grounds that they alone are capable of judging professional performance.[4] Finally, this prohibition limits aggressive competition and thereby prevents other transgressions, such as fraud and misrepresentation which grow out of advertising.

Rules against stirring up litigation that have been incorporated into the lawyers' Canons of Professional Ethics stem from an earlier period in English history.[5] They are directed against the solicitation and support of parties having claims to litigate. Although these norms still have significance, they had greater utility during the Middle Ages when they were used to combat rampant perversion of the machinery of justice. These rules were based upon the realization that the court is a battleground wherein parties can inflict heavy losses upon one another. Therefore, many believed that the courts should not be used as a means for unscrupulous parties to press unjustifiable suits in order to plunder the innocent.

But ambulance chasing, like other social acts, is even more normatively complex. Social acts subsumed under one norm have to be differentiated from other acts in their class if they are to be fully understood. Thus, for example, both the lawyer who advertises his specialty in tax law by hanging out a neon sign and the attorney who has his divorce cases written up in the newspapers to publicize his specialty when his clients would prefer to keep their sordid personal affairs private, are guilty of advertising. Yet the divorce lawyer also violates his fiduciary (trust) obligation to his client. Ambulance chasing, however, contains other structural components having functional consequences which contribute to its interpretation.

Some of the ends accomplished by ambulance chasing are socially desirable for the injured claimant. It is functional insofar as chasers can prevent insurance companies from taking advantage of injured claimants. Thus, some insurance claims adjustors try to conclude settlements with claimants who are without legal representation, getting them to sign releases in which the injured relinquishes his claim to damages in return for the sum offered to him by the insurance company. By getting to the injured party before the claims agent and providing legal representation, the chaser enables the injured party to get more for his case than he would if he dealt directly with the insurance company. While some injured parties may be able to get these releases they have signed overturned in court, many of them, ignorant of their legal rights, continue to abide by their agreement with the insurance company even if dissatisfied.

Individuals have another disadvantage in dealing with large insurance companies. Given the lengthy delay before suits can be brought to trial, the insurance companies have considerable bargaining power at the beginning of a suit. They can press for a low settlement since they are under no compulsion to negotiate. (Generally, the amount of compensation insurance companies are willing to pay increases as the date of trial approaches.) Moreover, the corresponding position of the injured claimant is poor because his earning power may be gone or suspended at a time when his medical and living expenses are piling up. Hence, lack of funds may force him to settle for a lesser amount. Under these circumstances, a lawyer who proffers financial support to his client enables the client to hold out for a larger amount.

This function of personal injury solicitation conforms to the legal profession's goal to provide adequate legal services for persons in need of them—a frequently espoused value of the legal community as well as one of its felt problems. . . . Indeed, the functionality of ambulance chasing depends upon the goal not being achieved. As long as the legitimate provision of adequate legal services is recognized as a problem, the positive quality attributed to ambulance chasing is likely to remain.

THE BAR'S OPINION OF PERSONAL INJURY SOLICITATION

Data for the study came from two principal sources—from written opinions of Illinois Appellate Courts and from interviews with a stratified sample of Chicago lawyers. Out of 116 lawyers sampled, 87 per cent (101 subjects) were actually interviewed. Lawyers in different size firms were asked to give their opinion of personal injury solicitation. The question was part of a larger schedule concerned with legal ethics. The open-ended responses to this question were then classified by the researcher as being favorable or unfavorable. Since beliefs were ambivalent in some cases, classification was based on whichever beliefs appeared to prevail.

Among the sample, seventy-one lawyers had unfavorable opinions of solicitation, twenty-eight lawyers had favorable opinions, and two had no opinion. . . . Lawyers' opinions were related to their status in the profession. High-status lawyers disapproved of the practice more often than low-status lawyers. . . . Thus, lawyers with unfavorable opinions were more likely to belong to large firms, to practice corporate law or specialties related to corporate law exclusively, and to have a well-established clientele among business firms and upper-class persons. Lawyers with favorable opinions were more likely to belong to small law firms or to practice by themselves, to have at least some of their practice in nonbusiness areas of litigation, and to have a less-established clientele composed of lower-class individuals. Disapproval of personal injury solicitation was also positively related to a lesser degree to membership and participation in the Chicago Bar Association, the professional organization responsible for enforcing professional norms among Chicago lawyers. Generally, the closer the lawyer was to the plaintiff's side of personal injury practice where ambulance chasing occurs, the greater the likelihood of his being favorably disposed toward solicitation.

The majority of the sample . . . were opposed to personal injury solicitation. But it should be noted that among the lawyers in the sample specializing in personal injury plaintiff's work (which is only one segment of many), four-fifths (twelve lawyers) had favorable opinions of personal injury solicitation. Moreover, four-fifths of these specialists reported giving some sort of inducement to obtain personal injury cases.

Lawyers who had unfavorable opinions attributed different qualities to the practice of personal injury solicitation than did lawyers with favorable images. Lawyers with unfavorable images had one or more of the following three criticisms:[6]

First, disapproving lawyers, especially those from small, general practice firms, looked upon personal injury solicitation as unfair competition. The solicitation process was known to encompass a network of relationships organized around laymen who had actually procured the cases and who relied upon short-wave radios equipped to receive police accident reports or upon information received from hospital personnel, policemen, firemen, auto wreckers and repairmen, and undertakers having contact with the injured or their relatives at some point in time. Lawyers who had purchased cases from these illicit sources of supply were considered by these respondents to have an illegitimate monopoly over the personal injury field.[7] The following remarks were typical of those who felt they were excluded from obtaining these cases:

> We do very little personal injury because we don't have chasers. Personal injury is awful. You can't get a good case unless you buy it. The most controlled phase of law work is personal injury plaintiff's work. There is a tie-in between the [lay] chasers, the doctors, the undertakers, everybody. It's a system you can't break. Either they ought to make it ethical or they ought to police the field. I could get chasers if I wanted to. These cases don't fall into natural channels.

> If you've got volume and you're not a trial lawyer, you must have chased it. You just don't get to know so many Negroes and Puerto Ricans. I don't have much personal injury because I don't chase it. It's organized. They're taking business away from me.

Second, personal injury solicitation was denounced because lawyers associated it with the more serious transgressions of fraud and client-exploitation. For example, some lawyers thought that many chased claims were of dubious validity and that soliciting lawyers used perjured testimony:

> There is undue clogging of the courts with unnecessary litigation. A lot are false claims. It brings disrepute for the lawyer in the eyes of clients.
>
> They are bent on winning cases and they have no hesitancy to use allegations to fit the facts.

Other lawyers associated solicitation with "package dealing," an illicit practice allegedly performed by broker lawyers who make lump settlements by negotiating two or more claims together. This practice is suggested in the following response:

> The lawyer who gets volume personal injury necessarily can't do a good job for a client. The minimum going rate is $100 per contract and maybe only one out of five is profitable. He has to try for a fast turnover in order to make a profit.

And a few subjects considered the tax implications of solicitation which in their opinion made client-exploitation inescapable:

> The tax laws make client cheating definite. That's why I wouldn't fool with chasers. You can't deduct the money you pay to a chaser off of your income tax [as a business expense]. So you have to make it up somewhere. This means you have to cheat your client.

Finally, lawyers, especially high-status lawyers, were very much concerned about the public's image of the profession, even though they themselves had little or no contact with the personal injury plaintiff's segment. Lawyers in this high-status category were also most vociferous in their recommendation that solicitors receive strong punishment. As two lawyers commented:

> There's not as much enforcement of regulations against ambulance chasing. It puts the legal profession in disrepute. It's a seamy type of law and it's what the general public sees too often.
>
> There are 5 per cent who give a stinking aroma to the bar who ought to be disbarred. The Chicago Bar Association has enough evidence on these ambulance chasers and it hasn't done anything about it.

In contrast, lawyers categorized as having a favorable opinion of solicitation took a permissive attitude toward the practice. While few of these respondents could be said to have strongly approved of solicitation, they did show understanding of two other conditions structuring deviation; i.e., the needs of lower-status lawyers who could not get legal business and the needs of injured laymen who lacked knowledge of their legal rights. . . .

Some lawyers offered their own commonsense interpretation of Merton's Theory of Anomie[8] as their justification of solicitation. Blocked from getting corporate business and lacking the security of an assured salary, the lower-status lawyer had to pick up what legal business he could. This statement exemplifies this type of economic rationale:

> There's nothing reprehensible about personal injury solicitation if a young lawyer has no other way to get enough cases. The people with wills and corporations just won't do business with you.

Contrasted with the opinion that chasers exploited clients, other lawyers with favorable opinions thought that clients would receive good representation from a soliciting lawyer. These lawyers regarded solicitation as functional insofar as it served to counterbalance the abuses of insurance company adjustors who were out to settle claims for small amounts. The following statements reflect this view of the situation. . . .

> A lawyer demeans himself by chasing. However, people would not do anything about their case otherwise. Ignorant people have no knowledge of their claim. They might get small compensation for their injury from an adjustor. Chasers are better because a person is represented. There was a cleaning woman, an Italian immigrant in our building, who fell and injured herself. She told me about it, but by that time it was too late.

> Insurance adjustors created the bad situation. They are worse than the chaser. Chasing after [claims] releases is worse than chasing after cases. At least the chaser has the client's interest in mind.

THE PROCESS OF ENFORCING ETHICAL NORMS

Lawyers who commit major ethical offenses (including such transgressions as fraud and cheating clients, as well as personal injury solicitation) may be subjected to a rather elaborate enforcement process involving both the Illinois Supreme Court and the local bar associations. The court has given the bar associations the task of initiating action against deviant lawyers in their area. In the usual procedure, the Committee on Inquiry of a bar association investigates suspected lawyers. If the committee decides that there are grounds for action, it will prosecute the lawyer before the bar association's Committee on Grievances. As commissioners of the state supreme court, the grievance committee has the authority to hold closed trial proceedings where witnesses can be subpoenaed. In Chicago, the findings of the grievance committee are reviewed, and recommendations for discipline are made by the Board of Managers of the Chicago Bar Association. Where discipline is recommended, the case is docketed before the Illinois Supreme Court. The Bar Association counsel acts as *amicus curiae* (i.e., a friend of the court) in supporting the bar association's recommendations before the court. The lawyer responding to the charges against him is represented by counsel throughout all of the proceedings.

Although the lawyer community can be seen to play a significant role in the disciplinary process, there are definite limits to its influence. Despite the fact that these professional offenses are the proper concern of the lawyer community, its agency—the bar association—does not have the final authority to keep its own house in order. Nor are the courts likely to rubber-stamp the bar association's recommendations, given the way the proceedings are arranged. Unlike other appellate proceedings, the court is under no obligation to limit itself to decisions of law and not of fact. Therefore, it can come to its own decision concerning the "guilt" or "innocence" of the lawyer respondent, irrespective of the bar association's findings. Furthermore, the usual role of an *amicus curiae* has been modified. Where an *amicus curiae* has generally acted in an advisory third-party capacity, the *amicus curiae* in this situation is one of the two parties at bar. Thus, the *amicus curiae* may lose his favored advisory status and instead be put in the role of adversary *vis-à-vis* counsel for the opposite side.

In eight cases of personal injury between 1931 and 1956, the decisions handed down by the Illinois Supreme Court stand in sharp contrast to the recommendations of the bar associations and the majority opinion of the lawyer community. Where the bar associations had recommended disbarment or suspension from practice, the court's judgments were considerably more lenient. In seven out of the eight cases where the lawyer had only solicited, the court chose to issue only a verbal censure or to discharge the case entirely. The court's holding in the fifth case, *In re Veach*, established a precedent for permissive action. In this case, the court held that while solicitation of law business was highly reprehensible and improper, it was not an offense which imported venality, fraudulent practices, or moral turpitude. The effect of these decisions has been to inhibit the bar associations from taking action against other ambulance chasers. Since the cost of prosecution is great, bar associations have been reluctant to institute proceedings where there is little likelihood of success.[9]

The decisions demonstrate the validity of the proposition that the courts will restrain professional organizations in order to safeguard the liberties of individual professionals. Thus, in two of the cases where the court discharged the lawyer, *In re McCallum* and *In re Heirich*, the justices took note of the fact that the Chicago Bar Association had not come into court "clean-handed" in its use of fraudulent methods to obtain evidence against the respondents. Here, the court's decisions were predicated upon the belief that the lawyers were actually being prosecuted by the railroads and powerful railroad defense attorneys, who had used fraudulent means to obtain evidence against them. The court interpreted these proceedings as attempts on the part of the self-insured railroads to eliminate aggressive plaintiff's lawyers who were costing the railroads thousands of dollars annually in court awards. However, an official of the Chicago Bar Association made the following evaluation of the Court's handling of *In re Heirich* during an interview with the researcher:

> In the *Heirich* case, we had the evidence on him. Regardless of how we got it, the court should not have rebuked us. After all, we are the commissioners of the court. They made it into an adversary proceeding. It was the truth regardless of how we got it.

These findings also lend support to the explanation that the power of bar associations is limited because of the way disciplinary proceedings are structured. But the likelihood of bar associations' being overruled by the court is still a function of the substantive issue in question. Thus, the court has gone along with a majority of recommendations made by the bar associations for other types of attorney offenders, particularly in those cases where lawyers were found to have deliberately taken advantage of clients.

But as long as personal injury lawyers did not overreach their clients, the court took a tolerant attitude toward solicitation. The following excerpt from an opinion by Justice Bristow demonstrates that the court looked upon the personal injury situation as a game between solicitors and insurers. The opinion[10] denied a rehearing to the East St. Louis Bar Association after a successful soliciting lawyer from that area had been let off by the court with only a censure.

> Today, insurance companies, railroads, airlines, and other industries in whose operation some people are certain to be maimed or killed have highly organized mechanisms of defense. Claims agents, many of whom are not lawyers, do their simple duty when they try by fair means to obtain the lowest possible settlement for injured plaintiffs. Instances in which claims agents resort to unfair means range from cases in which the agent exerts excessive zeal to cases of shocking fraud. Even the most scrupulous claims agent cannot fairly represent both claimant and defendant. In any event, claims agents cannot hope to achieve advancement by effecting liberal settlements with claimants.
>
> On the other side, we find some overzealous "chasers," equipped with newspaper clippings, photostats of large settlement checks and other documentary evidence indicating that the lawyer they are representing is a "superman" never satisfied with anything short of six figures. It is a veritable scramble between the claims agent and the "chaser" to see which one can reach an injured claimant first. The net result of a timely arrival of the solicitor is that the claimant will eventually receive an

amount that a court and jury deem adequate and just. This presupposes that the case is placed in the hands of a lawyer of proven ability and unquestioned fidelity. The uncontradicted proof in this record demonstrates that respondent was such a person. Apart from the good, the only tangible harm that evolved from the solicitation in the instant case is that suffered by the St. Louis barrister who had a portion of his business sidetracked. I am not overlooking the impact of this ugly practice on our fine profession. Nevertheless, solicitation of personal injury cases is the natural reflex or defensive response to the unfair methods of claims adjustors, just as naturally as the human organism elaborates its own antibodies to combat disease. . . .

CONCLUSION

The present state of personal injury practice still remains an uneasy conflict between insurance companies and plaintiffs' attorneys. Periodic campaigns are launched to rid the profession of ambulance chasers, but the pattern persists. Some proposals have been put forward for changing the structure of personal injury practice in order to eliminate the problem; however, few changes have been adopted. One suggestion would eliminate the condition necessary for solicitation, the contingent-fee arrangement, and require personal injury victims who cannot afford legal representation to seek the services of legal aid. This solution is deficient because legal aid groups may not have the resources needed to match those of powerful insurance companies. Not only is legal representation obtained through charity unlikely to be of a very high caliber, but also it is likely to appear distasteful to many middle-class persons who also would not be able to afford the cost of an expensive court suit. Furthermore, if speedily instituted, this plan would deprive plaintiff's lawyers of their livelihood.

Another proposed solution is to erect a system for adjudicating personal injury suits similar to the workmen's compensation system, found in most states, which handles industrial accidents. Under this system, liability is assumed by the insured corporate defendants for most accidents in return for a low rate of compensation that is fixed by the state. However, this system would give the insurance companies just what they want, which is precisely why it is opposed by plaintiffs' lawyers. Insurance companies usually operate according to such a principle even though it is not institutionalized. Thus, they are frequently willing to settle most small claims irrespective of the validity of the claim and to concentrate their efforts upon contesting the big suits. But the adequacy of compensation would remain a bone of contention in a system where the rates are fixed.

Perhaps a better approach to the problem would be to prohibit insurance adjustors from making settlements until the claimants had received legal advice. A state bureau could be set up to serve as a clearinghouse for settlements to ensure injured parties a specified minimum amount of legal advice before negotiations toward settlement had begun. This bureau might also supervise lawyers' accounting of funds to their clients to prevent any client-exploitation by personal injury plaintiffs' lawyers. Once this system has been put into effect, assuring injured parties of legal assistance and regulating the activities of insurance companies, it would then be possible to enforce wholeheartedly rules against solicitation and to give them the deterrent quality they presently lack.

Notes

1. Jerome E. Carlin, *Lawyers on Their Own* (New Brunswick, N.J.: Rutgers University Press, 1962), pp. 181–182.

2. *Morris* v. *Pennsylvania R. Co.*, 10 Ill.App.2d 24, 134 N.E.2d 21 (1956).

3. See E. T. Hiller, *Social Relations and Structures* (New York: Harper & Row, 1947); Edward Gross, *Work and Society* (New York: Crowell, 1958); Ernest Greenwood, "Attributes of a Profession," in Sigmund Nosow and William H. Form, eds., *Man, Work, and Society* (New York: Basic Books, 1962), pp. 112–118.

4. Dietrich Rueschemeyer, "Doctors and Lawyers: A Comment on the Theory of the Professions," *Canadian Review of Sociology and Anthropology*, 1 (February, 1964), pp. 17–30; Greenwood, *op. cit.*

5. Barratry, or stirring up litigation, was a crime under the common law. Its counterpart is Canon 28, which is explicitly entitled *Stirring up Litigation*. The common-law offense known as "maintenance" referred to aiding the prosecution or defense of a suit by one who does not have an interest in the thing in controversy. Its counterpart is Canon 42, which stipulates that a lawyer may advance expenses to a client, subject to reimbursement, but he may not agree to pay the cost of litigation. "Champerty" was the common-law crime whereby someone who had no prior interest purchased a share of a thing in dispute, with the object of maintaining and taking part in the litigation. It was a form of maintenance. The counterpart of champerty in legal ethics is Canon 10, which forbids a lawyer to purchase an interest in the subject matter of the litigation in which he is conducting. This canon is in apparent conflict with Canon 13, allowing contracts for contingent fees.

By and large, the common-law offenses have not been incorporated into statutory law.

6. All three of these criticisms can also be found in a large number of articles in the literature of the legal profession condemning personal injury solicitation (ED. NOTE: A considerable sampling of this literature is given in the original article).

7. Carlin, *op. cit.*, pp. 85–90.

8. Robert K. Merton, *Social Theory and Social Structure* (New York: The Free Press, 1957), pp. 139–149.

9. Statement made by a bar association official during a personal interview.

10. *In re Cohn*, 10 Ill.2d, 186, 194, 139 N.E.2d 301, 303 (1957).

IV

WHITE-COLLAR EXPLOITATION AND ITS VICTIMS

The growing concentration in the United States upon protection of consumers from exploitative and fraudulent commercial practices represents the convergence of numerous social and political developments during the past decade. Attention to problems of poverty has led to the belief that low income is a function not only of truncated opportunities but also of deeply entrenched mechanisms which compound original barriers against achievement of a decent standard of living. Poor persons do not, for instance, have access to adequate consumer information, the wherewithal or the time to comparison-shop, or the resources to take advantage of bulk-buying or more attractive credit opportunities. Penned into their own neighborhoods, they are often at the mercy of local dealers, who charge prices and engage in schemes that are patently exploitative.

The slow but inexorable adjustment of American society to the imperatives of its stated commitment to racial equality has also brought about increased awareness of the problems of minority-group members in the commercial world. The investigation of the McCone committee following the 1965 riots in Watts, a Negro neighborhood of Los Angeles, reported the sale of spoiled meat and produce and old bread, as fresh items, the high interest rates on furniture and clothing purchases, and the merchandising of shoddy materials at exorbitant prices. The committee noted complaints in Watts about exploitation by insurance companies and institutional lenders, and it suggested that the rampant destruction of business property during the riots may have been brought about in part as a retaliation against perceived injustices.

It is conditions such as these that are summarized by David Caplovitz, an associate professor of sociology at Columbia University, in the first article in this part, a reading which draws upon the author's monograph, *The Poor Pay More* (New York: The Free Press, 1963). Caplovitz' article is especially noteworthy for its attempt to view the relationship between the ghetto merchant and his customer from the perspective of both parties, rather than as a one-sided, shameless exploitative system. He points out that ghetto merchants must pay high insurance rates and that they have comparatively small turnover of items compared to the large downtown stores. A cycle of self-defeating commercial frustration is clearly indicated. Faced with better-than-usual possibilities of payment default, the merchant demands extremely high interest rates. These rates in turn lead to consumer distrust and distress and, inevitably, to higher-than-usual payment defaults. Equally interesting is Caplovitz' delineation of the role of the door-to-door peddler in establishing the comforting atmosphere of rural commodity exchange by bridging the gap between the uneasy minority-group member and the remote, anonymous, and threatening world of urban commerce.

It would be interesting, as a corollary to Caplovitz' study, to attempt to determine the impact of practices such as "bait advertising" upon the individuals engaged in it. How do such persons regard themselves and what do they think of the persons they so deliberately deceive? It is possible that they merely regard their victims as dupes, disingenuous persons available for the more clever and more wily to prey upon. Perhaps they add to this view the cynical belief that were they not doing this job, there would be many others quite ready to undertake it. Many Americans by now are familiar with the technique often employed by salesmen for some encyclopedia firms: the attempt to convince prospects that it is their endorsement of the product that is most desired so that the company can enhance its reputation in their neighborhood. It is suggested in this carefully rehearsed sales approach that in return for the endorsement (which actually is meaningless) the customer will be given a considerable bargain. Presumably persons watching others succumb to such appeals to their vanity and cupidity develop a considerable scorn for humanity in general, a kind of scorn said to be characteristic of confidence men who come to believe that all "marks" (victims) themselves have "larceny in their heart," and that confidence games are merely instances of smarter culprits taking advantage of less adept ones. Stage actors, in fact, are also said to develop on occasion a similar condescending distaste for members of their audience; as Rebecca West has remarked, "There is a mockery inherent in the art of acting, the players must make everybody weep but themselves; if they don't weep they must jeer inside themselves at the people who do weep!" The Caplovitz work, among others, suggests the importance of studies detailing the genesis, the career pattern, and the personal consequences for the depredator of systematic deception.

Caplovitz' preference is clearly for controls other than appeals to ethics and compassion in order to reduce exploitation of low-income families. During recent years, in accord with this view, the executive and legislative branches of the federal government have concentrated growing attention upon education of the consumer and upon increased sanctions against merchants taking undue advantage of purchasers. The two readings following Caplovitz' contribution are part of the federal effort to bring about changes in practices, such as packaging and lending, on the grounds that consumers should not go unaided in attempting to unravel the intricate web of sums, sizes, amounts, and rates—which are often established in the deliberate attempt to create confusion and self-defeating miscalculations.

The inability of the consumer to cope adequately with current merchandising stratagems was clearly illustrated in a 1965 study at Eastern Michigan University, in which thirty-three college-educated wives were given a list of twenty common items to buy at a supermarket. They were asked simply to purchase the most economical package of each of the products; that is, to get the largest quantity for the lowest price.

Of the 660 buying decisions the women made, 43 per cent were wrong. On the average, the women spent eleven cents more out of each shopping dollar than they needed to. If this extra expenditure were extended over the course of a year, it would mean that the shopping budgets of the women would be increased by almost 10 per cent.

Activities in the automobile industry, discussed in the reading from the 1966 report of the President's Committee on Consumer Interests, have persistently caught the eye of social critics in the United States. Automobiles are intricately interwoven into the fabric of American existence, and the automobile industry has been marked by inordinate competition, built-in obsolescence, and a notable disregard for safety factors when these conflict with pricing and sales considerations. Used-car salesmen in the United States are often regarded as the epitome of unscrupulous dealers, and it is part of our national folklore that set-back odometers, sawdust-packed brakes, and similar ruses and lies ("This car had just one owner, an old lady who only drove it around the corner to church and back each Sunday") are commonplace in the used-car business.

Deception, in fact, is considered to be rife at all levels of the automotive world. In a 1941 investigation, for instance, representatives of the *Reader's Digest* disconnected a coil wire in an automobile, a relatively easily diagnosed malady, and then took the automobile to 347 garages throughout the nation. Of these, 129 immediately noted the problem and either charged nothing or a nominal fee for the work. The remainder—63 per cent of the garages—overcharged, inserted unnecessary work, charged for work not done, for parts not needed, or perpetrated similar kinds of fraud.

Such pervasive dishonesty in the automobile industry, documented further in the material prepared by the Committee on Consumer Interests, is perhaps most strikingly summarized by President Johnson's observation that from 1961 through early 1966, four times as many American soldiers were killed in highway accidents than in the fighting in the Vietnam war. Part of the culpability for such deaths, it might be alleged, lies with automobile advertisers who, as the reading indicates, seem to deliberately encourage reckless and irresponsible use of automobiles.

The vulnerability of consumers in the United States has led to suggestions that we adopt the ombudsman idea originated in Scandinavia, which establishes a special office to represent the public in its conflicts with business or governmental agencies. An ombudsman, however, could aid only persons interested in self-protection. Many fraudulent schemes, such as those involved in so personal and sensitive an area as human illness, probably would not be altogether responsive to rational considerations. Fictitious panaceas cater notably to fears of death, to inabilities to cope either socially or psychologically with lingering illness, to feelings of impotence in the face of medically insoluble conditions, and to frustrations with implacable or inaccessible medical resources. Hope and infirmity combine in the health field to present a particularly vulnerable and often a particularly poignant target for white-collar offenses.

The willing involvement of victims in their own deception, often seen in the health field, is part of the underlying theme in the remaining chapters in Part 4, which are primarily concerned with public responses to specified kinds of white-collar crime.

It is often said that white-collar crime finds an especially hospitable climate in the United States because victims share with offenders a similar set of ethical attitudes and social aspirations and that offenders prey upon victims who themselves, in their own realms of operation, are equally dishonest. Though such a sweeping allegation may contain more fancy than fact, a survey of student responses to the Van Doren television quiz scandal indicates that there is a strong tendency to invoke lulling explanations to forgive (if blame is ever attached at all) some persons who blatantly offend formal ethical and legal codes. College students castigated the television producers, networks, and sponsors much more often than they directed their rebukes against Van Doren, though it was he who had most clearly compromised himself and who had compounded his original act by lying before the grand jury about it. Perhaps youth and personal charm made Van Doren too attractive to be cast as a villain. Perhaps a reluctance among the students to part with daydreams and to crash idols led to the transfer of blame to more impersonal and anonymous forces. How much the students' tendency to forgive Van Doren was a product of long-standing criminological stress on the overwhelming nature of debilitating external forces in the production of traditional kinds of offenders is an interesting issue. The Van Doren scandal and student reactions to it are reported in the article by Kurt and Gladys Engel Lang, the former a sociologist at the State University of New York, Stony Brook, and the latter at the Center for Urban Education.

Choice of violations of food laws by Donald J. Newman, a professor at the School of Criminal Justice, State University of New York, Albany, to assess public response to white-collar offenses fits with the Langs' emphasis on the degree of personal threat inherent in an act as a major key to opinions regarding its heinousness. Newman points out, however, that any purchaser might well have been endangered by the food violations he lists in his request for views regarding appropriate sentences. It is noteworthy that Newman's hypothesis that the public would favor penalties for food violators similar to those imposed on traditional kinds of offenders is not substantiated. Preferred sanctions generally were inclined toward more stringent sentences than those usually imposed by the courts, however. The Newman study clearly suggests the necessity for additional investigations regarding public opinion in simultaneous regard to both white-collar and traditional crime. Alterations over time in such assessments could provide clues to changing values in the society and might also offer insights concerning techniques of social control and suasion in regard to aberrant or criminal behavior.

The extent to which political and professional reactions to offenders should pay heed to public evaluations of the given behavior is touched upon briefly by Newman in a discussion that opens up fundamental issues of public policy. Newman seems inclined to the view that public opinion, however noteworthy, should form but one element—and perhaps a minor one—in the amalgam of items determining legislative, judicial, and correctional actions. More weight might reasonably be given to validated information about the consequences of various offenses and the consequences of various responses to them. In this sense, there appears to be support for the position stated by Margery Fry, an English reformer who dedicated her life to the improvement of penal policy, in the concluding observation in her book, *Arms and the Law*:

We are looking toward a system which shall renounce the ideas of weighing wickedness and turn instead to estimating danger, which shall at once acknowledge our ignorance and employ our knowledge to the full; strong enough for gentleness and wise enough for tolerance.

17

THE MERCHANT AND THE LOW-INCOME CONSUMER

David Caplovitz

The data to be presented grew out of the efforts of three settlement houses in New York City to do something about the consumer problems of the poor people in their neighborhoods. In 1960, these settlements commissioned the Bureau of Applied Social Research of Columbia University to carry out a survey of the consumer practices of low-income families as a prelude to a program of action. Two of these settlements were located in East Harlem and one on the Lower East Side. In all, we interviewed 464 families living in low-income public housing projects in these two areas. In order to get the merchants' views of the marketing situation, we carried out more informal interviews with some of the many merchants of furniture and appliances located in East Harlem, along Third Avenue and 125th Street. The density of furniture and appliance stores in this area is probably greater than anywhere else in the country.

The median income of the families we interviewed was about $3,300 in 1960, the year of the study. Most of them were members of racial or ethnic minorities. Forty-five per cent were Puerto Rican, 30 per cent

Reprinted from *Jewish Social Studies*, 27 (January, 1965), pp. 45–53.

Negro, and 25 per cent white, exclusive of Puerto Ricans. Relatively few, only 17 per cent, were natives of the city. The rest were migrants, generally from the South or from Puerto Rico. Their educational level was quite low. Only 17 per cent of the family heads had completed high school and about half did not continue their education beyond grade school.

Their place of origin, their ethnicity, their low educational level, all suggest that these consumers are products of more traditionalistic cultures, poorly trained in the ways of urban, bureaucratic society. This fact underlies many of the problems they encounter as consumers.

CONSUMER PRACTICES OF THE POOR

We might suppose that families whose incomes average only about $3,300 could not possibly be consumers of expensive durable goods. But this reasoning overlooks that rapidly expanding American institution, the installment plan and the special forms it takes in low-income areas. "No money down" and "easy payments" are the slogans luring even the poor into the marketplace. Our survey disclosed that in spite of their poor economic position and poor credit status, most of the families were consumers of major durables. For example: 95 per cent owned at least one television set (5 per cent owned more than one); more than three in every five owned a phonograph; more than two in every five owned a sewing machine; more than two in every five owned an automatic washing machine; more than a quarter owned a vacuum cleaner; one in every seven families owned an automobile.

Most of the families had moved into public housing during the five-year period preceding the study, and most of them had bought a good deal of furniture in that period. The typical family bought sets of furniture for at least two rooms when it moved into the project and had spent approximately $500. Some 16 per cent had paid more than $1,000 for furniture bought at the time of the move. The prices they paid for appliances were quite high. Forty per cent paid more than $300 for their TV set and 13 per cent paid more than $400. A number of families owned expensive combination television and phonograph sets and one family reported paying $900 for such an appliance.

It is not surprising that these families relied heavily on installment credit when making such expensive purchases. Approximately two-thirds of the appliances owned by the families were bought on credit and 80 per cent had used credit to buy at least some of their major durables. Their dependence on credit and their traditionalistic backgrounds account for the fact that hardly any shopped for major durables in the downtown department stores and discount houses. They went instead to the local stores or to the appliance chain stores that advertise "easy credit" plans.

It may come as a surprise to learn that the door-to-door peddlers, the men with the traditional slogan of "a dollar down, a dollar a week," are still thriving among the poor, finding new customers among the more recent migrants from the rural South and Puerto Rico.

Fully half the families we interviewed had made at least one credit purchase from these door-to-door salesmen, and more than a third had made repeated purchases. Most families regretted buying this way when they discovered they were paying exorbitant prices. But some, approximately 20 per cent, have had rather continuous relationships with peddlers, whom they have come to regard as almost a friend. The peddler serves as a purchasing agent for these families, getting them practically anything they need. Unlike most of the local merchants and the more bureaucratic stores that offer credit, most of the peddlers do not use installment contracts. The exceptions are outdoor salesmen for large firms specializing in a particular commodity such as encyclopedias or pots and pans. These men are not interested in building up a clientele. Once the contract is signed, this kind of salesman gives the customer a coupon book with instructions for mailing monthly payments, and then he disappears. But the more usual peddler is the man in business for himself, hoping to establish permanent relationships with his customers. His credit is of a more traditional kind. When payments are late or less than the specified amount, he does not add on service charges. This flexibility is appreciated by the customers and explains why some continue to buy from peddlers even though they know they pay much more than they would at a store.

It would be of great interest to know whether the occupation of customer-peddler (as these salesmen call themselves) is still dominated by Jews as it was in the early decades of the century. Although I cannot give you any statistics on this, my guess is that a majority of the peddlers today, particularly those in business for themselves, are Jews but that a growing number of Puerto Ricans are also playing this role. However, I suspect that most of the Puerto Rican peddlers are outdoor salesmen for one or another of the local stores. At least I make this inference from the fact that many of the stores in East Harlem have signs in their windows announcing the need for Spanish-speaking canvassers.

CONSUMER PROBLEMS AND PATTERNS OF EXPLOITATION

Their lack of shopping sophistication and their vulnerability to "easy credit" would suggest that many low-income families encounter serious difficulties as consumers. The study found this to be true. One in every five had experienced legal pressures because of missed payments. Their goods were repossessed, their salaries were garnisheed or they were threatened with garnishments. Many of the families in this position had heavy credit obligations that reached crisis proportions when their income was suddenly reduced through illness or unemployment. The following account given by a twenty-seven-year-old Negro husband is typical:

> I first bought a bedroom set. I still owed money on it when I wanted a living room set. I went back to the store and bought the living room set on credit. *At that time I was working and making good money. That was two years ago. Six months ago I got sick and stopped working.* And so I couldn't pay anymore. . . . When I got sick, I still owed $288. Last week they sent a summons saying I have to pay $440, not $288. We have to pay, but what I'm going to do is pay the $288, not the $440.

Like many of these consumers, this young man did not understand that he is liable for the interest on his debt, as well as court costs and legal fees.

Inability to maintain payments was not the only problem these consumers encountered. A much larger proportion—almost half of the sample—encountered difficulties because of the unethical and illegal practices employed by the merchants. This group includes families who were seduced by "bait advertising" and high-pressure salesmen into buying much more expensive merchandise than they had intended to buy, families who were given erroneous information about the costs of their purchases, and families who were sold, as new, merchandise that had been reconditioned.

The many incidents of "bait advertising" uncovered in the study can be illustrated by this typical experience of a twenty-six-year-old Negro housewife:

> I saw a TV ad for a $29 sewing machine, so I wrote to the company and they sent down a salesman who demonstrated it for me. It shook the whole house, but I wanted to buy it anyway. But he kept saying it would disturb the neighbors by being so noisy and he went out into the hall and brought in another model costing $185. . . . I actually had to pay $220. He promised if I paid within a certain amount of time I would get $35 back. But since my husband was out of work, we couldn't pay within the time period, so I didn't get the refund. . . . I was taken in by the high-pressure sales talk.

It should be noted that these high-pressure techniques often result in converting cash customers into credit customers. People who have every intention of paying cash when they answer the advertisement for the cheaper item suddenly find themselves buying much more expensive merchandise on credit.

The great success merchants have with "bait advertising" is indicated by the remarks of one of the furniture salesmen to whom we spoke in East Harlem: "I don't know how we do it. We advertise three rooms of furniture for $149 and the customers swarm in. They end up buying a

$400 bedroom set for $600 and none of us can believe how easy it is to make these sales." The technique of persuading the customer to buy items more expensive than those advertised is known in the trade as "the switch sale," and judging from this account such sales are not hard to come by. Another merchant told us that the amount of goods sold a customer depends more on how much risk the merchant is ready to assume than on the buying intentions of the customer. The merchant ready to assume great risk can presumably persuade the low-income customer to buy more than he intended to buy when he first entered the store.

I am sure that the proportion of families who are victimized by unscrupulous salesmen is much greater than our study uncovered, simply because many of these families do not realize that they have been cheated. This discovery is often made by accident. For example, a family may learn that it was sold a reconditioned TV set only when so informed by the repairman or they may learn from a friend that a particular item could have been obtained elsewhere for much less. Occasionally, one of these consumers would learn that he was overcharged by having an item appraised. One middle-aged Negro housewife told us that she agreed to buy her daughter a watch that a door-to-door salesman was selling for $60. "I gave him $3 down and got a payment book in the mail. About a month later I had the watch appraised in a 125th Street store and I found it was worth only $6.50." This woman tried to break the contract but did not succeed. When she stopped payments the company sued her and won a judgment by default.

As this incident indicates, the two kinds of problems that low-income consumers encounter—failure to maintain payments and being victimized by the sharp practices of the merchants—are not necessarily independent of each other. Some families, capable of maintaining payments, stopped paying when they discovered that they had been cheated. But instead of gaining retribution, they were more often than not subjected to legal sanctions brought upon them by the merchant. This process can be seen in the experience of a twenty-eight-year-old Puerto Rican man:

> I bought a set of pots and pans from a door-to-door salesman. They were of very poor quality and I wanted to give them back but they wouldn't take them. *I stopped paying and told them to change them or take them back.* I refused to pay. . . . *They started bothering me at every job I had.* Then they wrote to my current job and my boss is taking $6 weekly from my pay and sending it to pay this.

It is not clear from his account whether he had lost some of his previous jobs because of the efforts to garnishee his salary; this does happen with some frequency. Many employers simply will not be bothered with garnishments and do not hesitate to fire workers whose salaries are attached.

As the previous incident suggests, the laws regulating installment sales unwittingly act in favor of such merchants, because these poor consumers have little understanding of their legal rights and how to exercise them. By taking matters into their own hands and stopping payments on faulty merchandise, they only bring additional troubles upon themselves.

There is another aspect to this unwitting bias in the legal structure. The merchants who offer "easy credit" frequently sell their contracts at a discount to a finance company. Many low-income consumers do not understand this procedure. They mistakenly believe that the merchant has gone out of business and assume that nothing can be done about their problem. The practice of selling contracts to credit agencies thus often has the consequence of absolving the merchant of his responsibilities to the consumer, not because the law gives him this right, but because the consumer does not understand what has happened.

In keeping with their inadequacies as consumers in a bureaucratic society, most of the poor families we spoke to had no idea what they could do about their consumer problems. When asked directly where they would go for help if they found themselves being cheated by a merchant, some 64 per cent said they did not know. They could not name any of the community agencies equipped to deal with these problems, such as the Legal Aid Society, the State Banking and Finance Department, the Small Claims Court, or the Better Business Bureau. The Better Business Bureau was the agency most often cited by the minority who had some idea where they could go for professional help.

THE LOW-INCOME MARKETING SYSTEM

As I noted earlier, we interviewed some of the merchants in East Harlem and I will conclude this review of our study by giving you a brief picture of the techniques they employ to insure that the business will be profitable in spite of their readiness to extend credit to relatively poor risks.

Some of the incidents I have cited suggest one way in which the merchants protect themselves and that is to have unusually high mark-ups on their merchandise. In this special system of sales and credit, cheap goods are sold at prices that in the larger market place are commanded by high-quality merchandise. In East Harlem, one of the areas studied, the merchants use a number system to price their goods, referring to "one number," "two number," and "three number" items. Each number stands for a 100 per cent mark-up over the wholesale price. For example, a TV set that costs the merchant $100 and is sold for $300 is a "two number" item. According to a former bookkeeper in such a store, the merchandise in East Harlem is never sold for less than "one number" and often for more. Another sign of an unusual pricing system in these stores is the absence of price tags, signifying that prices are not standardized; there are hardly any "one-price" stores in low-income neighborhoods.

But the high mark-up does not in itself insure that the business will be profitable. No matter what he charges, the merchant can stay in business only if he receives payments from his customers. The assumptions of any credit system—the customer's intention and ability to pay—cannot be taken for granted in this market.

To some extent the merchant can count on legal controls over his customers. But these often prove inadequate, since many of the customers are employed only irregularly and others depend on welfare. Furthermore, the merchant who frequently resorts to legal controls is likely to lose goodwill in the neighborhood. For this reason, the merchants interviewed were reluctant to make extensive use of their right to sue defaulting customers.

Thus, in addition to formal controls the merchants depend heavily on informal, personal controls over their customers. The merchants reported that they operate their credit business on a "fifteen-month year," anticipating that their customers will miss about one in every four payments. This is considered a normal part of the business and the merchants take it into account when they compute the mark-up.

Many merchants adopt the methods of the customer-peddlers, employing their own canvassers, who visit the families in their homes both to collect payments and to sell additional merchandise. As part of the informal system of control, the merchants encourage weekly payment plans with the customer's bringing the payment to the store. This continuous contact enables the merchant to get to know his customer. He learns when the customer receives his pay check, when his rent is due, when job layoffs, illnesses, and other emergencies occur; in short, he gathers all kinds of information that allow him to interpret the reasons for a missed payment. Since the customer comes to the store with his payments, the merchant is ready to make another sale when the first is almost paid for. As a result, many customers are continuously in debt to the merchant in a pattern reminiscent of the relationship between the sharecropper and the company store. We might almost call these traditionalistic consumers in our cities "urban sharecroppers."

Various devices are employed in this marketing system for sifting and sorting the consumers according to their risk and matching them with merchants willing to extend them credit. For example, when a merchant finds himself with a customer he considers to be too great a risk for him, he does not discourage the customer. Instead, he directs him to a merchant with a less conservative credit policy. The peddlers also steer their customers to local merchants. When their customers request major appliances that they do not handle themselves, the peddlers will refer them to an appropriate merchant who is ready to extend them credit. The referring merchants and peddlers receive a commission for their service, another factor affecting the final sales price.

In describing what I call the low-income marketing system, I have stressed the inequities in this system of exchange, its exploitative features. But how is the persistence of such a deviant social system to be explained? Is it merely a matter of evil merchants taking advantage of the gullible poor? I think the answer is more complicated. This system with its obvious exploitative practices is able to persist because it performs important social functions. In a society in which consumption is not only a matter of obtaining material conveniences, but also a means of gaining self-respect and winning the respect of others, this marketing system makes consumers of the people who fail to meet the requirements of the more legitimate economy. Even the welfare family is able to consume in much the same manner as its social peers who happen not to be on welfare. Through the various mechanisms I have mentioned, the poorest risks are shunted to the merchants who are ready to accept great risk. A close association probably exists between the amount of risk that merchants in this system are willing to accept and their readiness to employ unethical and illegal tactics. It may even be that under the present marketing arrangements in our society, unethical practices are an inevitable consequence of serving the wants of the poorest risks. Society now virtually presents the poor risks with the unpalatable choice of foregoing major purchases and thereby forfeiting whatever self-esteem is to be derived from consumption, or being exploited. In short, the behavior of the local merchants must be seen in the broader context of a society in which even the poor are conditioned to want durable goods as a way of gaining self respect. . . .

I suspect that a more thorough study might show that the poor often turn to the merchants with whom they deal for a variety of services apart from merchandise. In the cold, impersonal bureaucratic world with which they have difficulty coping, the poor may consider the merchants as their allies. In calling attention to this other side of the "exploitative" relationship, I have no intention of excusing the sharp practices employed by the merchants. Just as I suspect that the patterns of exploitation are not to be explained on the grounds of man's evilness, so I suspect that the merchants' acts of friendliness toward their customers stem more from the desire to build goodwill than from innate altruism.

In stressing the impersonal forces shaping the behavior of the merchants *vis-à-vis* the poor consumer, I do not mean to imply that the abuses of this marketing system must be accepted as inevitable. Ways must be found through legislation and education for making the merchants more responsible for their actions. The strains in the present system, I fear, will only be heightened as the Negro community becomes more self-conscious of its rights and more dissatisfied with the status quo. But I am not too optimistic about the possibilities of correcting these abuses through ethical appeals to the merchants. It is not an easy task to convince businessmen . . . to lower their profits in the name of ethical and humanitarian standards.

18

HOME MAINTENANCE AND REPAIR

President's Committee on

Consumer Interests

In recent years the home improvement and repair industry has enjoyed virtually unprecedented expansion and prosperity. There are now, according to the National Home Improvement Council, approximately 60 million homes in the United States. To improve these homes and keep them in good repair, $11.7 billion was spent by the American consumer in 1963. Of this amount, $6.8 billion was spent by owner occupants of single-family dwellings. This is an average of $224 for each unit for the year.

It has been estimated that $12.5 to $13 billion was spent on home repair and improvement in 1965. Owners of properties with one housing unit spent $7.2 billion in 1965, almost $250 per homeowner. The Federal Reserve Board reports that commercial lending institutions alone held more than $3.6 billion in home repair and improvement loans in 1965. Home improvement is, therefore, big business.

The average homeowner channels 1.5 per cent of his income each year into improving or repairing his home. Among the many reasons for this large investment are these:

Reprinted from *Consumer Issues 1966* (Washington, D.C.: U.S. Government Printing Office, 1966), pp. 41–57.

Homeowners have more to spend because of higher personal income.

Houses built during the boom of the 1950s are about a decade old and in need of repair and modernizing.

Lenders make funds readily available for home improvement and reportedly foresee no real shortage of home-improvement credit in the immediate future.

There is growing demand for older houses in established suburban areas which are restored or refurbished at great expense.

FRAUD ALSO SPREADS

Fraudulent and deceptive practices in the home repair and improvement field have also boomed. They have caused consumer losses estimated at $500 million to $1 billion yearly, or roughly between 4 per cent and 8 per cent of the entire business.

Each year $7 million is taken from California consumers solely through fraudulent and illegal aluminum-siding sales, according to the state's attorney general.

Complaints received by the better business bureaus throughout the country indicate the prevalence of fraud in the home-improvement field. The National Better Business Bureau reports that since 1953 home improvement has remained at the top of their Instances of Service list. In 1964, the bureaus processed 275,185 home-improvement inquiries and complaints, a remarkable 27 per cent increase and 7.3 per cent of the bureaus' total services. As Allan E. Backman, executive vice president of National Better Business Bureau, said: "No industry which is the subject of more than 30,000 complaints a year to Better Business Bureaus can afford to view the situation with complacency."

SCHEMES AND TECHNIQUES

Home-improvement swindles defy neat categories, for they touch every aspect of the ever-changing home-improvement industry. In Wisconsin, they are most prevalent in the furnace and furnace repair, window and door, roofing and siding, carpet and rug (permanently installed), and built-in vacuum cleaner businesses. Though home-improvement rackets may occur in any season, they typically peak in the spring and summer when itinerant repairmen and door-to-door salesmen take to the road. Most fraudulent home-improvement schemes have common characteristics: phony bargains, tricky financing, guarantees not honored, materials misrepresented, and performances exaggerated. Itinerant repairmen come in a variety of guises: the gutter, furnace, or chimney repairman; the roofing or siding expert; the quack tree surgeon; the bogus termite-control expert; home-remodeling specialist; driveway blacktoppers and oilers; installers of storm windows and awnings; fire- and burglar-protection devices; water softeners, central home vacuum units, and intercom systems. Their arsenal of sales techniques include:

"Model home" pitch—the owner is offered a special discount for the use of his home as a display.

Bogus contests—a "lucky winner" is offered various prizes and the "free" services or product of the salesman.

Factory deals or special wholesale prices, which are actually overpriced.

Bait-and-switch tactics—services or products are advertised at ridiculously low prices and then later disparaged in favor of a far higher-priced item or service.

Fictitious and inflated regular prices from which the homeowner is promised a "discount."

Misleading guarantees.

Misrepresentation of interest rates.

Free gifts and samples.

Scare tactics—a particularly vicious practice is to lead the consumer to believe that the lives of his family and himself are in danger if the services of the salesman are not purchased.

Salesmen posing as "official inspectors" or "graduates of home-improvement academies" or "representatives" of well-known manufacturers.

Referral selling—the consumer is led to believe that he can pay for all or part of the service or product through "commissions" gained from sales to persons whose names he has given the salesman.

REFERRAL SELLING

Thousands of persons each year are misguided into believing that they have found an easy way to make money through referral sales. Such schemes are particularly attractive to the unemployed homemaker who is led to believe she can "earn commissions."

Legislatures and enforcement agencies have attacked referral-selling schemes as deceptive and misleading. However, proving deception involves a case-by-case approach with knowledge of the probability of consumers earning sizeable sums—facts generally known only by the company sponsoring the referral sales. The President's Committee believes laws should be enacted outlawing such schemes, whereby consumers are led to believe they can make money merely by recommending names of friends and neighbors, but which all too often result in consumers having to pay out money for goods they had not intended to buy.

A recent landmark decision of the state of Washington Supreme Court presents a somewhat novel theory for outlawing referral selling.[1] The court stated that referral selling possesses the elements of prize, chance, and valuable consideration, which thereby brings it within the scope of the state's lottery laws. The court also held that the finance company which had been assigned the conditional sales contract could not enforce the contract against the purchaser because of the illegal taint of the referral-selling scheme. The court dismissed the "something for nothing" claim of the referral selling by pointing out the absurd and preposterous result if the claim were, in fact, true. The decision said:

> The Lifetone salesman told respondents that they could get something for nothing through the referral-selling scheme. Respondents are obligated to pay $1,187.28 for equipment costing $225.32. For ease of demonstration, respondents must earn twelve commissions of $100 each in order to get, as promised, something for nothing. This means that twelve respondents' referrals must purchase as respondent did; they, in turn, to get something for nothing, must find twelve more people to purchase, and so forth, as follows:

	Number of Purchasers
First round	1
Second round	12
Third round	1,728
Fourth round	20,736
Fifth round	248,832

> Soon the scheme will run itself out; the market will become saturated.

OTHER DOOR-TO-DOOR GIMMICKS

The model-home pitch, the "free" gifts and samples, the "official inspector" and the specially selected household gimmick all lend themselves to door-to-door selling. In fact, "model home" companies were accused in a majority of the home improvement and repair complaints received by the Minnesota attorney general's Consumer Fraud Bureau in recent years.

Recent cases involving the Holland Furnace Company illustrate how these schemes operate in practice. Holland salesmen would often gain entrance into a home by saying they were government agents, gas or utility company inspectors, or heating engineers.[2] They would tear down or dismantle the owner's furnace, often without his permission, on the pretext of inspecting it or cleaning it, then refuse to reassemble the furnace in order to pressure the owner into purchasing a Holland furnace or to coerce him into signing a release absolving Holland of liability. The salesmen also used scare tactics in selling, such as falsely representing that the old furnace would asphyxiate the customer's family, burn up, or blow up.

Holland Furnace Company did business in forty-four states, had 475 branch and subbranch offices, and had gross annual sales totaling at least $30 million. The Federal Trade Commission conducted hearings for nearly two years before a cease and desist order was rendered against Holland in 1958.[3] This order was then appealed to the FTC and thereafter twice to the United States Circuit Court of Appeals and once to the United States Supreme Court.[4] However, the company still failed to discontinue its fraudulent practices. This resulted in further litigation and the imposition of heavy fines on company officials for noncompliance with the 1958 order. At least five states (Illinois, Michigan, Minnesota, Washington, and Wisconsin) also obtained orders preventing Holland Furnace Company from continuing their fraudulent practices.

The total waste of money stemming from the Holland Furnace Company operation and the resulting litigation surrounding it is inestimable. It shows also that action after the fact is an unwieldy and largely ineffective method of controlling home-improvement fraud. Yet, under present law, action usually must be postponed until consumers have filed a substantial number of complaints.[5] State and federal agencies should have power to obtain preliminary civil injunctive relief in consumer fraud cases.

OTHER PROBLEMS

Many problems that arise from fraudulent home-improvement schemes are similar to other areas of consumer fraud: for example, assignment of the negotiable instrument to a holder in due course, which nullifies most of the consumer's defenses;[6] high interest rates and carrying charges;[7] failure to inform the purchaser accurately of the total installment price of the home improvement;[8] and general misrepresentation of the product and its performance capabilities.[9]

Other ills seem to be inherent to the home-improvement industry or, at least, to occur there most often. Long delays in completing improvements have plagued homeowners for years and have precipitated fraudulent use of completion certificates. Marked disparities between pictorial renderings and finished jobs have also caused consumer consternation and are a potential source of fraud.[10]

The labor involved in home improvements also raises mechanic's lien problems. This has been described as follows:

> As a company gets ready to pull up stakes, they stop paying local suppliers and these suppliers then file liens against the property which is improved. Thus, many homeowners are forced to pay twice. It is true that the homeowner can demand lien waivers before payment, but few homeowners secure this protection for themselves.[11]

FEDERAL GOVERNMENT PROTECTION

The Federal Trade Commission and, to a lesser extent, the Post Office Department are active in regulating the home-improvement industry. So, too, is the Department of Housing and Urban Affairs (HUD), where, for example, the Federal Housing Administration (FHA) withdraws loan insurance privileges from shady operations. Indirectly, however, two other federal agencies perform notable service in this area: the Justice Department because of its Criminal Division and Administrative Regulations Section, and the Agriculture Department because of its publication of various consumer information pamphlets and books.

The Federal Trade Commission's broad jurisdiction over "Unfair methods of competition . . . and unfair or deceptive acts or practices" brings home-improvement frauds affecting interstate commerce squarely within its scope. Unfortunately, the FTC lacks the staff to prosecute all but the largest and most notorious of the persons and firms violating the law it administers. Thus, cases as large as Holland Furnace Company take much of the commission's time, leaving many smaller, but equally dangerous, cases to state and local control. Because of such limitations, FTC has encouraged industry self-regulation and has issued trade-practice conference rules and industry guides.

The guides' purpose is to spell out clearly the commission's position on the legality of certain industry practices.[12] These have generally helped businessmen by translating complex laws into lay language. Yet business distrust of the commission's motives and interpretations remains.

The rules are efforts initiated by trade associations or the commission to achieve voluntary compliance.[13] These rules have helped eliminate industry-wide practices and fostered self-regulation. However, their effectiveness is limited, for a firm's failure to observe the rules cannot be enforced as per se violation of the law. . . .

Because legal action often entails prolonged litigation, the commission generally encourages informal negotiations culminating in voluntary compliance or stipulations for discontinuance of a certain practice. Nevertheless, during the past two years the commission has moved to prohibit home-improvement practices involving the sale of siding, storm windows, awnings, car-ports, floor covering and carpets, and the use of the "model home" pitch, bogus contests, deceptive referral schemes, bait-and-switch tactics, fictitious "regular" prices, misleading guarantees, misrepresentation of interest rates, and false designation of salesmen as graduates of a "home-improvement academy."

The President's Committee believes that while codes of ethics and practices are valuable, the industry has not shown it can regulate itself. FTC's efforts have proved vital, and Congress should expand appropriations for the commission so it can enlarge its protection of consumers.

THE POST OFFICE

The Postal Inspection Service conducts extensive investigations of alleged violations of the Mail Fraud Statute, which makes it a crime to use the mails to defraud. The Postal Inspection Service turns the facts adduced from such investigations over to the Criminal Division of the Justice Department for possible criminal prosecution where there is satisfactory evidence that the mails are being used to defraud.

The Postmaster General is also empowered to stop incoming mail from reaching the fraudulent operator or forbid payment of postal money orders or notes. He may also obtain a temporary restraining order and preliminary injunction directing detention of the defendants' incoming mail if he believes the law is being violated.

These are effective weapons to combat mail fraud. However, relatively few home-improvement schemes use the mails, and the post office cannot be expected to be a primary enforcement agency in the home-improvement field.

STATE AND LOCAL ACTION

There have been a number of proposed local ordinances regulating door-to-door salesmen and "temporary businesses." This movement toward local licensing by ordinance is national in scope and reflects the prevailing inability of present state and federal laws to control the problem. As early as 1947, the National Institute of Municipal Law Officers became concerned with the problem and conducted a survey which determined that twenty-four major cities had licensing ordinances. The institute also prepared a model licensing ordinance requiring bonding and investigation. In 1963, the League of Wisconsin Municipalities surveyed the problem and determined that forty Wisconsin cities had licensing ordinances and that about half of those ordinances required the posting of a bond.

The main arguments supporting licensing ordinances are that the consumer would then be able to identify the company with certainty, the license could be revoked as an effective enforcement sanction, and the consumer could sue for the proceeds of the performance bond if the contractor fails to perform. Fingerprinting and positive identification would single out those applicants convicted of criminally violating fraud and unfair trade-practices statutes. The bonding provisions would tend to insure that the contractor would not leave town before the job was completed. An ordinance could, in addition, require the posting of a liability as well as a performance bond, thereby protecting the consumer from those acts of the contractor resulting in property damage or personal injury.

The major arguments against such an ordinance are that municipal licensing would lead to a multiplicity of licenses for the average contractor, and that the giving of a license and an identification badge would lend false authority to the practices of the unscrupulous.

The Bureau of the Budget of the city of Milwaukee in its special report to the Common Council on the financial impact of the proposed licensing ordinance argued that considerable expense would be incurred by the city in the administration and enforcement of the new law. Advocates of local licensing and the bureau have pointed out, however, that the cost of the program can be borne by the industry through licensing fees.

The Milwaukee estimates of financial impact provide useful information on the question of whether local licensing is a practical method of curbing abuses in the industry. Milwaukee's Bureau of the Budget estimated that the city, with three-quarters of a million persons, had 3,000 home-improvement contractors and that each contractor employed an average of three salesmen. Because of the industry's high rate of personnel turnover, the bureau estimated that the city would be issuing 4,000 new licenses and 8,000 renewals annually. With a $5 fee for an original license and $3 for a renewal, the total cost of the program would be covered.

Nevertheless, it is questionable whether local licensing is an appropriate corrective. The sole sanction usually available is license revocation or refusal, and experience has shown it to be seldom used. In addition, uniformity of policy and administration is not assured, and the method is subject to misuse by unconscionable contracts. Thus, licensing only indirectly gets at the problems of the consumer. Furthermore, the method is indiscriminate in its failure to distinguish between legitimate and illegitimate businesses. . . .

STATE LEGISLATION REGULATING
CREDIT TRANSACTIONS

Fifteen states have enacted retail installment sales acts which cover services. In addition, a few states which do not otherwise regulate retail installment sales of services performed have enacted home-repair financing acts.

The most recent statute dealing with the home-improvement industry, the Michigan Home Improvement Finance Act of 1965, has several provisions that directly benefit the consumer. One is for a "cooling off" period, during which the consumer can change his mind. Another is for full disclosure of all charges and the basis of their determination. Others prohibit previously commonly employed waivers of rights, modify the "holder in due course" rule, and set the maximum permissible finance charges.

Regarding credit sales of home improvements, the maximum charge permitted is $8 per month or $100 per year computed on the principal amount of the contract even though the time balance is to be paid in installments. This, in effect, prohibits the application of the usurious time-price differential doctrine, which allows one price to be charged for cash, and a higher price, not considered to include interest, to be charged for deferred payments. The finance charges can accrue only during the period between the completion of the work and the date of the final payment due. The consumer has the right to pay the amount due in full at any time, and the finance charges must be appropriately adjusted.

Finally, the act essentially provides that the criminal acts of agents are deemed to be the acts of their principals, unless it appears that the individuals engaged in the management of the contractor or finance agency had neither actual nor constructive knowledge of the wrongful conduct or were reasonably unable to prevent the wrongful conduct.

INTERGOVERNMENTAL ACTIVITIES

Intergovernmental cooperation is not what it should be. Closer cooperation should be established between federal, state, and local governmental agencies dealing with consumer protection. The Federal Trade Commission's Office for Federal-State Cooperation, and Michigan's four-point program of statewide cooperation illustrate steps that could be taken.

Although home-improvement trade associations have vigorously opposed most legislation dealing with their industry, there is some indication of a growing acceptance that certain legislation is necessary. The general reaction of responsible persons in the industry is probably similar to that of Malcolm Stevenson of the Maine Merchants Association who stated that legitimate retail firms are willing to support regulation of home-improvement contractors "whether they believe it is sound or not, because of the fringe element which causes grief to Maine citizens." Hopefully, such statements indicate a growing responsiveness by the home-improvement industry to the needs of the consumer and a recognition of the need for legislation to curb existing abuses in the industry.

Notes

1. *Sherwood & Roberts-Yakima, Inc.* v. *Leach,* 409 P. 2d 160 (1965).

2. *Holland Furnace Co.,* 55 F.T.C. 55 (1958).

3. *See Holland Furnace Co.* v. *F.T.C.,* 295 F. 2d 302 (7th Cir. 1959).

4. *Ibid., cert. den.* 361 U.S. 928 (1960). See further *In re Holland Furnace Co.,* 341 F.2d 548 (7th Cir. 1965), *cert. den.* 381 U.S. 924 (1965).

5. John G. Kellogg, "Czar in Lambskin: Administrative Regulation of Commercial Activities in Wisconsin," *Wisconsin Law Review* (Winter, 1965), pp. 154–155.

6. "Translating Sympathy for Deceived Consumers Into Effective Programs for Protection," *University of Pennsylvania Law Review,* 114 (January, 1966), p. 414.

7. See Barbara A. Curran, *Trends in Consumer Credit Legislation* (Chicago: University of Chicago Press, 1965); Wallace P. Mors, "Recent Trends in State Regulation of Consumer Credit," *Journal of Finance,* 15 (May, 1960), pp. 191–205; Karl W. Cavanaugh, "Retail Credit Sales and Usury," *Louisiana Law Review,* 24 (June, 1964), 822–849.

8. Thomas L. Steffen, "Truth in Lending?—A Viable Subject," *George Washington Law Review,* 32 (April, 1964), pp. 861–892; "The Consumer in the Marketplace: A Survey of the Law of Informed Buying," *Notre Dame Lawyer,* 38 (August, 1963), pp. 555–617.

9. Friedrich Kessler, "The Protection of the Consumer under Modern Sales Law," *Yale Law Journal,* 74 (December, 1964), pp. 262–285; "Unconscionable Sales Contracts and the Uniform Commercial Code, Section 2-302," *Virginia Law Review,* 45 (May, 1959), 583–592.

10. This problem is also found in mail-order land-sales frauds. See U.S. Senate, Subcommittee on Frauds and Misrepresentations Affecting the Elderly, Special Committee on Aging, 89th Cong., 1st Sess. 1965, "Frauds and Deceptions Affecting the Elderly: Investigations, Findings, and Recommendations: 1964," *Report,* pp. 27–46.

11. Letter from Michael S. Berman, Special Assistant Attorney General of Minnesota, to James D. Jeffries, Assistant Attorney General of Wisconsin, February 24, 1966.

12. For a general analysis of the Guides see "Voluntary Compliance: An Adjunct to the Mandatory Process," *Indiana Law Journal,* 38 (Spring, 1963), pp. 394–403.

13. See "Trade Practice Rules and Trade Conferences: The FTC and Business Attack Deceptive Practices, Unfair Competition and Antitrust Violations," *Yale Law Journal,* 62 (May, 1953), pp. 912–953.

19

AUTOMOBILES

President's Committee on
Consumer Interests

The automobile, perhaps as nothing else, illustrates how present-day opulence and prosperity are coupled with shortages of consumer information, quality, and standards. Widely used for pleasure, the car is necessary to millions of people who depend on it for transportation to work, school, stores, and so on; so much so that the number of multiple-car families has almost doubled in the last decade—from 5.7 million to 11.8 million.

There are now more than 75 million cars on the road compared with less than 52 million a decade ago. Last year, Detroit sold some 9.3 million cars against 7.9 million in 1955, and imported cars tallied 559,430, almost a tenfold sales increase from 57,115 a decade earlier. The sheer size and importance to the national economy of the automotive industry, therefore, make its performance a matter of vital interest to consumers.

Reprinted from *Consumer Issues 1966* (Washington, D.C.: U.S. Government Printing Office, 1966), pp. 59–77.

BUYING A CAR

At $2,000 and up, an automobile is a major investment to the average consumer. With the exception of his home, the consumer probably makes no more important purchase in his life. Few consumers buy more than two homes in their lifetime. Yet millions of motorists trade their automobiles every three or four years. Since an increasing number of families own two cars, the problems of automobile purchase, financing and maintenance loom large indeed in the consumer's life. Buying a car is a major decision. The number of options runs high. There are hundreds of car styles domestically produced each year; and to these must be added the assortment of imports, plus used cars in both categories. No matter how desirable choice is, it must be based on knowledge if it is to be satisfying and meaningful.

SOURCES OF INFORMATION

Despite the fact that many car owners purchase as often as every two or three years, experience is a limited teacher. Recommendations (and complaints) of friends and relatives can only help a little.

There is no abundance of information published in general magazines and newspapers. Periodicals of the consumer-testing organizations—Consumers Union and Consumer Research—attract a circle of relatively diligent, better-educated consumers. These reports at best can only serve as guides rather than definitive recommendations. Small budgets allow the researchers to buy one car of a type and that sample may not be typical of the manufacturer's output. For the same budgetary reason, cars are tested for a few thousand miles, sufficient to demonstrate many features, but not enough to reveal defects which become apparent in the course of normal wear and tear. In addition, by the time these tests are completed and the reports issued, several months of the selling season have passed.

Translating technical data and specifications into layman's language and including it in advertising copy would be most helpful to the consumer, especially since shopping for a car generally begins with watching auto advertisements. To a large extent, these are not nearly as informative as they might be.

Manufacturers' advertisements tend to stress sex, status, thrills, and luxury. One, for example, for Ford's Mustang, pictures an attractive young woman beside a new car. The caption reads: "My brother thinks I bought my Mustang because it's the most popular new car ever. Mother thinks Mustang's easy handling sold me. Father thinks it was the lively 'Six.' I told them I got it because it was such a good buy. (But I really got it because it's sexy.)" In smaller type, the ad speaks of "Mustang's dashing good looks, breath-taking array of luxury, and more than seventy options."

Another example is the blatant sex appeal of the TV campaign "Join the Dodge Rebellion." Many car names alone promote speed and thrills—Fury and Cyclone GT to name but two—and the ad copy usually spells it out in more detail. According to Jeffrey O'Connell, co-author of *Safety Last—An Indictment of the Auto Industry*, "car advertisements deliberately encourage reckless driving among teenagers."[1]

In making style, speed, and similar values the rationale of production and annual innovations, and thereby promoting these values, the automobile industry insists it is giving people what they want.

It is apparent that advertisements using these appeals are successful in selling cars. Since the consumer has so few other sources of educational information about what to look for in buying a car, his basis for evaluation is primarily what he learns through the automobile advertisements. If the typical automobile purchaser were to be as informed as the industrial firm which buys a fleet of cars, automobile advertising might have quite a different cast. If as much money were spent on consumer information about construction, durability, and safety features as the automobile manufacturers now spend on advertising other, more subjective features of their products, competition in the automobile market might be operating along somewhat different lines than is now the case.

Dealer advertisements are as uninformative as manufacturers' and are sometimes misleading. The price of one model is occasionally featured in an ad beside pictures of more expensive models. Sometimes the featured price refers to one of a kind in the dealer's showroom; when the customer inquires about that car, he is switched to another, more expensive model.

Testimony to this was made by an automobile dealer at the Automotive Conference held by the Massachusetts Consumer Council. He said:

> What are the major problems? Dealers who, at the height of the season, will advertise extremely "hot cars" at exact cost or slightly above cost, creating confusion among the consumers as to whether this product is really hot or whether it is distress merchandise. In many of these cases, the dealers have been shopped by professional shoppers and only one of these cars, if any, is available to look at; and then it is usually a dirty, unattractive car out in the back which is shown to the customer only after strong insistence. Then in certain instances we find that if this car is wanted to be bought as advertised, the customer is then sold factory standard equipment and even a $100 conditioning, or get-ready, charge.

As in all buying, the salesman should be a source of information for the consumer, and the consumer encounters good and bad practitioners. Yet in perhaps no other field is there so much complaint from consumers about misrepresentation. This may result from the fact that in purchasing a car, the consumer has so much more at stake financially than he does in most other purchases and is therefore more prone to complain. Be that as it may, automobile salesmen have often, for example, been accused of promising many things contingent on the approval of the manager—approval which is denied so much later in the transaction that the consumer, at the very least, is at a psychological disadvantage and sometimes cannot easily turn back. A genuine difficulty arises if a trade-in is involved and appraisal is made a month or two before consummation of the transaction and delivery of the new car. In that time lag, the used-car market may have changed drastically and the value of the individual car dropped. Or the car itself may have been physically altered either by accident or by deliberate action of the customer; and the seller may therefore wish, or feel compelled, to revise his estimate of the trade-in allowance.

However, sellers are supposed to be experts, and they perhaps should be obliged to make firm offers on trade-ins, even if delivery of the new car is several weeks away (presuming only normal wear on the car in the meantime).

Sometimes the car sold as new is a used car. Demonstrators and floor samples at automobile shows are shined up and sold as new cars. Legislation should prevent the sale of such cars without proper identification.

BUYING USED CARS

Consumer problems are particularly acute in the purchase of used cars. Used-car dealers have allowed unscrupulous salesmen to use the classified columns of newspapers, particularly in weekend editions, to pose as private party sellers, under such intriguing headings as "Lady must sell," "Low mileage car," "Urgent necessity compels sale." While some used cars are sold by new car dealers, a large number are sold through used-car specialists. The two groups of dealers exhibit some hostility to each other. New-car dealers charge used-car dealers with gross injustices and abuses of the public. In public opinion polls, used-car dealers rank at or very near the bottom of the list of business occupations considered ethical and respectable by the public.

Consumer Reports publishes monthly summaries of legal actions and used-car dealers often figure prominently in them. For instance, the September, 1965, issue contained the following:

> The Washington state attorney general filed suit against Julio Grassi Motors, Inc., of Tacoma, doing business as G.M. Auto Sales. Some of the charges brought were that Grassi violated a state law requiring itemization of finance charges, insurance costs, taxes, and other charges, that he made false promises about repairs, and that he doctored cars with oil products, sawdust, and other compounds to conceal defective parts.

In New Rochelle, N.Y., the state attorney general won a consent agreement from Crabtree Motor Sales, Inc., that it would not misrepresent used cars as being "brand new executive cars" with "practically no mileage."[2]

The purchaser of a used car, in fact, is frequently at the mercy of the dealer from whom the car is purchased. Among other abuses of dealers are (1) turning back the odometer several thousand miles, (2) camouflaging or hiding, rather than repairing, defects in the car, (3) concealing the number of owners and the previous use of the vehicle—a fictitious "previous owner" (sometimes a friend or relative of the seller) acts for a fee and guarantees the car's good condition and low mileage.

The enormous increase in the use of rental and leased automobiles in the last few years has created an additional problem for the purchaser of used cars. Cases have been reported of rental and leased cars being overhauled and then sold as almost new demonstrators or executive cars.

Still another problem in the used-car field is the sale of used cars "as is." It is truly a case of *caveat emptor*, since the buyer commits himself to buying an article exactly as it is with no guarantees or assurances from the seller as to its condition or performance. Any contract stamped "as is" should make absolutely clear that the seller is making absolutely no warranties or guarantees.

It is clear that car purchasers need far more information about the product they are buying. Automobile manufacturers and dealers have an obligation to make their advertising and sales campaigns more informative. In addition, there is a need to enhance the legal rights of the buyer.

FINANCING A CAR

Financing cars presents almost every possible pitfall and snare in consumer credit, ranging from exorbitant interest rates to confessions of judgment. Abuses in automobile financing loom large in the complaint files of better business bureaus and consumer agencies. A few classic problems were described by Lt. Col. Clyde Griffith, Judge Advocate, Fort Myers, Virginia, during the 1965 congressional investigation into the Federal Services Corporation.[3] Although primarily concerned with one agency's dealings with military personnel, he was speaking of practices that are common to all sorts of financing, and for civilians as well as servicemen.

Col. Griffith began by assuming a soldier is buying a used car for $600. Financing it for two or three years in states having legal interest rates up to 4 per cent per month could bring interest charges to 144 per cent of the price: $4 \times 12 \times 3$. The soldier also must finance insurance over the same period so that "this purchase will not be $600 but it will run frequently twice that amount, let's say conservatively $1,200 to finance this over two to three years."

The colonel pointed out that "it is perfectly legal . . . the companies that engage in this usually sell their insurance at a very high price . . . and lots of times they require the soldier to buy the insurance that they . . . sell."

In addition, when signing the purchase contract, the soldier also signs a second document "which is a note not for $600 (the price of the car), but let's say $1,200, which is the price of the car plus all financial and insurance charges. The company that sells the car immediately transfers this note to a second company, a holder in due course who takes the note without defenses." The note says "for value received, I agree to pay $1,200."

When the soldier has paid $200, finds that he cannot pay out his installments and wants to surrender the car, he still owes as much as $800; that is, the original $1,200 less the $200 he paid, less the value received for the car at a subsequent sale, usually forced.

> Lots of times, there is only one bidder [and] the bidder is closely associated with the repossessing company. They take the car back, sell it with one bid at a forced sale. They are lucky if they get $200 for it. This is credited to the soldier's account. So he gets a total credit of $200 that he has paid in plus the $200 that was received for the car. . . . They could sue on this note and this soldier can't even go in and say: But this $800 represents two and a half years of unused interest, unused insurance.

The car having been repossessed, the soldier owes the money and doesn't have the car.

These practices may not affect the average car buyer; nevertheless they lend weight to the aforementioned need for a thorough study of the consumer credit field. For the average car buyer, a prime difficulty stems from the reluctance of most dealers to disclose the cost of credit. Indeed, the tendency of many—perhaps most—dealers is to emphasize "easy, low cost" terms, which frequently turn out to be neither.

Sometimes the price of an automobile is quoted in dollars per month with no indication of how many months the payments must run. There are numerous other ways of quoting prices and interest, only one of which is fully satisfactory—giving the accurate cash price of the car, the accurate price of credit, and the interest charges stated as an annual rate.

Beyond credit disclosure, however, is the question of financing rates and arrangements. It is a matter of serious concern that 50 per cent or more of the net revenue of some new-car dealers is derived from their share of the profits from the financing arrangements on their sales.

On the surface, at least, this raises the possibility that some automobile dealers might be as interesteed in selling credit as in selling cars. There can be no objection to this if people know how much they are paying for the car and how much they are paying separately for the credit. . . . The use of credit in connection with the purchase of automobiles calls for particular attention.

TIRES

It is a sad commentary that, as a cost-cutting device, inferior grades of tires are provided on many new cars. There is no defense for automobile makers' equipping new cars with tires that are not capable of safely carrying a full load of passengers under all conditions commonly encountered. In addition, "many cars sold today are equipped with tires which are not capable of standing up under speeds which the car can achieve."[4]

Some 1,100 different new tires are available, according to the Directory of the Rubber Manufacturers Association. Produced by fourteen manufacturers and sold under national brand names and private labels, each may also be available as retreads. Seeking to distinguish one from another, the most careful shopper finds insufficient instruction in available literature. He may read the few consumer magazines that report on tires, but these articles are neither definitive nor always up to date. There are no government publications on the subject, and industry literature is highly technical. As far as advertisements are concerned, they exemplify noninformation and misinformation. This deficiency is also characteristic of tire selling; in fact, an alliance between lack of standards and lack of consumer information overshadows tire merchandising.

No common terminology exists. Therefore the word "premium" can be used to describe any tire, regardless of its price or quality. The same is true of "supreme," "ultra premium," "deluxe," "first line," "second line," and so on. One company's premium tire may be inferior to another company's second line. Moreover, although "premium" connotes high quality, it may be a maker's lowest quality below "deluxe," "custom," and other superior-sounding categories. Yet, the industry's descriptive terms suggest grades or levels of quality.

Names mislead not only about quality, but also about construction and materials. A case in point is reference to ply, which is a layer of cord contained in the carcass. When cotton was used exclusively to make tire cord, four-plys were desirable for endurance. Despite the fact that rayon and nylon are stronger fibers pound for pound and can be as strong in two-ply construction as four-ply cotton, four-ply is still featured for all tires, sometimes in the phrase "two-ply four-ply rating." Far more important than ply is the type of fiber; denier, or thickness, of the fiber; how much strength it derives from special treatments and processing; the number of cord ends per inch of ply fabric; and the number of strands in the cord. Tires can be compared, in this respect, with carpeting. Carpet of bulked filament fibers that are strongly sewn (tufted) to the backing can produce stronger carpet than abundant wool staples sewn so loosely that they shed and leave bald spots.

The consumer may be further confused by the many trade names applied to the rubber used, such as Tufsyn Rubber, Duragen Rubber, Miracle Riv-Syn, Dynatuf Tread Rubber, among others. Often a fiber with a new name is said to be an advancement offering superior performance, but whether it is superior to the manufacturer's prior product or superior to products of competitors is not made clear.

Moreover, price is not a meaningful yardstick. "Manufacturers actually use different list prices: the no–trade-in price (dealers seldom attempt to sell at this price); and a suggested price to be used with trade-ins. The price . . . will probably be none of these, but another price determined by the local price situation and perhaps by [the consumer's] own bargaining power. The charge for replacement under the guarantee is prorated according to tread wear, but what [the consumer pays] is not a percentage of the price originally paid, as a rule, but of the code price, which is often higher. Thus, the guarantee may become worthless before it expires."

At the point of sale, the consumer gets insufficient enlightenment. A dealer or retail clerk in an auto supply store is often unable (or unwilling) to explain the difference between the brand he carries and others. He may distinguish the qualities (grades) of a particular brand, but this information is no basis for comparisons with other brands, since each has its own grades.

Even the one point about which the consumer feels sure—the size of the tire he needs—presents an element of uncertainty: whether he in fact gets that size. Although tire manufacturers have size standards, these standards allow so wide a degree of tolerance that a tire claiming to be one size may actually measure a whole size smaller. A serious hazard results if the consumer calculates the load capacity of his car on the basis of the tire size he requested but is actually riding on a smaller tire. Undersizing also is tantamount to overcharging. Assume, for example, that the consumer has asked and paid for a 9×14 at $40.30, but obtained an 8.50×14 which, properly sized, sells for $36.20. He paid an excess of $4.10. True, undersizing is not a widespread practice. However, the potential inherent in poor standards is as dangerous as no standards.

Standard sizes, a single grading system, and one laboratory testing procedure for determining basic features of quality and safety are necessary. Such standards should enable the consumer to compare these basic features: mileage, high-speed durability, body strength, tread width, body thickness, body durability, impact resistance and traction edges.

The Committee believes that Congress should pass legislation which requires minimum tire safety standards and prescribes tire performance grades.

MAINTENANCE AND REPAIR

Manufacturers lead the consumer to expect care-free performance from his car, but often he is disappointed. New-car buyers have complained that their vehicles were delivered with so many defects that after adjustments and repairs they were not new cars but repaired cars.

Most faults of new cars are traceable to the factory where poor quality control has shown itself to be a sorry by-product of the drive for profits. It seems to get worse as demand increases, according to a report by the *Wall Street Journal*, which said:

> Quality problems in the auto industry have been headline news in recent months. General Motors Corporation has recalled 16,000 of its 1965 Chevrolets to replace a defective door latch. Chrysler Corporation has written owners of 17,500 Dodges about needed repairs of a throttle linkage. Ford Motor Company has asked about 40,000 owners of 1965 Lincolns to bring in their cars to replace the brake fluid, and, last week, Ford said its dealers are asking 25,000 owners of 1966 Fords and 5,000 owners of 1966 Mercurys to return their cars for inspection for possible brake-line trouble.[5]

Because defective cars are often hazardous to drive, Senator Walter F. Mondale of Minnesota, has submitted the "fair warning" amendment to S.3005, the Traffic Safety Act of 1966. Explaining provisions of the bill, Senator Mondale said.

> My bill would require the manufacturer of automobiles to notify people who have cars which are defective. It places the burden of discovering the defect on the manufacturer because he has designed, produced, and inspected the automobile, and is in the best possible position to know of the defects in the automobile, and the remedies for correcting the defect. . . . [6]

Inaccurate odometers are one of the common defects. Assuming that the value of a used car is in part dependent on the miles it has been driven, an odometer reading that is higher than actual miles traveled deprives the customer of real value when his car is traded in. In a recent *Consumer Bulletin*, inaccurate odometers were found on all five 1966 automobiles tested. One tested model was found to be recording 5 per cent more mileage than actually traveled.

A better-designed locking system and tighter restrictions on master keys would benefit the consumer not only as individual but also as a taxpayer, since millions of dollars are spent annually to recover some 1,265 cars stolen daily throughout the country.

Car radios also raise problems on occasion. Some dealers reportedly prefer to install their own radios instead of those supplied and warranted by the factory because, they say, under the factory warranty it takes too long to get a defective radio replaced or repaired. Practiced by a reputable dealer, the substitution may work in favor of the consumer. However, less scrupulous dealers have been substituting what the trade calls "mongrel" radios to make a larger profit than on factory-installed units.

On the face of it, extended warranties and guarantees on cars provide additional protection for the consumer, at least if he is fully aware of the terms. But a big problem is precisely that—What are the terms? What is covered? What must be done to keep the warranty effective? The Chrysler 50,000-mile, five-year guarantee, for one, is supposed to go through several successive owners, if necessary. However, if the used car, when sold to the second owner, has an odometer that has been tampered with, that owner will think the car has more guaranteed mileage on it than is actually the case.

With new cars, one development that bears watching, as warranty periods grow longer and longer, is the potential limitation of choice of repairmen. To the extent the consumer is induced to feel obligated to have all maintenance on his car performed in the repair shop of the dealer from whom he purchased the vehicle—whether or not the terms of the warranty require him to do so—competition is weakened, ultimately to the detriment of consumers. The antitrust agencies should scrutinize this situation to be certain that any such developments do not hamper competition.

In used cars a special difficulty arises in the meaning of a guarantee to repair anything found defective at a charge for parts plus labor, allowing 15 per cent off regular prices. Since the "regular price" is seldom known to any individual and he therefore cannot know whether a 15 per cent discount is truly given, such terms should be banned from guarantees and warranties. As state consumer agencies have urged, a complete study should be made of warranties and guarantees covering new and used cars.

Unless the consumer is a mechanic or mechanically inclined, he can neither diagnose his car's ills nor judge the proficiency of repairs and whether the repair price was reasonable. So he must trust to the honesty and competence of the mechanic. The volume of complaints in this area makes clear that often this trust is misplaced.

One possible solution may lie in auto diagnostic centers. According to the American Automobile Association, fifty such centers are operating throughout the country. For a fee, the clinic certifies to the owner the true condition of his car and the true need for repairs. Although it lists the needed repairs, the clinic does not obligate the motorist to have the repairs made in its shop.

In addition to reducing unnecessary repair costs, such clinics can be used to arbitrate disputes between salesmen and customers over the trade-in values.

CONSUMER–DEALER–MANUFACTURER RELATIONS[7]

"Mounting Complaints of Poor Dealer Service" last fall stirred auto manufacturers to prod their dealers about service, reported the *Wall Street Journal*. In a lengthy article, the paper wrote:

> Never a particularly popular lot with the public, the dealers' reputation may now be worsening. Earlier this year, advertising executive David Ogilvy told a national convention of auto dealers about a special poll he had requested from the Gallup Organization. The survey showed that only 3 per cent of those interviewed considered new-car dealers "honest and trustworthy"—placing them, in the public esteem, well below some other frequently criticized groups that deal with consumers. . . .
>
> Complaints are coming largely on poor service, says an official of Chrysler Corp. Thomas A. Couple, a vice president of American Motors Corp., adds: "The plain fact is dealers aren't doing a good job of selling service." A growing number of customers agree; many find the red carpet laid out for them by dealer salesmen is yanked out under their feet after their cars have been delivered and found wanting.[8]

Customer problems with automobiles can concern the original manufacturer of the equipment and the car, the local dealer at the point of final sale, and both dealer and manufacturer. The customer is often buffeted between the dealer and manufacturer. Although many thoughtful industry spokesmen have criticized this, their comments have been to no avail.

Customers do not readily get satisfaction for their complaints and frequently get involved in a seemingly interminable round of correspondence. Or, the customer may be inconvenienced by lengthy, unproductive visits to the repair shop, visits which may even result in a loss of income when the automobile is the sole means of getting to work. The courtesy car arrangements of some dealers are not the general practice.

There is evidence that some undesirable and unethical practices in the sale of new and used automobiles result from a proliferation of dealerships throughout the country. At times this proliferation has been tolerated, if not caused, by the manufacturers themselves. For they have been known to sponsor new dealers in a market as a stimulant to the established dealers.

Manufacturers must take care not to have so many dealerships that some will have too little volume of new cars to provide a working profit for the concern. If dealers' profit margins become too slim, any tendency to engage in sharp practices to build up profit may be reinforced. At least one major manufacturer has been eliminating the less adequate and less profitable dealerships; and perhaps the whole industry would be improved if more stringent qualifications were attached to the granting of a dealer's franchise. . . .

SAFETY AND DESIGN

Dangers from either defects in manufacture or poor operating conditions are quite different from those which are inherent in design and exist no matter how precise the vehicle's assembly and care. This has not been made as clear as it should have been in recent congressional hearings and in numerous articles and books indicting the automobile industry. It must be emphasized, therefore, that cars can be designed not only to reduce accidents but also to reduce injuries and deaths. In the words of Representative James A. Mackay of Georgia:

> It is most important to understand that collisions are not synonymous with injury and death. Injury and death are, to a large extent, the result of ill-considered and hazardous interior (and exterior) design in automobiles. Changing this design is not particularly difficult, is not particularly complicated, nor is it particularly expensive.[9]

In the face of overwhelming evidence demonstrating the feasibility and practicability of designing safe automobiles, "the industry and its apologists [have been] forced to abandon the argument that the safety of the car could not be improved [or] to fall back to the prepared position that a safe car would be too expensive or so ugly no one would buy it."[10]

A survey by the Columbia Broadcasting System found 82 per cent of the participants wanted safety features as standard automobile equipment. Of these, 74 per cent said they could sacrifice style and convenience for safety features in order to retain price levels; 18 per cent said safety features should be added as standard equipment at increased prices. Only 5 per cent said safety features should be optional equipment. No opinion was expressed by 13 per cent.

That the industry has been forced to adopt safety innovations was demonstrated in *U.S. News & World Report,* which reported on 1967 safety innovations to be included during "another year of the sporty look." *U.S. News* stated that all but one of the safety feature items required by the General Services Administration on all 1967 cars bought for use by the federal government will "show up" on cars made in the United States. That last item, exhaust ("blow-by") devices, will be required by federal laws in 1968.[11]

The automobile makers' moral and ethical failures to the public are crystal clear. There are also human and economic losses to be laid at their doorstep. As President Johnson has said:

Each year 50,000 Americans die on our highways. Each year, 100,000 Americans are permanently disabled on our highways. Each year, nearly 4 million Americans are injured on our highways. . . . Another statistic—equally grim but not so familiar—is that since 1961, we have lost four times as many American servicemen in motor vehicle accidents as our enemies have been able to kill in all the fighting in Vietnam.

According to Richard L. Goen, senior operations analyst, Stanford Research Institute, who headed a study on highway safety, improvements in cars might reduce highway deaths by one-third.[12]

Automobile accidents cost an estimated $10 billion in 1965—in property damage; in loss of income due to absence from work; in legal, medical, and hospital costs; in costs of handling automobile insurance. This $10 billion is the equivalent of more than $200 for every American family, or more than $50 for every American man, woman, and child; nearly one-half of the cost of all new and used cars in 1965; more than the entire total of all doctor and dentist bills; about twice the sum spent for private education.

Public safety demands immediate and direct action in the form of federal legislation. Congress should pass legislation which prescribes safety features for cars and prohibits the sale of new cars that fail to include the prescribed safety features.

Notes

1. *The New York Times* (May 18, 1966).

2. *Consumer Reports,* September, 1965, p. 447.

3. U.S. House of Representatives, Subcommittee on Domestic Finance, Committee on Banking and Currency, 89th Cong., 1st Sess. 1965, "Investigation into Federal Service Finance Corporation," *Hearings,* pt. 1.

4. Sam Crowther and Irwin Winehouse, *Highway Robbery* (New York: Stein & Day, 1966), p. 74.

5. *Wall Street Journal* (April 25, 1966).

6. *Congressional Record,* U.S. Senate, April 5, 1966, p. 7213.

7. See Stewart Macauley, "Changing of Continuing Relationship between a Large Corporation and Those Who Deal with It: Automobile Manufacturers, Their Dealers, and the Legal System," *Wisconsin Law Review* (Summer, 1965), pp. 483–575, and (Fall, 1965), pp. 730–858.

8. *Wall Street Journal* (October 11, 1965).

9. *Congressional Record,* U.S. House of Representatives, May 18, 1966, p. 10453.

10. Jeffrey O'Connell and Arthur Meyers, *Safety Last* (New York: Random House, 1966), p. 111.

11. *U.S. News & World Report* (May 2, 1966), pp. 40–43.

12. *Ibid.* (May 27, 1966), p. 44.

20

WHAT THE HEALTH HUCKSTERS ARE UP TO

Changing Times

Two years ago on a day in June, John Bone, a seventy-eight-year-old farmer, walked into the office of a chiropractor in Shelbyville, Indiana, holding a postcard that said he was entitled to a free physical examination by "diagnostic specialists" who would be in town for one week only.

Mr. Bone had, in his words, "sprung" his back lifting some rocks on the farm and thought the local practitioner with the help of the visiting specialists could help him.

"So I went in," Mr. Bone recounted later, "and a lady said the doctor would see me in a minute. There were two doctors there (neither of them the local man) and in a little room the first one started to take my complaint on a card. I told him about my back and the pain seemed to be across my kidneys, and my stomach didn't feel good either and after supper a couple of times I had vomited. I had a little constipation, too. But all I wanted was an adjustment of my back. The doctor said all he did was take the history and give the examination. He took my blood pressure and that was all. I went into another room and this other fellow looked at my card and said right off I had to have an X ray for $10.

Reprinted from *Changing Times, the Kiplinger Magazine* (September, 1964), pp. 24–29.

"That didn't take long. Then he showed me two pictures and pointed out things I couldn't see. He said I had a bad liver and gall bladder and my kidneys weren't working right, but he had this wonderful machine that worked by colon irrigation and oxygen therapy, which he guaranteed would cure me in three months for $390, $35 discount if paid in cash.

"Well, that sure made me mad. I come in for a $5 office call and he tried to tell me I was falling apart. I told him my brother was an osteopath who would fix my back in twenty minutes and the whole thing was a fake and he was a damned crook. He offered to cut the fee in half but that only made me madder and I got out of there."

What John Bone sensed instinctively was that he had become embroiled in one segment of a many-faceted operation that annually relieves the American people of an estimated billion dollars for worthless nostrums, unnecessary pills and potions, "cures" for incurable ailments, and useless devices that pretend to diagnose or treat or both.

The health hucksters prey on the elderly, on persons afflicted with diseases like arthritis, cancer, and diabetes for which medical science has no sure answers, on the poor who can be taken in by offers of "free" diagnoses or trial treatments, on faddists, and on those whose vanity is sufficient to make them spend money on hair restorers, bust developers, potions alleged to increase sexual powers, complexion aids. In fact, they can take into camp just about everyone who doesn't bother to inform himself about what science can and can't do for human well-being and who doesn't stay on guard against smooth talk, high pressure, and rosy promises.

Some—like the outfit Mr. Bone got mixed up in briefly—are even able to fool an occasional physician or other health practitioner into believing that their nonsense is useful.

In a few cases, honest differences of opinion lead reputable medical men to push unorthodox, experimental treatments that have been officially rejected or are highly suspect.

John Bone was different from the majority of victims of quacks, or perhaps angrier than most. Usually people who have bitten and been taken are too ashamed to complain to law-enforcement agencies. Many won't admit their foolishness to their own doctors, a failure that can endanger their health even more.

Not Mr. Bone, though. His story goes on.

"Later in the day I met a friend and his wife had been through the same thing so we could see for certain it was all as crooked as a cow's hind leg. We went right to the police. They soon learned these fellows weren't licensed to practice and they went right up and arrested them."

That was not the end of the story by a long shot. Because postcards (10,000 of them) had been mailed throughout the Shelbyville area to advertise the traveling clinic, postal inspectors were able to gather evidence of mail fraud against a pair who had worked in California, Florida, and probably other states.

The results: Roy Wright DeWelles, age sixty, a one-time chiropractor from Kansas, was convicted by a federal district court in Indianapolis and sentenced last December 13 to ten years in prison. He has appealed his case, however, and is residing at his home at Pass Christian, the beautiful resort area near Gulfport, Mississippi. He remains under $10,000 bond pending the appeal.

Richard A. Broeringmeyer, DeWelles' accomplice who sometimes described himself as a naturopath, entered a plea of guilty to mail fraud charges and was sentenced to eighteen months in prison. He began serving his term in January. After more than fifteen years, DeWelles' remarkable machine, usually called the Detoxacolon, is no longer being sold to health practitioners at $2,500 a whack. But it is believed that beginning about 1948 DeWelles sold some 200 of the machines, taking in half a million dollars. He is also believed to have realized a million dollars in treatment fees, while the practitioners who bought the machines took in another million. In a single year—1955—DeWelles ran seventeen clinics in Florida like the Shelbyville one and took in at least $100,000 before the Florida State Board of Examiners moved in and local chiropractors stopped associating with him.

Undeterred, DeWelles in 1957 set up the Fremont Christian Clinic in Los Angeles and hired two aged, retired physicians to front for the operation. He concentrated on cancer patients and treated hundreds of them—at $1,000 each—with his machine and injections of unproved and unorthodox drugs. The business flourished, partly through the help of a radio evangelist (that's why the word "Christian" was used in the clinic name), until DeWelles and four associates were indicted in 1961 by a grand jury on charges of criminal conspiracy to cheat and defraud. After three months of stormy testimony, the trial ended in a hung jury and eventual acquittal for all defendants. Still pending against him in federal court in California is a charge of illegally shipping a drug in interstate commerce.

It was after this latter charge was brought against him that DeWelles started his traveling clinics in the Midwest and ran afoul of Mr. Bone and some other Shelbyville citizens.

At the trial in Indianapolis last winter, a faculty member from the Lincoln Chiropractic College in that city testified that DeWelles' machine, which was a pressure device to force water into the large intestine, was not a recognized form of therapy in the chiropractic profession. Medical testimony indicated that treatments with it could be dangerous for persons with ulcers, acute appendicitis, or colitis. There was testimony, too, that the X-ray pictures of the colon made by DeWelles were insufficient to diagnose many ailments. Yet, diagnose he did, everything from dermatitis to cancer, with only a blood-pressure measurement and the one X-ray to go on.

"A STUBBORN AND PERSISTENT BLIGHT"

That's how Anthony J. Celebrezze, Secretary of Health, Education and Welfare, characterized medical quackery recently. He had good reasons. Here are some of the startling statistics that go into the estimate of one billion dollars spent annually on useless or needless remedies:

A quarter of a billion dollars spent on quack remedies by some 6,000,000 of the nation's arthritis sufferers (half of all those stricken). Ten thousand persons are said to be selling potions and devices to arthritics.

Some 4,000 people make $50,000,000 a year on "cancer treatments." (Harry M. Hoxsey alone is said to have taken in $50,000,000 in ten years.)

At least $300,000,000 is spent each year by persons who prescribe patent medicines for themselves or go in for food fads.

Ten million Americans spend $350,000,000 a year on vitamins and minerals they probably don't need. (The fact is that most people get all the nutrients they need in their regular diets. Yet one company selling a food supplement door-to-door increased its gross income from $2,000,000 to $8,000,000 in one year.)

Already, the meter is ticking toward the billion-dollar mark without a mention of no-account diabetes treatments, mail-order dental plates and eye glasses, phony hemorrhoid treatments, "fountain of youth" products, gadgets, pills and "plans" to control obesity, and other schemes to separate people from their money by delusion or outright trickery.

A great many people—more today than ever before—are attacking the problem of how to keep consumers from throwing their money away in their search for health. Last October the second Congress on Medical Quackery gathered together experts from all over the country to consider how best to combat the problem. The American Medical Association has set up a special committee in addition to its long-existing investigation service. The United States Senate's committee on aging has held two hearings aimed at deciding whether new laws are needed to protect oldsters (who are especially vulnerable) from health frauds.

The Federal Trade Commission, the Food and Drug Administration, and the Post Office inspection service are stepping up efforts to enforce laws. Many prosecutions—as well as education programs—are under way.

But it is all a slow business. Due process of law takes a long time. It must if it is to be fair, but many people are impatient.

Dr. Frederick R. Stare, chairman of the Board of Nutrition, School of Public Health, Harvard University, and long in the forefront of the fight against nutritional quackery, expressed this impatience when he testified before the Senate committee with these words: "The first point that I would like to make is that for a naïve person, as far as government and regulations are concerned, I just cannot understand why it takes so damn long for our regulatory agencies to regulate."

THE "ELECTROMAGNETIC ERA"

Kenneth L. Milstead, Ph.D., special assistant to the commissioner of FDA, is hopeful that the heyday of fake medical devices that pretend to diagnose or heal by producing a weak magnetic field or emitting short-wave radio frequencies has finally ended. A series of court decisions bars use of a number of such worthless devices and allows the FDA to seize as many of them as it can find in use.

But the electromagnetic era has had a long life. It began in 1796 with the theories of Dr. Elisha Perkins, who thought that two metallic rods pulled downward over a diseased part of the body would yank out the illness. One of his customers was George Washington.

Schemes involving such devices got their biggest boost from the invention of the telephone and the electric light (which made possible the success of Dr. Hercules Sanche's Electropoise and Polizer for the "spontaneous cure of disease"). Later the radio helped Dr. Albert Abrams of San Francisco originate his system of Radionics, based on the theory that all disease is a "disharmony of electronic oscillation." Dr. Abrams, who died in 1924 leaving an estate of $2,000,000, operated the College of Electronic Medicine.

Dr. Abrams's clinic was taken over after his death by Fred J. Hart and operated as the Electronic Medical Foundation. Until the law clamped down, the clinic worked like this, according to facts the government developed.

Practitioners from all over the country would take a sample of blood from their patients and mail it on a piece of blotting paper to Hart's clinic in San Francisco. At the clinic the blotter would be placed in a device called the Radioscope, which was supposed to measure the "emanations" associated with different diseases given off by the dried blood. Metal plates connected with the box would be held by a clinic employee called a "reagent." The machine's operator would stroke the employee's abdomen with a plastic wand. When the wand "stuck" to a particular spot, an "electronic reaction" was indicated. This would tell the operator the exact identity, location and significance of any disease afflicting the patient—perhaps thousands of miles away. The practitioner who had sent

in the blood sample would be informed by postcard of the disease and
its treatment, and he would then proceed to treat the patient with one of
Hart's machines, which he had previously purchased.

There were thirteen different types of treatment machines: Oscilloclast, Oscillotron, Regular Push Button Shortwave Oscilloclast, Sweep
Oscillotron, Sinusoidal Four-in-One Shortwave Oscillotron, Galvanic Five-
in-One Shortwave Oscillotron, Depolaray, Depolaray Chair, Depolaray
Junior, New Depolaray Junior, Depolatron, Depolatron Chair and Elec-
tropad.

All of the machines were declared by FDA to be completely worthless, and the diagnostic device (the Radioscope) flunked its every test
during the FDA investigation. It couldn't tell the difference between
colored water and blood, between the blood of a living man and that of
a dead one. Blood submitted from an amputee resulted in a report of
arthritis in the foot and ankle the man had lost several years before.
Blood from a rooster brought a diagnosis of sinus infection and dental
caries.

Hart did not contest an injunction procedure, and the machines were
declared illegal under a consent degree. He is now director of the National Health Federation. An official spokesman for this organization has
stated that "the top echelon of the AMA and the FDA have apparently
joined hands in a deliberate, well-organized, criminal conspiracy to enforce a medical monopoly in all matters of health upon the American
people."

Robert W. Ellis, president of Ellis Research Laboratories, Inc., of
Chicago, for years sold a machine called a Micro-Dynameter for as much
as $875 to health practitioners. This device is a fairly sensitive galvanom-
eter mounted in an impressive cabinet. It was claimed that the machine
could discover disease in living tissue by measuring electrical current
produced by the abnormality. Actually, tests showed that the amount of
current flowing between the electrodes of the device only measured the
amount of perspiration on the skin of the person holding the electrodes.

The government sued to ban the machine from interstate commerce
and won its case in Chicago. An appeals court upheld the decision, and
in 1962 the Supreme Court refused to review the matter.

The court of appeals in upholding the lower court's ruling against
Ellis used this language: "The Micro-Dynameter is not safe for use even
in the hands of a licensed practitioner. A device whose labeling claims it
to be an aid in diagnosing as many diseases as this one, when in fact it
is not, is unsafe for use no matter who uses it. . . ."

After the court action, more than 800 of the machines were volun-
tarily destroyed by those who had purchased them, and another 300 were
seized. Some 5,000 more are believed to have been sold prior to the court
ruling.

Another group of devices—Neurolinometers, Electron-O-Rays, Quto-Electronic Instruments and Radioclasts—were all manufactured in Tiffin, Ohio, and distributed by Toftness Clinic at Cumberland, Wisconsin. The clinic, operated by Irving N. Toftness, a chiropractor, and members of his family, was designed to teach practitioners how to use the devices, which were sold for as much as $1,200 each. A federal district court in Toledo banned the devices in 1962, and since then about fifty Neurolinometers have been seized and twenty voluntarily destroyed. One seizure case is still being contested.

These are by no means all the names on the FDA's list of questionable health devices. Seizures have also been made of Royal Lee's Endocardiograph and the E-Meter used by L. Ron Hubbard and his Academy of Scientology. Both cases are being fought out in the courts, with Lee and Hubbard defending the worth of their machines. These and others are all based on the electromagnetic theory of diagnosis and treatment.

UNPROVED CANCER REMEDIES

When a disease cannot always be cured by orthodox medical men, when causes and means of treatment are vague and even diagnosis difficult, it becomes easy for the unorthodox to sell their theories. The tragedy is that a belief in them keeps so many despairing cancer victims from getting the early and proper treatment they must have to survive.

The American Cancer Society has evaluated negatively nearly twenty remedies promoted for treatment of cancer in the past three years. It has, in the words of Dr. Roald N. Grant, director of professional education for the society, attempted to be "open-minded as well as hard-headed." This is not easy when responsible scientific thought cannot always agree on which treatment is worthwhile and which is worthless. Moreover, the lay public is unusually—and understandably—prone to try unproved cancer remedies no matter how foolish.

All logic goes out the window when people truly believe that cancer can be cured with coffee enemas, a special diet that will also help you to live to 150, an all-grape diet, a head-shrinking compound from the Amazon. But some of the remedies sound more plausible than those, and a few are even backed by members of the medical profession who are convinced that they have an answer to cancer.

Hoxsey and others employed potassium iodide on cancer patients "to restore the body to physiological normalcy." Hoxsey's pills also contained licorice, red clover, burdock root, stillingia root, barberis root, poke root, cascara, Aromatic USP 14, prickly ash bark, and buckthorn bark. For external cancer Hoxsey used the same pills plus—as occasion demanded—

a yellowish powder containing arsenic sulphide, yellow precipitate, sulphur, and talc; or a red paste with antimony trisulphide, zinc chloride, and blood root; or a clear liquid made of trichloroacetic acid.

A Michigan physician developed some "antitoxins" which he called Glyoxylide, Malonide, and Benzoquinone. His therapy consisted of a dietary cleansing regimen, enemas, and injections. Glyoxylide, the chief method of therapy, contained one part of partially oxidized inositol (a vitamin) to a trillion parts of distilled water.

The most recent—and right now the best known—of what the American Cancer Society classifies as unproved remedies is Krebiozen. Krebiozen powder, according to the government, is mainly creatine, an amino acid derivative that is plentifully available from meat in an ordinary diet. The human body of itself produces in twenty-four hours 100,000 times as much creatine as the drug's label says there is in one Krebiozen ampule.

Neither the American Cancer Society nor the FDA has found acceptable evidence that any of these drugs—and others like Laetrile, Mucorhicin and Millrue—have "objective benefit" in the treatment of cancer in humans. In the case of Krebiozen, the Justice Department has been reviewing evidence gathered by the FDA to determine whether official action should be taken. Court proceedings have been instituted against the other three.

AND THE LIST GOES ON AND ON

The pain of arthritis can be alleviated by proper treatment, but no cure is yet possible and very often pain returns from time to time even with good medical care. These facts make the arthritis sufferer an easy victim.

Jerry Walsh, special educational consultant for the Arthritis and Rheumatism Foundation and himself a sufferer for more than twenty years of crippling arthritis, recently told the Senate committee on aging, "I can guarantee any of you gentlemen or anyone in this room that if you are in this bed of pain with arthritis, you will try anything to stop the pain, at any cost. You say, 'What have I got to lose?' "

The Oxydonor is a simple metal disc attached to a cylinder. To "reverse death process to life process," you attach the disc to the part of your body affected with arthritis and immerse the cylinder into cold water. The amazing gadget was sold—at $30 to $35 each—from 1892 to 1958. The Vrilium tube, or magic spike, is a brass container with one two-thousandths of 1 per cent barium chloride in it. It fetched $300!

Dr. Ernest T. Krebs Sr. of the John Beard Memorial Foundation in San Francisco was criminally prosecuted and fined in federal district court for distributing what he called Pangamic Acid or "vitamin B$_{15}$" and Vi-Cardia as cures for arthritis and heart disease. It was also Krebs who produced and distributed Laetrile for the treatment of cancer.

Liefcort is an alleged arthritis remedy manufactured in Canada by an American physician, who is a fugitive from United States justice for peddling a baldness "cure." It is highly dangerous and cannot be brought into this country legally, but many arthritis sufferers go to Canada and smuggle in their own supply. One such was a seventy-one-year-old woman who developed severe internal bleeding and died within four months after starting to take the pills.

Liefcort, which is made in the home of its developer, Robert E. Liefman, M.D., contains highly potent hormones, which should never be used without close supervision of a doctor.

Other remedies promoted for arthritis include such unlikely offerings as bee venom, "immune milk," sea brine, alfalfa, uranium pads, and copper bracelets. They are sold through the mail, door-to-door, and through so-called "clinics" by a small army of what the Arthritis and Rheumatism Foundation calls the "misery merchants."

HOW TO SPOT A QUACK

The moral to all of these horror stories is simple: Don't get taken. But it isn't always so simple to tell truth from fiction.

Oliver Field, head of the department of investigation of the American Medical Association, has long preached the application of six rules for spotting the outright quack:

If he uses a special or "secret" machine or formula he claims can cure diseases.

If he guarantees a quick cure.

If he advertises or uses case histories and testimonials to promote his cure.

If he clamors constantly for medical investigation and recognition.

If he claims medical men are persecuting him or are afraid of his competition.

If he tells you surgery or X-rays or drugs cause more harm than good.

21

VAN DOREN AS VICTIM:
STUDENT REACTION

Gladys Engel Lang
and *Kurt Lang*

On November 2, 1959, Charles Van Doren, the egghead idol of millions of television quiz fans, confessed to participation in a gigantic hoax, which enabled him to earn $129,000 by besting opponents on the program "Twenty-One." As it turned out, he was able to do this because he had received in advance correct answers that were denied to others. For a week or two, Van Doren was front-page news, the subject of small talk everywhere. In the prominence given it, the issue of Van Doren's duplicity overrode both foreign affairs and domestic issues. Though it is beyond question that the Van Doren exposure cut very deeply, the exact nature of the public reaction can stand pinning down.

Van Doren seems to have been pretty much absolved from guilt by the verdict of public opinion, in spite of the fact that professors and the academic community clearly condemned him. Moreover, the New York City press, in the days following his confession, tended to treat Van Doren as a tragic hero victimized by the television industry. Television and radio

Reprinted from *Studies in Public Communication*, 3 (Summer, 1961), pp. 50–58.

were perhaps somewhat less ready to place specific blame on anybody. But among the public at large, there was a large residue of sympathy for the fallen idol. According to a Sindlinger survey, only 18.6 per cent found Van Doren most to blame, with the overwhelming majority singling out the producers, the sponsors, and the network in that order of frequency. Students at Columbia University, where Van Doren taught, appeared to share this readiness to exonerate him. When the trustees accepted his resignation, students called a protest meeting which received wide television coverage.

This small study is based on a questionnaire administered to 225 students in nine classes in two institutions of higher learning both located in New York City. In asking students to express themselves in writing on various facets of the affair, we hoped to get fresh reactions before views had become hardened into an official collective definition and before the line college students were "expected" to take could be culled from their remarks as well as from those of their favorite commentators and columnists.

The students queried in this investigation are probably a somewhat better cross section of college students than the demonstrators at Columbia University. While no claim of representativeness is made, we can point out that (1) the sample included students in a private and in a public institution; (2) the questionnaire was administered in several sections of a required liberal arts curriculum in a core course in communication arts (required of students majoring in journalism, dramatics, and other trade subjects), and in sections of social science classes, some mostly for education majors and others primarily for majors in sociology; and (3) the students, ranging from freshmen to seniors, exhibited varying scholastic abilities. On the debit side, it must be noted that the sample was confined to New York City with only a small proportion of resident students rather than commuters.

The questionnaire covered, in its first part, certain background data, television viewing habits (especially regarding "Twenty One" and other quiz shows), prior involvement in discussions of the Van Doren affair, and exposure to mass-media coverage of the confession. The key part of the questionnaire listed seven cases in which public figures had been exposed in, or confessed to, some wrongdoing. The student was asked to assess the gravity of each "mistake," explaining his reasoning in defining it as greater than, less than, or comparable to that of Van Doren.

STUDENT REACTION

Students, like the population as a whole, were inclined to blame the sponsors, network, or producers more than Van Doren, but hardly because they were indignant at the industry. The most striking aspect of their responses is the readiness with which they forgave Van Doren and extended him their sympathy. When responses to the questionnaire were coded and tabulated, it was found that only one out of seven students (14 per cent) openly condemned Van Doren. When the remaining responses (86 per cent) were classified, it was found that they divided just about equally into three groups: (1) those completely sympathetic to Van Doren who saw no personal wrong in what he had done (26 per cent); (2) those who recognized that Van Doren shared some minor responsibility for his participation in the hoax, but were completely ready to forget and forgive (27 per cent); and (3) those who were sympathetic to Van Doren, but expressed some mild misgivings about his role in the affair (33 per cent). Six-sevenths of the students, then, can be classified as essentially sympathetic. To all of them Van Doren had acted the part of the tragic hero, caught by the force of circumstances greater than himself and finally overpowered by them. By publicly confessing, he had demonstrated his sincerity and thereby vindicated himself.

THE VICTIM

We begin by examining the reasoning employed in exonerating Van Doren; i.e., the extenuating circumstances which in the view of those queried mitigated his responsibility. Those students sympathetically inclined toward Van Doren drew on any one or more of six criteria:

1. *Legality.* Van Doren was absolved on the grounds that he had done nothing illegal. Some students said, for example, "He didn't steal; he was offered the money." In the same vein, some students who ignored the illegality of lying before a grand jury commended him for "having told the congressional committee the truth."

2. *Intent to do harm.* Van Doren had had no harmful intent; whatever deficiency in judgment he revealed, his motives, at least, had been honorable. The most common way of putting it was that "he didn't deliberately harm anybody."

3. *Moral realism.* Van Doren, whatever his motives, had done no harm because the deception occurred while he was acting as an entertainer. Said one, "He did not represent himself as anyone but a man with a phenomenal memory. He gave the public what it wanted. I believe that theatrics of this type aren't really so bad. Anyone stupid enough to believe most of show-biz's representations deserves to be fooled." Not all expressed the same cynicism, but simply insisted that the sponsor had won an audience that felt it had been entertained. The only harm that had come was to Van Doren. "He only risked his own job" was a phrase employed.

4. *Cast the first stone.* The reluctance of students to cast the first stone helped absolve Van Doren. Again the responses ranged from tender-minded indulgence to complete cynicism. The former pleaded that Van Doren was only human. His act on "Twenty-One," declared one student, "was a phase of human character and personality. I believe that the human race in general really shares his guilt. People do not put themselves in his position, but they are always ready to criticize. Perhaps some would have said 'no' when asked to take the bribe but how many would have regretted it?" The cynical version is capsuled in the phrase, "It is human nature to look for any easy buck."

5. *Moral relativism.* Students, insisting that there are no moral absolutes, shrank from any condemnation. One cannot judge a person's actions, they argued, but only understand them. For example, it was asked, "How can anyone say whether a man's acts are good, bad, or indifferent if they don't know his own principles and values?"

6. *Social determinism.* The cards were seen to be stacked against Van Doren so overwhelmingly that he was left with no choice. In the first place, Van Doren had to play by the rules prevailing in the world of mass entertainment. In the second place, unscrupulous producers, themselves victims of the tyranny of ratings, tempted him. Finally, Van Doren as well as those who collaborated in the hoax were all victims of a corrupt society. Since everybody (or societal standards) are to blame, Van Doren escapes without blame. We choose only a few of the many quotes that illustrate this point of view:

In the final analysis, Van Doren is not alone to blame. Van Doren, being the erudite man that he is, accepted the money probably because of his "low" salary at Columbia ("low" in the sense of not being commensurate with his intellectual abilities). . . . One might also say that the present status of teachers' salaries is also to blame, where it *forces* a man of such education and intellectual ability as Van Doren to do such a thing.

He was guilty of "selling his name" (which is, after all, what the producers found so attractive). It is unfortunate that a man of his prestige and position found it *necessary* to do so.

This much I'll say. If our society, yours and mine, if the public at large feels offended, by God they have it coming! But, unfortunately, apathy will reign supreme once more and nothing will be done to evaluate the sorely deficient educational system, the pitifully low cultural standards of this country. Moses Hadas in his talk on this campus said that "impeccable" taste was the prime characteristic of the cultured man in ancient Greece. Our taste is revealed in "The $64,000 Question" and "Twenty-One." Acquire culture vicariously! Diderot said if a provincial were to stick his hand into the cage of a lion and got bitten, would you blame the provincial or the lion? This is the question I'm pondering now.

THE BETRAYAL

The small minority who defied Van Doren's duplicity as a major rather than minor offense did so for one of two distinct reasons: (1) They saw in his performance a betrayal of the public trust; or (2) having been quiz fans, they felt personally betrayed.

The strongest moral indignation was expressed by quiz fans who had idolized Van Doren. There was a positive association between the number of quiz programs a student regularly watched and his degree of indignation. Still, in speaking of his offense, they aimed their indignation at the fact that the *public*, not they themselves, had been taken:

> He was not forced to appear on the program. A man of his intelligence and position can be expected to know when a hoax purely for entertainment ends and when a great deception begins. He emphasized his guilt by lying all the time, until now, about his part in the hoax. . . . Van Doren at this point seems as guilty as the producers since he developed a nation-wide admiration and used it to maintain his innocence.

A much larger group saw Van Doren's betrayal in less impersonal terms; i.e., as a betrayal of the academic profession, as a misuse of television, etc. Hence they did not consider Van Doren as the unfortunate victim of sharp operators. These feelings were elaborated by them:

> Considering the position he occupied as an educator, his actions would have to be condemned. Examples of exemplary conduct are to be set by people in positions enabling them to have an influence on future human behavior. Again, with the present-day stress on the development of intellectual areas, his action tends to depreciate the whole reason behind the stress, emphasizing use of nefarious rather than honest means to achieve status.

> The public never harbors the thought of associating education on a high level with dishonesty of educators. Van Doren's action has therefore unconsciously promoted this association.

Clearly, those who recognized the public character of his offense were forced to condemn Van Doren's actions. They stressed also that the decision to take part in the fraud, whatever the temptation, was Van Doren's and Van Doren's alone. The son of a respected scholar and himself a scholar, he could hardly plead moral ignorance. If anything, more should be demanded of him. He harmed many people, said one, when he "used the mass media to cheat the public, lied under oath, lowered the respect due the teaching profession and the intellect, and consciously chose to commit a moral wrong."

PERSONAL VERSUS PUBLIC MORALITY

The basis on which students arrived at their moral judgment becomes clearer when their assessment of Van Doren's "mistake" is compared with the seven other "mistakes" they were asked to assess. We were able to construct a Personal Offense Score for every student. Every mistake judged graver than that committed by Van Doren was scored as +1; every mistake judged less grave was scored as −1 If the two were considered "comparable," the scoring was 0. Ergo, a total score of +7 indicated that, by comparison to these other offenses, that of Van Doren appeared very minor, while a total score of −7 indicated a rather severe judgment against Van Doren. By the same token, an overall score of 0 could mean either that Van Doren's offense was judged more serious than half the others or that it was comparable in every instance.

Beginning with the "mistake" that students as a group judged most severely, the seven other "mistakes" are given in their ascribed order of severity; this is not the order in which they appeared in the questionnaire. The figure set in brackets behind each "mistake" represents the number of students who judged it graver than Van Doren's minus the number who judged it a lesser offense.

1. A successful candidate for United States Representative admitted that he had lied during the campaign about his opponent's being a Communist. (152)

2. A college student revealed that he had copied and sold questions of an upcoming New York State Regents Examination. (118)

3. A White House aide accepted a personal gift from a firm trying to get a defense contract from the government. (97)

4. An unknown artist painted original pictures in the style of a seventeenth-century Dutch master and, after certification by experts, sold them as that master's work. (76)

5. A public figure went to jail for having lied before a congressional committee about his past political associations. (62)

6. A United States Senator admitted that for several years he had received from a group of supporters a sum of money to help him meet his expenses in office. (36)

7. A real estate broker reported that he cleaned up a small fortune when he bought up land after being tipped off on plans for a slum clearance project on the site. (−36)

All but one of the seven "mistakes" were judged more severely than Van Doren's. The exception is the tip-off exploited by the real estate operator. The explanation is hardly to be found in the superficial similarity between receiving the two kinds of inside tips; other offenses were more often judged "comparable." It lies rather in the students' ability to visualize clearly the *personal* harm inflicted. In general, the greater the personal harm that could be imagined, the more severe the judgment of the student. Respondents tended to discount as "harmless" the kind of white-collar offense where direct harm to others was not apparent; i.e., where the individual harmed could not be directly identified. The majority of students did not assess the "crimes" in terms of their social or public implications. This is borne out not only by inspection of the rank order but comes out even more clearly in the explanations offered for their judgments.

For example, judgments of the United States Representative who falsely accused his opponent of Communism was so severe because students saw clearly that somebody could get hurt: "The candidate endangers the life chances of his opponent by accusing him of being a Communist. Whose life chances did Van Doren endanger except perhaps his own?" The fact that the sums Van Doren won might have been garnered by others more honest occurred to very few and, when recognized, made no difference. Again, in reading students' attitudes toward the theft and sale of the Regents Examination, one gets the impression that it was the failure to make answers available to everybody, thus giving some an unfair advantage in the exam (an extremely important determinant for entrance into college and attainment of scholarships) that accounted for the gravity of the offense. Thus, "Van Doren's offense did not actually cause any real harm (except to dignity) of those involved but the student's action would cause invalidation of the exam, thereby wasting time and effort of those taking the exam [if discovered] and a general inaccuracy of grading [if not discovered]."

The party harmed, whether it was the firm's losing a defense contract, the art dealer paying for a portrait that was a fake though supposedly original, etc., is usually cited as a reason for judgment. The items form something in the way of a cumulative scale, with the person's judging the least reprehensible item as a worse crime than Van Doren's also likely to judge the others more severely. Specific points of view somewhat extraneous to the case at hand, however, prevent the scale from being more reproducible than it is.

In particular, the "liberal-conservative" dimension affects judgments on several items. The item in which the largest number saw an analogy to Van Doren was the fake testimony of a congressional committee witness. Van Doren himself appeared to some as the scapegoat of a congressional witch-hunt. Because of their liberal outlook also, some saw visible harm in the actions of a speculator.

For instance, in the case of the White House aide's accepting a gift, an occasional student saw a specific "third party" being injured by the action; that is, another company which might have gotten the contract. In general, however, the Sherman Adams case was recent enough to affect the student's judgment according to his political beliefs. Also, many students judged lying before the congressional committee about past political affiliations the least offensive of the "mistakes." This was the crime which the largest number saw as comparable to that of Van Doren. Many introduced extraneous material into the question in the effort to mitigate its seriousness. "The public figure might have been trying to protect persons he felt innocent of guilt," was a typical interpretation. Others agreed with the student who wrote, "I believe a man's personal associations should be kept known to that person alone and if he doesn't wish to reveal the truth about his associations he has the privilege to do so." Van Doren, for these students, was also a victim of congressional inquiry, even more so than the man who went to jail for lying. Van Doren, "when summoned by the congressional committee did not perjure himself. Instead he told the truth." Thus the students, as "liberals," converted both into men suffering for their principles.

Though so many saw the real estate broker's transactions as his own business, a few socially conscious students looked upon this kind of corruption as one of the most serious offenses listed. Yet even here they translated its effects into personal harm: "There could be the possibility of his doing a great deal of harm to some of the people affected. For example, a child continues to live in the slums and as a result commits a crime for which he is sent to jail for the rest of his life."

THE BASES OF SYMPATHY

To account for student reaction, we offer first a sociological explanation. To say that there is an area of public life in a state of anomie and not subject to any recognized code of behavior is neither new nor particularly enlightening. While it is true that the Van Doren affair, more than anything else, helped dramatize the lack of effective regulation that prevailed in the field of television, it is also true that people were unable to see just how the television scandals represented any departure from the kind of business ethics they were willing to put up with. Lacking objective moral norms, the individual falls back on personal ones. Thus the majority of students, "liberals" and "conservatives" alike, apply a particularistic standard. Having been impressed with the need to succeed, the success of others, unless a personal offense to themselves or a third person is involved, serves as the reaffirmation of standards that are primarily personal. The politically liberal student is ready to see in the practices of the television industry a justification of Van Doren. At least this is a possibility for all those who do not feel personally betrayed.

From a psychological viewpoint, the public reaction that treated Van Doren more as martyr than offender is more than plausible. The fund of goodwill with which Van Doren's confession was met indicates some kind of identification. In asking forgiveness for Van Doren, people are, in effect, asking forgiveness for themselves. Van Doren had not played by the rules; yet he went on the quiz program as a representative of the academic world—supposedly a disinterested seeker after truth. His behavior proved that he could be bought. Not wishing to face the consequences of living in a world that stresses success and rewards it, even if it is attained by violating the rules, students identified with him, the victim, against a more formal moral code they never made. The reaction to Van Doren represents something similar to and yet different from the scapegoating motif. In scapegoating, the individual casts his sins on a scapegoat and then, to purge himself of moral guilt, seeks punishment of the victim. In the Van Doren case, the student identified with the scapegoat because in sympathizing with him he made common cause against the overly restrictive (as he defined them) moral dictates of society.

Finally, the universe from which our respondents came must not be overlooked. They were, after all, college students. In this milieu, they were being exposed to certain philosophical beliefs. Among these is the widely prevailing viewpoint that social determinism is the equivalent of moral relativism and that, in view of this, to make demands on the individual that are hard to live up to is somehow unfair. The influence of the doctrine of cultural relativism is especially evident in classes queried which contained a high proportion of majors in sociology.

These classes also contained a higher proportion of seniors. Not one of forty-three from these classes was in the group critical of Van Doren. The suggestion is offered for what it is worth: Social determinism not well understood leads students to locate responsibility in external circumstances; and in this instance led them to define Van Doren, whose side they took, as the underdog.

Each of the two authors of this paper were also participant observers. As such we can testify that in these two institutions the issue was discussed in many classrooms and that the overwhelming majority of the faculty (not only those in the social sciences) felt strongly enough about the Van Doren affair to lecture the students in quite negative terms. Many students responded by becoming rather ashamed of their initial pro-Van Doren sentiment. One-third of our respondents could be queried only on November 5, two days after the confession had made headlines. The percentage critical of Van Doren's action rose appreciably between the first and second day of administration, a difference not accounted for by differences in the composition of the classes.

At least among the students of two institutions, the faculty appears to have been partly successful in molding student opinion concerning

Van Doren. The idea that certain objective social norms must be defended even if, realistically, they are sometimes hard to live up to or that one might demand more from an academic person, especially one who came from a renowned literary family, is the kind of "undemocratic" thought alien to most students. One observes in mild form the pattern of guilt evasion whereby persons make common cause against the overly restrictive dictates of society.

22

PUBLIC ATTITUDES TOWARD A FORM OF
WHITE-COLLAR CRIME

Donald J. Newman

> Surely there are crimes of different kinds; but among
> all these kinds, there is, no less surely, a common ele-
> ment. The proof of this is that the reaction which
> crimes call forth from society, in respect of punish-
> ment, is, save for differences of degree, always and
> ever the same. The unity of effect shows the unity
> of cause.—*Emile Durkheim*

The inclusion of the concept of "white-collar crime" into the subject
matter of criminology has, of course, necessitated revisions of formerly
popular theories of criminal behavior and has redirected criminological
research to include white-collar offenses and offenders within its framework. Only bare beginnings have been made. By its nature, white-collar
crime is difficult to study; laws and offenses are complex and many times
violators are corporations rather than persons and are not to be found
conveniently housed in prisons awaiting the researcher. Furthermore,
white-collar crime is not an entity. There are many different variations of
occupational duplicity, ranging from embezzlement to the illegal formation of cartels. Research to date, with the exception of Sutherland's
definitive study, has concentrated chiefly on embezzlement and violations
of wartime regulations. The purpose of most of this research has been to
describe the violations, defend their inclusion as "real crimes" and thus

Reprinted from *Social Problems*, 4 (January, 1953), pp. 228–232.

a fit subject for criminologists, and to explain both the causes and the effects of such crimes in our culture.

The purpose of the present research is to deal with a somewhat different issue; namely, the reactions of a sample of citizens, some of them victims, all of them potential victims, to a certain form of white-collar crime. In this case, the offenses chosen were violations of the Federal Food, Drug and Cosmetic Act, revised 1938. All offenses used in the study pertained to food. A sample of consumers was asked to judge certain selected cases, not in terms of guilt or innocence, for all cases represented convictions, but in terms of how they would treat, or more likely punish, the offender in the cases. The consumers' responses were compared with actual decisions in the cases and with possible decisions provided in the federal law. The general hypothesis underlying the research was that consumer judgments would be more severe than actual administrative decisions and would, in fact, approximate punishments meted out for more conventional criminal offenses such as larceny or burglary.

PURPOSE OF JUDGING PURE FOOD LAW VIOLATIONS

Violations of food legislation were selected as the basis of this study primarily because they represent a form of white-collar offense which directly affects everyone in the society. To be sure, violations in restraint of trade, patent infringement, rebating, and other such crimes eventually affect practically all citizens, but harmful results are less direct than in cases of food adulteration and are concealed in increased prices, poorer selection of commodities, and other complex and less visible ways. Then too, food law violations represent a fairly "old" type of white-collar crime, dating from the original legislation of 1906, and is a type of offense occurring during peace as well as war. Presumably, public condemnation of violators of wartime regulations is more severe than in peacetime, since in war the public is more strongly united against common enemies and such violations are, in effect, forms of treason, or less strongly, profiteering. Both Clinard and Hartung have pointed to the high degree of public support of wartime regulations and the rather harsh public attitudes toward black-market cases dealt with civilly rather than by criminal prosecution.[1] The lack of consensus surrounding the federal regulation of business in peacetime is, however, a different matter. The open conflicts in Congress, by the press and radio, and on the debating forum concerning the passage of pure food laws raise doubt as to public support of this legislation. While no one wishes to eat adulterated food, of course, a great deal of lobbyist and advertising pressure was brought to oppose federal regulation of food manufacture. However, it is proposed here that, facing the fact of adulterated food, the consumer will react with severity against the violator regardless of how he may feel about regulatory legislation in abstract.

SELECTION AND PRESENTATION OF
CASES FOR JUDGMENT

Six cases of food law violation were randomly selected from the files of a federal District Attorney, abstracted, and presented in questionnaire form to a sample of consumers. The six cases represented three types of violation: misbranding, distasteful but not physically harmful adulteration (termed "aesthetic" adulteration), and physically harmful adulteration. Cases were abstracted and appeared to the consumer as follows:

> *Case I:* The _____ Canning Company and _____, owner, were found guilty of violating the Federal Food, Drug and Cosmetic Act in that low-grade peas were canned, branded, and sold as more expensive, high-grade, "fancy" peas. First conviction for the company. However, on the same day, three other canning companies owned by the same person were found guilty of the same offense.

> *Case II:* The _____ Dairy Products Company was found guilty of violating the Pure Food Law in that a pasteurized American cheese food that they manufactured and sold was found to contain maggots, cow hairs, cow manure, rodent hairs, and insect fragments. First offense.

> *Case III:* The _____ Company manufactured and sold a common milk food product containing a poisonous substance not necessary in the manufacture of the product. The poison was a boron compound. Although not ordinarily fatal, the amount contained in this sample could result in severe nausea and repeated doses lead to intestinal disorders. First offense.

Three other cases similar to these completed the questionnaire. Below each of the first three cases appeared a list of possible penalties ranging from "no penalty" through "a warning should be given" and "the product should be seized and destroyed" to fines, probation, jail sentences and to "persons responsible should be sentenced to _____ years in prison." Consumers were asked to check the punishment they felt to be proper or to write, in space allowed, any punishment or other treatment not covered on the list.

Each of the additional three cases carried a brief statement of the actual court or administrative decision in the case and respondents were asked whether they felt the decision to be adequate, too severe, or too lenient, and except for responses of "adequate" were asked to write in what they felt to be an appropriate penalty. Prior to reading the cases, of course, they were presented with a brief statement of the nature and purposes of pure food legislation and it was made clear that each case in the questionnaire represented a conviction so that the issue was not guilt or innocence, but sentence, if any, to be imposed.

THE CONSUMER SAMPLE

Persons selected as respondents were sampled on the basis of a residential base map on which population characteristics were calculated from a previous study.[2] The only qualifications for inclusion were adulthood and complete lack of involvement with occupations dealing with the manufacture, distribution, or sale of food stuffs. Each respondent was personally contacted, the purpose of the research explained, and a questionnaire and stamped envelope left which was to be completed and mailed to the researcher. Two hundred and five contacts were made and one hundred and seventy-eight valid responses received. Of interest in the questionnaire responses was the fact that over half (60 per cent) of the sample recalled reading about cases of adulteration, while 34 per cent recalled purchasing misbranded or adulterated food.

ANALYSIS OF CONSUMER RESPONSES

An analysis of the responses of the sample as a whole revealed that, when reactions for all six cases were averaged, the majority of the consumers (78 per cent) felt that penalties should have been more severe than the actual court decisions and yet fall within the maximum penalties provided by the federal law; that is, a one year prison sentence on a first conviction. Choices of penalties equal to or less harsh than the one actually imposed were made by approximately 22 per cent of the sample, while almost 20 per cent felt that the violators (e.g., company owners) should receive a prison term longer than a year, which is inconsistent with present legislation. Furthermore, in each individual case whether it was misbranding, aesthetic adulteration, or harmful adulteration, this same pattern of responses occurred. That is, in spite of variations in types of offense, the average consumer response, while within the penalty limit of the present statutes, was more severe than the actual administrative action. Combining those respondents whose choices were more severe than the actual decision and yet within the law and those whose responses were more severe than the law allowed, 78 per cent of the respondents indicated that they would have punished the violators more severely than was actually done in the cases presented.

An analysis of the sample by groups of differing incomes, various educational levels, and other similar demographic distinctions revealed no significant differences in severity of penalties selected. About 68 per cent of the sample were women, and again, no significant differences were found between choices of males and females, nor were differences discovered between the group of individuals who reported having purchased adulterated or misbranded foods and those respondents who did not report experiences with adulteration.

While there was some variation in the selection of penalties from case to case by respondents, the majority of the sample members were consistent in their judgments when specific penalties were tabulated as "less severe than actual decision" and so on.

CONCLUSIONS

In our analysis of the responses, while recognizing that the sample size forbids generalization to the entire population, we can suggest that:

1. Court and administrative decisions in pure food violations do not represent the will of the majority of the consumers. This cannot be extended to mean that consumers do not approve of the penalties provided by law, because the greatest percentage of their choices of penalties was within the upper limit of the federal law. It means then that this disapproval extends to the administration of the law, not the law itself.

2. Consumers react to pure food violations (as shown by their choice of penalties) without regard for their class position; that is, even though they vary greatly by income, occupation, and educational level, by degree of awareness and familiarity with these violations, and by amount of organized consumer activity, their choices of penalties do not differ significantly from one such grouping to another. This is in contradiction to the idea implicit in Sutherland's analysis where he points to the relative toleration of white-collar offenses by individuals in roughly the same socioeconomic stratum as the violators.[3]

3. Although pure food law violations are not an entity, that is, there are types of violations (misbranding, aesthetic adulteration, and physically harmful adulteration), approximately 60 per cent of the sample selected penalties of the same severity in relation to the actual decisions for all three types of cases and selected these penalties whether or not they knew the actual court or administrative decision.

4. The original hypothesis of the study, namely, that respondents would select penalties comparable to those traditionally imposed in conventional criminal cases involving offenses like burglary, larceny, and so on was not supported. While some respondents were apparently willing to sentence some violators to "ten years in prison," the majority chose penalties less severe than a prison sentence. Fines, warning, seizure of

the product, and jail terms, in various combinations, were the most popular responses. In effect, respondents viewed food adulteration as more comparable to serious traffic violations than to burglary. This can perhaps be taken as evidence in support of the position of Burgess and others that such violators are viewed as "lawbreakers" rather than "criminals."[4]

This, of course, does not lessen the criminal nature of food adulteration. Laws, at least partially penal, were broken, and the majority of respondents did choose formal penalties more severe than informal warnings now provided by legislation. Furthermore, many respondents indicated that, had the violations been "intentional" (the problem of proving intent is not necessary in food law violations but should "willful intent" be shown, the maximum sentences may be increased), they would have recommended stronger penalties. Sutherland's study of seventy large corporations which demonstrated the frequency of recidivism in white-collar crime (an average of fourteen convictions or judgments per corporation) effectively negates the question of accidental violation.[5] This persistence of violation seems greater than chance unless willfulness were present, although intent may never appear in the official record. In the present study, however, all of the cases were, by chance, first offenses, which probably tended to mitigate the respondents' reactions.

In the more conventional types of crime, the specific reactions of the individual victim ordinarily have little bearing on the punishment of the criminal. This punishment is the right of the state and is defined in law and similarly, to a great extent, in public opinion. Laws are enforced to the extent that the public, or at least a large proportion of the public, feels that conformity to them is necessary, expedient, or proper. When public opinion changes sufficiently, the laws change or their enforcement ceases. The era of Prohibition, with its eventual repeal, is probably the best illustration of this, although it is seen, too, in the many antiquated statutes such as the various "blue laws" of many communities, which legally define an act as criminal but which are never enforced.

In the case of the pure food offenses, however, which do not have such a long history in the mores of our society, the importance of public opinion is difficult to assess. Few would suggest that victim revenge, mob rule, or lynching laws would be a more effective means of control than the present state penal laws in cases of ordinary criminal violations, and the same would apply to food violations and other white-collar crimes. However, the complex nature of the development and enforcement of laws regulating business makes it necessary to examine such laws in the light of consumer opinion. If consumers favor much stricter enforcement or more severe laws, this does not mean that such measures should necessarily be taken or would in any way affect the pure food violation rates, but a knowledge of consumer attitudes might provide some guide to enforcement of present laws and to possible changes in future legislation.

In general, in this new sociological area of white-collar crime, we recommend further research regarding the consumer's role in, and attitudes about, such offenses.

Notes

1. Marshall B. Clinard, *The Black Market:* A Study in White Collar Crime (New York: Holt, 1952), p. 93; Frank E. Hartung, A *Study of Law and Social Differentiation*, Ph.D. Dissertation, University of Michigan, 1949, pp. 330–331.

2. John W. Teter, *The Ecology of Residential Areas in Madison, Wisconsin*, Ph.D. Dissertation, University of Wisconsin, 1947.

3. Edwin H. Sutherland, *White Collar Crime* (New York: Dryden Press, 1949), pp. 46–48.

4. Ernest W. Burgess, Comment on Hartung's "White Collar Offenses in the Wholesale Meat Industry in Detroit," *American Journal of Sociology*, 56 (July, 1950), pp. 32–33.

5. Sutherland, *op. cit.*, p. 20.

V

WHITE-COLLAR OFFENSES AND THE LEGAL PROCESS

Most forms of both traditional criminal behavior and white-collar crime are said to be outlawed because they injure persons who neither bargain for nor merit such harm or deprivation. More penetrating analysis, however, would seem to support the view that the imposition of criminal sanctions reflects, in large measure, historical circumstances and social values, including values related to the kinds of harm that people rightfully should be protected against. Air pollution, intrafamilial psychological torture, by-products of industrial freedom (decisions, for instance, regarding whether to close a plant or to relocate or to hire or fire persons with certain kinds of skills), access to medical resources, rights regarding use or destruction of what is defined as one's own property (such as cattle or grain or a house), and a myriad number of similar items are all usually well within legal boundaries in the United States, although they may produce harm to individuals or to the social system much more overwhelming than that brought about by other acts defined as criminal.

It is in this sense that the question of which kinds of behavior should be designated as white-collar offenses by official codes becomes important. The readings in Part V, dealing primarily with the delineation, processing, and treatment of white-collar offenses and including material from cultures other than the United States, cast some light on problems of nomenclature and present some information on how other societies have dealt with similar issues. In addition, two studies from Great Britain offer portraits of individuals incarcerated for white-collar offenses. Unfortunately, there are no comparable data available in the United States, but the British investigations tell something about mechanisms of English law and, by emphasis and selection of material, their authors provide clues to how persons in societies other than the United States regard white-collar crime.

The advertising industry, dealt with in the opening article in this part, has often been a scapegoat in reviews of white-collar offenses. For one thing, advertising is omnipresent; for another, it is often marked by blatant ruses—announcers mouthing qualifying phrases about their products, for instance—and by a good deal of gaucherie and lack of aesthetic taste. The alleged benefits derived from advertising are, at least, arguable advantages when measured against their financial and psychological costs. Mediators in disputes about advertising are apt to suggest that informed consumer choice requires that purchasers know that a product exists, how it performs, and how that performance rates against possible substitutes. They suggest that imaginary, emotional, or otherwise irrelevant advertising appeals constitute a public disservice. The problems involved obviously concern, first, agreement on criteria to determine social benefit and social harm; second, determination of proper methods for encouraging the desirable and discouraging the undesirable; and third, adjudication of what kinds of advertising fall into which category.

It is such an enterprise that marks the analysis of the use of "props" and "mock-ups" in television advertising, described in the opening article in the section by Bruce E. Fritch, an attorney now practicing in Los Angeles. Such devices were presumptively barred by dictum in a ruling of the Federal Trade Commission which grew out of an instance in which a piece of glass, covered with sand, and labeled "sandpaper" by the announcer, was employed to demonstrate the extraordinary ability of a shaving cream to deal with recalcitrant beards. The F.T.C. had acted upon its statutory obligation to control advertising in order to restrain "unfair methods of competition," methods which seemingly provide one product with undue advantage over another. Fritch questions whether the use of harmless substitutions, undertaken because of technical difficulties inherent in television photography, should fall under the ban of the Federal Trade Commission. The reading is noteworthy for its organized review of the classifications of damage which have come forth from earlier commission decisions and for its confrontation of the question of whether viewers, competitors, and the general public actually are harmed by such artifices. How such harm might be measured—in the case under review, for instance—is a question for the combined resources of social science and legal scholarship. Most often, of course, the issue is adjudicated in terms of the presumed expertise, clinical judgment, and common sense of commission members, with little or no attempt to gather more definitive information on the subject. It would be interesting to speculate, for instance, how the commission might respond if a public opinion survey demonstrated beyond peradventure that the sandpaper advertisement was disbelieved by most viewers and that, in actual fact, it was harming the sales and competitive position of the advertised product rather than enhancing its standing.

The second reading adds perspective to viewpoints which stress that many harmful white-collar acts escape proscription because of the power of business interests and that many white-collar offenders avoid prosecution and conviction because of their social status. Harris B. Steinberg, a practicing attorney in New York City, suggests that the defense of persons accused of white-collar crime presents unique pitfalls and that, in some regards, white-collar offenders are in a less advantageous position than traditional violators. He notes that the white-collar defendant is apt not only to be tried by a regular court, but is also susceptible to later disciplinary proceedings before a licensing board. Such consequences might be regarded as a form of double jeopardy, with dual punishment for the same act, much as if a plumber was penalized for a theft he committed while at work and then, following this, was forbidden ever again to practice his trade. It is interesting too that Steinberg, on the basis of his trial experience, disagrees with Sutherland and Dershowitz by insisting that trials of white-collar offenses are subject to full reports in the newspapers and that they tend to produce acute discomfort among defendants because of their presumed influence with colleagues. Steinberg also suggests that well-placed friends may be more harmful than useful to the white-collar defendant, a view which most traditional offenders would probably regard with a good deal of skepticism. It may be true that on certain occasions the notoriety of the white-collar violator precludes the more relaxed kind of plea negotiation that can redound to the benefit of anonymous malefactors. It is certainly true that throughout the system of justice, officials tend to be notably responsive to items such as public indignation. Prosecutions are initiated, sentences made harsher, and paroles delayed because public officials do not want to incur the wrath of public opinion, even if such opinion represents only a small (but vocal) minority. It is not Steinberg's position, however, that white-collar offenders are always in a disadvantageous judicial position vis-à-vis traditional offenders, and it seems self-evident that they have numerous substantial advantages, not the least of which is their ability to hire high-priced, effective legal counsel.

Official response to business and commercial behavior in countries other than the United States is indicated in the reading by George Feifer, a free-lance writer, who discusses the use of capital punishment in the Soviet Union for certain forms of business transgression. For Americans, the death penalty as a response to crimes (except treason) that do not involve physical injury but rather are viewed as detrimental to the economic well-being of the state and therefore of all its citizens is a somewhat novel concept. Feifer suggests that the implementation in the Soviet Union of severe penalties for economic crimes represents an attempt at reform, though he is doubtful about the general efficacy of the practice, despite indications that in certain areas— notably, flagrant black-market operations—the new sanctions have had a definite and discernible impact.

The final two readings in Part V, both examining populations of white-collar offenders in British prisons, raise questions regarding sampling that have continuously plagued criminological research. There is agreement, of course, that incarcerated offenders are a select segment of the offending population, and there is reason to believe that they represent the least adept of their kind. It is sometimes suggested that studies should nonetheless concentrate upon such offenders, because to do otherwise would affront the democratic ideal that a person is not guilty until so proven. On the other hand, there is something quixotic about eliminating from a study an individual who by all reasonable, extrinsic judgments has, in fact, committed the stipulated act, but who has avoided conviction because of, say, an appellate court ruling that there had been an unnecessary delay in his arraignment. Little argument might be raised that such a person deserved to be freed, but considerable argument might be advanced that it is reasonable to include him in a study sample if the research question is concerned with attributes of persons committing the illegal act or its causes. In the same manner, there is an obvious bias introduced into an etiological study if an innocent person, incorrectly convicted, is included in a study of offenders.

G. E. Levens, who worked in a British prison prior to his retirement, avoids precise definition of the term "white-collar criminal" in his study with a good-natured, if not altogether satisfying, disclaimer noting his intention to examine persons who seem to be white-collar offenders by general belief and not to become embroiled in the "pedantry" of definitional argument. As a result, the population Levens studies runs a wide gamut, and at points it deviates considerably from what most writers would regard as white-collar offenders. For one thing, Levens includes persons of "reasonably high social status" in his sample, regardless of their offense. Particularly noteworthy is Levens' finding that white-collar violators in British prisons are exclusively from the middle class. This may indicate the absence of violators better placed in the class structure or it may signalize their greater invulnerability to apprehension and conviction.

The study of thirty white-collar offenders at Leyhill Prison, conducted by John C. Spencer, a professor at the University of Edinburgh, is built upon a more substantial definitional foundation than that of Levens. Like Levens,

Spencer is taken by the absence of persons of high social standing and prominent economic position among the imprisoned white-collar offenders, and, in agreement with Clinard and Lane, he emphasizes the necessity for personality inventories for his study population. His data provide no particular insight along personality lines, but they do point to the drive for upward mobility among the offenders as a possible key explanation for their deviation. Spencer's work is important for its indication of the need, as seen by a foreign writer, for American criminologists to concentrate less on business crime and more generically on categories of white-collar offenses that include such things as trade union violations, bankruptcy frauds, tax evasion, and similar matters.

Spencer's final remarks are worth particular attention, because they combine in adjacent sentences the ofttimes contradictory impulses found in writing on white-collar crime. "The proper decision as to the appropriate method of control can only be made on a foundation of social research," he remarks in conclusion. This call for empirical investigation, however, is undercut in the sentence preceding, where Spencer observes that "certain forms of behavior are so antisocial in their consequences that neither internal regulation alone nor government control unsupported by criminal sanctions is enough."

23

ILLUSION OR DECEPTION:
THE USE OF "PROPS" AND "MOCK-UPS"
IN TELEVISION ADVERTISING

Bruce E. Fritch

An ice-cream manufacturer, hoping to advertise his goods on television, can hire the most creative agency and use the most advanced technical equipment, but still be unable to show the world his product. A few minutes under hot studio lights and he finds himself extolling the virtues of vanilla "consommé," hardly a gourmet's delight. He has lost what is sometimes called the "Unique Selling Proposition," a product's most salient and saleable quality.[1] But the plight of the ice-cream maker is not unique, for the technical difficulties confronting him are not peculiar to his product. Blue shirts, for example, look white on television; butter looks like white oleomargarine. To compensate, television advertisers successfully have used props and mock-ups, designed to appear on television as their products do in real life. The death-knell of this practice, however, may recently have been tolled by the Federal Trade Commission in *Colgate Palmolive Co.*, the "sandpaper" case.[2]

Involved was the legality of a television commercial in which Palm-

Reprinted by permission of the Yale Law Journal Company and Fred B. Rothman & Company from *Yale Law Journal*, 72 (November, 1962), pp. 145–161.

olive Rapid Shave" was applied to a piece of plexiglass covered with sand, which an announcer called "sandpaper." Use of this mock-up was necessitated by the inherent difficulties of television photography—real sandpaper is indistinguishable from smooth colored paper. An actor shaved the mockup clean in a stroke, claiming to prove that Rapid Shave is so highly moist that it can shave the heaviest beard in seconds. The commission held the commercial deceptive, finding that Rapid Shave, in fact, could not shave true sandpaper even after an hour of soaking. But the commission went much further. It stated that the use of the mock-up would constitute an illegal deception even if the shaving cream could actually shave real sandpaper as fast as it shaved the mock-up and in every other particular was exactly as depicted in the commercial. Thus the FTC, albeit in dictum, announced its intention to prohibit absolutely the use of any prop or mock-up in a commercial message on television except as background material.

The source of the FTC's general powers to regulate advertising is section 5 of the Federal Trade Commission Act, which formerly authorized the commission to prohibit "unfair methods of competition in commerce." This original grant of power restricted the commission to acting upon false advertising only if it was likely to injure competitors of the advertiser. But in 1938, Congress passed the Wheeler-Lea Amendment, which extended the commission's authority over "unfair or deceptive acts or practices in commerce." The extension was motivated by a desire to afford consumers greater protection from false advertising.[3] Although the indefinite language of the provision itself suggests a broader scope, discussion of the amendment in Congress indicates that the acts intended to be proscribed were those which cause or threaten to cause injuries to consumers:

> By the proposed amendment to section 5, the commission can prevent such acts or practices which injuriously affect the general public as well as those which are unfair to competitors. In other words, this amendment makes the consumer, who may be injured by an unfair trade practice of equal concern, before the law, with the merchant or manufacturer injured by the methods of a dishonest competitor.[4]

The amendment thus enabled the commission to prohibit advertisements merely by showing an injury to consumers, without first having to establish adverse effects upon competition in general. Moreover, since the emphasis was upon protecting consumers from injuries, the central concern was with the *effects* of advertisements rather than particular devices or methods employed by advertisers. The question posed by the "sandpaper" case would thus seem to be whether the use of props or mock-ups in television commercials injure or create a risk of injury to consumers or competitors. Standards for determining such an injury, unfortunately, are neither to be found in the statute nor in the legislative history, since Congress never made clear what it meant by "injury."

In deciding whether a particular practice constitutes an injury, several factors would seem relevant. The need to protect consumers from the harms of false advertising is, of course, clear and generally recognized. This goal necessitates a careful examination of the kind of injury, if any, attributable to the use of props or mock-ups. But aside from injury, the benefits and detriments of any particular form of advertising would not seem to be the concern of the FTC,[5] for the commission is limited to a policing function, designed to protect certain groups from deceptive practices in advertising and, at the same time, to allow advertisers maximum freedom in their choice of advertising content and media. These objectives, however, cannot be achieved unless some standard for prohibiting "deceptive" advertising is articulated. As defined and applied in the non-television false-advertising cases decided under section 5a, the criterion suggested by the legislative history—injurious effects upon consumers and competitors—not only affords ample protection to the consuming public and allows maximum freedom to advertisers, but also takes account of the technical difficulties presented by television as an advertising medium.

An examination of these cases reveals several general types of injuries that have come to be proscribed by the act. First, advertising claims which conceal latent dangers to consumers or mislead consumers into thinking a potentially dangerous product is entirely safe have been banned from the earliest days. In *Gelb* v. *FTC*,[6] for example, it was held that the makers of "Instant Clairol," a hair dye, must disclose in their advertisements that the product could inflict skin irritation upon persons allergic to its ingredients and blindness if used to color eyelashes or eyebrows.

Second, advertisements consistently have been held illegal if they contain a false claim which might induce a consumer to purchase a product under expectations that he will acquire something better than the product being offered. The "injury" to the consumer lies in his not getting what he bargained for. The clearest example of such advertisements are those ascribing a quality,[7] ingredient,[8] or effectiveness[9] to a product which in fact it does not possess.[10] Somewhat similar is testimonial advertising, which induces a consumer to purchase a product because of an opinion by someone he respects. If the testimonial is untrue, the consumer does not get what he expects in terms of the popularity or prestige of the product.[11]

Section 5a has also been applied against advertisements that tend to create a false impression about the advertised product which might motivate the consumer to make a particular purchase, regardless of whether he ultimately acquires everything he fully expected. The leading case, *Kerran* v. *FTC*,[12] involved an advertiser of "refined oil" who neglected to inform the public that his oil actually was second-hand, having been re-refined from used oil. The commission held that the advertiser could be compelled to disclose this fact, even though it was conceded that both "new" and "used" oil properly rerefined were equally effective lubricants. The dissenting opinion, arguing against disclosure, based its contention on the proposition that the consumer, who desires merely "good" oil, is not prejudiced by any erroneous impression an advertisement might give him so long as he acquires the "good" oil he wanted. That is, if what the consumer acquires squares with his expectations before purchase, he receives what he bargained for and there is no "public interest" in prohibiting advertisements that communicated to him some kind of falsehood. The majority, however, reasoned that the public "is entitled to know the facts . . . and . . . make its own choice with respect to purchasing . . . even though the choice is predicated at least in part upon ill-founded sentiment, belief or caprice." The injury, then, lies in the deprivation of a truthful factual basis upon which the consumer may rely in deciding to purchase the advertised product. *Kerran* also serves to show that a deception can consist not only in an express statement that is untrue, but also in a silence that leads a reasonable man to infer a false notion.

The fourth type of advertisements brought under Section 5*a* involves injuries to competitors. Advertisements which mislead a buyer into acquiring something other than he expects simultaneously divert potential sales from competitors who do not indulge in similar advertising practices. Competition, of course, is supposed to stimulate improvements in consumer goods by favoring sellers of superior goods over others in the same price range. The false advertiser, however, attains a better position in the competitive market not on the strength of a superiority inherent in his goods, but upon a fiction communicated through his advertisements. Finally, Section 5*a* has been held to prohibit false advertising that ascribes to competitive products inferiorities they do not in fact possess or which falsely disparages the competitors themselves.

These cases make clear, then, that some actual or potential injury to consumers or competitors has been the determinative factor in finding deception in an advertising practice, although the particular injury has taken various forms. In deciding the question of proper use of props and mock-ups in television commercials, however, the FTC has failed to carry forth this earlier focus upon effects. Instead, it has tended to categorize the cases with an undue emphasis upon the subject matter or devices employed in the commercial, without fully examining the effect of the advertisement on consumers and competitors. Yet there is no apparent reason for approaching television problems any differently from others, for the injuries are identical whether the advertising claim is communicated by the written word or through a combination of oral words and moving images. Thus, for example, an advertiser who uses a prop or mock-up to "demonstrate" or "prove" that his product possesses certain characteristics which it does not possess stands in the same position as one who makes such misrepresentations by use of the written word. In either case, the consumer is misled into buying something for which he did not bargain.

Although it is perhaps not feasible to list all conceivable injuries that could be produced by use of props and mock-ups in television commercials, it is necessary to identify a range of injuries from which the consumer may be protected in order that a fair standard of conduct for the advertisers as well as a workable guide for enforcement of the statute may be formulated. At one extreme is the actual physical injury to the consumer caused by a concealment of dangers inherent in the product; at the other is injury to the consumer's self-reliance resulting from his loss of an adequate factual basis for the purchase decision. In between fall many situations in which the injury to the consumer is frustration of justifiable expectations. The common denominator of all injuries within this spectrum is that they result from the consumer's acquiring a product which in some way is different from what was advertised. Prior to its decision in the "sandpaper" case, the FTC banned only those television commercials that involved the use of props or mock-ups that threatened to produce injuries falling somewhere within this spectrum.[13] But the dictum in the "sandpaper" case, suggesting that use of props or mock-ups as an integral part of a television commercial message causes injury even if there is communicated to the consumer no false impression as to the nature or quality of the advertised product, would extend this spectrum.

Such an extension would severely limit the effectiveness of television advertising. It is generally recognized that technical limitations of the television medium require use of props or mock-ups in order to communicate in any manner the image of certain objects. It is obviously impossible to transplant most natural and many artificial objects into a small television studio. Limitations of space require the use of artificial props designed to resemble mountains, houses, lakes, and so forth.[14] Time limitations prohibit showing the entire development in a sequence of events; instead, the technique of showing three successive views—"before," "middle," and "after," using three separate objects frozen at those stages of development—frequently is used. Sound problems often necessitate a singer's merely "lipping" a prerecorded song, to permit on-stage dancing or changing of scenery which would create disruptive noises were the microphones turned on. The same problems, of course, face television advertisers, and they try to solve them similarly:

> Like all visual arts, television relies on certain production techniques intended to compensate for limitations imposed by studio facilities and electronic distortions. As the public knows, performers wear blue shirts on television because a white shirt creates undesirable highlights and a blue shirt looks white. By the same token, yellow looks grey on television.

The same is true of foods in television commercials. Some preparations must be tinted so they will look as white as they do in real life. . . .

In other words, an advertising agency in every medium of advertising relies on special techniques to create reality, not to misrepresent but rather to represent accurately.

The advertiser in the "sandpaper" case attempted to justify the use of a plexiglass mock-up and any possible resultant injury on the ground that the problems of photography necessitated its substitution for real sandpaper. But in rejecting "technical difficulties" as a justification for any deception, the commission stated:

Assuming it to be the fact that there are indeed such limitations in television photography, the commission can appreciate that these "technical" difficulties could give rise to problems for sponsors and agencies in determining how most effectively to use television in advertising their products. The limitations of the medium may present a challenge to the creative ingenuity and resourcefulness of copywriters; but surely they could not constitute lawful justification for resort to falsehoods and deception of the public.

This zealous desire for the truth seems misplaced. True, the use of a prop or mock-up may be characterized as a falsehood. But it is another thing to say that the use of mock-ups constitutes a deception of the public. Such a view seems more concerned with what occurs in the television studio than with the message projected on the screen. Under this view, an advertiser may not use a prop or mock-up to show the actual qualities of a product or its performance, although it might be lawful for him to exploit the distortions of television projection to make a product or its performance appear superior on the screen, so long as he uses the real object in the studio. Clothes still gray and dingy after being washed in Brand X soap, for example, could then be televised even if they appear whiter and brighter than they really are. And if this also is deemed illegal, the advertiser is in the unenviable position of not being able to use the real object in an advertisement because that would be misleading and not being able to use a prop which appears like the real object on the screen because that too could be misleading. In short, he may not show his product or its performance on television.

The difficulties presented by the FTC's current view are in part attributable to a failure to distinguish between deception to the general public and to the consuming public, and therefore between "injury" to these groups. But the legislative history of section 5a, however scant, and the treatment of nontelevision advertising cases suggest that a commercial does not constitute a deceptive practice prohibited by Section 5a unless the falsity employed by the advertiser causes injuries to the consumer. The solution to the problem, then, depends upon isolating those injuries peculiar to consumers and not shared by the general public.

The distinguishing characteristic of a consumer is that he has or will acquire a product. Thus, any false claim in an advertisement must relate to this acquired product in order to constitute consumer injury. That is, the false claim must give the consumer a concept of the product different from what he actually acquires, for only such injuries are peculiar to the consumer class alone. As the spectrum of injuries identified earlier is defined in terms of this same relationship between the false claims in advertisements and the nature of the acquired product, the spectrum necessarily includes those consumer injuries envisioned by Section 5a. Considerations of fairness to advertisers in their attempt to compensate for the technical limitations of television require such a strict interpretation of Section 5a. As indicated earlier, some products are ill-suited to television photography, and to deny the use of props or mock-ups to their manufacturers would be to deny them the use of television,[15] or at least lessen its advantages by making tests or demonstrations impossible. The employment of a false element in a television commercial solely to compensate for technical difficulties, therefore, should be permitted so long as the presence of such a false element does not result in the kind of consumer injury falling within the spectrum.

A disregard for technical difficulties evidenced in the "sandpaper" dictum would expand Section 5a into an area in which the false element employed in the advertisement would not cause injuries peculiar to the consumer. Use of plexiglass, for example, instead of real sandpaper, does not injure the consumer of the shaving cream so long as, accepting the FTC's own hypothetical, it has all the properties depicted in the commercial. For any possible injury that may arise out of such a substitution is an injury common to all television viewers in being shown one thing while being told it is another. True, such a practice may constitute a "deceptive" practice in the broadest sense, but it does not in any way injure consumers, whose specific protection was the primary concern of the act. In this sense, the FTC has invaded the area of general television-viewer protection by expanding the scope of Section 5a beyond mere consumer protection.

The test suggested here is supported by a line of nontelevision cases holding that all elements of untruth need not be disclosed. In an early case, for example, involving a manufacturer of furniture who advertised his product to the trade as "mahogany" or "walnut" when in fact it was merely veneered plywood, the court reversed the FTC's disclosure order on grounds that everyone in the trade knew that the words "mahogany" and "walnut" referred to laminated wood.[16] Similarly, a court refused to prohibit an advertiser from calling his shoes "Kaffor-Kid" even though they contained no skin of young goats. The court decided the case upon evidence that the word "kid" communicated to the ordinary consumer qualities of texture and appearance, not the source of the leather, about which he was not concerned in the slightest. The court suggested that consumers understood that ordinary "kid gloves" or "kid shoes" do not contain leathers tanned from the skins of kids.[17] More recently, a court permitted unqualified use of the words "Elasti-Glass" to describe a product essentially made of plastic by noting that the word "glass" in the public mind derives from the appearance of the product, not from the manufacturing process or specific contents.[18] The determinative factor in all these cases was that the consumer was not misled into expecting something different from what he actually acquired, despite the false element in the advertisement.

Except for the dictum in the "sandpaper" case, the policy of both the courts and the FTC in allowing the use of what could be considered a misleading element in an advertisement to counteract technical limitations has been consistent with the test formulated here. In *Hutchinson Chemical Corp.*,[19] for instance, involving the "flaming auto" commercial, the FTC explicitly recognized time limitations inherent in television broadcasting. In order to "prove" that a car wax could withstand extreme heat and cold, gasoline was poured onto a car fender to which the wax had been applied. The gasoline was then ignited and, twelve seconds later, doused with cold water. The commission dismissed the charge that the demonstration was too short to prove what was purported. It said that if a fire lasting thirty seconds, a time period assumed sufficient to transfer requisite heat to the fender, would in fact prove the claim, the advertiser could limit the demonstration shown in the commercial to a shorter period to compensate for "time restrictions." In recognizing the need for flexibility in the enforcement of Section 5a in order to achieve a desirable balance between protecting consumers and allowing advertisers considerable freedom, this former policy of the FTC stands in marked contrast to the dictum of the "sandpaper" case.

Notes

1. See Martin Meyer, *Madison Avenue, U.S.A.* (New York: Harper & Row, 1958), pp. 49–53.

2. *Colgate-Palmolive Co., Trade Regulation Reporter*, vol. 3, § 15,643 (1961).

3. See Milton Handler, "The Control of False Advertising under the Wheeler-Lea Act," *Law and Contemporary Problems*, 6 (Winter, 1939), p. 96.

4. United States House of Representatives, 75th Cong., 1st Sess., *Report No. 1613*, p. 3 (1937).

5. The arguments in favor of advertising have been recited in many places. See, for example, Ralph S. Brown, "Advertising and the Public Interest: Legal Protection of Trade Symbols," *Yale Law Journal*, 57 (June, 1948), pp. 1165–1206; George Burton Hotchkiss, "An Economic Defense of Advertising," *American Economic Review*, 15 (March, 1925), pp. 14–22. Equally omnipresent has been the recitation of arguments

the other way; for example, Brown, *op. cit.*, and Frank P. Bishop, *The Economics of Advertising* (London: R. Hale, 1946), chap. 8. It is without regret that this raging controversy is side-stepped here.

6. 144 F. 2d 580 (2d Circ. 1944).

7. *FTC v. Algoma Lumber Co.*, 291 U.S. 67 (1934) (holding illegal advertisements using the words "California white pine" to describe a less desirable kind of pinewood called "pinus ponderosa").

8. *Jacob Siegel Co. v. FTC*, 327 U.S. 608 (1946) (reversing and remanding on other grounds where the circuit court had affirmed a cease and desist order against advertisements for fur coats, featuring the name "Alpacuna" when the product contained no vicuna fur).

9. Best known of these cases is *Carter Prods., Inc. v. FTC*, 268 F.2d 461 (9th Circ.), *cert. denied*, 361 U.S. 884 (1959), enforcing an FTC order that Carter eliminate the word "Liver" from the trade name of its "Little Liver Pills," when it was shown that the product had no curative or active effects upon the liver. Probably the most extreme case involved false advertising claims that a mineral water could cure some fifty-two infirmities, running the gamut from poison ivy to sterility. *Capon Water Co. v. FTC*, 107 F.2d 516 (3d Circ. 1939).

10. Also included in this category are false claims about where a product was made. *Houbigant, Inc. v. FTC*, 139 F.2d 1019 (2d Circ.), *cert. denied*, 323 U.S. 763 (1944) ("French" perfume made in the United States), *Cf. Edward P. Paul & Co. v. FTC*, 169 F.2d 294 (D.C. Circ. 1948) ("Du Barry" on labels held deceptive when the porcelain originated in Japan).

11. Cases have held that when a testimonial has been purchased or solicited, advertisements which imply otherwise are illegal. See Murray Stein, "Testimonial Advertising and the Federal Trade Commission," *George Washington Law Review*, 17 (April, 1949), p. 349 and fn. 41.

12. 265 F. 2d 246 (10th Circ. 1959).

13. At least two cases involved the use of a prop or mock-up to ascribe a quality to the advertising product which it did not possess. Consumers purchasing in reliance would not get what they expected. In 1959, the manufacturers of "Natural Wave," a hair-curling lotion, developed television commercials in which they used as a prop an ordinary drinking straw soaked in the lotion to demonstrate that the product penetrates hair, changing its structure and creating a "natural" curl. A consent decree was issued on the allegation that "Natural Wave" possessed no abilities to change the basic structure of human hair nor change naturally straight hair to naturally curly. . . . An initial contested cease and desist order recently was rendered against the "invisible shield" commercial. The hearing examiner ruled that by using a piece of transparent glass to shield an announcer from flying objects, the commercial tended to ascribe to the toothpaste it was advertising properties it did not possess (formation of an invisible protective shield around teeth). There has been one instance in which the commission registered its opinion that television props were being used to violate standards of testimonial advertising. This case resulted in a consent decree banning a commercial for "Rolaids," an indigestion remedy, in which an announcer appeared in a white coat, addressed as "doctor." The complaint alleged that these practices "convey to TV viewers that Rolaids are endorsed by the medical profession" when they were not, and therefore that they "have the capacity to deceive a substantial portion of the purchasing public and are deceptive practices in violation of the FTC Act."

14. See generally, Hoyland Bettinger, *Television Techniques* (New York: Harper & Row, 1947), p. 15; and William C. Eddy, *Television: The Eyes of Tomorrow* (Englewood Cliffs, N.J.: Prentice-Hall, 1945), pp. 211–228.

15. See Charles H. Wolfe, *Modern Radio Advertising* (New York: Funk & Wagnalls, 1949), p. 673; and F. R. Elliott, "Memory for Visual, Auditory and Visual-Auditory Material," *Archives of Psychology*, 29 (1936), pp. 52–54.

16. *Berkey & Gay Furniture Co. v. FTC*, 42 F. 2d 427 (6th Circ. 1930).

17. *Ohio Leather Co. v. FTC*, 45 F.2d 39 (6th Circ. 1930).

18. *S. Buchsbaum & Co. v. FTC*, 160 F.2d 121 (7th Circ. 1947).

19. 55 F.T.C. 1942 (1959).

24

THE DEFENSE OF THE WHITE-COLLAR ACCUSED

Harris B. Steinberg

The trial of a white-collar case, as I have been led to understand the term, is not necessarily one having anything to do with haberdashery—the haberdashery of either the defendant or his lawyer—but is rather one involving a crime such as tax fraud, stock fraud, mail fraud, customs fraud, or one or another of the more subtle, more complex types of cases arising out of business activity, where the defendant, until his indictment, has usually been a respected—or at least a previously unapprehended—citizen. The special features of such trials, after all the preliminaries are over and one is about to pick a jury, are the subject of this paper.

First, I should like to go back to what may properly be considered a preliminary but which, even so, merits a further word. That is the subject of fees.

In this sphere of white-collar crimes, it presents more than ordinary difficulties. The receipt of a proper fee brings with it the relaxed feeling that one is free to turn one's entire attention to the real adversary—the prosecution—rather than being continuously plagued with bickerings and

Reprinted from *American Criminal Law Quarterly*, 3 (Spring, 1965), pp. 129–138, with the permission of the American Bar Association and its Section of Criminal Law.

conflicts with one's own client, who should be a shoulder-to-shoulder ally, rather than an adversary even in the most limited sense.

Even the experienced and secure trial lawyer may be perplexed when it comes to setting a fair fee for the lengthy trial of a complicated case. How many days and nights of legal research will be necessary? How long will it take to learn all the facts and read the many papers involved? The businessman with no previous criminal record, with children in good schools, and a wife in the country club, will be at your door more frequently than most other clients to seek comfort and guidance on how to comport himself in his daily affairs. How many pretrial motions will be necessary, and what work is involved in them? Are there ancillary proceedings to be anticipated? A real estate broker, a lawyer, an accountant, a securities broker are all licensed by other agencies, and as publicity emerges concerning the facts of the indictment, they may be called to account before other agencies, and one must consider the time required to manage those problems, as well as furthering the forthcoming trial preparation.

My own feeling is that it is fairer to the lawyer and to the client to try to set a fee which is likely to be proper for all the reasonably foreseeable work up to the day of trial. This should be forthcoming early in the proceedings, and before one has entered a notice of appearance in court. Once one has actually appeared in the action, it may be embarrassing or difficult to withdraw because of money disagreements with a client, and one should strive at all costs to avoid such an event. Especially when this happens on the eve of trial is one likely to be embarrassed, because the prosecution may be heard to complain loudly that they are ready with their witnesses and that a change of lawyers will mean unwarranted delay.

The question of setting trial fees is not easy to handle either. A fee at one's usual daily rates may be unrealistic when the trial stretches into months, and once one has started the trial, there is no effective way to withdraw if the agreed refreshers are not forthcoming. A useful solution is to agree on a fee, payable in advance, for a trial period which seems realistic, in view of the best estimates which are offered by prosecution and defense. If the trial turns out to be unduly protracted beyond that estimated period, a further weekly fee can be set.

In every case, one must make a tentative decision, as early as possible and as objectively as possible, whether one has a really good chance to win a jury verdict, or whether public passion or the evidence is expected to be so strong that a jury verdict of acquittal is a forlorn and unrealistic hope and the only honest expectation is that, on appeal from a conviction, a good, serious and worthwhile law point is involved in the case and will merit serious consideration by the appellate court. This will help determine, to some extent, what kind of a record you make, how ready you will be to make concessions of fact, to waive technicalities of proof, and how assiduous you will be to make objections and take exceptions. Ideally, one should be able to drive forward toward both objectives-in tandem but, practically, it has been my observation that this is not always, or even very often, possible.

Too often, the impatience of the judge will be made manifest, with attendant effect on the jury, if one doggedly hews to every one of one's rights. This may lead to crusty and peremptory decisions to sit for inordinately long hours, to be grudging of ordinary courtesies, like a day off for a child's graduation, or starting an hour late on occasional mornings so one can take care of other pressing matters.

I lean toward cooperative effort with the court, wherever possible without sacrificing the client's real interests, in avoiding lengthy technical proof, and meeting the prosecutor more than halfway in shortening trials. It has been the experience of many lawyers trying complicated cases that the longer and more unwieldy the proceedings become, the more difficult it becomes to avoid the feeling on the jury's part that so much time, money, and effort have gone into the trial that it would be unbecoming to let the defendant off. And the recent trend of appellate decisions has been firmly away from reversing convictions because of errors in the admission or exclusion of evidence. Indeed, any sort of error, even one of real substance, does not loom awfully large in a very long record on appeal. Harmless error seems more harmless and less erroneous, in retrospect, if it is buried in thousands of pages of trial proceedings.

Accordingly, I recommend agreeing readily on the receipt of photostat copies of documents when that will save time, not pressing about the full panoply of foundations for evidence where a record of a reputable bank or brokerage house is offered, and dispensing with the calling of shorthand reporters to verify that an official transcript of minutes was accurately transcribed. Such generosity generally leads to similar courtesy when one starts producing records and proof on behalf of the defense and may prevent the kind of dull bickering, before the jury, which causes them to lose interest in everything including your contentions.

Usually, too, the demonstration of a genuine desire to cooperate in speeding up the trial will result in more generosity in furnishing "Jencks Act" material a little in advance—perhaps the night before the witness is called. This, if it is possible to arrange, will save you anxiety and trouble. It is vexing to have to read grand jury minutes in the courtroom while the jury stares at the ceiling and the judge drums impatiently with his fingertips and asks irritably why it takes you more than twelve minutes to read a hundred and fifty pages of testimony.

Most often the complicated white-collar case will involve more than one defendant—indeed, the usual one involves about a half-dozen or more defendants, each represented by his own lawyer. The managing of the order of cross-examination and the order of opening and summation should ideally be left to agreement among counsel, rather than be left to the chance order of naming defendants in the indictment. In this way, the strongest counsel can make the fullest cross-examination, and needless repetition is avoided. If counsel cannot agree—and prima donnas are found more often in the courtroom than on the concert stage—the court may impose an order which is strategically undesirable. I have usually found that a generous and realistic recognition of the relative seriousness of the cases against various defendants and the abilities of various lawyers make it possible for the defense lawyers to agree among themselves. Even where the defenses of different defendants are to some degree antagnostic, or at least not compatible, it is still possible and highly desirable for counsel to refrain from hindering each other.

Recently, I tried a case with a lawyer for a codefendant who was inclined to be somewhat theatrical and flamboyant and given to the large and magnificent gesture. Midway in the trial, I found it necessary to object on the record to many of his shotgun questions, after agonized *sotto voce* pleadings had had no effect. The situation which unfortunately ensued made the real opponents in the courtroom the two defendants, rather than the prosecution and defense. It became inevitable that both could not be acquitted. What really left the proceedings wide open was the other lawyer's final gesture. With a flourish and a loud statement that he at least had nothing to hide, he offered in evidence a number of papers which I had succeeded, in pretrial proceedings, in having suppressed. My anguished screams for a mistrial and my repeated cries for a severance were ignored. It is worth a comment here that the chances of a mistrial, or a severance, once a complicated and lengthy trial has commenced, are very slight—a shotgun marriage is arranged at the time of the indictment, and the defendants are usually bedfellows to the bitter end, whether they like it or not.

Three of the most vexing problems in lengthy trials are (1) whether to put the defendant on the stand, (2) the nature of the defense, and (3) newspaper publicity.

As to (1), I know that many lawyers feel that unless a defendant testifies in his own behalf, he has little or no chance of success. This may be so, and I have heard able and respected lawyers say so, vehemently and often.

Generally, it is true, the defendant has no criminal record, is prepossessing, and can tell his story clearly; and it would seem to be an easy decision to let him testify. However, most white-collar cases involve a pattern of conduct that may be more widespread and more horrendous than the specific crime or crimes charged in the indictment. The vexing problem is what will one open oneself to by way of cross-examination on collateral matters. The chilling prospects which often loom in this connection have led me, on many occasions, to advise the defendant against testifying in his own behalf. I cannot honestly say, by the results I have witnessed, that I can make any hard-and-fast rules about the desirability of the defendant's testifying or not. At any rate, that decision is ultimately the defendant's own—one can only advise. There is an exception where one knows, from the client's own lips, that what he proposes to say on the stand is a lie. In that event, clear ethical strictures prevent one from continuing in the case and becoming a party to perjury, if the client insists on that course of conduct.

The second problem I noted above—the nature of the defense—is an interesting and important one. Remember that it is up to the prosecutor to prove guilt beyond a reasonable doubt. He must have a firm, fixed theory—he must be prepared to prove exactly how something happened or he cannot prevail. The defense has an entirely different objective. The defendant, in my submission, should never try to prove what happened. Usually, he cannot prove someone else's guilt or his own innocence. He should try to knock holes in the prosecution's structure. He can knock various kinds of holes into it—they need not be consistent with each other. Every hole creates a reasonable doubt. Two or three kinds of separate and alternative weaknesses in the prosecution's case go more strongly to show how unwarranted is a conviction than one kind of weakness.

A friend of mine, who is an able and experienced lawyer, and a dogged perfectionist by nature, was trying a celebrated tax fraud case a few years ago. The courtroom scuttlebutt at the close of the government's case was generally in agreement that effective cross-examination had so weakened the prosecution's case that it had barely survived a motion to dismiss and could scarcely be expected to convince a jury. The lawyer was graciously acknowledging admiring congratulations on the efficiency of his cross-examination, which had left the *modus operandi*, urged by the government, in considerable doubt.

Fired by the universal admiration and apparently resolved to do the job "no-hands," he then proceeded, on defense, to show what *did* happen, according to the defense theory. A long, complex demonstration followed, with a feeling of disbelief and embarrassment becoming heavier and more palpable every hour. It was clear that the jury was not prepared to accept the proffered explanation, regardless of how they had felt originally after the prosecution's story had been completed. A conviction resulted, which might not have been necessary. In the inevitable postmortems over the drinks, he gave it as his own opinion that he had bitten off too much on the defense and should have rested on the weakened prosecution case. I felt he was right in that appraisal.

The matter of newspaper and television publicity in white-collar cases is one of the most annoying. Usually, such trials are the subject of full reports in the press. These have probably begun before you were in the case, at the time of investigation, or possibly when the indictment came down. If it is something of interest to the financial community, continuous references will appear in the financial pages. Let us assume that you have done your best by way of pretrial motions to procure a dismissal or a change of venue or delay of trial, because of improper newspaper reports, but that you have been unsuccessful. Such an assumption is not hard to make, based on the trend of judicial decisions.

At any rate, one can only be alert during the trial to read all reports, and if anything prejudicial appears, to bring it promptly to the court's attention and, if necessary, have *voir dire* inquiries of the jurors as to whether they have seen the offending article, or heard the improper radio or television report. The only thing I should like to impress on you in this connection is that whatever scant chance you have of getting somewhere with such incidents is completely dissipated if you yourself contribute anything to the publicity. For that reason I have made it a rigid and unvarying rule to make absolutely no comment whatsoever to any reporter about any case I am in. Whatever I have to say is on the record, in court, in some manner which bears on some issue of the case, in a proper proceeding.

This rigid rule is often unpopular with your own client, as well as with the press. Businessmen clients who are accustomed to publicity as a good thing to be sought often, and who are fearful of bad publicity, are crushed when they read the usual garbled and erroneous black-and-white oversimplifications of the daily press or the thirty-second verbal report on TV. They (or their cronies or business associates) want you to correct the record. All experienced attorneys know that one can only lengthen the normally short attention span of the reporters by engaging in this sort of controversy-by-statement or press release. In addition to being ethically improper, the making of statements about a pending case is of no practical use to your client, and, furthermore, it may serve to vitiate a good legal point if an improper release by the prosecution has caused prejudicial matter to reach the jury's ears.

Akin to the client's anxieties about press reports, with which one must try to cope, are his suggestions that he knows Senator So-and-so or Judge X or Commissioner Y, has played golf with him, and served as godfather to his third grandchild; he inquires what he can ask the putatively willing senator, judge, or commissioner to do for him. I need hardly tell you that most often (1) the extent of the acquaintanceship is not nearly as close as the panicky defendant imagines; (2) even where it is very close, the public official fervently wishes that it could be expunged from his memory; and (3) there is not a single thing he could properly do even if he wished to. As gently as possible, but as firmly as a rock, it is often necessary to discourage the client about any ideas he has along these lines. If the ideas persist, one may have to withdraw from the case.

Let us assume that the client decides, even reluctantly, to follow your advice and try the case on the merits. What next? Matters of mechanics, while not too important in a short trial, become more so in a long one. I like to keep fairly full notes of the trial in a notebook—listing exhibits by number and description, and a fairly complete summary of the evidence as it comes in, identifying whether it was direct, cross, or redirect, and on what morning or afternoon it went in. I do this even where I get day-by-day copies of the minutes. I leave to an associate the digesting of day-by-day minutes where we have them, underlining in red pencil those paragraphs which I should like to return to on cross-examination or in summation.

I find that constant rereading of my own handwritten notes fixes details in my head—just as my elaborate notebooks got me through law school. This may be because I have a visual mind and only an average memory, appropriate to my age. Others may have different systems, which work equally well or better for them.

Along with these notes, I keep copies of exhibits, labeled and numbered in separate filing folders and keep these folders in an expanding filing envelope as I go along. Just as I mark off certain portions of testimony for later use in summation and cross, I do the same with exhibits. This process of winnowing, analyzing, discarding, and changing goes on continually, consciously and subconsciously, throughout the trial. Often, I awake with a start, at 3:00 A.M., hop out of bed, and feverishly note that the date of Exhibit 35 has a significance I hadn't perceived before, making it worthy of comment, by juxtaposing it with defendant's Exhibit C. At other times, I change my mind about the effect of an argument I had been hugging to my breast, prepared to thunder it out on summation. It doesn't seem so hot, when one thinks that the prosecutor can demolish that argument by reference to Exhibit 18.

I keep a section of my notebook at the back with random jottings of ideas for summation. From the minute the trial begins, I keep thinking of what I will say and what I will not say on summation.

That greatest of all advocates, the late John W. Davis, once said that the way to try a case is to think of what summation you would like to make, and then put in only those pieces of evidence which will enable you to make those arguments. To me, this is a profound truth of trial work, particularly true in long and complicated cases.

The summation is, in my opinion, the single most important part of the case. We have long since passed from the days of silver-tongued orators with high-flown phrases, shouting, weeping, and carrying on like revivalists. That sort of approach is for the most part merely embarrassing to listeners. But let no one believe for a moment that the low-keyed, conversational style now in vogue can carry the day, if it is a vehicle for low-keyed, matter-of-fact recitals, stringing together dates, names, and events. That sort of approach may well be useful and desirable for a prosecutor, but it will do nothing for a defense lawyer. The summation must sound like facts, but it must be largely compounded of emotion, barely kept in check, but tense and quivering with earnestness that is real and compelling. I am a little sheepish when I tell you that I am often on the verge of tears when I sum up, although I do not shed them.

I think it most important to organize your summation carefully. List and name all the witnesses and deal with what each one of them said— indeed, all the evidence for you and against you—even though you do so by lumping certain types of witnesses together and treating them together. Have the exhibits you intend to read from neatly gathered in the order in which you expect to use them. Have clearly typed or clearly marked excerpts of word-for-word testimony that you will read, readily at hand, in order to eliminate fumbling and breaking the tension which you want to induce in a slowly mounting tide.

For this reason I make use of few, if any, written notes. Dropping one's eyes to look over your notes breaks the spell you would like to create. A mongoose who stops to put on its bifocals and fumbles about in a file of loose papers kills few, if any, cobras. . . .

Character or, more properly, reputation evidence is often useful in cases of this type, because the defendant will usually have a clean prior record. There is a tendency, often noted, to treat such testimony as a rather unconvincing makeweight. I believe it can be useful, and may sometimes furnish the difference between winning and losing, especially where the prosecution relies on self-confessed lawbreakers, or indicted co-conspirators who are "singing for their supper." Where such testimony is used, I like to avoid the sporadic, casual interjection of character witnesses at inappropriate times, which is often allowed to suit the convenience of such witnesses.

"Your Honor, can we break into Mr. So-and-so's cross-examination of the present witness so we can take a character witness out of turn? Dr. X has to leave, and it will only take a minute." This request is often heard and usually granted, with little grumbling and resistance. My trouble with this procedure is as follows: First, the character witness who is not willing to wait like other witnesses is, in effect, saying, "I am willing to be a witness, but I begrudge the time necessary." This reflects, subtly, on his real regard for the defendant. If he really thought a great deal of him, he would willingly submit to a little inconvenience on his behalf. Second, a succession of character witnesses, in their proper order, has a cumulative effect not achieved by having their testimony come in at random, spaced far apart. It almost amounts to acknowledging the slightness of their contribution to the proof when one does not present them with the logic and order inherent in the adducing of other proof. It goes without saying that these witnesses should be seen before they are brought to the stand, and one should explore carefully with them the proper basis for their evidence. In other words, since they testify to reputation, rather than their own appraisal of the defendant, they should be ready to tell when and with whom they discussed the defendant and how they learned of the defendant's reputation. Good character witnesses can be the subject of an important part of the summing up, and when this is followed by a reference in the court's charge to the proper scope of such testimony, it sometimes makes the difference between victory and defeat.

One final word—about the requests to charge. One section of my notebook is devoted to jottings of possible subject matters for requests, and as the trial progresses I try to isolate and formulate subjects for requests. I do not bother with boiler plate, but only with those things that I believe present real legal issues of interest, and I try to ring the changes on several variants of each request to make sure that the legal question is stated in as simple, spare language as possible.

Early—indeed, very early—in the case, the judge and his clerk will keep pressing, with ever more insistence (sometimes with what amounts to almost a neurotic fervor), for your written requests to charge. Often the third or fourth day you will probably hear the court putting on record at the close of each session, a recital of how often he has asked for written requests and how pained he is that they are not yet in his hands. This, despite the fact that you still have about three or four weeks to go on the prosecution's direct case. I try to go to great lengths to appease the court by giving him written requests as early as I can. Rarely, however, will this phase of the trial be completely satisfactory to everyone.

CONCLUSION

I would summarize the white-collar case as follows:

1. They are generally longer than others.

2. They usually involve several defendants, with the attendant problems of having several lawyers working together or at cross-purposes.

3. The defendant usually has no prior criminal record but generally does have other, similar transactions in his background, raising problems as to his taking the stand and the scope of his cross-examination.

4. There will usually be a great number of exhibits to manage.

5. Usually, the Jencks materials are important and will provide much material for cross-examination.

6. In most cases, the facts themselves will clearly emerge, and the question of intent will be paramount.

7. In judging this question of intent, jurors who can relate to the defendant or his situation are oftentimes sympathetic.

8. A cooperative, dignified, and straightforward conduct of the defense, aimed at eliminating waste of time and insistence on rights that have little real relevance to the merits, will serve to capitalize on this sympathetic feeling and not forfeit it.

9. In those cases where the loss of the case before the jury seems so likely as to make it wise to put chief reliance on saving law points for appeal, it is, of course, necessary to be more insistent on crossing *t*'s and dotting *i*'s, but even here one serves one's client and the cause of justice best by being as cooperative as possible.

10. The defendant's troubles in a white-collar case will not be ameliorated—in fact, they may be vastly increased—if he yields to panicky ideas of getting "help" from supposedly influential friends or if he seeks to engage in the futile, frustrating, and questionable activity of managing the press by public relations methods. Furthermore, you can do your proper part as a member of the profession by seeing that it is not done.

25

RUSSIA SHOOTS ITS BUSINESS CROOKS

George Feifer

When Stanislaw Wawrzecki was executed in Warsaw late in March, 1965, Polish intellectuals blanched and muttered bitterly. Wawrzecki had been convicted as the mastermind of a conspiracy to divert meat belonging to state stores to sell for private profit; over a decade, the court found, the conspiracy had netted some 3.5 million zlotys (officially $150,000). His execution was apparently Poland's first in some 10 years for an economic crime, and it provoked strong resentment.

"What is the price now for human life in Poland?" asked a Warsaw resident. "Is it a ton of meat or only half a ton?"

"This is something for Asia, but not for a European country," another Pole protested.

"Asia" was probably a euphemism for "Russia" where (confirming Polish scorn for Muscovite barbarity) executions for economic crimes are now common. Only two weeks after Wawrzecki's execution, one T. Chkekheidze, the chief engineer of a Soviet candy factory, was convicted of masterminding a ring that had embezzled $76,000 by substituting

Reprinted from *The New York Times* Magazine (May 2, 1965), pp. 32–33, 111–112. © 1965 by The New York Times Company.

treacle for honey and margarine for butter, and siphoning off cognac destined for strong chocolates. Close to 200 Soviet citizens in the last four years are believed to have been sentenced to death for economic crimes.

The death penalty has not always been so liberally applied in Soviet Russia; but more often than not, it has. Capital punishment was abolished in 1917, restored in 1918, abolished again in 1920, restored in the same year, abolished in 1947 and reintroduced in 1950. During the years it existed (I refer here to punishment awarded by the ordinary court system, not the extralegal organs of terror and state security), the range of crimes for which it was applied fluctuated widely, from a few capital crimes to seventy-four categories under Stalin.

When the new Fundamentals of Criminal Legislation were enacted in 1958, after intensive debate about liberalizing Stalinist practices, the death penalty was not listed among the forms of criminal punishment. To demonstrate that execution was to be a highly restricted and temporary expedient, it was made the subject of a separate article: "As an exceptional measure of punishment until its full abolition, the application of the death penalty by shooting is permitted . . ."—but only for treason, espionage, sabotage, terroristic acts, banditism, and intentional murder with aggravating circumstances. Then, in 1961 and 1962, the Presidium of the Supreme Soviet promulgated, with little warning, a series of decrees extending the death penalty to economic crimes.

What are economic crimes? The decrees themselves explain them as well as anything else: speculation in currency, gold, or securities, professionally or on a major scale; theft and pilfering of state or communal property; counterfeiting of currency or securities for sale, or sale of counterfeit currency or securities; bribery.

The imposition of the death penalty for these noncapital offenses strikes most Westerners as cruel and inhuman. More shocking, the first application of the new decrees was *ex post facto*. The members of a group of currency speculators who were executed in Leningrad in 1961 had been sentenced earlier to fifteen years' imprisonment. In spite of Article 6 of the Federal Bases of Criminal Law—"A law establishing culpability for an act or increasing punishment has no retroactive force"— the Presidium of the Supreme Soviet passed a special decree permitting the death penalty for these men, and they were shot. The same procedure was resorted to in the execution of several gangs earlier sentenced to imprisonment for systematic plunder of state property.

The Soviet public was far less concerned by the new decrees, even by the executions, than many Western observers. Indeed, the execution of candy-racketeer Chkekheidze caused no noticeable public interest. Probably no one besides members of his family was gravely disturbed.

Among "ordinary," nonintellectual Russians, the decision to use extreme measures to suppress economic crime was hardly discussed. Russians have long been fatalistic: *Nichevo podelaiesh* (Nothing can be done about it) is their usual attitude. Like Russia's cruel climate and thin soil or the poverty of peasant life, criminal punishment is accepted as a "given" about which nothing can be done because higher powers have willed it. It has always been so in Russia, Czarist and Soviet; in this sense, the new decrees are not really new.

Even Soviet jurists are quiet about the extension of the death penalty. There have been sharp debates within the Soviet legal profession about critical problems of criminal law and procedure; the presumption of innocence, the significance of confession, the moment at which counsel should be permitted an accused person are among the major topics of debate. But no jurist, even the most liberal, has appeared in print to challenge directly the extension of the death penalty.

Even at professional conferences, where debates occasionally extend to the very principles of Socialist legality (and where exchanges occasionally become acrimonious), I have never heard the decrees, or the executions, challenged. For they lie in one of those areas where policies are established *na verkhu* (at the summit). Intense press and professional campaigns are mobilized to implement such policies, and no one needs to be warned that opposition will not be tolerated.

Not in public, anyway. Once, I asked a group of law students: "Doesn't *anyone* among you object to the application of the death penalty to economic crimes?" No one answered. But later, in private conversations, it turned out that a few, at least, did object. "Don't be misled," said one graduate student. "Lots of us are repelled by capital punishment. It's just as inhuman and regressive here as anywhere else. But you just can't talk about it at this moment. [It was late 1962, at the zenith of the campaign against economic crime.] In time, when this fury blows over, you'll hear solid arguments against it."

Why was "this fury" against economic crimes whipped up so soon after the major legal reforms of 1958?

For one thing, the extension of the death penalty in this area was but one phase of a general swing to harshness in Soviet penal policy. Zigzag has been the pattern of that policy since 1917, and in the 1961 "zag" the death penalty was extended not only to economic crimes, but also to aggravated cases of rape, major crimes committed by dangerous recidivists, crimes committed by persons while serving sentences for earlier serious crimes, and crimes committed against members of the Voluntary People's Brigades called *druzhiniki*.

Moreover, Soviet judges have begun awarding increased sentences for lesser crimes throughout the criminal code; and the use of conditional sentences and probation, widely encouraged from 1959 to 1961, has been drastically restricted. According to Moscow lawyers, the enthusiastic cam-

paign to "go easy on the criminals" starting in 1958 produced not the
desired efforts at reform, but an increase in crime rates.

But economics did play a special role in the new penal policy—economics plays a special role in all Soviet policies, and although Soviet commentators like to demonstrate that Western criminal policies faithfully
serve the changing needs of the capitalist class, the relationship of law
to economics seems more direct in their own country. The economic
crimes for which death has been imposed in the last four years run to a
pattern, with many, often ingenious, variations. Consider, for example,
a few of the most celebrated cases. Two residents of Riga established an
elaborate underground lipstick factory in the basement of one of their
homes. With the aid of workers in a legitimate factory, they diverted
supplies to their private plant—59,000 tubes in 1960 alone—and manufactured their private brand for the eager Russian market. The director
of the official plant received 1,500 rubles a month as his share of the
profits. The two ringleaders were executed, and five others received long
labor-colony sentences.

An underground textile plant in Tashkent manufactured some 310,000
yards of silk cloth—among other textiles of "left-handed production"—
which netted the conspirators nearly a million rubles in profit. Eleven
death sentences were imposed by the court.

An illegal clique of "businessmen" turned a Moscow mental asylum
into a secret knitwear factory of remarkable proportions: fifty-eight machines produced fashionable sweaters from 460 tons of wool. Private trade
relations were established with fifty-two factories, collective farms, cooperatives, and stores, some of which featured the sweaters in their
windows. Ten death sentences were imposed: four of fifteen years' imprisonment and ten others of lesser terms.

A clique centered in Moscow established a sprawling network for
speculating in gold and foreign currency. According to Soviet press reports,
its dealings, which included the purchase of valuables and smuggling of
Soviet currency abroad, as well as trading in gold and hard currency, ran
to millions of rubles. At least two of the speculators were shot, and an
undetermined number of others received long labor-colony sentences.

An inspector at government wheat mills sold part of one mill's flour—
running to thousands of tons—to other members of a gang and concealed
the loss by adding moisture to the remaining flour and by bookkeeping
subterfuges. He was shot, and his accomplices were awarded lengthy
sentences.

The catalog of these crimes is long and varied, ranging from the
systematic cheating of kopeks on pickles to vast industrial and commercial
enterprises thriving within the official Socialist manufacturing and distributing channels. Carloads of scarce goods are diverted from one factory
to another and from major cities to outlying regions where they fetch

huge profits; factories are operated privately in off-hours to manufacture black-market products from embezzled raw materials; goods and materials are stolen outright from the state in a hundred bold and subtle ways. And since the Soviet economy is a dense mesh of bureaucratic chains of command, control procedures and supercontrol procedures, the conspiracies are invariably jacketed in a pyramiding system of bribes involving directors of enterprises and trusts, auditors, investigators, control commission officials, bookkeepers, detectives, party inspectors—all of whose function is to prevent just such cheating.

In a Socialist economy—more precisely, in an economy planned to the extent that the Soviet one is planned—all economic transactions command national concern, and the reason for criminal sanctions against private enterprise is obvious: One deviation here means thousands of them there. Divert a ton of wool from a state factory to one in a private garage, and you have rendered invalid a staggering amount of paper planning. It is not your private business, but the community's.

But what inspired the sudden, furious drive against economic crimes precisely in 1961, when the Soviet economy was thriving as never before? I think several currents of Soviet political, legal, and economic history ran together to produce the decision. No one seriously questions that the decision was made by Khrushchev personally. And Khrushchev, as his successors have confirmed, was an impulsive leader. He was determined to change the nature of the Soviet economy—indeed, the very direction of the march to Communism—and this, I think, was a major motivation of the death-penalty decision, as of many others during his reign.

The crucial measures of economic and political success, before Khrushchev, had been quantitative: tons of steel poured, barrels of petroleum refined, tons of coal mined and kilowatts of energy produced. (And often it was not so much what was actually produced that mattered, but what was claimed on paper to have been produced.) But Khrushchev the pragmatist, the leader with the common touch, the prophet of "goulash Communism" became less and less interested in millions of tons of raw materials produced and more and more interested in what was being manufactured from the raw materials—in what was on sale in ordinary stores. He was genuinely devoted to creating an affluent society, to defeating capitalism in economic competition, if not for 9 million 120-inch wheelbase cars a year, at least for a comfortable life for all citizens.

Thus, when he found that almost nothing capable of producing pleasure of ownership was being sold in Soviet stores and concluded that one of the reasons was that the Socialist channels of manufacture and distribution were shot through with conspiracies diverting state goods for private profit, he lost all of his limited patience. "Our society will not and cannot tolerate such shameful survivals of the past," he fumed. "They must be fully eradicated."

No doubt he was all the more enraged when he found that the jurists who had reformed Stalin's harsh criminal laws had overreformed. In 1958, the maximum sentence for noncapital crimes was reduced to fifteen years, and it was absurd, Khrushchev surely felt, that masterminds of million-ruble conspiracies could take their risks (and not very grave risks, since they were usually well-protected by "family circles" of officials supposedly responsible for preventing violations) with this relatively short maximum and the probability of parole at half-sentence. The law needed to be sharpened, Khrushchev reasoned, and examples had to be found to deter potential cheaters. And so the death penalty was enacted, and an intense campaign launched to encourage judges to use it.

Or was the drive against economic crime mere camouflage for a new outburst of anti-Semitism? Judging by surnames in Soviet press reports, more than 60 per cent of the defendants executed for economic crimes have been Jewish. This astonishing figure, taken with the pointed emphasis on Jewish names in reporting the cases, the thinly disguised and sometimes openly vicious anti-Semitic tone of cartoons and satire, and the drastic restrictions on Jewish religious and cultural life, led many Western observers to conclude that the campaign was, in fact, a vendetta against Russian Jewry.

A portion of Moscow Jews confirm this charge tearfully. On the other hand, other Soviet Jews—including Jewish lawyers—feel that the party had not expected the campaign to involve such a disproportionate percentage of Jews and, indeed, that it now feels some consternation that events have developed this way. They assert, too, that Soviet Jews make up a far greater percentage of those responsible for consumer manufacture, wholesaling and retailing, and a far greater percentage in the territories where economic crimes are being prosecuted systematically, than their proportion (roughly 2 per cent) of the Soviet population as a whole.

A third explanation, offered by Soviet jurists, seems to me most perceptive: While the party leadership had not planned the campaign against economic crimes with the Jews in mind, it has to some extent become an outlet for anti-Semitism on the part of the police, investigators, prosecutors, judges and other second-level officials, many of whom were reared in peasant milieus, and there absorbed rural Russia's obsessive distrust of Jews.

The fact that Jews are likely to hold middle-level positions in trade—runs this argument—makes them more vulnerable to prosecution than higher officials who, though they may be profiting more, are better protected. Prosecutors and judges can fight for Socialist legality, frighten concealed swindlers, and vent their anti-Semitism all at one time.

Has the campaign been successful? Apparently one kind of cheating has been drastically curtailed. In the late 1950s, a visiting American could hardly walk through downtown Moscow without being stopped half a dozen times by Russians offering to buy dollars. Now, after the executions, such encounters are exceedingly rare, and I have been told that the Soviet black market has developed a considerable fear of handling dollars. But in the absence of statistics—and all meaningful Soviet criminal statistics are absent—no one besides a handful of Soviet officials can evaluate the full effect of the campaign.

What the effect of the new Soviet experiments in market techniques (freeing enterprises to make their own procurement and sales arrangements, with profit the major criterion of efficiency) will be on economic crimes and the death sentence is, of course, a matter of speculation. There are reasons to expect, however, that the new scheme may reduce the rate of economic crime. At the least, it should decrease the number of conspirators involved in a given case; for, freed from rigid controls from above, the directors of enterprises will have less need to bribe state officials.

And if the new freedom and the emphasis on profit provide a legitimate outlet for commercial initiative in response to consumer demand, the phenomenon of economic crime may be reduced in more positive ways. Embezzlement, bribery, theft of the people's wealth, disruption of the plan, corruption of Socialist mores—all this may be channeled, in some significant measure, into competition for Socialist profit, a concept now elevated to glory.

But it is the potential long-range effect of the new economic arrangements which offers the best hope that the death penalty for economic crimes will be abolished. In the measure that the profit scheme helps relieve the chronic Soviet shortage of consumer goods, the *raison d'être* of economic cheating will be correspondingly diminished. For—as Westerners found during World War II—it is shortage more than planning that inspires black markets and conspiracies to exploit precious public goods for private profit. As Aristotle put it: "Poverty is the parent of revolution and crime." Eliminate shortages and you eliminate the sources of economic crime.

That, at least, is the theory. So far, there has been no Marxist-Leninist society with an adequate supply of consumer goods to test the theory in practice.

26

101 BRITISH WHITE-COLLAR CRIMINALS

G. E. Levens

It would be quite normal for an author, as he embarks upon a reading carrying a title such as this, to plunge immediately into the currents of pedantry and attempt a rigid definition of two terms which convey a recognizable, but perhaps evaluative, meaning to most of his readers: "white-collar crime" and "white-collar criminals." I will largely shirk this task by pointing to the difficulties of definition and suggesting a way they may be avoided.

Academic discussion of white-collar crime has generally been channeled along two different and mutually confusing avenues: the first being one in which "white collar" is attributable to the offender, and the second in which it refers to the offense. The snag, quite obviously, is that a white-collar offender can commit both white-collar offenses (such as business crimes, contraventions of trade regulations, embezzlement, fraudulent conversion of money or property, etc.) and offenses which we might call "ordinary" (such as sex offenses, motoring offenses, simple larceny, and so on). On the other hand, a number of white-collar offenses can equally

Reprinted from *New Society* (March 26, 1964), pp. 6–8.

be committed by persons of acceptably white-collar status (like solicitors, managers, clerks, accountant, and by others who would not normally qualify for such a description (postman, general dealers, dairy roundsmen, shop assistants, etc.).

I believe that the criterion uppermost in most people's minds when they are considering this concept is that each offender has occupied a reasonably high social status, irrespective of the crime of which he has been convicted. In my research into the postdischarge prospects of prisoners who had previously been in white-collar occupations, I found it more expedient to think in terms rather of the "middle-class offender."

The sample under discussion in this article represents 101 middle-class prisoners who were discharged from six prisons during the period from February to June, 1962. The only criterion governing their selection was that each man could be reasonably classified—in terms primarily of his employment position, but also of his general cultural background—as being of at least lower-middle–class status.

PROFILE OF THE PRISONERS

Now, let us look at these men and see what characteristics they share, and in which ways they differ from other convicted prisoners.

In comparing the ages of the men in this sample of white-collar workers with the most closely coterminous figures available for the prison population as a whole (very short-term prisoners excluded), it becomes apparent that the average convicted middle-class offender is somewhat older than the average prisoner—about six or seven years older, in fact; the median ages for the two groups was around thirty-six and twenty-nine years respectively. This difference may also be illustrated by comparing the numbers who fall within the two age groups, 21 to 29 and 30 to 49. Just half of all men in prison fall within the former range, while only 37 per cent of the white-collar men do so; but the latter age range accounts for only approximately 42 per cent of all prisoners, yet comprises over 58 per cent of the men in the middle-class sample.

The reason for the difference in these two patterns lies undoubtedly in a conjunction of the motivation of much "white-collar" crime (of which we shall be saying more later) together with the presentation of the necessary opportunity to commit such offenses. For it is, generally speaking, only after the completion of a number of years' service in administrative, managerial, and/or professional employment that a degree of financial trust is placed in a man, and that he is therefore able to take a predatory advantage of it. This sort of situation is more likely to arise during a man's thirties and forties.

We use the term "white collar" to cover a very wide range of occupational groupings, and it is of more use in designating a minimum level of occupational status than in describing a strictly homogeneous type of employment. E. H. Sutherland, the American sociologist who was the first to consider white-collar crime within the framework of a systematic general theory of criminal behavior, admitted the embezzler and the forger to his ranks of the white-collar criminal, but nevertheless saw the businessman as typifying this category of offender. Occupational descriptions of the 101 subjects in the sample show that only one in five of these men can be classified as self-employed men running their own businesses. And, of these, the majority are of fairly junior status—usually men in small firms which they manage by themselves or with just one or two others, taking on only a few employees if at all, and generally struggling to put their enterprises on a sound financial footing, without possessing a very strong business acumen to back up these endeavors. The typical image of the corrupt and unethical tycoon, as shown in the Sutherland formulations, does not hold good for the United Kingdom—though one could easily argue that this sort of man does frequently infringe the law in his financial and commercial dealings, but that he is astute enough to avoid being caught. We shall return to this point later.

Another "typical" image of the white-collar criminal is that of the professional man—the solicitor, the accountants, etc.—who, having perhaps embroiled himself in financial difficulties, makes fraudulent use of his clients' or his employer's moneys to resolve those problems. (One might also include the abortionist doctor in this group.) It comes as a minor surprise therefore to discover only eleven men who would be categorized in this way, seven of them being solicitors or solicitors' managing clerks.

LESS RISK AT THE TOP

One fact which does seem to stand out fairly strongly is that in each of the occupational groupings in this sample, except the professional one, it is the man in the middle and junior echelons who predominates—thirty-three out of thirty-seven clerical, managerial, and administrative workers; sixteen out of twenty-one businessmen; eighteen out of twenty-two salesmen. One supposes that among professional men it is generally only in the highly qualified and therefore more responsible positions that the opportunity to commit offenses arises (i.e., the responsibility of being entrusted with funds, signing checks, not having day-to-day supervision of one's accounts, etc.).

The picture of the not-too-lowly clerk who makes off with the week's takings or fiddles receipts in order to divert some extra cash into his own pocket is quite a departure from that of the senior official or professional man manipulating large sums of money or of businessmen engaged in ruthless trading and commerical dealings. Again, we are left with the problem of deciding whether this latter group of men, occupying senior positions in their fields, do in fact only rarely commit offenses as these figures suggest or whether they are just as criminal as the others, but do not get caught (or, when they are convicted, are dealt with in other ways, such as by means of heavy fines, rather than sent to prison). The Sutherland thesis closely follows this latter opinion, but a number of the imprisoned businessmen in the sample indicated to the author (quite independently of each other) that it is primarily when a business, whatever its size or nature, is in its infancy and not yet firmly established upon a sound financial basis that the need to overstep the obscure and tenuous boundary between business ethics and actually illegal activity is greatest. In other words, men occupying senior positions in business just do not *need* to offend against business and financial laws so often. I am more cynically inclined to the opinion, however, that these men occupy senior positions simply because they are more astute and efficient in the ways of business than the others, and, likewise, they know how and when to play against the law with the greatest profit and the least risk.

Finally, we should note the fairly large proportion of salesmen in the sample—over one-fifth of the total. Although most of these were far removed from the door-to-door level of sales representative, it is nevertheless probably true that this group as a whole represents in terms of class origin a more marginal, less-established type of middle-class status than that of most of the other men in the sample. These are generally men who left school at fifteen or sixteen and who have perhaps passed through periods as manual workers before adopting white-collar employment.

Another of the characteristics which we are inclined to attribute to the middle-class offender is that of a previously clear record. We imagine him as being in trouble for the first time; and even if he has committed offenses in the past, this at any rate is the first time he has been convicted. On the whole, the sample bears out this observation, but it is nevertheless interesting in the light of this image to see that forty-four of the 101 men had previously been convicted in a court of law (including two who had served civil prison sentences). Even if we subtract from this number ten men whose most serious convictions had been for minor motoring offenses, drunkenness, betting offenses, etc., we are still left with the fact that approximately one-third of all the men in the sample had previous convictions of a more serious nature recorded against them, and of these nineteen (or just under one in five) had served prison sentences. One man had already paid seven separate visits to jail for increasingly longer periods of time, and eight others had been to prison more than once previously.

It goes without saying that these recidivists were not to be found among the professional men, civil servants, senior managerial and administrative workers, etc., simply because they would normally have been barred from further employment in these fields after their first conviction of any gravity. The recidivists, therefore, are located more among the ranks of the self-employed businessmen, salesmen, and junior- and middle-rung clerks. This proportion of one in five conforms very closely to the accepted rate of reconviction among first-time prisoners (20 to 25 per cent) and would suggest that in this respect, at least, the population of white-collar convicts is not very different from the prison population as a whole.

What were the crimes that took these men to prison? Being of white-collar status, did they commit offenses of a white-collar nature too? The answer, briefly, is yes. Roughly three-quarters of these men had committed offenses broadly definable as white collar; that is to say, either offenses arising essentially from their tenure of white-collar employment, offenses by businessmen, crimes of a fraudulent nature, or cognate offenses such as forgery, tax, and bankruptcy frauds. Five of the seventy-four men in this category had also been convicted of offenses under other headings, such as sexual offenses, simple larceny, assault, etc. One man had not only run off with the firm's wages, he had also been drawing a regular income from the fraudulent use of National Insurance stamps, had committed bigamy (incidentally, his second offense of this nature; that is, four wives in all), and had tied up the whole thing by failing to surrender to bail.

The largest group by far was that of offenses by employees, their employers being the usual victims. Under this heading are to be found most of the cases of embezzlement, larceny as servant, falsification of accounts, forgery, etc. This group accounts for thirty-seven of the 101 men, a good deal more than the next largest single group—that of businessmen who had committed offenses during the course of their commercial and financial dealings (seventeen in all). Again, it is interesting to see that Sutherland's conception of white-collar crime as largely comprising offenses by the corrupt businessman is hardly supported by this evidence. In fact, the figure of seventeen cases of crimes by businessmen out of a total of 101 subjects is swollen by a number of small-time businessmen, working on their own account without an established firm and often without other partners or employees, whose offenses would have been more accurately grouped under the head of false pretenses by con men were it not for the fact that they had been committed in the course of the men's business activity, as an intrinsic part of their profit-making enterprise so to speak.

There were eleven cases in the sample involving sexual offenses, nine of these being concerned with young children, but the patterns of both motivation and commission of these particular sorts of crimes bear little relationship to those of the more frequently occurring white-collar offenses, even though a number of the men had found their victims among persons with whom they had come into contact during the course of their employment or, alternatively, through social activities of a mainly middle-class nature. (The author here has in mind the teacher indecently assaulting his pupils, the part-time scoutmaster and his pack, etc.). Strictly speaking, one should classify sex offenses committed during the course of white-collar employment (i.e., by teachers, doctors, and so on) as white-collar crimes, but the author has felt it more suitable to group homogeneously all sex offenses in view of the fact that the attitude of the general public toward such crimes per se is probably more critical than is its condemnation of the violation of (moral) trust which has been involved.

The ten cases of "ordinary" offenses were found usually, though not invariably, to have been committed by the type of man who was of a more marginal middle-class status—junior clerks, salesmen, and so on. With one exception, the solidly middle-class man was not to be found among these numbers.

CULTURAL IMAGE

These figures help to confirm that the general pattern of criminal deviation for the middle-class man is quite different from that of the lawbreaker from a lower social stratum. To a large extent, this distinction may be attributable to the factor of opportunity, but we should certainly not overlook the importance of a culturally induced attitude on the part of these men as to what is admissible as criminal behavior and what is not. For it is apparent that the middle-class man, seeking a solution to his financial difficulties, tends generally to confine himself to the violation of the financial trust placed in his employment position and to commit only "clean" crimes. As we have seen, he usually refrains from undertaking other, more usual, forms of illegal enterprise, like larceny or house breaking. The reason for this is probably a combination of factors:

These other "ordinary" crimes are the work, more often than not, of the young man, a man who is stronger, fitter, and therefore physically better equipped for such activity than the office-bred white-collar worker verging upon middle age.

All crimes require a knowledge of the "tricks of the trade," and the white-collar worker is much more likely to know how to manipulate the figures in his account book or to forge financial documents than he is to be *au fait* with the art of safe blowing, lock breaking, or the disposal of stolen goods.

As Sutherland has pointed out, the middle-class white-collar man moves among and associates with others who are acquainted, at first or second hand, with the nature and techniques of such white-collar offenses. He is much less likely to come into continuous contact with people who have knowledge of "ordinary" or more violent crimes.

One should give some attention to the observation of D. R. Cressey in his outstanding study of the violation of financial trust, *Other People's Money*, that although the white-collar offender knows that embezzling the firm's funds is "wrong," nevertheless he reconciles this knowledge with his own depredatory activity by means of rationalizations, which reduce the guilt feelings that such criminal behavior must engender. "They didn't give me the raise I was due for last year"; "they're a big firm, they can afford it"; "they're covered by the insurance"; "everyone is on the fiddle here, so why not me too?"; or "I've put in more work than they've paid me for." Naturally, the psychological rationalization of an offense involving the use of even a moderate amount of violence, or threatened violence, or which produced a victim immediately describable in interpersonal terms, would be infinitely more difficult to achieve.

DRAIN OF SELF-CONFIDENCE

One cannot escape the impression that most of the prisoners in the sample did not conceive of themselves as criminals. This epithet still conveyed to them, as to most people, the image of the thug, the bank robber, the demoniacal and notorious villain who clubs old ladies in dark alleys and makes off with the house money; the sort of person, in fact, with whom they were now obliged to live every day but from whom they continued to distinguish themselves, even while sharing the same cell. The word "criminal" certainly does not conjure up the mental picture of a solicitor's quietly converting his client's money nor, for that matter, of a minister of religion indulging in his favorite hobby with the boys and girls after choir practice.

Nevertheless, this self-confidence was certainly less securely maintained among those who were in prison on a second or further occasion, and one or two of those who were later reconvicted passed comments on their second time around which indicated that they were beginning to accept the possibility, as one put it, that "maybe I am just a criminal after all." No longer were they anxious to point out that they represented just the visible ninth of the criminal iceberg and that they were simply the unlucky ones who had been caught.

A final point should be made upon the motivation for these crimes. What were the precipitating factors which led these men to resort finally to criminal means for the resolution of the financial crises affecting them? (For of the ninety-seven men who provided the necessary information, seventy-five were in financial difficulties of one kind or another, often to a very serious extent.)

Table 1 gives some indication of the causes for their difficulties, and in particular it is interesting to note the indirect effects upon these men of the competition for social status in suburbia (for 41 per cent of the men lived in a suburban area, mostly around London and in the Home counties). This is expressed most strongly in the large proportion of men whose difficulties arose from the fact that their economic position was constantly summed up in the equation: "Expenditure = Income + X." Heavy spending on entertainment, dining out, and drinks frequently goes alongside serious financial commitments on the mortgaged semidetached, cars, and miscellaneous other middle-class "essentials."

Drinking and gambling alone account for what may seem a fairly small percentage of the total, and, again, the more conventional picture of the white-collar employee who "borrows" from the till in order to gamble and perhaps regain his losses, is not, from these figures, a very accurate one, accounting for no more than 11 per cent of the entire sample (15 per cent of those quoting the experience of financial difficulties).

Table 1. Causes Given for Financial Troubles, as Per Cent of Total Number of Men

Cause	Per cent[a]
Heavy social expenditure	41
Business failings	21
Low or irregular income	21
Heavy home liabilities	16
Gambling	15
Drinking	9
Other reasons[b]	5
(Insufficient information)	5

[a] Some men quoted more than one cause, so the percentages do not add up to 100.
[b] For example, blackmail, keeping two homes.

27

A STUDY OF INCARCERATED WHITE-
COLLAR OFFENDERS

John C. Spencer

The few major studies of white-collar crime have dealt with the crime rather than the criminal. The very nature of the crime makes this inevitable, since it is easier to study the social institutions to which individuals belong than to gain access to the individuals themselves. The thirty white-collar criminals who constituted the sample for my exploratory study at Leyhill Prison had all been convicted and sentenced to imprisonment by the courts. I took advantage of the availability of a captive population in a prison, recognizing at the same time the limitation of a sample consisting entirely of men who had been apprehended, convicted, and sentenced to imprisonment. Since a basic assumption of this paper has been that white-collar criminals are more likely than ordinary criminals to remain outside the courts, this is a serious limitation. A prevalent attitude of the sample during my interviews at Leyhill was: "We were just careless—doing what everyone else in business does—but we were unlucky."

Reprinted from John C. Spencer, "White-Collar Crime," in Tadeusz Grygier, Howard Jones, and John C. Spencer (eds.), *Criminology in Transition* (London: Tavistock Publications, 1965), pp. 251–264.

The extent to which such remarks as this were merely rationalization and therefore valueless as an indication of the prevalence of this kind of behavior among other members engaged in the same occupation is impossible to assess. In the case of embezzlement, for example, Cressey has emphasized rationalization as an essential element in his hypothesis.[1] In this study I observed that there were important variations in the extent to which my informants recognized their offense as deviant behavior in the groups to which they belonged.

The study was carried out during the spring of 1959, following a course of winter lectures given to the prison staff for the Extension Department of Bristol University. Leyhill Prison is classified as a minimum security regional training prison. It consists of a group of converted army hospital hutments in the grounds of a country mansion near the village of Leyhill. Its extensive grounds are surrounded by no more than low walls or hedges. It maintains an active training program and the visitor is continually aware of a high level of morale among staff and prisoners.[2] The Leyhill population contains a very large proportion of first offenders and men who are good security risks. The white-collar criminal is well suited to the training regime. He sees himself as the elite of the prison. At the time of my visit, for example, there were strong views expressed in favor of the exclusion of sex offenders from the prison cricket team. A not uncommon remark made by my informants was, "We wouldn't steal like the embezzlers" or "Ours isn't a nasty offense like the sex offenders." In their language, it should be noted, they avoided the use of prison jargon.

The proportion of offenses committed by the 260 inmates of Leyhill was:

Larceny, breaking and entering	20%
Sex offenses (excluding incest)	20%
Fraud and false pretenses	20%
Incest	16%
Other	24%

SELECTION OF THE SAMPLE

The choice of criteria for selecting the sample was at first sight difficult. The definition was based on Sutherland—an offense committed by a person of high status in the course of his occupation. It was made easier by the fact that the number of men in English prisons who fit this definition is small. Unfortunately, no statistics as to size or distribution are available, since it is a definition which cuts across the recognized classification of types of crime and criminal. The prison commission advised me that the largest number would be found at Leyhill.

The criteria selected for the sample were: offense, occupation, and social status. After discussion with the Department of Public Prosecutions, the three most appropriate offenses all appeared to come within the general category of fraud: conspiracy to cheat and defraud, offenses under the Prevention of Fraud (Investment) Act, and fraudulent conversion when tried before an assize court. My main object was to exclude persons who deliberately set out to make money by fraud. The offense of fraud assumes many forms, some serious and others relatively minor.[3] It is certainly not synonymous with white-collar crime though closely related to it.

It was necessary, therefore, to take into account both occupation and social status. Though occupation is itself the most important determinant of social status, and might have been expected to constitute alone an adequate criterion, I found it necessary, after reading the prison records, to make a judgment as to suitability for inclusion in the sample on the basis of social status in the neighborhood or in local associations. For example, although in general I excluded clerks from the sample, I included a solicitor's clerk on the grounds of his prominent position on the local cricket team and the status achieved through professional relationships.[4] For inclusion in the sample it was essential that the man should have committed the offense in the course of his occupation.

The sample was obtained by taking the first thirty cases on the prison register who fitted the above criteria. This register was maintained in chronological order. Cases not fitting the criteria were discarded. An analysis was made of the records of all the thirty cases, but only twenty-four men were interviewed; six men were discharged before the interviewing was complete. Each man was asked by the governor if he would be willing to take part. There were no refusals. The interviews lasted for about one hour to one-and-a-half hours. Some men were interviewed a second time. An open-ended questionnaire was used covering the following areas: circumstances of offense, family of origin and own family, siblings, education, friends, social groups, occupation, and aspirations for themselves and/or their children.

THEORETICAL FRAMEWORK

In developing a theoretical framework for this study I was influenced by the approach of the structural-functional school of sociology, by Sutherland's theory of differential association, and by Sellin's discussion of culture conflict and crime. I started from Aubert's assumption that white-collar crime is both "crime" and "not crime" and that, in Merton's words, "certain phases of social structure generate the circumstances in which infringement of social codes constitutes a 'normal response.' "[5] An approach of this kind stresses the social system rather than the individual criminal and views white-collar crime as appropriate behavior within the system.

Now there are clearly obstacles to the development of this kind of framework which are inherent in the nature of the sample. It is impossible to study a social system through the experience of a single informant. The occupations of the sample differed widely and men were drawn from all parts of the country. It was, however, possible to adopt a more limited approach and to see the behavior which led to the individual's imprisonment within the context of the social groups with which he has been or would like to be identified. . . .

Every individual is identified with a number of social groups and is supposed to conform not only to the rules which it shares with other groups, but also to those which are peculiarly its own. The more complex the culture, the more likely the norms of these groups may conflict, no matter how much overlap there may be as the result of common acceptance. The problem, then, is to identify and clarify them, and the sociological analysis of criminal norms must penetrate beyond the labels of the law to the type of social value to which the violation does harm. Through this kind of approach we may move toward a greater understanding of what Sutherland called the white-collar criminal's "selective obedience to law."

Sociological studies of crime have generally depreciated the significance of personality factors in the explanation of white-collar crime. This has arisen for two reasons: first, because they have been primarily concerned with social systems rather than with individuals; second, a more unsatisfactory reason, because they have tended to adopt Sutherland's view that personal traits are unimportant.[6] This second reason is unsatisfactory because it assumes a naïve approach to personality theory. In fact, we know little about the personality of the white-collar criminal. He has been neglected by psychologists and psychiatrists.

In this study, though primarily concerned with the norms of behavior, I tried not to ignore such facts about personality as emerged in the course of the interview. I started from the assumption that the white-collar criminal is a normal personality and from Leitch's observations on the very small incidence of actual psychoneurotic and psychotic illness, and from the deliberate exclusion of typical psychopathic personalities from Leyhill.[7] But psychiatric concepts of abnormality, in studies of conventional offenders, fail to do justice to the subtleties of personality of the white-collar criminal.

In this study there is no systematic theory of personality. Observations about the personality of the informants are related mainly to their capacity to handle the conflict of norms presented by membership in different social groups.[8] Abnormal conduct, though from one point of view is the violation of a conduct norm, from another point of view is the expression of a personality which has "incorporated cultural elements which lead their possessor to engage in abnormal instead of in normal conduct."[9] The individuals in my sample were drawn from a heterogeneous group of occupations and from very different social backgrounds. My assumption was that the stability of personality of the white-collar criminal will vary directly with the coherence of the group norms with which he has identified. That is, I expected to find that the more stable individuals were identified with more coherent group norms.

FORMAL CHARACTERISTICS OF THE SAMPLE

Age. They were predominantly a middle-aged and elderly group. Two-thirds of the sample were over forty-five years old. Only one man was under thirty. Three were between fifty-five and sixty-five. Judged, at least by previous convictions, they were late-comers to crime.[10]

Previous Convictions. Twenty-five of the sample had no previous convictions. Of the remaining five men, three had previous convictions for motoring offenses and two had received short sentences of imprisonment for frauds committed some twenty years previously.

This much is to be expected in view of the principles of selection for Leyhill. Of greater interest is the question as to how long they had been committing their offenses. Here there were wide variations. One informant, a stockbroker in his late fifties and probably the wealthiest member of the sample, indicated that the type of behavior for which he was finally convicted had been of very long standing. For the majority, however, the offense or offenses that led to their conviction were the culmination of a series of dubious business enterprises over the previous three or four years.

Offenses. The two most characteristic offenses committed by the sample were fraudulent conversion and conspiracy to defraud. Five of the sample were also convicted of false pretenses in addition to fraud. Four were convicted of either embezzlement, forgery, or falsification of accounts. The case for including these last three offenses is certainly arguable. On Cressey's definition they would have been excluded. Sutherland, on the other hand, included embezzlement, pointing out the large sums of money which have been embezzled and the serious consequences of violation of trust. He observed that it was an interesting exception to white-collar crime in respect of power relationships and contrasted the power of white-collar criminals with the weakness of their victims.[11] My own justification for including these four in the sample was their social standing in their community.

This brief statement on the offenses committed emphasizes the salient characteristics of the sample. Fraud was their main offense and the circumstances of the offense as presented in court made abundantly clear the fraudulent nature of their transactions. No one reading an account of these circumstances would have labeled their behavior as merely "para-criminal." The offenses were more than just "technical" in character.

Length of Sentence. Twenty-five out of the sample of thirty were serving sentences between three and five years. The remaining five had sentences of seven and eight years . . .

Occupation and Occupational Record. After reading the occupations entered in the prison records, it very quickly became clear that no sample of top businessmen from large corporations would be available at Leyhill. In short, this could not be a sample of men fulfilling Sutherland's stereotype of the "merchant princes and captains of finance and industry." Perhaps it does, however, contain their "lesser followers."[12]

The sample was graded on the Hall-Jones occupational scale.[13] This scale contains seven classes . . . and is a grading of occupational status not of social class, but occupation has an important bearing on class. The result of this grading shows that the sample fell into the three highest classes as follows: Class 1, six men; class 2, thirteen men; class 3, eleven men. The occupations ranged from solicitor to haulage contracter. It was not always easy to determine the class represented by the occupation. At least two-thirds of the sample owned or managed a business firm. Several were listed in the prison records as a company director. "Company director" by itself can mean many things. Since the class of a business owner or director or manager depends, on the Hall-Jones scale, on the number of people employed, size of firm was as important factor. The list also contains such occupations as estate agent, shop owner, auctioneer, surveyor, and accountant. Perhaps the outstanding characteristic of the sample was the number of men working on their own or with a partner. There were no executives of well-known corporations.

Their occupational records showed considerable evidence of upward mobility. Many of them had started as skilled manual workers and some had risen to positions of considerable affluence. The example of Mr. X——— is typical of this pattern of mobility: He had left an elementary school at fourteen and trained for seven years as an apprentice machinist. After working as a machinist in a factory he set up on his own as a motor engineer. On psychiatric grounds he was not called up for military service. In due course he built up a company of 300 trucks by buying up government vehicles at the end of the war. The money with which to do this was obtained from finance corporations. The success of this operation led to loans for nonexistent vehicles. At the time of his conviction for conspiracy to defraud, his debts amounted to a total over £140,000.

The fathers of the men in this sample, on the other hand, were drawn mainly from Classes 4 and 5, a fact which emphasizes the upward mobility of our group.

Education. The same emphasis on upward mobility is shown by an analysis of their education. Fifteen men left elementary school at age fourteen. Four had been educated at a technical school, eight at a private school, and three at a public school. Two went to a university.

Marriage. None of the sample was unmarried, twenty-one were living with their wives, one was a widower, and eight were separated. Of these eight men, three were living with a woman. These facts tell little about their marriage relationships, but they support the general impression gained in the interviews of reasonably stable relationships between husbands and wives. This is certainly in marked contrast to the marriage relationships of the habitual offender.[14]

DISCUSSION

The evidence of this group of thirty men may be looked at from two points of view: first, as individual white-collar criminals and, second, as the social framework of white-collar crime.

The outstanding characteristic of these thirty men, as is obvious from this brief analysis of certain formal data about them, is their upward mobility. This observation was an unexpected one. It did not constitute a basic assumption underlying the study. I had expected to find in my sample a much larger group of men in leading commercial and financial positions and with a superior social and educational background.

This upward mobility is closely related to what also appears to be an outstanding feature of their personality, their ambition, their drive, their desire to mix with people of higher social position than their own and to give their children an expensive private education, and their willingness to take financial risks in the process. In contrast to their own ambitions and even reckless behavior, I continually noticed the apparent stability and security of their siblings as they discussed their family histories. They lived more expensively than their brothers and they often spoke of their brothers' ability to stick to a routine task without ambitions for success and achievement. One informant said, for example, "My brother and I are different temperaments. He is much more placid than me. He is a sounder character and would stick to things much more." Their families had, with one exception, no record of criminal convictions so far as I could learn. The exception was Mr. Y———, convicted of fraudulent conversion together with his brother. The two brothers, who were both builders, induced clients to part with money in order to have an alleged share of the profits from property deals. Some of the properties were not for sale and others were not available. The clients lost £10,000 in these deals when the firm went bankrupt.

Of particular interest to me were the norms of the groups to which the sample belonged or with which they identified themselves. The evidence points to the noticeable conflict of norms which a large number of the sample experienced in the course of their occupation and their social life. The conflict was particularly acute in the case of occupation and family life. Several men spoke of living two lives and of the ignorance of their wives and other relatives of their business relationships.

They were, in general, popular members of social groups. Their clubs included two prominent London clubs, Masonic lodges, Rotary, and a host of minor political, social, and sports clubs of various kinds. One member of the sample was a past master of a city livery company in London. Club membership was considered important mainly for the social prestige which it carried and for the opportunity of mixing with people of superior status. It was all part of the same process of upward mobility for which the expensive house and automobile and other symbols of status were also thought to be necessary. A small number of the sample took part in the social life of church and chapel. All the evidence points to the fact that they kept separate the norms of the different groups to which they belonged, particularly those of employment, recreation, and family.

Some members were better able to accept the conflict of norms involved in membership of contrasted groups. They spoke confidently of their "two lives." Others were more anxious about the conflict, and the strain of "keeping up appearances" as respectable and successful professional or businessmen had, in a few cases, resulted in nervous breakdown. Some felt the stigma of prison very acutely, whereas others merely expressed hostility at the injustice of their conviction and sentence. All rationalized their behavior in one way or another.

The most common form of rationalization was the excuse that they were merely doing what everyone else did. Mr. Z———, for example, a property developer convicted of conspiracy to defraud, who had induced clients to put down deposits on houses which were found to be nonexistent at the time of his firm's bankruptcy, said,

> What I did—having a separate bank account for all the deposits taken and using the money to build the houses—is what every builder does. If it succeeds, no one minds. If it fails, there is a prosecution. I know of many companies which have gone into liquidation where there was no prosecution. Our ideas have been sound, but we have been poor administrators; we didn't set out to rob and swindle.

> I make a strong moral distinction between fraudulent conversion and theft or embezzlement. We wouldn't dream of stealing anything.

The same excuse was applied to such behavior as the manipulation of expense accounts and the splitting of commissions.

Nevertheless, in spite of the rationalizations of this kind, the sample differed widely in feelings of guilt. There was a tendency for the professional members in the sample, perhaps as a consequence of the disciplinary procedure and ethical rules of their professions, to express a greater feeling of guilt than the businessmen. For the professional man, there was a double penalty—imprisonment and also exclusion from the profession.

To generalize about personality on such slender evidence is clearly impossible. But two points deserve emphasis. First, there was a noticeable absence of the feelings of rejection and emotional deprivation commonly found in studies of the recidivist. Two men, however, a solicitor and a civil servant, spoke of the effect that poverty and financial worries in their families had had on their subsequent determination to bring up their own families in comfort. Several mentioned the very high expectations that their mothers had for them, and one of these spoke of a dominating father with a very modest ambition for his son's future. Second, there was the evidence of risk taking, which some of the sample in the course of the interviews called a "gambling instinct." There was, moreover, a kind of ruthless determination in some of the sample to achieve their goal. One man, an estate agent, said, "I would say I am amoral. Is this going to be good for Joe? I can smell money and I can buy brains—professors are as cheap as peanuts. Everyone can be bought—at a price."

But it would be a mistake to see the adventurous and ruthless gambler as typical of the white-collar criminal. Such men did not account for more than one-third of the sample. About equal in number were the muddlers and the incompetent men, with no firm principles or standards, whose gradual drift from unethical into dishonest behavior was accentuated by threatened business failure or the withdrawal of credit by a hire-purchase finance corporation. Unfortunately, we have no data on their level of intelligence, but it seems likely that there was a wide variation in the level of intelligence of the group.

In examining the social framework of the white-collar crime analyzed in this sample, three closely related features deserve attention. The first is the prevalence of bankruptcy in the sample. Sixteen of the sample of thirty had become bankrupt. The losses to creditors were considerable, including several sums between £10,000 and £120,000. Seldom did the assets amount to more than one-tenth of the liabilities. The view has been expressed that the line of demarcation between insolvency and fraud is at times very arbitrary and that the decision to prosecute is greatly dependent on the attitude of creditors and the facility with which assets may be realized to cover liabilities. The inference to be drawn from these brief observations is the urgent need for criminological study of bankruptcy and the extent of the antisocial consequences of both voluntary and involuntary liquidation.

The second is the absence of adequate public control over the activities of the hire-purchase finance corporations and over dealings in property and real estate. Nearly half the cases in our sample fall into the category of real estate and of business financed by hire-purchase credit, particularly road haulage and television sets. It is almost impossible in certain cases to believe that adequate inquiries were made by finance corporations into the capacity of these men to manage a business or into the state of their finances. It is certainly not difficult to see the reasons which led to reckless behavior in businesses where either the gains were considerable or finance was plentiful until a national "credit squeeze" was suddenly applied.

The third feature is the very high proportion of small firms and professional men operating singly or with a partner. In the case of solicitors, the Law Society in England has recognized the problem of the single lawyer and recommended the advantages of partnership. The businessmen in this sample were in a very different position from the "captains of finance and industry" in Sutherland's study. They were subject to different kinds of incentive and control from those experienced by executives of large corporations. Such success as many of them had was relatively short-lived, and all eventually failed in their struggle for status and prestige. As members of small firms, they were easily at the mercy of an unscrupulous partner or managing clerk; some of them suffered crippling losses at the hands of customers and clients. On the other hand, their victims—with the exception of those who received compensation from the Law Society's fund—obtained little redress in the face of considerable financial loss.

CONCLUSION

Each successive generation has the task, as Mannheim observed, of working out afresh its views on the problem of crime and of translating them into legislation.[15] The challenge of white-collar crime to criminology is unique in several ways. First, unlike most types of crime, there is no clear consensus as to the kind of behavior that should be considered criminal. The more difficult ethical and legal problems which confront us arise in the "grey" areas where the rules are confused, rather than in areas where behavior is known to be criminal. In the second place, the relationship between the white-collar criminal and his victim is quite different from the usual relationship between criminal and victim. The victim of a white-collar crime frequently hopes to gain financially from the relationship. . . . Third, the regulation and control of white-collar crime requires methods quite different from the ordinary process of law enforcement. It is to this problem that future study and research should be particularly directed.

The fact that white-collar crime has come to be almost synonymous with the crimes of businessmen is indicative, at least to sociologists, of the fact that a major threat to our values has come from this segment of society, especially in the United States. This is an unfortunate and even misleading assumption. The field is in fact a much wider one: There is every reason to include also such important problems as tax evasion and avoidance, bankruptcy, bogus advertisements, political corruption, and trade-union activities.

The problem of regulation and control may be viewed on three levels: internal methods of regulation by the industry or profession, administrative control by an appropriate government agency, and judicial control by the use of the criminal law and criminal sanctions. Each of these three methods has its appropriate function but their interrelationship is frequently neglected. The growth of disciplinary procedures in the professions is unequivocal evidence of agreement over the necessity for control over ethical and professional behavior. The procedures adopted by all the professions, although differing in detail, are modeled on the experience of the General Medical Council. Yet this development was initially a slow process. The early history of the General Medical Council since its foundation in 1858 shows how slow it was to make use of the quasi-judicial powers it had received by the act under which it was instituted.[16]

In business and finance the development of regulation and control is similarly a slow process. While there is strong opposition to government interference, there is also a growing recognition of the value of internal methods of regulation. Advertising provides an apt illustration of this general trend. The formation of the Advertising Standards Authority in Great Britain is one such important development. In the United States, the Federal Trade Commission has tightened its control over advertising, particularly over deceptive advertising on television. But certain forms of behavior are so antisocial in their consequence that neither internal regulation alone nor government control *unsupported by criminal sanctions* is enough. The proper decision as to the appropriate method of control can only be made on a foundation of social research.

Notes

1. Donald R. Cressey, *Other People's Money: The Social Psychology of Embezzlement* (New York: The Free Press, 1953), chap. 4.

2. See A. Leitch, "The Open Prison," *British Journal of Delinquency*, 2 (July, 1951), pp. 25–33.

3. With permission from the chief commissioner of the metropolitan police, I compared the size of frauds for which there had been convictions in the metropolitan police area during the years 1955 and 1956 to 1957 (the only years for which complete data are available). As will be seen from the following table, large frauds over £10,000 form a very small part of the total.

Year	Total number of frauds	Frauds over 100	Over 1,000	Over 10,000
1955	3,232	231	32	1
1956	3,330	250	43	6
1957	4,112	91	26	5

With few exceptions the largest frauds were for fraudulent conversion.

4. Edwin H. Sutherland, "White-Collar Criminality," in Albert Cohen, Alfred Lindesmith, and Karl Schuessler, eds., *The Sutherland Papers* (Bloomington, Ind.: Indiana University Press, 1956), p. 51, fn. 1.

5. Robert K. Merton, *Social Theory and Social Structure* (New York: The Free Press, 1957), pp. 131–194.

6. Sutherland, "White-Collar Criminality," *op. cit.*, p. 58; Edwin H. Sutherland, *White Collar Crime* (New York: Dryden Press, 1949), chap. 15.

7. Leitch, *op. cit.*, pp. 31–32.

8. See Dorothy Emmet, *Function, Purpose and Powers* (London: Macmillan, 1958), p. 285.

9. Thorsten Sellin, *Culture Conflict and Crime* (New York: Social Science Research Council, 1938), p. 40.

10. See Norval Morris, *The Habitual Criminal* (London: G. Bell, 1951), p. 367.

11. Sutherland, "White-Collar Criminality," *op. cit.*, p. 57.

12. *Ibid.*, p. 48.

13. John Hall and D. Cardadog Jones, "Social Grading of Occupations," *British Journal of Sociology*, 1 (March, 1950), pp. 31–55.

14. Morris, *op. cit.*, pp. 350–353.

15. Hermann Mannheim, *Criminal Justice and Social Reconstruction* (London: Routledge, 1946), p. 4.

16. C. P. Harvey, "The Disciplinary Committee and the Courts," *British Medical Journal*, 2 (November 22, 1958), pp. 1257–1259.

VI

CONTROVERSY REGARDING THE CONCEPT OF WHITE-COLLAR CRIME

The five readings in this last part are occupied with questions concerning the proper definition of white-collar crime. They are apt to strike a posture of disingenuous innocence, while vigorously pursuing their respective ends, as if their authors cannot quite understand how it is that others are unable to comprehend the self-evident positions that they put forward. As background regarding the scope and definition of white-collar crime, the readings come to grips with common elements to an unusual degree and they lay out carefully for the reader diverse polemical considerations involved in the study of white-collar crime.

It is notable that the authors are usually members of either the legal profession or the sociological discipline, with one foot firmly planted in their area of major concentration and the other less firmly rooted in or seeking out the second area. In particular, the authors are men conversant to a noteworthy degree with two fields of knowledge who tend to snipe at members of one with specialized information and insights from the other.

The Sutherland-Tappan debate opens the section. Sutherland's knowledge of law was not formidable, but he had enough command of it to offer forceful arguments regarding logical flaws in a professional approach often so bound up in day-to-day pursuits and so committed to historical precedent that it was apt to blur the distinction between the defined and the definitive. Both Sutherland and Tappan, it might be noted, are rather agile at paraphrasing opposing views, so that they stand in their least attractive form when they are finally marshaled for rebuttal.

The tenacious and inexorable nature of Sutherland's approach commands respect as he drives his polemical steamroller. Obviously irritated by criticism of his earlier work, Sutherland sets out to demonstrate that white-collar crime truly is "crime." Perhaps the most treacherous and vital moment in his presentation occurs when he argues that civil fines are really the same as criminal fines except that the stigma of criminality has been extracted from them. It is, of course, true that all fines involve deprivation and that they therefore penalize, under whatever guise. If, however, civil fines are to be regarded as equivalent to criminal sanctions, except for the removal of stigma, then Sutherland would appear obligated to maintain that any official sanction involving loss or hurt is a criminal sanction. Justice Warren in *Trop v. Dulles*, in fact, enunciated essentially this view, with the observation that "inquiry must be directed to substance" and that "a statute that prescribes the consequences that will befall one who fails to abide by these regulatory provisions is a penal law." "Even a clear legislative classification of a statute as nonpenal," Warren wrote, "would not alter the fundamental nature of a plainly penal statute."

Therefore, it is not Sutherland's position that is necessarily out of line; his default lies in not grappling with its extraordinarily far-reaching implications for the study not only of crime and deviance, but also of virtually all forms of human activity that may result in retaliatory actions.

Sutherland is also apt to regard the generally more benign treatment accorded to white-collar offenders in contrast to traditional offenders as at least partially traceable to class and behavioral homogeneity between the authorities and the white-collar violators, a conclusion of considerable interest but one not clearly demonstrated. Certainly it is true that during the Depression period in the United States the prosecution of business firms increased considerably, perhaps, as Sutherland maintains, because business was in a period of its lowest status. Nonetheless, capital punishment of traditional property offenders, for example, also increased markedly during the same period. It seems likely that it is something more fundamental and pervasive than the status of businessmen that conditions the ebbs and flows of prosecutory actions against white-collar offenders.

More than any other scholar, Paul W. Tappan (1911–1964) incessantly called criminologists to task for their neglect of legal concerns in their work. Tappan, who had earned a doctorate in both law and sociology, spent the major portion of his career at New York University before moving to the University of California in Berkeley, a few years before his death. Tappan spearheaded campaigns against sexual psychopath statutes (a crusade, incidentally, in which his most notable intellectual companion was Sutherland) and iniquitous and euphemistic practices in juvenile courts, which he believed (and the Supreme Court subsequently—in the *Gault* decision in 1967—so held) were violative of due process of law.

The Tappan article forcefully states a position that only comes to peripheral grips with Sutherland's work, despite the illusion it creates of a penetrating rebuttal. Tappan is notably effective in documenting the varying definitions that Sutherland accorded to white-collar crime, and he marks the tendency to group together as criminal all forms of behavior by a person who, in his colorful language, may be "a boor, a sinner, a moral leper, or the devil incarnate" but who, despite this, need not be a criminal. But when he comes to the core of his differences with Sutherland, Tappan sidesteps direct confrontation. For one thing, Tappan moves from Sutherland to concentrate his fire on Harry E. Barnes and Negley K. Teeters, authors of a rousing, "fire-eating" criminological textbook in the troglodyte tradition of sociology, that makes no pretense of scientific exactitude or analysis. More important, Tappan avoids adjudication of precisely what is criminal and what is not, the issue that preoccupied Sutherland. Sutherland probably would not have disputed Tappan's theme that white-collar crime should in fact be violative of criminal statutes; it is that the two differ (though Tappan's precise position is unclear) on what it is that is a criminal statute.

The third reading, written by Robert G. Caldwell of the University of Iowa, a sociologist who also has a law degree, is included primarily because—besides attempting to read sociologists a lesson in law, one whose effectiveness may be somewhat blunted by its occasional condescension—it recapitulates many of the arguments leveled against the concept of white-collar crime and offers interesting prospects of resolution. Caldwell's article is one of a group dealing generally with white-collar crime. Other readings—notably those by Hermann Mannheim, Donald Newman, Frank Hartung, and Richard Quinney—are indicated in the Bibliography and should be read for an understanding of the manner in which various scholars see the past work and future prospects of this area of study.

The final two readings in Part VI collide over a number of issues that merit strong emphasis. The first, written by Sanford H. Kadish, a professor of law at the University of California in Berkeley, besides representing legal writing at its very best, thrusts the study of white-collar crime directly into the mainstream of economic considerations and views it in a much broader perspective than has usually been the case.

It may be that the chronological age of academic concern with white-collar crime is largely responsible for its curious disjunction with other work on crime. In the early writings traditional crimes were considered patently malevolent and authors concentrated their attention upon distinguishing offenders from "normal" persons. Invective was commonplace and self-righteousness pervasive. Subsequently, writers were apt to take a more neutral stand toward violations and violators. Following this—and the matter is very much at this point today—sophisticated inquiry has been directed toward elimination of criminal sanctions against certain kinds of offenses (such as homosexual behavior between consenting adults, drunkenness, abortion, and attempted suicide) and has been concerned with the efficacy of diverse kinds of sanctions applied to different kinds of offenses.

White-collar crime studies, appearing late on the scene, have mainly traveled through only the earlier stages of inquiry. Sutherland, most notably, was apt to regard white-collar violations rather uncritically as acts which society chose to outlaw, and deservedly so, though he was too perceptive not to be aware that such decisions were at least arguable. It was merely that he chose not to argue them. Most other writers totally bypass ideological and pragmatic issues underlying the delineation of white-collar offenses.

It is noteworthy that Kadish served as a general consultant to the President's Commission on Law Enforcement and Administration of Justice during 1966 and 1967 and helped to fashion the commission's stand regarding the decriminalization of a variety of offenses presently coming within the criminal codes. His article on white-collar crime attempts to address the same kinds of questions that were asked of statutes outlawing acts because of moral considerations. Kadish raises a number of teasing issues. He wants to know, for example, how much deterrence is involved in the stigma presumably attached to criminal conviction for economic violations. He picks away at the prevalent view that white-collar crime statutes are poorly enforced because of congruence between the values of the enforcers and the violators by suggesting that the very existence of the laws, despite "the ardent protests of important economic interests in the past thirty years is some evidence that [business] is not all-powerful." He also challenges the view that business interests are united in monolithic consensus.

How the same set of facts may be variously interpreted is clearly shown by Kadish's reasoning concerning public response to white-collar offenses. The relative degree of public indifference to such behavior, he maintains, is the product neither of insensitivity nor of business machinations, but rather inheres in the relative absence of moral opprobrium in the acts themselves, when these acts are viewed not in terms of their long-range or subtler consequences, but as willfully evil forms of behavior. Most writers appear to believe that the community should be outraged by white-collar crime; Kadish views as more important the stipulated fact that the public is *not* outraged. In the absence of such public indignation, he is hesitant to favor use of criminal sanctions, though he grants that campaigns calculated to create a sense of outrage might be in order. Kadish is particularly concerned with the "danger of debilitating the moral impact of the criminal conviction and hence decreasing the overall effectiveness of the criminal law."

Many of Kadish's points are given a critical re-examination in the final chapter, written by Harry V. Ball, a sociologist at the University of Hawaii, and Lawrence M. Friedman, a member of the law faculty at the University of Wisconsin.

Ball and Friedman find little utility in Kadish's attempt to isolate and distinguish a class of offenses labeled "economic crimes," and they are adept at putting on display a plethora of statutes whose contents, depending upon a point of view, may be considered economic, common law, or health and safety measures. Much of their discussion is occupied with attempts to qualify the broad generalizations of the Kadish presentation. Ball and Friedman make telling points throughout with empirical illustrations of the fluidity of some of Kadish's observations when elements of the defined ingredients are given specific rather than general content. They falter at times, however, in their attempt to amalgamate white-collar offenses with a broader range of criminal actions and, almost inadvertently, seem to regard economic crimes as a behavioral entity of some kind, about which important things may be said.

Finally, the reading by Ball and Friedman presents warnings that both summarize and herald scholarship regarding white-collar crime. Their concluding cautionary note states a thesis to which other writers have often turned. The search for general theories of crime is a futile exercise, Ball and Friedman maintain. Intellectual advance in the understanding of all human behavior represents the most pressing necessity for sound comprehension of criminal behavior. In criminological research, attempts must be made to determine distinguishing characteristics of crimes such as murder, trespass, and corporate monopoly, and of persons who commit such offenses. The sanctions under analysis must be stated with precision, and the ingredients of the offenses must be spelled out clearly. In essence, their call is a statement of fundamental demands of intelligent inquiry, whose essential but elusive quality is so well indicated by the range of results and viewpoints represented throughout the present volume.

28

IS "WHITE-COLLAR CRIME" CRIME?

Edwin H. Sutherland

The argument has been made that business and professional men commit crimes which should be brought within the scope of the theories of criminal behavior.[1] In order to secure evidence as to the prevalence of such white-collar crimes, an analysis was made of the decisions by courts and commissions against the seventy largest industrial and mercantile corporations in the United States under four types of laws: namely, antitrust, false advertising, National Labor Relations, and infringement of patents, copyrights, and trademarks. This resulted in the finding that 547 such adverse decisions had been made, with an average of 7.8 decisions per corporation and with each corporation's having at least one.[2] Although all of these were decisions that the behavior was unlawful, only forty-nine, or 9 per cent, of the total were made by criminal courts and were *ipso facto* decisions that the behavior was criminal. Since not all unlawful behavior is criminal behavior, these decisions can be used as a measure of criminal behavior only if the other 498 decisions can be shown to be decisions that the behavior of the corporations was criminal.

Reprinted from *American Sociological Review*, 10 (April, 1945), pp. 132–139.

This is a problem in the legal definition of crime and involves two types of questions: May the word "crime" be applied to the behavior regarding which these decisions were made? If so, why is it not generally applied and why have not the criminologists regarded white-collar crime as cognate with other crime? The first question involves semantics, the second interpretation or explanation.

A combination of two abstract criteria is generally regarded by legal scholars as necessary to define crime; namely, legal description of an act as socially injurious and legal provision of a penalty for the act.[3]

When the criterion of legally defined social injury is applied to these 547 decisions, the conclusion is reached that all of the classes of behaviors regarding which the decisions were made are legally defined as socially injurious. This can be readily determined by the words in the statutes—"crime" or "misdemeanor" in some, and "unfair," "discrimination," or "infringement" in all the others. The persons injured may be divided into two groups: first, a relatively small number of persons engaged in the same occupation as the offenders or in related occupations; and, second, the general public either as consumers or as constituents of the general social institutions which are affected by the violations of the laws. The antitrust laws are designed to protect competitors; they are also designed to protect the institution of free competition as the regulator of the economic system and thereby to protect consumers against arbitrary prices, as well as being designed to protect the institution of democracy against the dangers of great concentration of wealth in the hands of monopolies. Laws against false advertising are designed to protect competitors against unfair competition and also to protect consumers against fraud. The National Labor Relations Law is designed to protect employees against coercion by employers and also to protect the general public against interferences with commerce due to strikes and lockouts. The laws against infringements are designed to protect the owners of patents, copyrights, and trademarks against deprivation of their property and against unfair competition, and also to protect the institution of patents and copyrights which was established in order to "promote the progress of science and the useful arts." Violations of these laws are legally defined as injuries to the parties specified.

Each of these laws has a logical basis in the common law and is an adaptation of the common law to modern social organization. False advertising is related to common-law fraud, and infringement to larceny. The National Labor Relations Law, as an attempt to prevent coercion, is related to the common-law prohibition of restrictions on freedom in the form of assault, false imprisonment, and extortion. For at least two centuries prior to the enactment of the modern antitrust laws, the common law was moving against restraint of trade, monopoly, and unfair competition.

Each of the four laws provides a penal sanction and thus meets the second criterion in the definition of crime, and each of the adverse decisions under these four laws (except certain decisions under the infringement laws to be discussed later) is a decision that a crime was committed. This conclusion will be made more specific by analysis of the penal sanctions provided in the four laws.

The Sherman antitrust law states explicitly that a violation of the law is a misdemeanor. Three methods of enforcement of this law are provided, each of them involving procedures regarding misdemeanors. First, it may be enforced by the usual criminal prosecution, resulting in the imposition of fine or imprisonment. Second, the Attorney General of the United States and the several district attorneys are given the "duty" of "repressing and preventing" violations of the law by petitions for injunctions, and violations of the injunctions are punishable as contempt of court. This method of enforcing a criminal law was an invention and, as will be described later, is the key to the interpretation of the differential implementation of the criminal law as applied to white-collar criminals. Third, parties who are injured by violations of the law are authorized to sue for damages, with a mandatory provision that the damages awarded be three times the damages suffered. These damages in excess of reparation are penalties for violation of the law. They are payable to the injured party in order to induce him to take the initiative in the enforcement of the criminal law and in this respect are similar to the earlier methods of private prosecutions under the criminal law. All three of these methods of enforcement are based on decisions that a criminal law was violated and, therefore, that a crime was committed; the decisions of a civil court or a court of equity as to these violations are as good evidence of criminal behavior as is the decision of a criminal court.

The Sherman Antitrust Act has been amended by the Federal Trade Commission Law, the Clayton Law, and several other laws. Some of these amendments define violations as crimes and provide the conventional penalties, but most of the amendments do not make the criminality explicit. A large proportion of the cases which are dealt with under these amendments could be dealt with instead under the original Sherman Act, which is explicitly a criminal law. In practice, the amendments are under the jurisdiction of the Federal Trade Commission, which has authority to make official decisions as to violations. The commission has two principal sanctions under its control: the stipulation and the cease and desist order. The commission may, after the violation of the law has been proved, accept a stipulation from the corporation that it will not violate the law in the future. Such stipulations are customarily restricted to the minor or technical violations. If a stipulation is violated or if no stipulation is accepted, the commission may issue a cease and desist order; this is equivalent to a court's injunction except that violation is not punishable as contempt. If the commission's desist order is violated, the commission may apply to the court for an injunction, the violation of which is punishable as contempt. By an amendment to the Federal Trade Commission Law in the Wheeler-Lea Act of 1938, an order of the commission becomes "final" if not officially questioned within a specified time and thereafter its violation is punishable by a civil fine. Thus, although certain interim procedures may be used in the enforcement of the amendments to the antitrust law, fines or imprisonment for contempt are available if the interim procedures fail. In this respect, the interim procedures are similar to probation in ordinary criminal cases. An unlawful act is not defined as criminal by the fact that it is punished, but by the fact that it is punishable. Larceny is as truly a crime when the thief is placed on probation as when he is committed to prison. The argument may be made that punishment for contempt of court is not punishment for violation of the original law and that, therefore, the original law does not contain a penal sanction. This reasoning is specious, since the original law provides the injunction with its penalty as a part of the procedure for enforcement. Consequently, all of the decisions made under the amendments to the antitrust law are decisions that the corporations committed crimes.[4]

The laws regarding false advertising, as included in the decisions under consideration, are of two types. First, false advertising in the form of false labels is defined in the Pure Food and Drug Act as a misdemeanor and is punishable by a fine. Second, false advertising generally is defined in the Federal Trade Commission Act as unfair competition. Cases of the second type are under the jurisdiction of the Federal Trade Commission, which uses the same procedures as in antitrust cases. Penal sanctions are available in antitrust cases, as previously described, and are similarly available in these cases of false advertising. Thus, all of the decisions in false advertising cases are decisions that the corporations committed crimes.

The National Labor Relations Law of 1935 defines a violation as "unfair labor practice." The National Labor Relations Board is authorized to make official decisions as to violations of the law and, in case of violation, to issue desist orders and also to make certain remedial orders, such as reimbursement of employees who had been dismissed or demoted because of activities in collective bargaining. If an order is violated, the board may apply to the court for enforcement and a violation of the order of the court is punishable as contempt. Thus, all of the decisions under this law, which is enforceable by penal sanctions, are decisions that crimes were committed.

The methods for the repression of infringements vary. Infringements of a copyright or a patented design are defined as misdemeanors, punishable by fines. No case of this type has been discovered against the seventy corporations. Other infringements are not explicitly defined in the statutes on patents, copyrights, and trademarks as crimes, and agents of the state are not authorized by these statutes to initiate actions against violators of the law. Nevertheless, infringements may be punished in either of two ways: First, agents of the state may initiate action against infringers under the Federal Trade Commission Law as unfair competition and they do so, especially against infringers of copyrights and trademarks; these infringements are then punishable in the same sense as violations of the amendments to the antitrust laws. Second, the patent, copyright, and trademark statutes provide that the damages awarded to injured owners of those rights may be greater than (in one statute as much as threefold) the damages actually suffered. These additional damages are not mandatory, as in the Sherman Antitrust Law, but on the other hand they are not explicitly limited to wanton and malicious infringements. Three decisions against the seventy corporations under the patent law and one under the copyright law included awards of such additional damages and on that account were classified in the tabulation of decisions as evidence of criminal behavior of the corporations. The other decisions, seventy-four in number, in regard to infringements were classified as not conclusive evidence of criminal behavior and were discarded. However, in twenty of these seventy-four cases the decisions of the court contain evidence which would be sufficient to make a *prima facie* case in a criminal prosecution; evidence outside these decisions, which may be found in the general descriptions of practices regarding patents, copyrights, and trademarks, justifies a belief that a very large proportion of the seventy-four cases did, in fact, involve willful infringement of property rights and might well have resulted in the imposition of a penalty if the injured party and the court had approached the behavior from the point of view of crime.

In the preceding discussion, the penalties that are definitive of crime have been limited to fine, imprisonment, and punitive damages. In addition, the stipulation, the desist order, and the injunction, without references to punishment for contempt, have the attributes of punishment. This is evident both in that they result in some suffering on the part of the corporation against which they are issued and also in that they are designed by legislators and administrators to produce suffering. The suffering is in the form of public shame, as illustrated in more extreme form in the colonial penalty of sewing the letter *T* on the clothing of the thief. The design is shown in the sequence of sanctions used by the Federal Trade Commission. The stipulation involves the least publicity and the least discomfort, and it is used for minor and technical violations. The desist order is used if the stipulation is violated and also if the violation of the law is appraised by the commission as willful and major. This involves more public shame; this shame is somewhat mitigated by the statements made by corporations, in exculpation, that such orders are merely the acts of bureaucrats. Still more shameful to the corporation is an injunction issued by a court. The shame resulting from this order is sometimes mitigated and the corporation's face saved by taking a consent decree.[5] The corporation may insist that the consent decree is not an admission that it violated the law. For instance, the meat packers took a consent decree in an antitrust case in 1921, with the explanation that they had not knowingly violated any law and were consenting to the decree without attempting to defend themselves because they wished to cooperate with the government in every possible way. This patriotic motivation appeared questionable, however, after the packers fought during almost all of the next ten years for a modification of the decree. Although the sequence of stipulation, desist order, and injunction indicates that the variations in public shame are designed, these orders have other functions as well, especially a remedial function and the clarification of the law in a particular complex situation.

The conclusion in this semantic portion of the discussion is that 473 of the 547 decisions are decisions that crimes were committed. This conclusion may be questioned on the ground that the rules of proof and evidence used in reaching these decisions are not the same as those used in decisions regarding other crimes, especially that some of the agencies which rendered the decisions did not require proof of criminal intent and did not presume the accused to be innocent. These rules of criminal intent and presumption of innocence, however, are not required in all prosecutions under the regular penal code and the number of exceptions is increasing. In many states a person may be committed to prison without protection of one or both of these rules on charges of statutory rape, bigamy, adultery, passing bad checks, selling mortgaged property, defrauding a hotel keeper, and other offenses.[6] Consequently, the criteria that have been used in defining white-collar crimes are not categorically different from the criteria used in defining other crimes, for these rules are abrogated both in regard to white-collar crimes and other crimes, including some felonies. The proportion of decisions rendered against corporations without the protection of these rules is probably greater than the proportion rendered against other criminals, but a difference in proportions does not make the violations of law by corporations categorically different from the violations of law by other criminals. Moreover, the difference in proportion, as the procedures actually operate, is not great. On the one side, many of the defendants in usual criminal cases, being in relative poverty, do not get good defense and consequently secure little benefit from these rules; on the other hand, the commissions come close to observing these rules of proof and evidence although they are not required to do so. This is illustrated by the procedure of the Federal Trade Commission in regard to advertisements. Each year it examines several hundred thousand advertisements and appraises about 50,000 of them as probably false. From the 50,000 it selects about 1,500 as patently false. For instance, an advertisement of gum-wood furniture as "mahogany" would seldom be an accidental error and would generally result from a state of mind which deviated from honesty by more than the natural tendency of human beings to feel proud of their handiwork.

The preceding discussion has shown that these seventy corporations committed crimes according to 473 adverse decisions and has also shown that the criminality of their behavior was not made obvious by the conventional procedures of the criminal law, but was blurred and concealed by special procedures. This differential implementation of the law as applied to the crimes of corporations eliminates, or at least minimizes, the stigma of crime. This differential implementation of the law began with the Sherman Antitrust Law of 1890. As previously described, this law is explicitly a criminal law and a violation of the law is a misdemeanor no matter what procedure is used. The customary policy would have been to rely entirely on criminal prosecution as the method of enforcement. But a clever invention was made in the provision of an injunction to enforce a criminal law; this was not only an invention, but also a direct reversal of previous case law. Also, private parties were encouraged by treble damages to enforce a criminal law by suits in civil courts. In either case, the defendant did not appear in the criminal court, and the fact that he had committed a crime did not appear in the face of the proceedings.

The Sherman Antitrust Act, in this respect, became the model in practically all the subsequent procedures authorized to deal with the crimes of corporations. When the Federal Trade Commission Bill and the Clayton Bill were introduced in Congress, they contained the conventional criminal procedures; these were eliminated in committee discussions, and other procedures which did not carry the external symbols of criminal process were substituted. The violations of these laws are crimes, as has been shown above, but they are treated as though they were not crimes, with the effect and probably the intention of eliminating the stigma of crime.

This policy of eliminating the stigma of crime is illustrated in the following statement by Wendell Berge, at the time assistant to the head of the antitrust division of the Department of Justice, in a plea for abandonment of the criminal prosecution under the Sherman Antitrust Act and the authorization of civil procedures with civil fines as a substitute.

> While civil penalties may be as severe in their financial effects as criminal penalties, yet they do not involve the stigma that attends indictment and conviction. Most of the defendants in antitrust cases are not criminals in the usual sense. There is no inherent reason why antitrust enforcement requires branding them as such.[7]

If a civil fine were substituted for a criminal fine, a violation of the antitrust law would be as truly a crime as it is now. The thing which would be eliminated would be the stigma of crime. Consequently, the stigma of crime has become a penalty in itself, which may be imposed in connection with other penalties or withheld, just as it is possible to combine imprisonment with a fine or have a fine without imprisonment. A civil fine is a financial penalty without the additional penalty of stigma, while a criminal fine is a financial penalty with the additional penalty of stigma.

When the stigma of crime is imposed as a penalty, it places the defendant in the category of a criminal and he becomes one according to the popular stereotype of "the criminal." In primitive society "the criminal" was substantially the same as "the stranger,"[8] while in modern society "the criminal" is a person of less-esteemed cultural attainments. Seventy-five per cent of the persons committed to state prisons are probably not, aside from their unesteemed cultural attainments, "criminals in the usual sense of the word." It may be excellent policy to eliminate the stigma of crime in a large proportion of cases, but the question at hand is why the law has a different implementation for white-collar criminals than for others.

Three factors assist in explaining this differential implementation of the law: the status of the businessman, the trend away from punishment, and the relatively unorganized resentment of the public against white-collar criminals. Each of these will be described.

First, the methods used in the enforcement of-any law are an adaption to the characteristics of the prospective violators of the law, as appraised by the legislators and the judicial and administrative personnel. The appraisals regarding businessmen, who are the prospective violators of the four laws under consideration, include a combination of fear and admiration. Those who are responsible for the system of criminal justice are afraid to antagonize businessmen; among other consequences, such antagonism may result in a reduction in contributions to the campaign funds needed to win the next election. Probably much more important is the cultural homogeneity of legislators, judges, and administrators with businessmen. Legislators admire and respect businessmen and cannot conceive of them as criminals; that is, businessmen do not conform to the popular stereotype of "the criminal." The legislators are confident that these businessmen will conform as a result of very mild pressures.

This interpretation meets with considerable opposition from persons who insist that this is an egalitarian society in which all men are equal in the eyes of the law. It is not possible to give a complete demonstration of the validity of this interpretation but four types of evidence are presented in the following paragraphs as partial demonstration.

The Department of Justice is authorized to use both criminal prosecutions and petitions in equity to enforce the Sherman Antitrust Act. The department has selected the method of criminal prosecution in a larger proportion of cases against trade unions than of cases against corporations, although the law was enacted primarily because of fear of the corporations. From 1890 to 1929, the Department of Justice initiated 438 actions under this law with decisions favorable to the United States. Of the actions against business firms and associations of business firms, 27 per cent were criminal prosecutions; while of the actions against trade unions, 71 per cent were criminal prosecutions. This shows that the Department of Justice has been comparatively reluctant to use a method against business firms which carries with it the stigma of crime.

The method of criminal prosecution in enforcement of the Sherman Antitrust Act has varied from one presidential administration to another. It has seldom been used in the administrations of the presidents who are popularly appraised as friendly toward business; for example, McKinley, Harding, Coolidge, and Hoover.

Businessmen suffered their greatest loss of prestige in the Depression which began in 1929. It was precisely in this period of low status of businessmen that the most strenuous efforts were made to enforce the old laws and enact new laws for the regulation of businessmen. The appropriations for this purpose were multiplied several times and persons were selected for their vigor in administration of the laws. Of the 547 decisions against the seventy corporations during their life careers (which have averaged about forty years) 63 per cent were rendered in the period of 1935 to 1943, that is, during the period of the low status of businessmen.

The Federal Trade Commission Law states that a violation of the antitrust laws by a corporation shall be deemed to be, also, a violation by the officers and directors of the corporation. However, businessmen are practically never convicted as persons, and several cases have been reported (such as the "6 per cent case" against the automobile manufacturers) in which the corporation was convicted and the persons who direct the corporation were all acquitted.[9]

A second factor in the explanation of the differential implementation of the law as applied to white-collar criminals is the trend away from reliance on penal methods. This trend advanced more rapidly in the area of white-collar crime than of other crime because—due to the recency of the statutes—it is least bound by precedents and also because of the status of businessmen. This trend is seen in the almost complete abandonment of the most extreme penalties of death and physical torture; in the supplanting of conventional penal methods by nonpenal methods, such as probation and the case work methods which accompany probation. These decreases in penal methods are explained by a series of social changes: the increased power of the lower socioeconomic class upon which most of the penalties were previously inflicted; the inclusion within the scope of the penal laws of a large part of the upper socioeconomic class, as illustrated by traffic regulations; the increased social interaction among the classes, which has resulted in increased understanding and sympathy; the failure of penal methods to make substantial reductions in crime rates; and the weakening hold on the legal profession and others of the individualistic and hedonistic psychology, which had placed great emphasis on pain in the control of behavior. To some extent overlapping those just mentioned is the fact that punishment, which was previously the chief reliance for control in the home, the school, and the church, has tended to disappear from those institutions, leaving the state without cultural support for its own penal methods.[10]

White-collar crime is similar to juvenile delinquency in respect to the differential implementation of the law. In both cases, the procedures of the criminal law are modified so that the stigma of crime will not attach to the offenders. The stigma of crime has been less completely eliminated from juvenile delinquents than from white-collar criminals because the procedures for the former are a less complete departure from conventional criminal procedures, since most juvenile delinquents come from a class with low social status, and because the juveniles have not organized to protect their good names. Because the juveniles have not been successfully freed from the stigma of crime, they have been generally held to be within the scope of the theories of criminology and, in fact, provide a large part of the data for criminology; because the external symbols have been more successfully eliminated from white-collar crimes, white-collar crimes have generally not been included within these theories.

A third factor in the differential implementation of the law is the difference in the relation between the law and the mores in the area of white-collar crime. The laws under consideration are recent and do not have a firm foundation in public ethics or business ethics; in fact, certain rules of business ethics, such as the contempt for the "price chiseler," are generally in conflict with the law. These crimes are not obvious, as is assault and battery, and can be appreciated readily only by persons who are expert in the occupations in which they occur. A corporation often violates a law for a decade or longer before the administrative agency becomes aware of the violation; in the meantime the violation may have become accepted practice in the industry. The effects of a white-collar crime upon the public are diffused over a long period of time and perhaps over millions of people, with no person's suffering much at a particular time. The public agencies of communication do not express and organize the moral sentiments of the community as to white-collar crimes in part because the crimes are complicated and not easily presented as news, but probably in greater part because these agencies of communication are owned or controlled by the businessmen who violate the laws and because these agencies are themselves frequently charged with violations of the same laws. Public opinion in regard to picking pockets would not be well organized if most of the information regarding this crime came to the public directly from the pick-pockets themselves.

This third factor, if properly limited, is a valid part of the explanation of the differential implementation of the law. It tends to be exaggerated and become the complete explanation in the form of a denial that white-collar crimes involve any moral culpability whatever. On that account it is desirable to state a few reasons why this factor is not the complete explanation.

The assertion is sometimes made that white-collar crimes are merely technical violations and involve no moral culpability (i.e., violation of the mores) whatever. In fact, these white-collar crimes, like other crimes, are distributed along a continuum in which the *mala in se* are at one extreme and the *mala prohibita* at the other.[11] None of the white collar crimes is purely arbitrary, as is the regulation that one must drive on the right side of the street, which might equally well be that one must drive on the left side. The Sherman Antitrust Law, for instance, is regarded by many persons as an unwise law and it may well be that some other policy would be preferable. It is questioned principally by persons who believe in a more collectivistic economic system; namely, the communists and the leaders of big business, while its support comes largely from an emotional ideology in favor of free enterprise which is held by farmers, wage-earners, small-business men, and professional men. Therefore, as appraised by the majority of the population it is necessary for the preservation of American institutions and its violation is a violation of strongly entrenched moral sentiments.

The sentimental reaction toward a particular white-collar crime is certainly different from that toward some other crimes. This difference is often exaggerated, especially as the reaction occurs in urban society. The characteristic reaction of the average citizen in the modern city toward burglary is apathy unless he or his immediate friends are victims or unless the case is very spectacular. The average citizen, reading in his morning paper that the home of an unknown person has been burglarized by another unknown person, has no appreciable increase in blood pressure. Fear and resentment develop in modern society primarily as the result of the accumulation of crimes as depicted in crime rates or in general descriptions, and this develops both as to white-collar crimes and other crimes.

Finally, although many laws have been enacted for the regulation of occupations other than business, such as agriculture or plumbing, the procedures used in the enforcement of those other laws are more nearly the same as the conventional criminal procedures, and law-violators in these other occupations are not so completely protected against the stigma of crime as are businessmen. The relation between the law and the mores tends to be circular. The mores are crystallized in the law and each act of enforcement of the laws tends to re-enforce the mores. The laws regarding white-collar crime, which conceal the criminality of the behavior, have been less effective than other laws in re-enforcement of the mores.

Notes

1. Edwin H. Sutherland, "White-Collar Criminality," *American Sociological Review*, 5 (February, 1940), pp. 1–12; and "Crime and Business," *Annals of the American Academy of Political and Social Science*, 217 (September, 1941), pp. 112–118.

2. Cf., Edwin H. Sutherland, *White Collar Crime* (New York: Dryden Press, 1949), pp. 15–182.

3. The most thorough analysis of crime from the point of view of legal definition is Jerome Hall, *Principles of Criminal Law* (Indianapolis: Bobbs-Merrill, 1947).

4. Some of the antitrust decisions were made against meat packers under the Packers and Stockyards Act. The penal sanctions in this act are essentially the same as in the Federal Trade Commission Act.

5. The consent decree may be taken for other reasons, especially because it cannot be used as evidence in other suits.

6. Livingston Hall, "Statutory Law of Crimes, 1887–1936," *Harvard Law Review*, 50 (February, 1937), pp. 616–653.

7. Wendell Berge, "Remedies Available to the Government under the Sherman Act," *Law and Contemporary Problems*, 7 (January, 1940), p. 111.

8. On the role of the stranger in punitive justice, see Ellsworth Faris, "The Origin of Punishment," *International Journal of Ethics*, 25 (October, 1914), pp. 54–67; George H. Mead, "The Psychology of Punitive Justice," *American Journal of Sociology*, 23 (March, 1918), pp. 577–602.

9. The question may be asked, "If businessmen are so influential, why did they not retain the protection of the rules of the criminal procedure?" The answer is that they lost this protection, despite their status, on the principle, "You can't eat your cake and have it, too."

10. This trend away from penal methods suggests that the penal sanction may not be a completely adequate criterion in the definition of crime.

11. An excellent discussion of this continuum is presented by Jerome Hall, "Prolegomena to a Science of Criminal Law," *University of Pennsylvania Law Review*, 89 (March, 1941), pp. 563–569.

29

WHO IS THE CRIMINAL?

Paul W. Tappan

What is crime? As a lawyer-sociologist, the writer finds perturbing the current confusion on this important issue. Important because it delimits the subject matter of criminological investigation. A criminologist who strives to aid in formulating the beginnings of a science finds himself in an increasingly equivocal position. He studies the criminals convicted by the courts and is then confounded by the growing clamor that he is not studying the real criminal at all, but an insignificant proportion of nonrepresentative and stupid unfortunates who happened to have become enmeshed in technical legal difficulties. It has become a fashion to maintain that the convicted population is no proper category for the empirical research of the criminologist. Ergo, the many studies of convicts which have been conducted by the orthodox, now presumably outmoded criminologists, have no real meaning for either descriptive or scientific purposes. Off with the old criminologies, on with the new orientations, the new horizons!

This position reflects in part at least the familiar suspicion and misunderstanding held by the layman sociologist toward the law. To a large

Reprinted from the *American Sociological Review*, 12 (February, 1947), pp. 96–102.

extent it reveals the feeling among social scientists that not all antisocial conduct is proscribed by law (which is probably true), that not all conduct violative of the criminal code is truly antisocial, or is not so to any significant extent (which is also undoubtedly true). Among some students the opposition to the traditional definition of crime as law violation arises from their desire to discover and study wrongs which are absolute and eternal rather than mere violations of a statutory and case law system which vary in time and place; this is essentially the old metaphysical search for the law of nature. They consider the dynamic and relativistic nature of law to be a barrier to the growth of a scientific system of hypotheses possessing universal validity.[1]

Recent protestants against the orthodox conceptions of crime and criminal are diverse in their views; they unite only in their denial of the allegedly legalistic and arbitrary doctrine that those convicted under the criminal law are the criminals of our society and in promoting the confusion as to the proper province of criminology. It is enough here to examine briefly a few of the current schisms with a view to the difficulties at which they arrive.

I

A number of criminologists today maintain that mere violation of the criminal law is an artificial criterion of criminality, that categories set up by the law do not meet the demands of scientists because they are of a "fortuitous nature" and do not "arise intrinsically from the nature of the subject matter."[2] The validity of this contention must depend, of course, upon what the nature of the subject matter is. These scholars suggest that, as a part of the general study of human behavior, criminology should concern itself broadly with all antisocial conduct, behavior injurious to society. We take it that antisocial conduct is essentially any sort of behavior which violates some social interest. But what are these social interests? Which are weighty enough to merit the concern of the sociologist, to bear the odium of crime? What shall constitute a violation of them—particularly where, as is so commonly true in our complicated and unintegrated society, these interests are themselves in conflict? Roscoe Pound's suggestive classification of the social interests served by law is valuable in a juristic framework, but it solves no problems for the sociologist who seeks to depart from legal standards in search of all manner of antisocial behavior.

However desirable may be the concept of socially injurious conduct for purposes of general normation or abstract description, it does not define what is injurious. It sets no standard. It does not discriminate cases, but merely invites the subjective value judgments of the investigator. Until it is structurally embodied with distinct criteria or norms—as is now the case in the legal system—the notion of antisocial conduct is useless for purposes of research, even for the rawest empiricism. The emancipated criminologist reasons himself into a *cul de sac*: having decided that it is footless to study convicted offenders on the ground that this is an artificial category—though its membership is quite precisely ascertainable, he must now conclude that, in his lack of standards to determine antisociality, though this may be what he considers a real scientific category, its membership and its characteristics are unascertainable. Failing to define antisocial behavior in any fashion suitable to research, the criminologist may be deluded further into assuming that there is an absoluteness and permanence in this undefined category, lacking in the law. It is unwise for the social scientist ever to forget that all standards of social normation are relative, impermanent, variable, and that they do not, certainly the law does not, arise out of mere fortuity or artifice.[3]

II

In a differing approach certain other criminologists suggest that "conduct norms" rather than either crime or antisocial conduct should be studied.[4] There is an unquestionable need to pursue the investigation of general conduct norms and their violation. It is desirable to segregate the various classes of such norms, to determine relationships between them, and to understand similarities and differences between them as to the norms themselves, their sources, methods of imposition of control, and their consequences. The subject matter of this field of social control is in a regrettably primitive state. It will be important to discover the individuals who belong within the several categories of norm-violators established and to determine then what motivations operate to promote conformity or breach. So far as it may be determinable, we shall wish to know in what way these motivations may serve to insure conformity to different sets of conduct norms, how they may overlap and reinforce the norms or conflict and weaken the effectiveness of the norms.

We concur in the importance of the study of conduct norms and their violation and, more particularly, if we are to develop a science of human behavior, in the need for careful research to determine the psychological and environmental variables which are associated etiologically with nonconformity to these norms. However, the importance of the more general subject matter of social control or "ethology" does not mean that the more specific study of the law-violator is nonsignificant. Indeed, the direction of progress in the field of social control seems to lie largely in the observation and analysis of more specific types of nonconformity to particular, specialized standards. We shall learn more by attempting to determine *why* some individuals take human life deliberately and with premeditation, *why* some take property by force and others by trick than we shall in seeking at the start a universal formula to account for any and all behavior in breach of social interests. This broader knowledge of conduct norms may conceivably develop through induction, in its inevitably very generic terms, from the empirical data derived in the study of particular sorts of violations. Also, our more specific information about the factors which lie behind violations of precisely defined norms will be more useful in the technology of social control. Where legal standards require change to keep step with the changing requirements of a dynamic society, the sociologist may advocate—even as the legal profession does—the necessary statutory modifications, rather than assume that for sociological purposes the conduct he disapproves is already criminal, without legislative, political, or judicial intervention.

III

Another increasingly widespread and seductive movement to revolutionize the concepts of crime and criminal has developed around the currently fashionable dogma of "white-collar crime." This is actually a particular school among those who contend that the criminologist should study antisocial behavior rather than law violation. The dominant contention of the group appears to be that the convict classes are merely our "petty" criminals, the few whose depredations against society have been on a small scale, who have blundered into difficulties with the police and courts through their ignorance and stupidity. The important criminals, those who do irreparable damage with impunity, deftly evade the machinery of justice, either by remaining "technically" within the law or by exercising their intelligence, financial prowess, or political connections in its violation. We seek a definition of the white-collar criminal and find an amazing diversity, even among those flowing from the same pen, and observe that characteristically they are loose, doctrinaire, and invective. When Professor Sutherland launched the term, it was applied to those individuals of upper socioeconomic class who violate the criminal law, usually by breach of trust, in the ordinary course of their business activities.[5] This original usage accords with legal ideas of crime and points moreover to the significant and difficult problems of enforcement in the areas of business crimes, particularly where those violations are made criminal by recent statutory enactment. From this fruitful beginning, the term has spread into vacuity, wide and handsome. We learn that the white-collar criminal may be the suave and deceptive merchant prince or "robber baron," that the existence of such crime may be determined readily "in casual conversation with a representative of an occupation by asking him, 'What crooked practices are found in your occupation?' "[6]

Confusion grows as we learn from another proponent of this concept that, "There are various phases of white-collar criminality that touch the lives of the common man almost daily. The large majority of them are operating within the letter and spirit of the law" and that "In short, greed, not need, lies at the basis of white-collar crime."[7] Apparently, the criminal may be law-obedient but greedy; the specific quality of his crimes is far from clear.

Another avenue is taken in Professor Sutherland's more recent definition of crime as a "legal description of an act as socially injurious and legal provision of penalty for the act."[8] Here he has deemed the connotation of his term too narrow if confined to violations of the criminal code; he includes by a slight modification conduct violative of any law, civil or criminal, when it is "socially injurious."

In light of these definitions, the normative issue is pointed. Who should be considered the white-collar criminal? Is it the merchant who, out of greed, business acumen, or competitive motivations, breaches a trust with his consumer by "puffing his wares" beyond their merits, by pricing them beyond their value, or by ordinary advertising? Is it he who breaks trust with his employees in order to keep wages down, refusing to permit labor organization or to bargain collectively, and who is found guilty by a labor relations board of an unfair labor practice? May it be the white-collar worker who breaches trust with his employers by inefficient performance at work, by sympathetic strike or secondary boycott? Or is it the merchandiser who violates ethics by undercutting the prices of his fellow merchants? In general these acts do not violate the criminal law. All in some manner breach a trust for motives which a criminologist may (or may not) disapprove for one reason or another. All are within the framework of the norms of ordinary business practice. One seeks in vain for criteria to determine this white-collar criminality. It is the conduct of one who wears a white collar and who indulges in occupational behavior to which some particular criminologist takes exception. It may easily be a term of propaganda. For purposes of empirical research or objective description, what is it?

Whether criminology aspires one day to become a science or a repository of reasonably accurate descriptive information, it cannot tolerate a nomenclature of such loose and variable usage. A special hazard exists in the employment of the term, "white-collar criminal," in that it invites individual systems of private values to run riot in an area (economic ethics) where gross variation exists among criminologists as well as others. The rebel may enjoy a veritable orgy of delight in damning as criminal most anyone he pleases; one imagines that some experts would thus consign to the criminal classes any successful capitalistic businessman; the reactionary or conservative, complacently viewing the occupational practices of the business world, might find all in perfect order in this best of all possible worlds. The result may be fine indoctrination or catharsis achieved through blustering broadsides against the "existing system." It is not criminology. It is not social science. The terms "unfair," "infringement," "discrimination," "injury to society," and so on, employed by the white collar criminologists cannot, taken alone, differentiate criminal and non-criminal. Until refined to mean certain specific actions, they are merely epithets.

Vague, omnibus concepts defining crime are a blight upon either a legal system or a system of sociology that strives to be objective. They allow judge, administrator, or—conceivably—sociologist, in an undirected, freely operating discretion, to attribute the status "criminal" to any individual or class which he conceives nefarious. This can accomplish no desirable objective, either politically or sociologically.[9]

Worse than futile, it is courting disaster, political, economic, and social, to promulgate a system of justice in which the individual may be held criminal without having committed a crime, defined with some precision by statute and case law. To describe crime the sociologist, like the lawyer-legislator, must do more than condemn conduct deviation in the abstract. He must avoid definitions predicated simply upon state of mind or social injury and determine what particular types of deviation, in what directions, and to what degree shall be considered criminal. This is exactly what the criminal code today attempts to do, though imperfectly of course. More slowly and conservatively than many of us would wish—that is in the nature of legal institutions, as it is in other social institutions as well. But law has defined with greater clarity and precision the conduct which is criminal than our antilegalistic criminologists promise to do; it has moreover promoted a stability, a security and dependability of justice through its exactness, its so-called "technicalities," and its moderation in inspecting proposals for change.

IV

Having considered the conceptions of an innovating sociology in ascribing the terms "crime" and "criminal," let us state here the juristic view: Only those are criminals who have been adjudicated as such by the courts. Crime is an intentional act in violation of the criminal law (statutory and case law), committed without defense or excuse, and penalized by the state as a felony or misdemeanor. In studying the offender there can be no presumption that arrested, arraigned, indicted, or prosecuted persons are criminals unless they also be held guilty beyond a reasonable doubt of a particular offense.[10] Even less than the unconvicted suspect can those individuals be considered criminal who have violated no law. Only those are criminals who have been selected by a clear substantive and a careful adjective law, such as obtains in our courts. The unconvicted offenders of whom the criminologist may wish to take cognizance are an important but unselected group; it has no specific membership presently ascertainable. Sociologists may strive, as does the legal profession, to perfect measures for more complete and accurate ascertainment of offenders, but it is futile simply to rail against a machinery of justice which is, and to a large extent must inevitably remain, something less than entirely accurate or efficient.

Criminal behavior as here defined fits very nicely into the sociologists' formulations of social control. Here we find *norms* of conduct, comparable to the mores, but considerably more distinct, precise, and detailed, as they are fashioned through statutory and case law. The agencies of this control, like the norms themselves, are more formal than is true in other types of control: The law depends for its instrumentation chiefly upon police, prosecutors, judges, juries, and the support of a favorable public opinion. The law has for its *sanctions* the specifically enumerated punitive measures set up by the state for breach, penalties which are additional to any of the sanctions which society exerts informally against the violator of norms which may overlap with laws. Crime is itself simply the breach of the legal norm, a violation within this particular category of social control; the criminal is, of course, the individual who has committed such acts of breach.

Much ink has been spilled on the extent of deterrent efficacy of the criminal law in social control. This is a matter which is not subject to demonstration in any exact and measurable fashion, any more than one can conclusively demonstrate the efficiency of a moral norm.[11] Certainly the degree of success in asserting a control, legal or moral, will vary with the particular norm itself, its instrumentation, the subject individuals, the time, the place, and the sanctions. The efficiency of legal control is sometimes confused by the fact that, in the common overlapping of crimes (particularly those *mala in se*) with moral standards, the norms and sanctions of each may operate in mutual support to produce conformity. Moreover, mere breach of norm is no evidence of the general failure of a social control system, but indication rather of the need for control. Thus, the occurrence of theft and homicide does not mean that the law is ineffective, for one cannot tell how frequently such acts might occur in the absence of law and penal sanction. Where such acts are avoided, one may not appraise the relative efficacy of law and mores in prevention. When they occur, one cannot apportion blame, either in the individual case or in general, to failures of the legal and moral systems. The individual in society does undoubtedly conduct himself in reference to legal requirements. Living "beyond the law" has a quality independent of being non-conventional, immoral, sinful. Mr. Justice Holmes has shown that the "bad man of the law"—those who become our criminals—are motivated in part by disrespect for the law or, at the least, are inadequately restrained by its taboos.

From introspection and from objective analysis of criminal histories one can not but accept as axiomatic the thesis that the norms of criminal law and its sanctions do exert some measure of effective control over human behavior; that this control is increased by moral, conventional, and traditional norms; and that the effectiveness of control norms is variable. It seems a fair inference from urban investigations that in our contemporary mass society, the legal system is becoming increasingly important in constraining behavior as primary group norms and sanctions deteriorate. Criminal law, crime, and the criminal become more significant subjects of sociological inquiry, therefore, as we strive to describe, understand, and control the uniformities and variability in culture.

We consider that the "white-collar criminal," the violator of conduct norms, and the antisocial personality are not criminal in any sense meaningful to the social scientist unless he has violated a criminal statute. We cannot know him as such unless he has been properly convicted. He may be a boor, a sinner, a moral leper, or the devil incarnate, but he does not become a criminal through sociological name calling unless politically constituted authority says he is. It is footless for the sociologist to confuse issues of definition, normation, etiology, sanction, agency and social effects by saying one thing and meaning another.

V

To conclude, we reiterate and defend the contention that crime, as legally defined, is a sociologically significant province of study. The view that it is not appears to be based upon either of two premises: first, that offenders convicted under the criminal law are not representative of all criminals and, second, that criminal law violation (and, therefore, the criminal himself) is not significant to the sociologist because it is composed of a set of legal, nonsociological categories irrelevant to the understanding of group behavior and/or social control. Through these contentions to invalidate the traditional and legal frame of reference adopted by the criminologist, several considerations, briefly enumerated below, must be met.

1. *Convicted criminals as a sample of law violators*:

a. Adjudicated offenders represent the closest possible approximation to those who have in fact violated the law, carefully selected by sieving of the due process of law; no other province of social control attempts to ascertain the breach of norms with such rigor and precision.

b. It is as futile to contend that this group should not be studied on the grounds that it is incomplete or nonrepresentative as it would be to maintain that psychology should terminate its description, analysis, diagnosis, and treatment of deviants who cannot be completely representative as selected. Convicted persons are nearly all criminals. They offer large and varied samples of all types; their origins, traits, dynamics of development, and treatment influences can be studied profitably for purposes of description, understanding, and control. To be sure, they are not necessarily representative of all offenders; if characteristics observed among them are imputed to law-violators generally, it must be with the qualification implied by the selective processes of discovery and adjudication.

c. Convicted criminals are important as a sociological category, furthermore, in that they have been exposed and respond to the influences of court contact, official punitive treatment, and public stigma as convicts.

2. *The relevance of violation of the criminal law:*

a. The criminal law establishes substantive norms of behavior, standards more clear-cut, specific, and detailed than the norms in any other category of social controls.

b. The behavior prohibited has been considered significantly in derogation of group welfare by deliberative and representative assembly, formally constituted for the purpose of establishing such norms; nowhere else in the field of social control is there directed a comparable rational effort to elaborate standards conforming to the predominant needs, desires, and interests of the community.

c. There are legislative and juridical lags which reduce the social value of the legal norms; as an important characteristic of law, such lag does not reduce the relevance of law as a province of sociological inquiry. From a detached sociological view, the significant thing is not the absolute goodness or badness of the norms but the fact that these norms do control behavior. The sociologist is interested in the results of such control, the correlates of violation, and in the lags themselves.

d. Upon breach of these legal (and social) norms, the refractory are treated officially in punitive and/or rehabilitative ways, not for being generally antisocial, immoral, unconventional, or bad, but for violation of the specific legal norms of control.[12]

e. Law becomes the peculiarly important and ultimate pressure toward conformity to minimum standards of conduct deemed essential to group welfare as other systems of norms and mechanics of control deteriorate.

f. Criminals, therefore, are a sociologically distinct group of violators of specific legal norms, subjected to official state treatment. They and the noncriminals respond, though differentially, of course, to the standards, threats, and correctional devices established in this system of social control.

g. The norms, their violation, the mechanics of dealing with breach constitute major provinces of legal sociology. They are basic to the theoretical framework of sociological criminology.

ADDENDA

A special class of cases that illustrates very well both the problem of definition and of legal policy is that of so-called "white-collar crime." Much attention has been devoted to such "crime" in recent years, and properly so, for peculiarly difficult problems of public policy as well as causation and treatment are involved in this area.[13] However, there is possibly less consistency involved in analyses of white-collar "criminality" than there is in any other category of crime. The white-collar criminologists represent one particular group among those who contend that the criminologist should study antisocial behavior rather than criminal law violation as such.[14] In seeking definitions of white-collar crime, one finds a rather remarkable diversity, but characteristically the definitions are loose and sometimes doctrinaire.

Unfortunately, norms of proper behavior in the economic fields of production, distribution, and advertising have been difficult to develop, partly because the commercial revolution took place so rapidly. Drawing lines between efficient and practical competitive behavior by the sharp but skilled and honest businessman, on the one hand, and the criminal practices of the dishonest and overpowerful, on the other, has proved extremely difficult. Interpretations and enforcement of the modern laws directed against various forms of white-collar crime have revealed the complex and controversial character of such policy, in part but not entirely by any means, because of the wealth and power of many of those who are brought to trial. The excessive tolerance that has developed for a loose economic and political morality is also at fault to a great extent. Unlike most forms of crime, white-collar depredations commonly have a diffused impact upon many in the society but little direct or obvious injury to single individuals. Moreover, and this is a peculiarly subtle problem, much of the white-collar conduct disapproved by some criminologists does have economic value. Often the policy question is one of balancing gain and loss from the behavior involved. Finally, it should be noted that our court and correctional systems have little to offer in the way of effective treatment, training, or even of deterrence in the handling of individuals of the sort here involved.

Our definitions of crime cannot be rooted in epithets, in minority value judgments or prejudice, or in loose abstractions. Within a system of justice under law, crime must be defined quite precisely and in accordance with the explicit formulations of the legislature. Such crime will not include all behavior that is antisocial, for reasons that we have noted, nor even all conduct that should be made criminal.

Notes

1. For the manner in which the legal definition of the criminal is avoided by prominent sociological scholars through amazingly loose, circumlocutory description, see, for instance, Florian Znaniecki, "Social Research in Criminology," *Sociology and Social Research*, 12 (March, 1928), p. 307.

2. See, for example, Thorsten Sellin, *Culture Conflict and Crime* (New York: Social Science Research Council, 1938), pp. 20–21.

3. An instance of this broadening of the concept of the criminal is the penchant among certain anthropologists to equate crime with taboo. See, especially, Bronislaw Malinowski, *Crime and Custom in Savage Society* (New York: Harcourt, Brace, 1926), and "A New Instrument for the Interpretation of Law—Especially Primitive," *Yale Law Journal*, 51 (June, 1942), pp. 1237–1254. Compare William Seagle, "Primitive Law and Professor Malinowski," *American Anthropologist*, 39 (April–June, 1937), pp. 275–290, and *The Quest for Law* (New York: Knopf, 1941); Karl N. Llewellyn and E. Adamson Hoebel, *The Cheyenne Way: Conflict and Case Law in Primitive Jurisprudence* (Norman, Okla.: University of Oklahoma Press, 1941); and Hoebel, "Law and Anthropology," *Virginia Law Review*, 32 (June, 1946), pp. 835–854.

4. Sellin, *op. cit.*, pp. 25ff.

5. Edwin H. Sutherland, "Crime and Business," *Annals of the American Academy of Political and Social Science*, 217 (September, 1941), pp. 112–118.

6. Edwin H. Sutherland, "White-Collar Criminality," *American Sociological Review*, 5 (February, 1940), pp. 1–12.

7. Harry Elmer Barnes and Negley K. Teeters, *New Horizons in Criminology* (Englewood Cliffs, N.J.: Prentice-Hall, 1943), pp. 42–43.

8. Edwin H. Sutherland, "Is 'White Collar Crime' Crime?" *American Sociological Review*, 10 (April, 1945), pp. 132–139.

9. In the province of juvenile delinquency we may observe already the evil that flows from this sort of loose definition in applied sociology. See Roscoe Pound, "Introduction," in Pauline V. Young, *Social Treatment in Probation and Delinquency* (New York: McGraw-Hill, 1937), pp. xxiii–xxxi. See also Paul W. Tappan, *Delinquent Girls in Court* (New York: Columbia University Press, 1947); and "Treatment without Trial," *Social Forces*, 24 (March, 1946), pp. 306–311.

10. The unconvicted suspect cannot be known as a violator of the law, to assume him so would be in derogation of our most basic political and ethical philosophies. In empirical research it would be quite inaccurate, obviously, to study all suspects or defendants as criminals.

11. For a detailed consideration of the efficacy of legal norms, see Jerome Michael and Herbert Wechsler, "A Rationale of the Law of Homicide," *Columbia Law Review*, 37 (May, 1937), pp. 701–761, and 37 (December, 1937), pp. 1261–1325.

12. For other expositions of this view, see articles by Jerome Hall: "Prolegomena to a Science of Criminal Law," *University of Pennsylvania Law Review*, 89 (March, 1941), pp. 549–580; "Criminology and a Modern Penal Code," *Journal of Criminal Law and Criminology*, 27 (May–June, 1936), pp. 1–16; and "Criminology," in Georges Gurvitch and Wilbert E. Moore, editors, *Twentieth-Century Sociology* (New York: Philosophical Library, 1945), pp. 342–365.

13. The author wishes to make it clear here, since there has been some misconstruction of his view in literature on the subject, that he believes white-collar crime, properly and precisely defined, to be not only a legitimate but an important phase of criminological inquiry. He deplores the loosely normative connotations that have been attached to the concept by some of Sutherland's interpreters, and he believes that they have resulted in some confusion so far as needed empirical research in this area is concerned.

14. Barnes and Teeters, *op. cit.*, 3d ed. (1959).

30

A RE-EXAMINATION OF THE CONCEPT OF WHITE-COLLAR CRIME

Robert G. Caldwell

The concept of white-collar crime, which was originated by Professor Edwin H. Sutherland before World War II, is now widely used in sociological literature, and by many students it is considered to be a valuable contribution to the theory of criminal behavior. However, some sociologists and many members of the legal profession have been critical of its implications and have urged that it be more strictly defined or entirely discarded. It is the purpose of this article to re-examine the concept of white-collar crime, to consider its legal and sociological implications, and to analyze the controversy arising from its usage.

WHITE-COLLAR CRIME DEFINED

According to Sutherland's original definition, white-collar crime is "a violation of the criminal law by a person of the upper socioeconomic class in the course of his occupational activities."[1] To this he added the expla-

Reprinted from *Federal Probation*, 22 (March, 1958), pp. 30–36.

nation that "the upper socioeconomic class is defined not only by its wealth but also by its respectability and prestige in the general society." By this definition, therefore, a fraud by a wealthy confidence man of the underworld or a murder by a businessman in a love triangle would not be a white-collar crime, but a fraud by a realtor in the sale of a house or a murder by a manufacturer in strike-breaking activities would be.

Most white-collar crimes involve a breach of trust which is usually accompanied and consummated by misrepresentation. This misrepresentation occurs, for example, in the financial statements of corporations, in advertising and other sales methods, in manipulations on the stock exchange, in short weights and measures, in embezzlement and misappropriation of funds, in the bribery of public officials, in the violation of price regulations, in tax frauds, and in the misapplication of funds in receiverships and bankruptcies.

Sutherland, Clinard, Hartung, and other sociologists assert that white-collar crimes are very serious, persistent, and prevalent in American society. In order to support their views, they point to the conditions revealed by numerous governmental investigations and to their own independent research into various aspects of our economic system. They insist not only that the financial losses resulting from white-collar crimes reach staggering proportions, but also that these losses are the least important of the consequences of such crimes. Ordinary crimes cause some inconvenience to the victims and, occasionally, if they involve serious bodily attacks or are repeated in quick succession, they cause a general community disturbance. White-collar crimes, on the other hand, according to Sutherland and other sociologists, spread feelings of distrust, lower public morale, and produce social disorganization.

The white-collar criminologists further contend that although white-collar crimes are very prevalent and very costly, few of the perpetrators are prosecuted or convicted in the criminal courts. This, they claim, is true because (1) the criminal courts are very lenient toward persons accused of white-collar crimes, (2) no effective method of dealing with offending corporations under the criminal law has as yet been devised, (3) efforts to make the criminal law more effective in cases involving corporations have been blocked by business interests, and (4) action in the civil courts and regulations by boards and commissions are widely relied upon to protect society against white-collar crimes.

On the basis of this analysis, Sutherland and those who are in agreement with him conclude that those who commit white-collar crimes are relatively immune because of the class bias of the courts and the power of the upper classes to influence the implementation and administration of the law and that, therefore, the difference in criminality between the lower and upper classes is made to appear greater in the record than it really is. This, in turn, in their opinion, has contributed to a distortion of the criminological theories of causation, since criminologists to a great extent have restricted their data to cases dealt with in criminal and juvenile courts, agencies which are used principally for offenders from the lower economic strata. In other words, they believe that the theory of causation which attributed criminal behavior in general either to poverty or to the psychopathic and sociopathic conditions associated with poverty is "based on a biased sample which omits almost entirely the behavior of white-collar criminals."[2]

The foregoing discussion indicates that there are two major issues involved in the controversy over the concept of white-collar crime; namely, (1) the moral issue and (2) the scientific issue. Each of these issues must be clearly identified and separately treated because, although they are related, each requires a different kind of answer.

THE MORAL ISSUE

The moral issue has arisen from the contention that our criminal laws and their administration are biased and unfair and that they tend to favor the rich and the influential and to discriminate against the poor and the friendless. Those that assume this point of view argue that many acts are the same, or nearly the same, as other acts that are now called criminal and should, therefore, be similarly labeled and condemned, even though the legislatures and the courts fail to do this. This is justified by some writers on the grounds that an act should be called criminal regardless of whether the provisions concerning it are in the criminal law, the civil law, or governmental agency regulations, as long as it can meet these two requirements: (1) Is it proscribed or prescribed by a duly constituted legislative body? and (2) Has the legislative body declared it to be punishable and specified the sanctions to be imposed?[3]

Furthermore, it is urged by those who favor the concept of white-collar crime that we should stigmatize as white-collar criminals both those who are convicted in the criminal court and those who might have been so convicted but, instead, through pressure or influence, were able to avoid conviction or for various reasons were taken into a civil court or before an administrative board, bureau, or commission. To a large extent, this point of view on the moral issue is a result of the strong influence exerted in American criminology by the Positive school, which focuses attention upon the criminal, while ignoring the legal definition of crime.[4]

The foregoing arguments are seductive in their simplicity, but their limitations become apparent when a careful examination is made of the terms "crime" and "criminal." In our society, the criminal law is a body of rules regarding human conduct which are prescribed, interpreted, and administered by our elected and appointed representatives and enforced by penalties imposed by governmental authority. A crime may be generally defined as the commission or omission of an act which the criminal law forbids or commands under pain of a punishment to be imposed by the state by a proceeding in its own name.[5]

It is obvious that not every act or failure to act could, or should, be regulated by the criminal law. Crimes are only those acts or failures to act that are considered to be so detrimental to the well-being of society, as judged by its prevailing standards, that action regarding them cannot be entrusted to private initiative, civil courts, or government agencies and bureaus, but must be taken by organized society in accordance with especially devised procedures. In fact, even if the victim of a crime takes no action, opposes it, forgives the criminal, or tries to conceal the crime, the state can and may press the charges.

How Do We Know a Crime Has Been Committed?   On the basis of what has been said thus far, it might appear that anyone who commits a crime is a criminal, but this definition immediately suggests an important question: How do we know that a person has committed a crime? Thus, in any particular case, it becomes clear that the definition of a criminal as one who violates the criminal law is not adequate. We must supplement it by establishing definite, exact, stable criteria to determine whether the accused actually committed a crime.

But why is it so important to have definite, exact, stable criteria to determine the guilt of the accused? The answer to this question can be found in the fact that a person's rights and reputation are involved. To apply the term "criminal" to a person is not only to lower his social status by publicly stigmatizing him, but also to declare that his guilt has been proved, that certain of his rights have been forfeited, and that he should be punished. The law, which defines the term "crime," is deeply aware of the serious implications of the term "criminal." Down through the years, it has carefully, and at times painfully, built up a definite procedure to determine the guilt of the accused and at the same time to protect his rights. By clearly defining terms, by precisely formulating methods, and by judiciously introducing changes, the law has promoted stability, dependability, and security of justice in its criminal procedure.[6]

In this procedure one of the important rules of evidence is that which requires proof of the *corpus delicti*. This term defined literally means "the body of the offense" or "the substance of crime." Although in popular language it is used to describe the visible evidence of the crime, such as the dead body of a murdered person, it is properly applicable to any crime and relates particularly to the act element of criminality. This means that it must be proved that a certain prohibited act has been committed and that it was committed by a criminal human agency. Furthermore, in addition to establishing the *corpus delicti* in a particular case, the state must also prove beyond a reasonable doubt that the accused was the human agent who committed the act or procured it to be committed.[7]

When this has been accomplished, according to the exacting regularities of legal procedure and due process,[8] the "accused" becomes the "convicted." Then—and not until then—does the "alleged criminal" become the "criminal." Anything short of this will often be inaccurate and unjust. Certainly, charges of crime by the press, the public, and the police do not meet the standard of rigorous precision that is required. Decisions by civil courts and administrative agencies, based as they may be upon a slight preponderance of evidence and not upon proof beyond a reasonable doubt as convictions must be in the criminal court, "can show no more than civil wrong." And "evaluations of assorted deviation from social mores" by sociologists "are concerned with broader and looser constructs than crime."[9]

Crime Must Be Defined by the Criminal Law.   Consequently, it must be insisted that no person is a white-collar criminal or any kind of criminal until he has been properly adjudicated as such in the criminal court. This is as true in the case of a corporation charged with some type of criminal behavior as it is in the case of a person accused of murder. On this point Tappan states, "In studying the offender, there can be no presumption that arrested, arraigned, indicted, or prosecuted persons are criminals unless they also be held guilty beyond a reasonable doubt of a particular offense."[10]

This is not to deny that there are imperfections in the criminal law and its procedure. But the remedy for this is not to disregard the preventive devices that the law has created to shield the innocent. The correct approach to this problem lies in the improvement of the criminal law, in the stricter enforcement of its provisions, and in the vigorous but unbiased and impartial prosecution of the accused.

Sutherland's original definition of white-collar crime, quoted earlier, had some merit inasmuch as it did not depart entirely from the principles of criminal law. Since then, however, other definitions have appeared which make no attempt to do this. Clinard, in discussing the black market, defines white-collar crime as "a violation of the law committed primarily by groups such as businessmen, professional men, and politicians in connection with their occupations."[11] Hartung, using what he terms a narrower definition of the concept, defines white-collar crime as "a violation of law regulating business, which is committed for a firm by the firm or its agents in the conduct of its business."[12] Clinard, then, would make any businessman, professional man, or politician who engages in any illegal activity in connection with his occupation a white-collar criminal, while Hartung would confine the term to a firm or its agents that violate a law regulating business in the conduct of the firm's business. Like Sutherland, both Clinard and Hartung disregard the important element of conviction. Furthermore, it is quite clear that the criminal law is in no way concerned with much of the activity to which they refer since many illegal acts and violations of business regulations are not defined as crimes by the criminal law.

Even Sutherland abandoned his earlier position and later defined crime as any act which the law describes as socially injurious and for which it provides a penalty. Thus, he made the violation of any law, civil or criminal, a crime when it is "socially injurious" and carries a penalty.[13] But he did not stop with this. Later still, in writing of the dangers of white-collar criminality, he said, "Some of the offenses are not even a violation of the spirit of the law, for the parties concerned have been able by bribery and other means to prevent the enactment of laws to prohibit wrongful and injurious practices."[14] Here, then, the term "white-collar criminal" has deteriorated to the point where it can be used to refer to anyone who engages in what the observer considers to be unethical or immoral behavior. As Tappan says, white-collar crime becomes "the conduct of one who wears a white collar and who indulges in occupational behavior to which some particular criminologist takes exception."[15] Now, at last, the shrewd businessman, the inefficient work-man, the immoral politician, the unethical doctor or lawyer—all can be condemned as criminals by a stroke of the pen. The result, states Tappan, may be "fine indoctrination or catharsis achieved through blustering broadsides against the 'existing system' [but] it is not criminology and it is not social science."[16]

Morality and Ethics Are Not the Same as Law. However, what has been said here should not be regarded as an attempt to minimize the immoral and unethical practices of many American businessmen which have been exposed and justly condemned by a series of shocking investigations. The point is that morality and ethics are not the same as the law, and an immoral or unethical person is not necessarily a criminal. But should criminologists not study what they consider to be antisocial behavior with the view to having it defined as crime by the law? Yes, by all means, but until it has been so defined some terms other than "crime" and "criminal" should be used in describing it. Failure to do this can result only in the corruption of the terms "crime" and "criminal," the integrity of which the law has sought so vigilantly to preserve, and to open the door to endless confusion. That the danger of this is real is eloquently attested to above by the fact that the white-collar criminologists cannot agree among themselves as to the meaning of the terms "white-collar crime" and "white-collar criminal." Unless they can come to some agreement regarding these terms and define them according to the principles of criminal law, they should disregard the concept of white-collar crime entirely because "vague omnibus concepts defining crime are a blight upon either a legal system or a system of sociology that strives to be objective."[17]

Furthermore, the legal profession is already entrusted by society with the responsibility of interpreting and administering the criminal law. In order to protect all parties concerned, the legal profession has always insisted upon a strict interpretation of the meaning of the term "crime" and has carefully constructed around it a technical procedure designed to reduce the possibility of injustice. It is not likely that the legal profession will change the meaning of the term "crime" at the mere suggestion of persons outside the profession. In fact, the expanded meaning of the word might actually tend to undermine the understanding and confidence between two professional groups whose increased cooperation is so important in the improvement of our laws and their administration.

Difficulties in Estimating the Extent of White-Collar Crime. As a result of the way in which the term "white-collar crime" is variously defined by different sociologists, there are major difficulties involved in any attempt to estimate the amount of this type of crime in the United States. For example, if we use Sutherland's original definition, we find these obstacles: (1) White-collar crime is a nonlegal term which refers to certain criminal acts, such as embezzlement and bribery, but does not specifically name the criminal acts to which it has reference; (2) it refers to a certain type of person, namely, a member of the upper socioeconomic class, but does not provide us with specific criteria by which to determine the social class of the person involved; and (3) the criminal law in defining acts that are usually referred to by the term "white-collar crime," with few exceptions, does not make any distinction regarding the social class of the offenders. Other definitions of white-collar crime present similar difficulties. It should be clear, therefore, why there are no official sources of criminal statistics by which to estimate the amount of white-collar crime.

If sociologists were to use the term "white-collar crime" to refer to acts that are defined as crimes by the law, official complications of white-collar offenses known to the police might then be included in the *Uniform Crime Reports*.[18] Although this arrangement would not provide a complete coverage of white-collar crimes, however defined, nor satisfy all the strict requirements set up by the white-collar criminologists, it would furnish official and highly reliable data that could be employed in a systematic and continuing revelation of the enormity of these crimes and in agitation for any necessary reforms in the criminal law and its administration.

All this, of course, does not mean that we should forbid research and discussion regarding what *ought* to be called criminal. On the contrary, these activities should not merely be conducted but should be encouraged. By such efforts the law can be brought more closely into line with the needs and desires of our people, and the justice of its administration can be more securely established. These goals can be achieved, however, only if the influence of public opinion is exerted through our legislatures and courts and not by mere attempts to change the meaning of the term "crime" through academic decree or fiat.

Jerome Hall has pointed out that there is a basic conflict in American criminology as a result of its failure to integrate the diverse streams of thought which have come to be known as the Classical and Positive schools.[19] In the resolution of this conflict, both the crime and the criminal must be emphasized if the interests of the individual and those of society are to be balanced properly. "The criminal and his social relationships must be emphasized if we are to understand why he commits a crime and how his behavior may be modified. And crime as a legal concept must be emphasized if we are to understand how to protect society against the criminal and the defendant against his accusers and those who wield authority."[20]

THE SCIENTIFIC ISSUE

The scientific issue springs from the contention that those who commit white-collar crimes are relatively immune because of the class bias of the criminal law and its administration, and that this in turn has led to a distortion of the criminological theories of causation since these theories have been based to a great extent on the official records of the criminal and juvenile courts and law-enforcement agencies. While this contention has merit, the remedy is to be found in the further development of an independent science of human behavior and not in the mere tinkering with legal statistics as suggested by the white-collar criminologists.

The criminal law and the data about crimes and criminals accumulated during the law-enforcement process are useful in scientific research, but, as Thorsten Sellin has explained, "the application of scientific criteria to the selection and classification of these data independently of their *legal* form is essential to render them valuable to science." If the investigator in the field of criminology is to contribute to the science of human behavior, he must free himself from the concepts and terminology created by the criminal law. He must define his own terms and base them on the intrinsic character of his material so that they will designate properties in that material which are assumed to be universal. "The legislator and the administrator on the one hand, the scientist on the other, speak different languages, fundamentally irreconcilable. This is as it should be, for they are pursuing essentially different ends. . . . Confinement to the study of crime and criminals and the acceptance of the categories of specific forms of 'crime' and 'criminal' as laid down in law renders criminological research theoretically invalid from the point of view of science."[21]

The irreconcilable difference between the language of the criminal law and that of science can be no more sharply delineated than by a comparison of the meanings given the concept "cause" in these two fields.

> By "cause" science means the sufficient antecedent conditions necessary for the evocation of a given phenomenon. When these conditions are sufficient, the phenomenon appears; when they are insufficient, it does not. It refers, therefore, to a functional relationship between the phenomenon studied and the conditions necessary for its appearance. These conditions must be thought of in terms of their interaction in the total situation. Some exert more influence than others, but the functioning of all is necessary to produce the phenomenon, which would be different if there were the least modification in the total situation.[22]

The law, on the other hand, gives the concept "cause" a much more limited meaning. It recognizes that an act often has consequences that reach far and touch the lives of many persons, but the law does not hold a person responsible for every consequence of his act. "In a philosophical sense, the consequences of an act go forward to eternity and its causes extend back to the beginnings of time. But human responsibility cannot be measured by such standards. To do so would result in infinite liability for all wrongful acts, stir up boundless conflicts, and fill the courts with endless litigation."[23] Liability for the consequences of any act must be limited in terms of some idea of justice or social policy, which tends to be an expression of the dominant values of the group. In the light of what is considered to be justice in any society, a person's act is said to be the proximate or legal cause of the consequences, and if those constitute a crime and the requisite intent is present, he is held to be criminally responsible. But it is obvious that in any particular case this procedure may disregard certain factors that would be included by the application of the scientific concept of cause. The law, therefore, by its very nature and without necessarily being subject to any class bias or any unethical or immoral pressures or practices may produce official data which do not meet scientific standards. Thus, the psychiatrist in certain cases may find himself in conflict with the legal concept of insanity, which may serve socially defined ends as agreed upon by most of the members of all socioeconomic classes but which does not square with the scientific concept of mental disease.

NEED OF INDEPENDENT SCIENTIFIC
TERMINOLOGY

One more question needs to be examined. Why not strip the terms "crime" and "criminal" of their legal meanings in scientific research and give them a content which is acceptable to scientists? In answer to this question, it must be insisted that such a redefinition of terms, as in the case of the moral issue, would lead only to misunderstanding and confusion, and that everything that could be accomplished by it could be secured much more easily and effectively by the use of an independent scientific terminology. This is the course that has been followed by the psychiatrist who avoids the legal term "insanity" in his scientific research, even though he may agree that certain persons who have been declared insane by the law are mentally diseased and employs data regarding them which are taken from official legal sources. Sellin, while suggesting that criminologists study the violation of conduct norms in order to put criminology on a scientific basis, calls attention to the dangers involved in the loose usage of the term "crime." In his opinion it is wiser to retain this term for the violations of the norms that are embodied in the criminal law and to use the term "abnormal conduct" for violations of all norms whether legal or not.[24] Thus, he would study all deviations from conduct norms[25] as measured by concepts created by sociologists. To the extent that these deviations are already defined as crimes by the law, he would refer to them as such in his scientific investigation but, in his examination of the nature and causes of conduct deviations, he would in no way be restricted by the concepts of criminal law nor would he seek to alter its terminology. Naturally, this study of conduct deviations would involve not only the identification of conduct norms (both legal and nonlegal), but also the analysis of the sociohistorical setting in which these norms have developed.[26] The results achieved by such scientific research might then be utilized by the law in the modification of its own concepts and principles. In this way, science and the law could work hand in hand, while at the same time directing their efforts toward the attainment of their own goals.

ISOLATIONISM IN SOCIAL SCIENCE FIELD

Regardless of what our views may be on the subject of white-collar crime, in this controversy, as in so many others in the field of sociology, we are forcefully reminded of the immaturity of the social sciences. Since so little is known about the intricacies of normal behavior, we should not be overawed by any branch of science, any school of thought, or any type of methodology and thus neglect other promising leads. Instead, at present, we should use all available resources in every field of knowledge and organize them in a coordinated attack along all approaches to the study of human behavior. In this attack, teamwork by scholars in the social sciences and the law can do much to break down the isolationism that has so often characterized research in the field of criminology and contributed to unfortunate misunderstandings and needless disputes.

Notes

1. Edwin H. Sutherland, "Crime and Business," *Annals of the American Academy of Political and Social Science*, 217 (September, 1941), p. 112.
2. Edwin H. Sutherland, "White-Collar Criminality," *American Sociological Review*, 5 (February, 1940), p. 9.
3. Frank E. Hartung, "White-Collar Offenses in the Wholesale Meat Industry in Detroit," *American Journal of Sociology*, 56 (July, 1950), p. 25.
4. Jerome Hall, *General Principles of Criminal Law* (Indianapolis: Bobbs-Merrill, 1947), pp. 542–551; Clarence R. Jeffery, "The Structure of American Criminological Thinking," *Journal of Criminal Law, Criminology, and Police Science*, 46 (January–February, 1956), pp. 658–672, and "Crime, Law, and Social Structure," *Journal of Criminal Law, Criminology, and Police Science*, 47 (November–December, 1956), pp. 423–445.
5. Justin Miller, *Handbook of Criminal Law* (St. Paul, Minn.: West, 1934), p. 16.
6. Paul W. Tappan, "Who Is the Criminal?" *American Sociological Review*, 12 (February, 1947), p. 100.
7. Miller, *op. cit.*, pp. 93–94.
8. Thomas M. Cooley, *Constitutional Limitations*, 3d ed. (St. Paul, Minn.: West, 1933), p. 626.
9. Paul W. Tappan, "Crime and the Criminal," *Federal Probation*, 11 (July–September, 1947), pp. 41–44.
10. Tappan, "Who is the Criminal?", *op. cit.*, p. 100.
11. Marshall B. Clinard, *The Black Market: A Study of White Collar Crime* (New York: Holt, 1952), p. 127. In presenting this definition, Clinard says, "Contrary to popular thinking, however, the use of a criminal sanction is not essential for a black market violation of law to be considered sociologically as a 'crime.'"
12. Frank E. Hartung, "White-Collar Crime: Its Significance for Theory and Practice," *Federal Probation*, 17 (June, 1953), pp. 31–36.
13. Edwin H. Sutherland, "Is 'White Collar Crime' Crime?" *American Sociological Review*, 10 (April, 1945), p. 132.
14. Edwin H. Sutherland, *Principles of Criminology*, 4th ed. (Philadelphia: Lippincott, 1947), p. 37.
15. Tappan, "Who Is the Criminal?", *op. cit.*, p. 99.
16. *Ibid.*
17. *Ibid.*
18. Although in the strict sense of the word an act is not a crime until it has been properly adjudicated as such in the criminal court, *offenses known to the police*, as shown by the *Uniform Crime Reports*, are the best available index of crime in the United States.
19. Hall, *op. cit.*, p. 542.
20. Robert G. Caldwell, *Criminology* (New York: Ronald Press, 1956), p. 24.
21. Thorsten Sellin, *Culture Conflict and Crime* (New York; Social Science Research Council, 1938), pp. 23–24.

22. Caldwell, *op. cit.*, p. 13.

23. *Ibid.*, p. 120.

24. Sellin, *op. cit.*, p. 32.

25. Other writers have used the term "deviant behavior" to refer to departures from the norms of a society. See, for example, Marshall B. Clinard, *Sociology of Deviant Behavior* (New York: Holt, 1957).

26. Clarence R. Jeffery, "The Development of Crime in Early English Society," *Journal of Criminal Law, Criminology, and Police Science*, 47 (March–April, 1957). pp. 647–666.

31

SOME OBSERVATIONS ON THE USE OF CRIMINAL SANCTIONS IN ENFORCING ECONOMIC REGULATIONS

Sanford H. Kadish

Those who have had occasion to look for answers to the problems of the use of sanctions, taken to include the whole range of official modes of securing compliance with norms of conduct, have commonly agreed for some time now that there are few to be found. In view of the antiquity of the legal experience, which for the most part has always entailed the use of sanctions of one kind or another, this is a remarkable verdict. Indeed, works written at the turn of the eighteenth century by Jeremy Bentham[1] are still the basic works in the area, a sobering observation which could scarcely be made of more than a handful of subjects of inquiry. In this state of affairs it is not surprising that we are largely ignorant of the impact of the penal sanction, which is only one aspect of the larger problem of sanctions, and still less so that we know little about the use of the penal sanction in an area of relatively recent development—economic regulatory legislation. These are only sectors of a much larger unexplored terrain.

Moreover, unnecessary confusion has become an ally of ignorance

Reprinted from the *University of Chicago Law Review*, 30 (Spring, 1963), pp. 423–449.

in impeding understanding of these areas. Because strong ideological differences separate the proponents and opponents of economic regulation, judgments about the effect of penal sanctions in achieving compliance tend to turn upon judgments about the merits of the substantive regulation. Liberally oriented social scientists, otherwise critical of the case made for the deterrent and vindicatory uses of punishment of ordinary offenders, may be found supporting stern penal enforcement against economic violators.[2] At the same time conservative groups, rarely foes of rigorous punishment for ordinary offenders, appear less sanguine for the criminal prosecution when punishment of business offenders is debated.[3]

This statement of the underdeveloped state of the art is by no means designed as an introduction to an ambitious effort to close the ancient gap in understanding. Quite the contrary, it is meant rather to excuse the modest ambit of these observations. What I would like to accomplish is to outline the special characteristics of economic regulatory legislation relevant to the use of the criminal sanction, to indicate what implications they have for effective use of the criminal law, and to suggest relevant concerns in the use of this sanction beyond the goal of enforcing the specific regulatory norm.

I

The kind of economic regulations whose enforcement through the criminal sanction is the subject of this inquiry may be briefly stated: those which impose restrictions upon the conduct of business as part of a considered economic policy. This includes such laws as price-control and rationing laws, antitrust laws, and other legislation designed to protect or promote competition or prevent unfair competition, export controls, small-loan laws, securities regulations, and, perhaps, some tax laws. Put to one side, therefore, are regulations directly affecting business conduct that are founded on interests other than economic ones; for example, laws regulating the conduct of business in the interest of public safety and general physical welfare. Also to one side are laws indirectly affecting business conduct by their general applicability; for example, embezzlement, varieties of fraud, and related white-collar offenses.

The class of regulations so defined possesses several characteristics that have a direct bearing upon the uses and limits of the criminal sanction as a means of achieving compliance. The first is the very feature suggested as the identifying characteristic of such legislation; that is, the nature of the interest protected. Certainly the use of criminal sanctions to protect interests of an economic character is not a contemporary departure. The extension of the classic larceny offense by courts and legislatures to embrace fraud, embezzlement, and similar varieties of misappropriation that threatened newly developing ways of transacting business is a well-documented chapter in the history of the criminal law.⁴ Indeed, the process continues today.⁵ But there is an important difference between the traditional and expanded property offenses and the newer economic regulatory offenses, a difference reflecting the shift from an economic order that rested on maximum freedom for the private entrepreneur to one committed to restraints upon that freedom. The traditional property offenses protect private property interests against the acquisitive behavior of others in the furtherance of free private decision.⁶ The newer offenses, on the other hand, seek to protect the economic order of the community against harmful use by the individual of his property interest. The central purpose, therefore, is to control private choice, rather than to free it. But the control imposed (and this too has significance) is not total, as it would be in a socialistic system. Private economic self-determination has not been abandoned in favor of a wholly state-regulated economy. Indeed, the ideal of free enterprise is maintained, the imposed regulations being regarded as necessary to prevent that ideal from consuming itself. Whether the criminal sanction may safely and effectively be used in the service of implementing the large-scale economic policies underlying regulatory legislation of this kind raises fundamental questions.

A second relevant feature of these laws concerns the nature of the conduct restrained. Since it is not criminal under traditional categories of crime and, apart from the regulatory proscription, closely resembles acceptable aggressive business behavior, the stigma of moral reprehensibility does not naturally associate itself with the regulated conduct.⁷ Moreover, the conduct is engaged in by persons of relatively high social and economic status; since it is motivated by economic considerations, it is calculated and deliberate rather than reactive; it is usually part of a pattern of business conduct rather than episodic in character; and it often involves group action through the corporate form.

The third noteworthy attribute of this legislation is the role provided for the criminal sanction in the total scheme of enforcement. Typically, the criminal penalty is only one of a variety of authorized sanctions which may include monetary settlements, private actions (compensatory or penal), injunctions, inspections, licensing, required reporting, or others. Its role, therefore, is largely ancillary and takes either or both of two forms. On the one hand, the criminal penalty may serve as a means to insure the functioning of other sanctions, as, for example, penalties for operating without a license or without prior registration or reporting. On the other hand, the criminal sanction may serve as a separate and supplementary mode of enforcement by directly prohibiting the conduct sought to be prevented, as in the Sherman Antitrust Act. Furthermore, implicit in the legislative scheme is the conception of the criminal sanction as a last resort to be used selectively and discriminatingly when other sanctions fail. In some legislation, of course, the message of selective enforcement is explicit in the law. Finally, the responsibility for investigation, detection, and initiating prosecution is often vested in a specialized agency or other body rather than left with the usual institutions for policing and prosecuting criminal violations. Moreover, these bodies commonly are not specialized organs of criminal enforcement, but are the agencies broadly charged with administering the legislative scheme.

This statement of the relevant features of the laws under inquiry, in terms of the interest protected, the behavior regulated, and the contemplated role of the criminal penalty, is not meant to suggest that these laws are ultimately unique in the problems they raise for criminal enforcement. Apart from the nature of the interest protected, most, if not all, of these characteristics may be found in other areas of the criminal law. And even though the nature of the interest protected is by definition unique, many of the problems it poses, such as making morally neutral behavior criminal, are common to other areas as well. All that is suggested is that if one asks, "What problems are raised for the effective use of the criminal sanction as a mode of achieving compliance in this area?" the beginnings of an answer are to be found in these congeries of characteristics. It remains now to suggest what bearing they have.

II

I propose to deal with the relevance of these characteristics in terms of three major problems: the problem of defining the proscribed conduct, the problem of corporate criminality and the problem of moral neutrality.

The Problem of Defining the Proscribed Conduct. The fact that the protected interest is the preferred functioning of the economic system and entails only partial restriction upon the operation of American business bears directly upon the task of defining the proscribed behavior with sufficient specificity to meet the requirement of fair notice generally applicable to criminal legislation. Where the criminal sanction is used to police other enforcement devices (as, for example, when it becomes criminal to market a security issue without registration or to do business without a license), the standard is met without difficulty. But the requirement of specificity is notably difficult of fulfillment where the crime itself purports to define the substantive economic behavior sought to be avoided. A notable example is the Sherman Antitrust Act's prohibition of "restraint of trade or commerce" and "illegal monopolization." Only to a small degree, if at all, is the difficulty remediable by better draftsmanship. As Thurman Arnold observed, "Antitrust policy touches fields and boundaries which recede as you approach them and disappear each time you try to stake them out."[8] The reason for this arises from several sources: First, the economic policy is itself unclear, constituting largely a vague aspiration for a proper balance among competing economic goals.[9] Second, illegality must turn on judgments that are essentially evaluative in character, rather than upon purely factual determinations. Third, the inevitable development of novel circumstances and arrangements in the dynamic areas under regulation would soon make precise formulations obsolete, even to the limited extent they proved feasible. . . .[10]

The requirement in an otherwise unconstitutionally vague definition of criminal conduct that the defendant must be shown to have acted willfully or knowingly has sometimes been held to remedy the defect of definition. Thus the Supreme Court found no unfairness in convicting a motor company for failing to reroute their explosive-laden truck "as far as practical, and where feasible" to avoid congested areas, where it was necessary to prove that this was done "knowingly"[11] or in convicting a taxpayer for attempting to evade taxes by making "unreasonable" deductions for commissions paid to stockholders as compensation for service, where the action was taken "willfully."[12] A requirement that the defendant have intentionally committed the act with a full and correct understanding of the factual circumstances is of no help to a defendant faced with an unclear definition of the conduct forbidden. On the other hand, however vague the line between what is permissible and what is criminal, where the actor is aware that his conduct falls squarely within the forbidden zone he is in no position to complain.[13] "A mind intent upon willful evasion is inconsistent with surprised innocence."[14] Apparently, therefore, it is *scienter* in this sense, that is, knowledge by the actor that he is violating the law, which is held in these cases to eliminate the vagueness problem. Yet this premise probably affords defenses to a larger group than intended, since a defendant who knew nothing of the existence of the law would be in as good a position as one who did not know that his action came within its terms.[15] If the prosecution must prove that the defendant knew his conduct fell within the terms of the law, it could hardly do so without proof as well that he knew of its existence. A legislature, however, could presumably resolve the semantic impasse by making it a defense that the defendant did not know his acts fell within its terms or perhaps, more narrowly, that he could not reasonably know it, though not a defense simply that he did not know of the law's existence.

Another approach to mitigating the difficulties of a vague formulation is through administrative choice of cases to prosecute. If the enforcement agency initiates criminal prosecution solely where the meaning of the statute has become acceptably clear through judicial interpretation, the unfairness of the original unclarity may be thought adequately reduced. An example is the announced policy of the Department of Justice to institute criminal prosecutions for Sherman Antitrust Act violations only where there is a per se violation, such as price fixing, a violation accompanied by a specific intent to restrain competition or monopolize, the use of predatory practices, or where the defendant has before been convicted of a Sherman Antitrust Act violation. This approach, unlike the legislative requirement of *scienter*, is of no avail where the vagueness of the statutory formulation renders the law constitutionally unenforceable. It is also dependent upon the existence of means other than criminal prosecutions to develop clarifying interpretation. In the Sherman Antitrust Act this is provided through the civil suit as a parallel means of enforcing the identical standard of conduct. This, in turn, however, may be a mixed blessing. One of the purposes of looseness and generality in the formulation of the standard is to create a flexibility that will allow judicial interpretation to keep pace with the changes in the character of the area under regulation. Courts may prove understandably reluctant to sustain expansive, although desirable, interpretations where the consequence will be to subject defendants to criminal as well as civil sanctions.

There are several alternatives to civil litigation as a means of producing clarifying interpretation. The most obvious is to delegate to the responsible administrative agency the authority to issue so-called "legislative regulations" in implementation of the statutory scheme. Providing criminal penalties for violations of these regulations then eliminates the vagueness problem to the extent of the clarity of the regulation. There is still, to be sure, a requirement of some specificity in the legislative standard from which the agency derives its authority. But this raises the different, though related, issue of delegation of powers, where requirements of specificity are considerably less than those applicable to criminal statutes. The declaratory order, in which the agency renders an advisory judgment on the legality of a contemplated course of action, is another possibility. This has utility both in providing further clarification of the applicability of regulations and in rendering interpretive guidance of the law when it, rather than a regulation, is the direct source of the prohibition. Section 5 of the Administrative Procedure Act provides a precedent for such an order, although the use authorized therein is considerably more limited than it might be.

Still another alternative is flatly to prohibit certain kinds of activity, except where an administrative agency, interpreting and applying general legislative standards, expressly allows it, as by issuing a license. The criminal penalty may then be imposed for the clearly defined offense of engaging in the activity without authorization. This, of course, is to use the criminal sanction, as previously suggested, as a means of enforcing another, noncriminal sanction. It is readily usable in such narrow areas as marketing securities or engaging in other particular types of business. It is impractical where the thrust of the prohibition goes to ways of conducting any and all kinds of business, as in the Sherman Act.

The Problem of Corporate Criminality. Conduct reached by economic regulatory legislation is typically group conduct often engaged in through the corporate form. This raises the formidable issue of corporate criminality. From the legislative viewpoint, the principal questions are twofold. First, what difficulties beset enforcement agencies in affixing criminal liability upon responsible actors where the principal violator is the corporation? Second, in any event, what are the possibilities of effective enforcement through the imposition of criminal penalties upon the corporation itself?

Fixing criminal liability upon the immediate actors within a corporate structure generally poses no special problem. But the immediate actors may be lower echelon officials or employees who are the tools rather than the responsible originators of the violative conduct. Where the corporation is managed by its owners, the task of identifying the policy formulators is not acute. But where the stock of the corporation is widely held, the organization complex and sprawling, and the responsibility spread over a maze of departments and divisions, then there may be conspicuous difficulties in pinpointing responsibility on the higher echelon policy-making officials.[16] The source of the difficulty is the conventional requirement that to hold one person criminally liable for the acts of another he must have participated in the acts of the other in some meaningful way, as by directing or encouraging them, aiding in their commission, or permitting them to be done by subordinates whom he has power to control. The difficulty is exemplified in the now famous antitrust prosecution of the electrical equipment manufacturers. Here the high policy makers of General Electric and other companies involved escaped personal accountability for a criminal conspiracy of lesser officials that extended over several years to the profit of the corporations, despite the belief of the trial judge and most observers that these higher officials either knew of and condoned these activities or were willfully ignorant of them.[17]

It cannot be known to what extent this legal obstacle to convicting the policy initiators actually reduces the efficacy of the criminal sanction in achieving compliance. Certainly, it would prove more significant in those areas, like antitrust, where giant corporations are the principal targets of the law, than in areas where they are not. But other factors may be more influential in preventing widescale successful prosecution of individual corporate officials under the antitrust laws; for example, there have been strikingly few convictions of corporate officials, even of officials of closely held corporations and the lesser officials of large, public corporations.

At all events, one means of reducing the difficulty would be to alter by statute the basis of accountability of corporate directors, officers, or agents. An amendment, for example, of the antitrust law was recently proposed which would have changed the present basis of accountability (that such persons "shall have authorized, ordered or done" the acts) to make it suffice that the individual had knowledge or reason to know of the corporate violation and failed to exercise his authority to stop or prevent it. This falls short of outright vicarious liability, since accountability is made to turn on fault in not knowing and acting rather than on a relationship simpliciter. Essentially it makes a negligent omission the basis of accountability. Still, a standard of accountability resting on precisely how much the far-flung operations of a nationwide corporation an official should reasonably be aware of approaches vicarious liability in its indeterminateness, since neither the common experience of the jury nor even specialized experience affords substantial guidance. In effect, it introduces an element of uncertainty concerning accountability into laws that often, like the Sherman Antitrust Act, are already marked by uncertainty concerning the conduct forbidden. . . .

Fixing criminal liability upon the corporation itself has posed fewer legal obstacles in the enforcement of regulatory legislation. The earlier conceptual difficulties of ascribing criminal intent to a fictitious entity have been largely removed by the developing law. And whatever doubt may exist is readily met by expressly providing for corporate liability in the regulatory statute. But the problem of corporate accountability—that is, when the entity is liable for conduct of its agents at various levels of responsibility—is analogous to the problem of holding corporate officials accountable for the acts of lesser agents. It has been resolved more sweepingly in the case of the entity. For acts of its high managerial agents, it is, by definition, accountable since a corporation cannot act by itself. For the acts of its lesser agents, the tendency has been, at least in the regulatory offenses, to hold the corporation accountable for the acts of employees within the scope of their employment or while acting as employees. Whether the consequential imposition of vicarious responsibility upon the corporate entity, as well as upon shareholders, is justified raises the question of the deterrent efficacy of convicting and fining the corporate entity.

The case for corporate criminality rests presumably upon the inadequacy of the threat of personal conviction upon the individual actors. As said earlier, difficulties of proof under legal principles of accountability have interfered with effective prosecution of high corporate officials. And the commonly observed jury behavior of convicting the corporate defendant while acquitting the individual defendants, even where proof is apparently strong, further supports the case for the alternate sanction. Moreover, "there are probably cases in which the economic pressures within the corporate body are sufficiently potent to tempt individuals to hazard personal liability for the sake of company gain, especially where the penalties threatened are moderate and where the offense does not involve behavior condemned as highly immoral by the individual's associates."[18]

Yet the question remains of the effectiveness of corporate criminality as a supplementary deterrent.

The only two practically available modes of imposing criminal sanctions upon the corporate defendant are through the stigma of conviction and the exaction of a fine. The former, classified by Bentham as the "moral or popular" sanction, operates, as he suggested, through the adverse reactions to the conviction of persons in the community.[19] Whether there is any substantial moral opprobrium attached to violation of economic regulatory legislation (even where individuals are convicted) I defer until later. Assuming there is, can it be said to have any appreciable significance when directed to a corporate entity? There is no substantial empirical basis for answering this question.[20] It seems unlikely that whatever moral stigma may attach to a convicted corporation would be felt in any effectual way by the corporate individuals, especially in large corporations where responsibility is diffused. On the other hand, the point has been made[21] (though denied as well)[22] that the corporate stigma may operate as a deterrent by impairing the reputation of the corporation in its business operations and hence adversely affecting its economic position. Until there is more to go on, one can only guess at the validity of this observation, though there is reason to expect that the impact of the conviction would operate differentially, depending on the size of the corporation, the extent of competition and the dominance of its market position, the degree to which its conviction attracted public notice, and the like.

The exaction of a corporate fine serves in part to give color to the moral stigma of conviction. Insofar as this is its role, its value depends upon the existence and power of the stigma to deter. On the other hand, the use of the corporate fine apart from the stigma of conviction raises no issue peculiar to the criminal sanction, since civil fines afford identical deterrent possibilities. Whether it would prove effective to increase the economic hazard of misconduct by authorizing higher fines than those now commonly authorized depends on such considerations as the general ability of the corporation to recoup its losses through its pricing policy and the likelihood that courts would impose the higher fines. An alternative recently proposed would substitute for the fine a governmental proceeding designed to compel the corporation to disgorge the profits attributable to its violation. These alternatives raise substantial questions concerning sanctions, but not the criminal sanction, strictly speaking.

The Problem of Moral Neutrality. Viewed in the large, the characteristic of the conduct typically proscribed by economic regulatory legislation most relevant for the purposes of criminal enforcement is that it is calculated and deliberative and directed to economic gain.[23] It would appear, therefore, to constitute a classic case for the operation of the deterrent strategy. Nonetheless, it is a widely shared view that the strategy has not worked out in fact, that the criminal sanction has not proved a major weapon for achieving compliance. Part of the explanation may be attributable to the difficulties of enforcement suggested above, such as the resistance to vaguely defined standards of criminality, the difficulty of fixing culpability upon high corporate officials, and the muffled and absorbable impact of corporate criminal sanctions. But it is likely that other factors play a more dominant role.

A common explanation of the failure of the criminal sanction is simply that the powerful business interests affected do not want these laws enforced and employ their power and position in American life to block vigorous enforcement. Influence is exercised over the legislatures to keep enforcement staffs impoverished and sanctions safely inefficacious. Enforcement officials, as prospective counsel for business interests, and judges, as former counsel, identify with these interests and resist criminal enforcement. Moreover, news media, under the control of these same groups, work to create hostility to these laws and their vigorous enforcement and sympathy for the violators. In short, "those who are responsible for the system of criminal justice are afraid to antagonize businessmen. . . . The most powerful group in medieval society secured relative immunity from punishment by 'benefit of clergy,' and now our most powerful group secures relative immunity by 'benefit of business.' "[24]

It would be dogmatic to assert that influences of this kind do not exist, but it may be doubted that they play a dispositive role. Business surely constitutes a powerful interest group in American life; but the profusion of regulatory legislation over the ardent protests of important economic interests in the past thirty years is some evidence that it is not all-powerful. Opposing forces have been able to marshal considerable public sentiment against a variety of business practices. Moreover, it is perhaps an oversimplification to identify all business as united in monolithic opposition. There is less a single business interest than a substantial variety of business interests. What then, in addition to business propaganda and influence, has accounted for the failure of the criminal sanction? Or, if we must have a villain, how has it been that business, which has not always gotten its way, has been this successful in devitalizing the use of that sanction?

It is a plausible surmise that the explanation is implicated in another feature of the behavior regulated by these laws; namely, that it is not generally regarded as morally reprehensible in the common view, that, indeed, in some measure it is the laws themselves that appear bad or, at least, painful necessities, and that the violators by and large turn out to be respectable people in the respectable pursuit of profit. It is not likely that these popular attitudes are wholly products of a public-relations campaign by the affected business community. The springs of the public sentiment reach into the national ethos, producing the values that the man of business himself holds, as well as the attitude of the public toward him and his activities. Typically, the conduct prohibited by economic regulatory laws is not immediately distinguishable from modes of business behavior that are not only socially acceptable, but also affirmatively desirable in an economy founded upon an ideology (not denied by the regulatory regime itself) of free enterprise and the profit motive. Distinctions there are, of course, between salutary entrepreneurial practices and those which threaten the values of the very regime of economic freedom. And it is possible to reason convincingly that the harms done to the economic order by violations of many of these regulatory laws are of a magnitude that dwarf in significance the lower-class property offenses. But the point is that these perceptions require distinguishing and reasoning processes that are not the normal governors of the passion of moral disapproval, and they are not dramatically obvious to a public long conditioned to responding approvingly to the production of profit through business shrewdness, especially in the absence of live and visible victims. Moreover, in some areas, notably the antitrust laws, it is far from clear that there is consensus even by the authors and enforcers of the regulation—the legislators, courts and administrators—on precisely what should be prohibited and what permitted, and the reasons therefor. And as Freund observed, "If a law declares a practice to be criminal, and cannot apply its policy with consistency, its moral effect is necessarily weakened."[25]

The consequences of the absence of sustained public moral resentment for the effective use of the criminal sanction may be briefly stated. The central distinguishing aspect of the criminal sanction appears to be the stigmatization of the morally culpable.[26] At least, it tends so to be regarded in the community. Without moral culpability, there is in a democratic community an explicable and justifiable reluctance to affix the stigma of blame. [27] This perhaps is the basic explanation, rather than the selfish machinations of business interests, for the reluctance of administrators and prosecutors to invoke the criminal sanction, the reluctance of jurors to find guilt, and the reluctance of judges to impose strong penalties. And beyond its effect on enforcement, the absence of moral opprobrium interferes in another more subtle way with achieving compliance. Fear of being caught and punished does not exhaust the deterrent mechanism of the criminal law. It is supplemented by the personal disinclination to act in violation of the law's commands, apart from immediate fear of being punished. One would suppose that especially in the cast of those who normally regard themselves as respectable, proper, and law-abiding the appeal to act in accordance with conscience is relatively great. But where the violation is not generally regarded as ethically reprehensible, either by the community at large or by the class of businessmen itself, the private appeal to conscience is at its minimum and being convicted and fined may have little more impact than a bad selling season.[28]

Are there modes of dealing with these consequences of making morally neutral behavior criminal? A commonly suggested remedy for inadequate enforcement is a campaign of strict enforcement aided by strengthened prosecution staffs and, perhaps, more severe penalties. But to the extent that the deficiency in enforcement is attributable to the moral inoffensiveness of the behavior, the major limitation of such a call to arms is that it is addressed to the symptom rather than the cause. How will legislatures be convinced to expend substantial sums for criminal enforcement or prosecutors to go for the jugular or courts and juries to cooperate in the face of a fundamental lack of sympathy for the criminal penalty in this area? Enlarged resources for prosecution may well afford staff enthusiasts an opportunity for more vigorous enforcement, but one may doubt that it can achieve more than a minor flurry of enforcement.[29]

An attack on the cause, insofar as moral neutrality is the cause, would presumably require a two-pronged program: one directed at the obstacle of popular nullification; the other at inculcating the sentiment of moral disapproval in the community. Each, of course, would inevitably have an effect upon the other. The former might proceed, not simply by allocating greater enforcement resources, but by arrangements that would reduce the traditional discretionary authority of the various bodies involved in criminal law enforcement. For example, the decision to prosecute might be exclusively centered in the agency responsible for the whole regulatory program; conservative legal interpretation might be dealt with by authorizing agency-interpretative regulations which are made relevant in criminal prosecutions; the temporizing of juries might be avoided by eliminating, where possible, jury trials, the judge's sentencing discretion might be curtailed by mandatory minimum penalties. There is, of course, the substantial task of persuading legislatures to abjure the traditional mediating institutions of the criminal law in an area where, the moral factor's being largely absent, they might be thought to have their historic and most useful function to perform. But if enacted, one might reasonably suppose that such legal arrangements could result in a somewhat more frequent and rigorous use of the criminal sanction and a heightening of the deterrent effect of the law.

The other prong of the program, the cultivation of the sentiment of moral disapproval, is perhaps closer to the heart of the matter. To some extent, the more frequent enforcement and the more stringent punishment of violators may tend to serve this objective, as well as its more direct in terrorem purposes, especially where cases are selected for enforcement with this end in view.[30] Whether a governmentally mounted campaign should be employed as well to give widespread publicity to successful convictions and to shape the public conscience in other ways may be questioned from various viewpoints, but it surely would be consistent with the basic strategy of using criminal sanctions in these areas.

How effective a campaign of selected prosecutions and attendant publicity would prove in creating a changed climate is problematical. Certainly one can not confidently deny that the spectacle of frequent conviction and severe punishment may play a role in molding the community's attitudes toward the conduct in question. Experience offers uncertain guidance. Tax evasion has a history that provides some support. We have come a considerable distance, though not all the way,[31] from the day when an English judge could observe from the bench, "there is not behind taxing laws, as there is behind laws against crime, an independent moral obligation."[32] The change was accompanied in this country by a gradual tightening of the criminal sanction. In 1924, tax evasion was upgraded from a misdemeanor to a felony and maximum imprisonment raised from one to five years; reforms in 1952 converted the criminal prosecution from a tax recovery device and weapon against the professional racketeer to a means of general deterrence of tax evasion by widespread and selected enforcement against all levels of violators.[33] While the tax evasion prosecution is still something of a special case, the record of successful prosecution has become genuinely impressive and the tax-evasion conviction a sanction of some consequence. Experience such as this, however, gives little more than support for the plainly plausible assumption that criminal enforcement may play some part. One can not be sure of the extent to which other factors, not necessarily present in areas other than tax, created the conditions for optimum use of the criminal sanction as a moralizing weapon or, indeed, of the extent to which other influences rather than, or in addition to, the criminal sanction, produced the changed climate. . . .

III

I have reserved for last those issues and concerns that arise out of goals other than the effectiveness of the criminal sanction in achieving compliance. Those which most prominently compete for consideration are, first, the sentiment of fundamental fairness—in a word, justice; and, second, the retention of the vitality of the criminal law in its traditional sphere of application. They come into play in connection with two aspects of the use of the criminal law to enforce economic regulatory laws; namely, the loosening of minimum requirements for culpability in the cause of enforcement efficiency and the criminalizing and punishing of behavior that does not generally attract the sentiment of moral reprobation.

Requirements of Culpability. At several points, attention has been called to the obstacles to effective prosecution created by certain conventional requirements of the criminal law; for example, the requirement of specificity in defining the prohibited conduct and the requirement of minimum conditions of accountability in holding persons responsible for the acts of others. Whatever basis these requirements have in the area of traditional crime, may they properly be diluted or dispensed with in the area of economic regulatory crime? The issue is fundamentally the same as that posed by the use of strict criminal liability, though, interestingly enough, this appears to have been much less commonly employed in economic regulation than in those controls on business directed to public health and safety.

The case for the irrelevance of these traditional requirements is reflected in the observation of a trust-buster of an earlier generation: "The rights of the accused, which are of the utmost importance where liberty of an individual is in jeopardy, are irrelevant symbols when the real issue is the arrangement under which corporations in industry compete."[34] In essence, the concept is that the purpose behind the criminal sanction in this area is not penalization, but regulation. Unlike the area of conventional crime against person and property, where criminalization serves to reassure the community, to express condemnation, and to set in motion a corrective or restraining regime, as well as to deter proscribed behavior, here the concern is solely with this last factor. "[T]he problem of responsibility is not the general social phenomenon of moral delinquency and guilt, but the practical problem of dealing with physical conditions and social or economic practices that are to be controlled."[35]

A countervailing consideration commonly adduced in discussions of strict liability is equally applicable where culpability requirements are otherwise withdrawn by statutes that do not adequately announce what is prohibited or that impose varieties of vicarious responsibility. Absent these requirements, it cannot be said except in a strictly formal sense that the actor made a choice to commit the acts prohibited. Hence, it is said that the law has no deterrent function to perform, offering no lesson to the actor or to other persons beyond the Pickwickian instruction that even if he does the best he can or anyone could to comply with the law, he may nonetheless be punished. Yet the argument does not quite persuade, for it may as plausibly be argued that the consequence of dispensing with the requirement of proof of culpability eases the task of the enforcing authorities, rendering successful prosecution more likely and, by discouraging insistence on trial and simplifying the issues when trials are held, enhances the efficiency of prosecution. In a word, certainty of conviction is increased. This may readily exert an added deterrent force upon the actor faced with a choice, since the chances of escaping punishment for a culpable choice, intentional or negligent, are decreased. And even where there is no immediate choice, the effect could sometimes be to influence persons to arrange their affairs to reduce to a minimum the possibilities of accidental violation; in short, to exercise extraordinary care.

Further, the persistent use of such laws by legislatures and their strong support by persons charged with their enforcement make it dogmatic to insist they can not deter in these ways.

Closer, perhaps, to the core of the opposition to dispensing with culpability is the principle that it is morally improper and ultimately unsound and self-defeating to employ penal sanctions with respect to conduct that does not warrant the moral condemnation that is implicit, or that should be implicit, in the concept of a crime. The issue is whether these considerations are adequately dealt with by the contention that laws dispensing with culpability are directed to regulation rather than penalization.

The contention plainly proves too much. If the sole concern is a nonreprobative deterrent threat, then it follows that the sanction should be drastic and certain enough to overcome the motive of economic gain, and not necessarily that the sanction should be criminal. Civil fines, punitive damages, injunctions, profit-divestiture programs, or other varieties of noncriminal sanctions would thus appear to offer equivalent possibilities of enforcing the regulatory scheme. Indeed, these alternatives might enhance the possibilities, since proof and evidentiary requirements are more onerous in criminal prosecutions than in civil suits. The conclusion appears difficult to resist that insistence on the criminal penalty is attributable to a desire to make use of the unique deterrent mode of the criminal sanction, the stigma of moral blame that it carries. If so, the argument of regulation rather than penalization turns out in the end to be only a temporary diversion that does not escape the need to confront the basic issue: the justice and wisdom of imposing a stigma of moral blame in the absence of blameworthiness in the actor.

So far as the issue of justice is concerned, once having put the moral question the footing becomes unsteady. Is the moral difficulty inconsequential, requiring simply the side-stepping of an otherwise useful symbol that happens to stand in the way of attaining immediately desirable goals? Does it yield to a pragmatic evaluation in terms of an estimate of the soundness of departing from principle to some degree in particular cases in order to attain goals of greater consequence?[36] Does it present an insuperable objection entailing commitment to values of such profundity that compromise is unthinkable? For present purposes it is perhaps enough to put the questions, though three points may be suggested: First, the starkness of the moral issue is to some degree assuaged by regarding laws dispensing with culpability as empowering enforcement officials to use their discretion to select for prosecution those who have in their judgment acted culpably. Plainly, however, the issue is not escaped since it remains to justify dispensing with the safeguards of trial on this single and crucial issue. Second, the recognition of the moral impasse does not necessarily require agreement that the criminal *law* should use its weapons for the purpose of fixing moral obloquy upon transgressors. It is sufficient that it is broadly characteristic of the way criminal conviction operates in our society. Third, and in consequence, the moral difficulty exists only so long as and to the extent that criminal conviction retains its aura of moral condemnation. The impasse lessens to the extent that the element of blame and punishment is replaced by a conception of the criminal process as a means of social improvement through a program of morally neutral rehabilitation and regulation. (Though such a development has important implications which I mean to return to shortly.)

Concerning the issue of ultimate wisdom, the point frequently made respecting strict liability is equally applicable to the dilution of these aspects of culpability typically at issue in economic regulatory legislation. The dilution is not readily confined within the narrow area for which it was designed, but tends to overflow into the main body of conventional crimes. The distinction between offenses that regulate and those that penalize in the traditional sense proves inadequate to divide the waters. For example, traditional concepts of liability in the main body of criminal law tend to receive a new and diluted form when construed as part of a regulatory statute. Moreover, the habituation of courts and legislatures to crimes dispensing with culpability in the regulatory area may readily dull legislative and judicial sensitivity to the departures from minimum culpability requirements already fixed in the main body of the criminal law. . . .

The Criminalization of Morally Neutral Conduct. But let it be assumed that the traditional grounds of culpability have been adhered to so that the defendant can fairly be held accountable for a choice to violate the economic prohibition. May there be costs, even so, in terms of principle and other goals, in employing the criminal sanction where the violative behavior does not attract in the community the moral disapprobation associated with a criminal conviction? How different and how similar are the considerations involved in dispensing with culpability? The question is the obverse of an aspect of the relation between criminal law and morals which has been much considered—the use of the criminal law to prohibit and condemn behavior that is widely (either actually or formally) viewed as morally reprehensible, where secular interests, in the sense of concerns beyond the immorality of individuals, do not exist.[37] Here the issue is the use of the criminal sanction to prohibit and condemn behavior that threatens secular interests, but that is not regarded as fundamentally and inherently wrong.

The central consequence of diluting or eliminating requirements of culpability is, as suggested, the criminalization and punishment of persons who cannot be said to warrant the condemnation thereby imported. It is this consequence that gives rise to the hard question of principle and practical consequences. In a sense a similar consequence follows from punishing conduct that is not itself blameworthy, even when culpably engaged in: Persons are stigmatized with conviction for conduct not regarded as deserving the moral stigma. The problem of principle, however, is of considerably smaller dimension, since the choice to act in defiance of the criminal prohibition may be regarded as in some measure furnishing an independently adequate ground for condemnation. (Yet it is necessary to add that the ground exists only in cases where the culpability requirements are extended to include knowledge or culpable disregard of the existence of the prohibition, an extension only occasionally made in regulatory legislation.)

The danger of debilitating the moral impact of the criminal conviction and hence decreasing the overall effectiveness of the criminal law can not readily be put aside. As Henry Hart has noted, "The criminal law always loses face if things are declared to be crimes which people believe they ought to be free to do, even willfully."[38] It may be mitigated to a degree by maintaining a proper proportion in the punishment authorized for various offenses in accordance with the moral culpability of the behavior. The limitations of such a strategy are, first, that there is always a strong pressure to raise authorized penalties when violations become widespread or conspicuous and, second, that there is an irreducible minimum in the moral condemnation comported by conviction of crime. Such considerations have led one observer to "decry the trend toward an increasingly undiscriminating employment of this branch of the law, and to repudiate the suggestion that criminal law should be applied more extensively in the areas of ordinary economic relationships."[39]

Of course, it may be answered that the conviction of violators of laws of this character serves as a means of moral instruction to the community; in short, that the onus of conviction is transferred to the behavior prohibited. That there will be a transference would appear quite likely, but that it should necessarily or generally be expected to involve imparting moral onus to the behavior rather than moral indifference to the conviction is considerably less so. The more widely the criminal conviction is used for this purpose and the less clear the immorality of the behavior so sanctioned, the more likely would it appear that the criminal conviction will not only fail to attain the immediate purpose of its use, but will degenerate in effectiveness for other purposes as well.

There is another cost not paralleled in the dilution of culpability requirements. The behavior under discussion involves restraints upon the free operation of business without at the same time denying commitment to a free enterprise system. The demarcation of the line between the legitimate, indeed the affirmatively desirable, and the illegitimate in business conduct is continually in flux and subject to wide controversy in the community. To say there is no complete consensus on what business decisions should be regulated and what left free of regulation is to say what is minimally true. It would not follow from this that a legislature should abstain from enacting such controls as command a majority. But the appropriateness of the criminal sanction as a means of enforcing the imposed control is another matter. I have already suggested that the criminal remedy in this situation tends to be ineffective and destructive of its overall utility as a sanctioning device. Here the point is different. To the extent it is effective in generating strong moral commitments to the regulatory regime it supports, it has the dangerous potential of introducing a rigidification of values too soon, of cutting off the debate, or at least restricting the ease of movement to new positions and a new consensus.[40] This seems to me the wisdom of Allen's caveat that "the function of the criminal law in these areas is not to anticipate but to reflect and implement the consensus already achieved in the community."[41]

A word in conclusion on lines of legislative action. The widescale abandonment of the criminal sanction in those areas where its cost is excessive is as unlikely as it is desirable. Legislative habit and the simple logic of here-and-now expediency have a compulsion not to be denied by contemplation of long-range consequences in areas removed from the immediate target of legislative concern. A more acceptable and hence more fruitful course is the development of means of reducing the costs of the use of the criminal sanction in economic regulations, which do not demand that it be abandoned altogether. If such means exist, one would expect they would be found in ways of dealing with the central fact principally responsible for the predicament, the irreducible core of condemnation in a criminal conviction. One possible approach is to institutionalize a system of gradation of convictions, just as systems of grading punishment have long been a part of the law. There is no adequate basis for accomplishing this under present law. The distinction between offenses *mala prohibita* and *mala in se* carries something of the flavor, but it is an informal rather than an institutionalized distinction and lacks any clear meaning. The felony-misdemeanor distinction has an established statutory basis. However, the categories have largely lost significance in distinguishing degrees of blameworthiness, some misdemeanors embracing crimes of serious moral import and some felonies embracing relatively minor transgressions. Moreover, there is need for a category of offense carrying considerably less weight than a misdemeanor. The petty-offense category, which appears in many statutes, is essentially a petty misdemeanor, retaining its label as a crime and being punishable with imprisonment. In those cases in which the label has been removed, the substance (that is, provision for imprisonment) has not. The Model Penal Code has attempted to meet the inadequacies of existing law by adding to its three categories of crime (felonies, misdemeanors, and petty misdemeanors) a separate noncriminal category designated a "violation," which is punishable only by a sentence of fine (under $500 or any higher amount equal to double the pecuniary gain made by the offender) or civil penalty and which does not "give rise to any disability or legal disadvantage based on conviction of a criminal offense." The design of this proposal "reflects the purpose of the code to employ penal sanctions only with respect to conduct warranting the moral condemnation implicit in the concept of a crime." Since strict liability even for crimes properly so regarded presents the same problem, the same solution is applied by treating crimes committed without culpability as "violations."

While novel in American law, the German law has for some years adopted an approach quite similar to that proposed by the Model Penal Code. Separate from a three-level classification of crimes, properly so called (*Straftat*), is another category of offense, the "regulatory violation" (*Ordnungswidrigkeit*). These regulatory violations are not punishable by imprisonment. A fine is the sole available sanction, indeed a fine which bears a special designation (*Geldbusse*, literally "monetary repentance") as opposed to the penal fine (*Geldstrafe*, literally "monetary punishment"). These fines are not registered in the punishment registry and are imposed at the first instance by the responsible administrative agency subject to the right of the violator to object and to be tried in the courts.

The feasibility of using the category of regulatory violation for sanctioning economic regulation is, of course, the principal issue. Here the German experience may offer some evidence for decision. Unfortunately, there appear to be no empirical studies of the relative effectiveness of its use in Germany. But to judge from the statute books, it is the typical noncivil sanction for economic misconduct. All antitrust violations, for example, are regulatory violations, as are violations of other restrictions upon economic behavior, such as certain behavior prohibited by the foreign trade law, laws governing the operation of loan banks, laws governing the closing of shops, transportation rate laws, and other laws. Particularly suggestive is the strategy used in connection with certain kinds of economic offenses as a means of individualizing the determination of whether a defendant's behavior is to be treated as a crime or a regulatory violation. For violations of certain price-control laws, import restrictions, and unlawful overcharging, a legislative determination of the appropriate category of the offense is withheld in favor of a judicial determination in each case. The law requires an offense under these laws to be dealt with as a regulatory violation unless the nature either of the conduct or of the defendant warrants dealing with it as a crime. It is a crime when the conduct "by virtue of its scope or consequences is likely to prejudice the goals of the economic system, especially those of market or price regulations" or when the defendant is a "repeated or professional violator or acts in culpable selfishness or otherwise irresponsibly, and by his conduct shows that he lacks respect for the public interest in the protection of the economic system, especially of the market or price regulations." With all their vagueness these provisions suggest a need in any system that employs a noncriminal category of violation and uses it to deal with economic violations, for a flexible device whereby violations may, with changed public sentiment and in consideration of the extremity of the circumstances, be raised to the category of crime.

One can hardly say that this approach through a *tertium quid* is the clear answer to the problem of using criminal sanctions to enforce economic restrictions. There are many imponderables with respect to its effectiveness both as a preventive and as a means of reducing the costs of an indiscriminate use of the criminal sanction. On the side of preventive effectiveness, is the reprobative association of a genuine criminal conviction a needed weapon of enforcement? Would the semicriminal category of offense convey enough of a sense of wrongness to perform its tasks? Can these laws be enforced efficiently enough without such associations? Is the loss of the power to imprison a substantial loss? Does what is left of the criminal process still provide efficiencies not available in the pure civil remedy? Will the regulatory offense prove politically acceptable to legislators and administrators as an alternative to outright criminalization? On the side of reducing costs, how much will it help that a new label has been created so long as the criminal process is used or that imprisonment is not available as a sanction, when in fact it is rarely used anyway? And finally, is whatever is lost in effectiveness worth what is gained in other respects? One cannot be dogmatic in answering these questions. But one can, I think, insist that these are the kinds of questions which must be asked about this alternative as well as others if we are to escape the limited options inherited from different days in the use of the criminal sanction.

Notes

1. See, for example, Jeremy Bentham, *An Introduction to the Principles of Morals and Legislation* (Oxford, 1789).

2. Harry Elmer Barnes and Negley K. Teeters, *New Horizons in Criminology*, 3d ed. (Englewood Cliffs, N.J.: Prentice-Hall, 1959), p. 43; Marshall B. Clinard, *The Black Market: A Study of White-Collar Crime* (New York: Holt, 1952), p. 243; George Bernard Shaw, *The Crime of Imprisonment* (New York: Philosophical Library, 1946), p. 34; Edwin H. Sutherland and Donald R. Cressey, *Principles of Criminology*, 5th ed. (Philadelphia: Lippincott, 1955). Feelings sometimes run high; see, for example, Edwin H. Sutherland, *White Collar Crime* (New York: Dryden Press, 1949), p. 85: "This change in the economic system from free competition to private collectivism has been produced largely by the efforts of businessmen. Although they have not acted *en masse* with a definite intention of undermining the traditional American institutions, their behavior has actually produced this result."

3. See *Wall Street Journal* (February 7, 1961).

4. For example, Jerome Hall, *Theft, Law, and Society*, 2d ed. (Indianapolis: Bobbs-Merrill, 1952).

5. Compare *People* v. *Ashley*, 42 Cal.2d 246, 267 P.2d 271 (1954), with *Chaplin* v. *United States*, 157 F.2d 697 (D.C. Circ. 1946).

6. *Cf.* J. Willard Hurst, *Law and the Conditions of Freedom in the Nineteenth Century* (Madison: University of Wisconsin Press, 1956), p. 21.

7. But see Sutherland, *op. cit.*, p. 45.

8. Quoted in John T. Cahill, "Must We Brand American Business by Indictment as Criminal?" in American Bar Association, Section on Antitrust Law, *Proceedings* (Chicago: American Bar Association, 1952), p. 30.

9. Robert H. Jackson and Edward Dumbauld, "Monopolies and the Courts," *University of Pennsylvania Law Review*, 86 (January, 1938), p. 237: "[I]t must be confessed that there is no consistent or intelligible policy embodied in our law by which public officials and businessmen may distinguish bona fide pursuit of industrial efficiency from an illicit program of industrial empire building." See *ibid.* at p. 232, quoting Senator Wagner: "Half of the laws enacted by Congress represent one school of thought, the other half another. No one can state authoritatively what our national policy is."

10. Hermann Mannheim, *Criminal Justice and Social Reconstruction* (London: Routledge, 1946), p. 159.

11. *Boyce Motor Lines* v. *United States*, 342 U.S. 337 (1952).

12. *United States* v. *Ragen*, 314 U.S. 513 (1942).

13. See *Screws* v. *United States*, 325 U.S. 91, 103–104 (1945).

14. *United States* v. *Ragen*, 314 U.S. 513, 524 (1942).

15. Cf. *Boyce Motor Lines* v. *United States*, 342 U.S. 337, 345 (1952) (Justice Jackson, dissenting).

16. See Richard A. Whiting, "Antitrust and the Corporate Executive," *Virginia Law Review*, 47 (October, 1961), p. 931; Alan M. Dershowitz, "Increasing Community Control over Corporate Crime," *Yale Law Journal*, 71 (December, 1961), p. 291.

17. See Myron W. Watkins, "Electrical Equipment Antitrust Cases—Their Implications for Government and for Business," *University of Chicago Law Review*, 29 (Autumn, 1961), p. 106.

18. Model Penal Code, Section 2.07, comment at pp. 148–149 (Tentative Draft No. 4, 1955).

19. Bentham, *op. cit.*, p. 25 (1907 ed.).

20. See Victor H. Kramer, "Criminal Prosecutions for Violations of the Sherman Act: In Search of a Policy," *Georgetown Law Journal*, 48 (Spring, 1960), p. 539.

21. Wolfgang Friedmann, *Law in a Changing Society* (Berkeley, Calif.: University of California Press, 1959), p. 196; Glanville Williams, *Criminal Law: The General Part*, 2d ed. (London: William Stevens, 1961), pp. 863–864.

22. Dershowitz, *op. cit.*, p. 287, fn. 5.

23. But see Robert E. Lane, "Why Business Men Violate the Law," *Journal of Criminal Law, Criminology, and Police Science*, 44 (July, 1953), pp. 151–165.

24. Sutherland, *op. cit.*, pp. 46–47.

25. Ernst Freund, *Legislative Regulation* (New York: Commonwealth Fund, 1932), p. 253.

26. See Henry M. Hart, Jr., "Aims of the Criminal Law," *Law and Contemporary Problems*, 23 (Summer, 1958), p. 404.

27. Mannheim, *op. cit.*, pp. 167–168: "Emile Durkheim has pointed out that 'the only common characteristic of all crimes is that they consist . . . in acts universally disapproved of by members of each society . . . crime shocks sentiments which, for a given social system, are found in all healthy consciences.' Although this requirement of universal disapproval may appear somewhat exaggerated, there can be no doubt that without the backing of at least the major part of the community legislation, in a democracy, must fail."

28. In his study of OPA regulation, Clinard concluded that punishment was largely ineffective beyond causing business to adopt shrewd manipulative evasions. He concluded that control required "the voluntary compliance with the regulations of society by the vast majority of the citizens." Clinard, *op. cit.*, p. 261. See also George B. Vold, *Theoretical Criminology* (New York: Oxford University Press, 1958), p. 257.

29. The short-lived Arnold era of vigorous criminal antitrust enforcement is a case in point. See Thurman Arnold, "Antitrust Law Enforcement, Past and Future," *Law and Contemporary Problems*, 7 (Winter, 1940), pp. 5–23.

30. *Cf.* OPA Manual, quoted by George H. Dession, *Criminal Law, Administration and Public Order* (Charlottesville, Va.: Michie Casebook, 1948), p. 200.

31. Congressman Thomas J. Lane of Massachusetts was convicted and imprisoned for tax evasion. He was renominated and re-elected to the House the next fall (*The New York Times* [October 17, 1962]). But having regard to Mayor Curley's experiences, Massachusetts may be a rather special case.

32. Mannheim, *op. cit.*, p. 146.

33. See Joseph H. Murphy, "Criminal Income Tax Evasion," *Northwestern University Law Review*, 48 (July–August, 1953), pp. 317–341, for a description of the reforms. As to the effects of the reforms, see Robert M. Schmidt, "Current Department of Justice Criminal Income Tax Policies," *Taxes*, 38 (April, 1960), pp. 299–311.

34. Assistant Attorney General Wendell Berge, quoted in Attorney General's National Committee to Study the Antitrust Laws, *Report* (Washington, D.C.: Government Printing Office, 1955), p. 353.

35. Freund, *op. cit.*, p. 302; Friedman, *op. cit.*, p. 198.

36. Holmes believed that the objective standard of criminal liability which disregards the personal peculiarities of the actor demonstrates that the existence of moral wrong is not a condition of punishment (Oliver Wendell Holmes, *The Common Law* [Boston: Little, Brown, 1923], p. 45). He found support for this in the proposition that "no society has ever admitted that it could not sacrifice individual welfare to its own existence" (*Ibid.*, p. 43). *Cf.* Richard A. Wasserstrom, "Strict Liability in the Criminal Law," *Stanford Law Review*, 12 (July, 1960), p. 739.

37. See the debate between Lord Devlin and Professor Hart in Patrick Devlin, *The Enforcement of Morals* (London: Oxford University Press, 1959); and H. L. A. Hart, *Law, Liberty, and Morality* (Stanford, Calif.: Stanford University Press, 1963).

38. See Hart, "Aims of the Criminal Law," *op. cit.*, p. 418.

39. Paul W. Tappan, *Crime, Justice, and Correction* (New York: McGraw-Hill, 1960), pp. 15–16. For a suggestive discussion of alternative ways of achieving favorable business sentiment, see Robert E. Lane, *The Regulation of Businessmen: Social Conditions of Government Economic Control* (New Haven, Conn.: Yale University Press, 1954), pp. 118–130.

40. The danger of the use of the criminal law to destroy a repugnant philosophy is exemplified in the revealing observation of Barnes and Teeters, *op. cit.*, p. 49: "White-collar crime flows from a competitive economy and philosophy that reveres success based almost exclusively on money. The job of the courts of justice, legislators, and a regenerated public is to wipe out this insidious philosophy before it is too late." *Cf.* Oliver Wendell Holmes, *Speeches* (Boston: Little, Brown, 1913), p. 101: "As law embodies beliefs that have triumphed in the battle of ideas and then have translated themselves into action, while there is still doubt, while opposite convictions still keep a battle front against each other, the time for law has not come; the notion destined to prevail is not yet entitled to the field."

41. Francis A. Allen, "Offenses against Property," *Annals of the American Academy of Political and Social Science*, 339 (January, 1962), p. 76.

32

THE USE OF CRIMINAL SANCTIONS IN THE ENFORCEMENT OF ECONOMIC LEGISLATION: A SOCIOLOGICAL VIEW

Harry V. Ball and
Lawrence M. Friedman

Concern over the use of criminal sanctions in the enforcement of business legislation is by no means new. As late as 1961, however, Whiting remarked that "the history of antitrust enforcement to date should not cause undue alarm to the corporate executive."[1] Two recent prosecutions have intensified the discussion and called Whiting's conclusion into question. In *United States* v. *McDonough Co.* one president and three vice presidents of several comparatively small garden-tool manufacturing firms received ninety-day jail sentences and a fine of $5,000 for deliberate price fixing and market rigging. The defendants entered pleas of *nolo contendere*. The government felt that a fine would be "a sufficient deterring factor"; the defendants argued against a jail sentence, pointing out that no jail sentence had been imposed in *nolo contendere* cases during the fifty-nine-year life of the Sherman Antitrust Act. The judge ignored both the government and the defendants. His position was that Congress would not have provided for imprisonment in the original act and retained it

Reprinted from *Stanford Law Review*, 17 (January, 1965), pp. 197–223. Copyright 1965 by the Board of Trustees of the Leland Stanford Junior University.

thereafter unless that penalty was intended to be used whenever a sentencing court believed jail sentences proper.

In the second and more famous case, the *Electrical Equipment Antitrust Cases*, the government demanded jail sentences in several instances. Moreover, the prosecutor asked the court to refuse pleas of *nolo contendere* from the individual defendants. The government argued that acceptance of such pleas "would neither foster respect for the law nor vindicate the public interest" in the light of the fact that the grand jury's indictments "charge violations of rigging and price fixing as serious as any instances ever charged in the more than half a century life of the Sherman Act." The judge agreed. The sentences imposed included, in addition to fines and probation, seven sentences to imprisonment for sixty days and thirty-one suspended sentences for various periods.

Many major newspapers paid little or no attention to the convictions and sentences;[2] some critics of the prosecution saw "ominous overtones" in the fact that men had been sent to jail for "something that has been going on for years as an accepted business practice";[3] and a convicted president of one of the twenty-nine accused corporations questioned the right of the government to enact such "regulations," much less to send a person to jail for their violation and asserted that "price stabilization" was an essential element of "free enterprise."[4]

Perhaps these price-fixing (price-stabilizing) and market-rigging (market-stabilizing) cases are not typical of the broader class of criminal-penal laws regulating business. The defendants knew they were violating the law, they acted in secret collusion, huge sums of money were involved, and the Justice Department strove mightily to equate the conduct in the second case to a fraud against the government. Quite different are mine-run violations of regulations affecting business, especially those involving strict liability where intentional violation is not an essential element of the crime. At least these may raise more clearly the problem of what Kadish has called "moral neutrality."[5] The issue is whether severe criminal sanctions ought to be imposed on those who violate the legal but not the moral code. In the view of Kadish and others, a key factor in any discussion of the propriety and effectiveness of the use of criminal sanctions in enforcing business regulations is the relationship between prevailing morality and the norms of the criminal law. Are economic crimes *morally* wrong? If they are, should men be sent to jail for committing them?

First, when we speak of using criminal sanctions, we may be referring to more than one meaning of the term use. One may distinguish between (1) authorization by the legislature of the employment of criminal sanctions, and (2) their application by the administrator. That is, the law may be said to "use" a sanction when a statute authorizes its use; in a second sense, the sanction is "used" only when it is actually applied.

Discussing antitrust laws, for example, one might debate whether it is proper to append criminal sanctions for violations of the regulations at all; and even those who concede that it is proper may question whether it is right to unsheath the sword in particular cases. Thus, those who are distressed because even a small proportion of the implicated officials of the electrical industry were imprisoned are probably opposed to any authorization of criminal sanctions in regulating business affairs; they can hardly argue that these particular offenders merited any special leniency. On the other hand, persons who complain because criminal sanctions are rarely invoked in mine-run antitrust cases and who look upon this as an indication of favoritism to "white-collar criminals" are questioning the administration of the sanctions while conceding—or even urging—the propriety of their authorization. Problems of the legislative authorization of criminal sanctions and problems of the administrative decisions to apply the sanctions ought to be analyzed separately.

Second, what do we mean by the term "criminal sanctions"? Statutes aimed at economic regulation often provide multiple, alternative sanctions. Sometimes mandatory sequences of use are prescribed. The sanctions may include cease and desist orders (enforced through contempt proceedings), injunctive divestiture proceedings, awards of damages or treble damages, monetary fines or forfeitures (which may or may not involve imprisonment for nonpayment), seizures of goods, revocations of business or occupational licenses, prison sentences, and probation with a threat of fine or imprisonment for the violation of probation. Of these, some classes of fines, direct imprisonment, and probation with threat of fine or imprisonment for the violation of the conditions of probation are generally considered "criminal" sanctions.

However, fines or money forfeitures are widely used also as sanctions in actions formally classified as "civil proceedings." Criminologists generally approve of the use of fines as a sanction for violation of laws punishing deliberate, calculated, antisocial "profit making," because the fine divests the violator of his profits; it is a penalty which plausibly can be said to deter profit-making misconduct. However, this defense of the propriety of the fine fails to distinguish a criminal fine from a civil forfeiture or from treble damages or other forms of punitive damages, which may also deter. One may, of course, ask whether money penalties are appropriate sanctions against a business organization; and there are other subsidiary questions; for example, should the state or the victim receive the money? But such questions are irrelevant to a discussion of whether the sanction of a money penalty should be "civil" or "criminal." Therefore, when one asks whether certain conduct should be subject to criminal sanctions, one is not asking whether the conduct should be subject to a money penalty. The civil law "punishes" breach of contract and torts with damage awards, but no one imagines that money damages here are criminal sanctions. For these reasons we are eliminating the fine or money penalty from our consideration of criminal sanctions.

When discussion is directed to the question of the use of "criminal" sanctions, then, the issues raised are essentially these: (1) Must the evidence establish the defendant's guilt beyond a reasonable doubt, and shall the defendant be entitled to all the procedural safeguards of criminal law? (2) Shall the defendant and his conduct be publicly labeled as criminal? (3) Shall the defendant, upon conviction, be subject to imprisonment or conditional probation with the threat of loss of liberty for violation of the conditions?

Finally, what is the meaning in this context of "economic regulation"? Kadish feels there is more than one kind of economic regulation and limits his discussion of enforcement problems to regulations "which impose restrictions upon the conduct of business as part of a considered economic policy." Kadish certainly has the right to specify types of regulation, and for his purposes they may constitute a unitary category. However, his reasons for isolating them—the uniqueness of the protected interest and their origin as part of a considered economic policy—cannot be defended upon empirical grounds. Let us test some of his examples in the light of his claimed differentiae.

For Kadish, the economic crime par excellence is the antitrust violation. The text of the Sherman Antitrust Act reflected legislative awareness of existing common-law doctrine concerning restraint of trade.[6] The enactment of a much-debated federal criminal statute on the subject owed more to political forces and theories operating in the late nineteenth century than it did to economic theory, policy, or ideology. The primary interest involved was and is "the emergence of the modern corporate organization as presenting a problem in the distribution of power," the continuing problem of individual freedom of choice, and the functioning of democratic processes in a society where large corporations had tremendous wealth and power, including political power. The basic problem has been and is "that of the control of the conduct of the business organization rather than a problem of preserving 'competition.'" This was clearly recognized at the time of the enactment of the Sherman Antitrust Act by proponents and opponents alike. William Graham Sumner, for example, opposed "federal interference" because he was firmly convinced that industrial "bigness" was economically desirable[7] and that government was too weak to resist being taken over by a business plutocracy if it sought to interfere with the trusts.[8] Arguably, considered economic policy entered the picture when the courts rejected arguments based on bigness per se and explicitly read the concepts of reasonableness and control into federal antitrust law.[9] "Dissolution is not a penalty but a remedy" to be employed only "if the industry will . . . need it for its protection."[10] Economic policy in its purest form entered the arena not as the primary purpose of the legislation but as an alleviation against its strictness in the face of good faith on the part of the regulated. Much of the vagueness of antitrust regulation must be ascribed not to efforts to restrict business but to efforts to prevent the use of the "political" Sherman Antitrust Act to hamstring productive efficiency.

Laws regulating maximum prices or rents represent the same basic situation. They are necessary to restrict the power of persons to use property in ways contrary to the public interest because some emergency condition has eliminated the freedom of the normal market. The crisis situation is viewed as a general threat to national health, safety, and welfare—even survival. In such a situation, extraordinary powers are assumed by the agents of the politically organized community against, for example, "speculative, unwarranted, and abnormal increases in rents; exactions of unjust, unreasonable, oppressive rents and rental agreements; overcrowding occupation of uninhabitable dwellings; speculative, manipulative, and disruptive practices by landlords of housing accommodations; and other acts and conditions endangering the public health, safety, welfare and morals" of the community. . . . Private housing has, in the legislature's opinion, become vested with a public interest.

The preceding suggests the difficulty of maintaining Kadish's claimed distinction between "economic" laws which are part of "considered economic policy" and "economic" laws relating to health and physical safety. In which category, for instance, belong the laws limiting the employment or the hours of work of women and children? These were propounded as health laws, to be sure, but another important factor was a considered economic policy giving job preference to male heads of households over the competition of women and children.[11] In general, "considered economic policy" and health and safety factors are inextricably bound together in the history of all types of regulation. For example, occupational licensing and similar laws are curious mixtures of economic policy and health and safety measures. The Wisconsin barber statute makes it unlawful "for any barber to use any instrument or article that has not been disinfected in accordance with . . . sanitary standards"; but the statute makes it equally unlawful to "advertise a definite price for any barbering service by means of displaying a sign containing such prices so that the same is visible to persons outside the barbershop." The two sections of this law are, to be sure, analytically separable; but the whole statute is animated by one spirit, in which an economic aim (protecting barbers from competitors) is mixed with a public-welfare aim (improving sanitary conditions of public barbershops).

In short, Kadish's attempt to distinguish the "economic" from other forms of regulation produces numerous inconsistencies. Thus, a rent-control law directed against unjust rents is viewed by Kadish as referring to morally neutral behavior and as part of a considered economic policy;

a tenement-house law that requires minimum standards of quality, regardless of the amount of rent, is presumably a health measure. In similar fashion, that part of most rent-control laws which makes it criminal for a landlord to seek to evict an existing tenant under certain circumstances would also be a regulation of morally neutral behavior. But how would Kadish classify an "open occupancy" statute that makes it criminal for a landlord to discriminate on the basis of race in the initial selection of tenants?

Moreover, it is even difficult to distinguish Kadish's "pure" form of economic crimes from his "traditional property offenses." These offenses, such as robbery, blackmail, forgery, and passing worthless checks, were intended, in his words, to protect property interests "against the acquisitive behavior of others," so as to further "free private decisions." To say that the traditional property offenses protect property (and thus aid private decisions) begs the question. These offenses are part of the system by which the legal order defines what objects and interests a particular social system chooses to protect as property. All social systems protect property as they define it; in so doing they map out what types of economic exchanges are protected (these they further) and what types are not (these they discourage). In our present society, you may induce a young lady to break her date and instead to go out with you on Saturday night. This is no crime (so long as she is over a certain age and you do not entice her from her family for immoral purposes) nor does it give her initial date a basis for civil action, for he had no property right in her agreement to attend the movies with him. In fact, you, the aggressor, have the benefit of the protection of the law from any physical intimidation by the first young man to keep you from "stealing his girl." But it is a crime to steal a wristwatch, a ten-dollar bill, or the sexual privileges of another man's wife. The noncriminality of inducing a girl to break a date (in legal terms, the fact one cannot have a property interest in a rendezvous) frees private citizens to engage in vigorous courtships and vigorous competition for eventual wives and sweethearts. Laws against adultery prevent or attempt to control the exercise of "free private decisions" in competition for sexual privileges by establishing property rights. Adultery is a form of trespass.

The traditional property offenses take their definition of property from the underlying assumptions of a given society and seek to use the criminal law to channel economic behavior along lines consistent with these assumptions. Therefore, they are arguably the product of considered economic policy, though so rooted in the social order that no one actually bothers much to consider them. The traditional criminal law has always aimed at regulating economic exchanges in the broadest sense. Most offenses against property (and even offenses against persons) apply social controls to limit or otherwise regulate the manner in which economic exchanges may take place, the terms of sale, and the type of commodity which may legitimately form the subject matter of a sale. Whether or not one has a marketable property interest that he may offer to another for purchase or whether he has merely a "possession" that he may not lawfully offer for sale is often a matter of the criminal law.

So, for example, you are not allowed to make a person buy his reputation (blackmail). The criminality of blackmail represents a social judgment that one may not manipulate as an income-producing asset knowledge about another person's past; you may not sell to that person forbearance to use your knowledge of his guilt. If, on the other hand, you acquire knowledge of a person's illustrious ancestry or use in business the skills necessary to ascertain the ancestry of others, you may set yourself up as a genealogist and bargain with others on the basis of your skill or information. The difference between a genealogist and a blackmailer— between a genteel and a criminal profession—reflects a difference in the notions of legitimate exchange within our society. In other societies, of course, the criminal law adopts a quite different definition of what is and what is not a legitimate exchange.

Even within our own society, subtle distinctions are made among types of economic exchange that are criminal, those which lead to civil penalties only, and those which lead to no penalties at all, but are positively encouraged by the legal order. The distinctions may at times appear anomalous. In Wisconsin if you give a worthless check to a tavern owner, you may be criminally responsible for your act, even though you are drunk on liquor he has sold you and even though he continues to sell liquor to you on the strength of the "credit" of your check. If, however, you buy liquor on open credit from this same tavern owner, he may not even collect his debt from you through regular civil court processes. Credit sales of liquor are against public policy, and liquor debts, like gambling debts, are unenforceable. However, much of the apparent anomaly of this situation is reduced when the researcher finds that it is also criminal for a tavern owner knowingly to serve a certified alcoholic or allow him to be served.

In short, Kadish's attempt to distinguish the "traditional property offenses" from his pure "economic policy" offenses turns out to be an instance of circular reasoning. The basic difference is presumably found in the fact that the traditional offenses are naturally associated with a "stigma of moral reprehensibility," while the economic offenses are "morally neutral." But he asserts that the traditional offenses possess this natural association in part precisely because they are criminal under traditional categories of crime. This seems to mean at its core that his "morally neutral" conduct is so simply because it is newly proscribed behavior. Kadish adds, however, that the new crimes are morally neutral also because they "closely resemble acceptable aggressive business behavior." But the key word here is "acceptable." Throughout one finds the hidden assumptions that business conduct not included in traditional property offenses was by definition not considered unethical or morally reprehensible, and, conversely, that all conduct proscribed by traditional property offenses is currently considered unethical or morally reprehensible. But this is precisely one of the central issues to be discussed in considering the relationship between popular morality and the criminal law relative to economic regulation.

This means that defining a pure category of economic crimes is of little value to a sociological examination of the use of criminal sanctions regulating economic transactions. It is more fruitful to begin with a broader inquiry: How does any given legal regulation affect the conduct of business and businessmen, what is its relationship in this regard to the prevailing morality, and what are the implications of this relationship to the use (in both senses) of criminal sanctions?

In pursuing this inquiry, we do not assume that there are any pure "economic crimes." Some criminal statutes, like the Sherman Antitrust Act, regulate the conduct of businessmen exclusively or almost so. Others, like price-control laws, regulate business transactions and control the conduct of both businessmen and nonbusinessmen, for example, consumers. Still others only rarely have special relevance to a businessman in the conduct of his business; e.g., laws against murder. To deny that there is a category of pure economic crimes is not to say that laws against murder and laws against monopoly do not reflect different social forces in their inception, diffusion, moral basis, and enforceability. But it does mean that these matters should be resolved by empirical evidence and not by definition.

LEGAL REGULATION, BUSINESS CONDUCT, AND PREVAILING MORALITY

We have shown the futility of looking for pure economic crimes and have framed our inquiry in terms of the relationship between specific legal regulations, business conduct, prevailing morality, and criminal sanctions.

By "prevailing morality" we mean the current attitudes of the public (or any relevant portion of the public) toward given courses of conduct in specified circumstances. The circumstances must be given close attention. For example, a study of various samples of the population of Akron, Ohio, in the mid-1930s indicated that prevailing opinion did not believe it "wrong" for West Virginia coal miners to steal coal from inoperative mines for their own use, though it was thought "wrong" if the theft were for resale for profit.[12] It was overwhelmingly recognized that in both instances the taking was a crime. On the other hand, the populace believed it "wrong" for a corporation to close its plant and move to another community because of a strike, though it was widely recognized that such a course of action was legal. As one might expect, the opinions varied with the position of the individual in the social structure of the community.

Clearly, it is important to learn which segments of the population determine the prevailing morality on any given issue. In discussions of what "ought" to be the relationship between morality and criminal law, a number of different, supposedly important "publics" have been designated. Some writers have placed special emphasis upon enforcement administrators, especially judges, while others have spoken in vague terms; e.g., of the offender's "fellowmen."[13] Kadish appears to be talking mostly about the public of the "regulated." Another writer has referred to "majority feelings of disgust or revulsion in the community."[14] Another has, in addition to distinguishing the administrators, sought to divide citizens into the regulated, the militant regulators, and the indifferent.[15] At least it is clear that communities, in generating standards of morality, are not to be considered as sets of isolated individuals; rather, communities are made up of persons of varying statuses and group memberships.

What is the evidence concerning the relationship between compliance with economic regulation and approval or disapproval of the regulation by the regulated? Here the general regulation of a specified area of conduct should be distinguished from particular rules or restrictions in effect at a particular point in time. We shall first consider attitudes toward general regulation. This is a relevant consideration, since the degree of approval reflects the attitude of the regulated toward the moral justification of the regulation.

The few empirical studies that have been made fail to indicate any simple relationships between the general attitudes of businessmen toward a given area of regulation and the willingness or propensity of businessmen to violate the regulations. . . .[16] These studies make only a negative point, that compliance and noncompliance are not wholly determined by whether persons subject to regulation approve of it, that is, whether they deem the regulation consistent with their moral code. The extent to which compliance is related to approval, however, ought to be taken into account. Regulatory laws are directed toward businessmen (just as laws against murder are directed toward members of society generally), and businessmen constitute the "public" within which compliance must be measured. To be sure, there is a wider "public" for purposes of measuring support for enforcement. Thus, complete and intransigent refusal by businessmen to obey might lead to more than collapse of regulation; severe social conflict might result if the narrower "public" (businessmen) refused to obey regulatory laws widely supported by the broader "public" (the general population). Moreover, the studies indicate that "disapproval" of laws by the regulated does not necessarily result in defiance and rebellion. Grumbling acceptance of the income tax, food and drug laws, and the Clayton Act may serve the purposes of the legal order perfectly well; wild enthusiasm for regulatory measures is not necessary.

Empirical evidence tends, therefore, to show that moral approval by the regulated is not a necessary condition of general compliance. It is also true that general compliance—even coupled with deep public moral support—does not of itself mean that application-use of criminal sanctions (as defined above) is an appropriate technique to ensure achievement of the social ends underlying given regulations with maximum efficiency. This fact is often recognized in discussion of certain sexual crimes, such as adultery, fornication, and consensual homosexuality. The general public condemns such sexual conduct, and most people comply with the law. Yet arguments are continually and powerfully advanced against punishing these acts through criminal processes. These arguments will be familiar to most readers. Essentially, it is argued that enforcement does more harm than good; for example, it encourages blackmail, snooping, arbitrary and unfair punishment of unlucky or unpopular offenders, and overzealous police work.

What underlies these arguments can be highlighted by considering a less flamboyant example, nonsupport of children. Here too the failure of the criminal law bears directly on the problem of economic regulation and the criminal process. Our "prevailing morality" does, of course, condemn a person's willful failure to provide support for his children; a man who neglects his children is guilty of highly immoral conduct in the eyes of the public. Most people sacrifice heavily to provide advantages for their children, and judges in good conscience vigorously denounce offenders. Yet the problem of nonsupport shows no sign of vanishing. Correctional administrators complain that child-support offenders fill too many jail cells; welfare administrators do not want to require mothers receiving Aid-to-Dependent-Children benefits to take legal action against nonsupporting fathers, feeling that such action would handicap their programs. Increasingly, law and administration seek devices to induce public condemnation of nonsupport with noncriminal sanctions (or at least without felony conviction). Here again, the use of criminal sanctions does not seem to provide an adequate solution to problems raised by conduct clearly condemned by prevailing morality.

It is easy to see why the "use" of criminal sanctions (in our second sense of "use") may actually impede the attainment of the ends supported by public policy and morality. The criminal law is more than a set of propositions, more than a moral code, more than a catalog of rights and wrongs. A set of precepts and definitions lies at the heart of the criminal law; but criminal law is also a technique, a mechanism; and it is administered through highly organized institutions. Criminal justice does not consist only of penal statutes, it is also judges, bailiffs, sheriffs, police-men, district attorneys, jails, workhouses, courtrooms, files, fingerprints. . . . Any realistic discussion of the application-use of criminal sanctions must take into account the impact on the accused of one of the law's most effective sanctions: the bringing of the accused into contact with the enforcement institutions of the criminal law. The difficulty with the use of criminal sanctions in child-support cases is the impeding effect of exposing the violator to the apparatus of the criminal law; its repressive and cumbersome techniques may interfere with the goals of persuasion, negotiation, and voluntary compliance on the part of the erring father.

This does not mean that making an act formally criminal may not have, in some cases, subtle aftereffects. Labeling conduct as "criminal" may change the public attitude toward the man who breaks the law as well as the attitudes of those who are themselves tempted to break the law. We shall examine these aftereffects later. For the present, it is enough to note that there is no necessary connection between the label "crime" and public morality nor between the forces which tend to induce compliance with statutory precepts. Criminal law, particularly as it relates to economic crime, is a set of techniques to be manipulated for social ends.

The history of criminal law is in fact a history of the reasons why techniques of criminal law enforcement have been brought to bear in particular areas to advance social goals. One factor dictating the use of criminal sanctions has been unduly ignored in most treatments of crime. This is the fact that the cost of enforcing the criminal law is borne by the state and that the initiation of criminal process and its administration are conducted by servants of the state. This is, in fact, a major social distinction between criminal and noncriminal law. To say that breach of contract is not a crime is not a statement about the morality of breach of contract, though we may consider breach of contract highly immoral under certain circumstances. Liability for breach of contract in the twenti-eth century has been imposed in some situations where the prior law did not impose liability, because of popular feelings that certain kinds of breach of contract are "unfair" (that is, immoral) and should therefore give rise to liability. The use of the concept of "unjust enrichment" affords a good illustration. The noncriminal nature of breach of contract means that the initial decision to "punish" a man who breaches his con-tract lies in the private sector and is, in fact, the exclusive decision of the man whose contract has been breached. In addition, once the aggrieved party decides to pursue his action in court, he must bear the expenses him-self (though he hopes to recover some of them if he wins). He must hire his own lawyer and make arrangements to pay him. The state provides judges and courtrooms as a service, but the state has no interest in whether the plaintiff chooses to terminate his case before judgment or whether he chooses to levy execution on the goods of the defendant after judgment. The victim of theft, on the other hand, does not hire the state to punish the thief. It is generally true of theft that the state will not prosecute unless a private citizen complains. But there are many areas of criminal law where this is not so. Murder is an obvious example.

We do not suggest that the only difference between criminal law and noncriminal law is that the former has socialized the process of enforcement, but this is an important distinction between the two areas, particularly with respect to economic regulation. Often the morality or immorality of proscribed conduct has little to do with whether the law labels the conduct criminal or leaves enforcement in private hands.

A striking example is usury. In Wisconsin, for example, usury was considered a socially dangerous and immoral practice by most of the population, as far as we can judge, through most of the nineteenth century.[17] It was not, however, a crime. It was discouraged by severe civil penalties under some of the statutes; under one statute, based on a New York model, the usurer was barred from recovering either principal or interest and thus might lose the entire amount of his loan. Common statutory provisions called for treble damages, as in modern antitrust law. Provisions for punitive or multiple damages tend to encourage (and are meant to encourage) private enforcement. But since usury was punished only by civil sanctions, penalties inured to the private citizen who pursued his remedy. He made the choice of suing or not suing, and he saw the matter through the courts.

In 1895, usury was made a crime in Wisconsin, punishable by fine. It would be a rash assumption to say that usury became a crime because in 1895 a heightened sense of the immorality of usury suddenly gripped the public. The true explanation is more subtle. In the Middle West of the nineteenth century, usury has been primarily a problem of the rate of interest on farm mortgages. By the turn of the century, it became pre-eminently a problem of urban consumption loans. Those who suffered from usury were unable to handle enforcement themselves because of their social and economic status. Loans were small; the borrowers were in large measure landless urban workers, many of them foreign-born. By contrast, the farmers in the 1850s and 1860s had had a larger voice in the affairs of the community and had been willing, to judge from court records, to enforce the usury laws. Making usury a crime was thus a legislative judgment that it was best to socialize remedial action, not because of the immorality of usury, but because under existing social conditions civil enforcement had failed.

Lending money at interest is an economic act, and usury is an economic wrong under the law of the American states. The historical development just related demonstrates that the progression from civil to criminal sanctions does not necessarily represent any change in the moral status of the act proscribed. Usury was stamped with immorality both before and after it was made criminal in Wisconsin.

It is probably more typical of economic regulatory crimes that the forbidden conduct is not considered "immoral" either before or after the imposition of criminal sanctions. Statute books are filled with economic crimes whose congruence with popular morality is either completely absent or so muted that one need not consider it. Take, for example, the Wisconsin statute which makes it a crime for any publicly supported hospital to "furnish to its inmates or patrons . . . any oleomargarine." Offenders are liable to fine "not to exceed $200 or imprisoned in the county jail not to exceed six months, for the first offense"; for subsequent offenses, fines may range up to $500, with imprisonment "not less than thirty days nor more than six months." The origins and purposes of the statute are perfectly obvious, but it is dubious to assert that it arose out of popular morality; and whether the public brands the purveyor of oleomargarine to patients in public (as opposed to private) hospitals with any special obloquy is even more dubious. Another Wisconsin statute forbids the sale of baking powder unless the label lists the ingredients, is printed "in the English language, with black ink, in type not smaller than eight point, bold-faced, Gothic capitals," and contains "the name and address of the manufacturer of such baking powder, and the words: 'This baking powder is composed of the following ingredients and none other.'" This crime bears the same penalties as the crime of giving oleomargarine to hospital patients. There may be considerable popular revulsion against the selling of poisonous or harmful or deceptive foods, but surely neither before nor after the passage of the act were there any deep well-springs of disgust against selling imported baking powder with a French label in small typefaces or printed in green ink instead of black. The purpose of the act is regulatory; as in the case of the criminal usury law, administrative considerations probably led to the choice of criminal sanctions. Theoretically, the state could give the buyer of baking powder that did not conform to statutory standards a civil action for damages or the right to rescind his purchase. This would certainly fail to accomplish the purpose of the statute, since the buyer of a small amount of baking powder would never bother to sue the seller. The criminal law is here used as an administrative technique, as a way of socializing the costs of enforcement, which are too great for individuals profitably to bear.

Frequently, however, the general criminal processes will prove too cumbersome and inefficient to attain the state's policy goals. The next step is to vest responsibility for enforcement and administration in an administrative agency. Although mislabeling of baking powder formally remains a crime in Wisconsin, one can be fairly certain that enforcement and policing of baking-powder labels (if any) are carried out by the staff of the appropriate executive department or agency, not by the district attorneys of the various counties.

The shift to administrative enforcement takes place partly because criminal sanctions drag with them all the traditional safeguards surrounding the defendant. Proof beyond a reasonable doubt, trial by jury, and other forms of protection are required. The socialization of remedies thus has the dysfunctional result of making large-scale enforcement difficult for reasons irrelevant to the purpose of making the proscribed acts criminal. Thus, transfer to an administrative agency is likely to occur as soon as such an agency is available. The criminal sanctions remain as threats—they are "used" in the sense of being authorized, but no longer "used" in the sense of wholesale application to offenders.

It is not, however, only the administrators of economic regulation who sharply distinguish between their authorization to invoke criminal sanctions and the selective application of these sanctions. We are coming more and more to recognize how highly selective is the process by which criminal sanctions are actually invoked. Even classic crimes of violence and immorality—murder, robbery, arson—are "administered" by public officials. Often only flagrant cases receive the full treatment. But the full treatment also serves as a threat to induce compliance by voluntary means. The existence of criminal sanctions applicable to the proscribed conduct warns the potential offender of the availability of the full treatment, but officials are free to use lesser means or no means as the situation may demand. Thus, the administration of criminal justice is in many ways analogous not only to the criminal aspects of economic regulation, but even to noncriminal regulation by administrative agencies. In general, criminal justice involves the delegation of large areas of discretion to the administrator.[18] Almost anything that can be said about vagueness, uncertainty, and selectivity of enforcement in economic regulation by administrative agencies can also be said about the traditional areas of criminal law. Statutes creating administrative regulation often admit frankly that vast discretion is vested in the administrators—they use such terms as "public interest," "convenience," and "necessity." Although the traditional criminal law does not specify that enforcement is selective, this difference is largely a matter of form. Statutes which set up administrative agencies are almost never content to give these agencies rule-making and civil-enforcement power; the statutes almost invariably add a catch-all section making violation of the statute or of the rules and regulations of the agency a crime. Like all criminal statutes, these administrative criminal laws leave the process of selection in the hands of administrators, even though no explicit mention is made of the fact.

The purpose of providing for criminal sanctions is at least twofold. First, it adds dimension to the full treatment available. This strengthens the agency's position by giving it one more weapon. Flagrant, unpopular violators of the law or the rules can be told they may go to jail, or at least face the obloquy, the annoyance, the physical restraints of the criminal process. Secondly, the criminal section of the statute enables the agency to use, when necessary, the general law enforcement machinery of the state. Of course the agency will invoke criminal sanctions only in exceptional cases. A criminal trial is a slow process, heavily laden with procedural safeguards for the defendant. It is not only the business community which is chary of criminal sanctions; the administrators themselves avoid them for the same reasons that lead welfare workers to deplore excessive use of criminal law in nonsupport cases. But the fact that the agency may not wish to use the criminal process often is no reason to deny them the power to invoke it in the proper case; thus, legislatures regularly authorize criminal sanctions and thereby create new regulatory crimes.

INTERACTIONS BETWEEN CRIMINAL LAW AND BUSINESS CONDUCT

Historically, growth in the number of regulatory crimes represents a broadening of the techniques for the enforcement of state policy. Nevertheless, the word "crime" has symbolic meaning for the public, and the criminal law is stained so deeply with notions of morality and immorality, public censure and punishment, that labeling an act criminal often has consequences that go far beyond mere administrative effectiveness. As noted in our discussion of criminal sanctions generally, imprisonment or threat of imprisonment and the public stigma of the criminal process are the real issues about which the discussion of criminal sanctions in regulating business revolves. It is generally accepted today that fear of criminal prosecution is an effective deterrent to businessmen, professional men, and the middle class.[19]

The very effectiveness of criminal sanctions in restraining the behavior of businessmen accounts in large part for the concern over the use of criminal-penal sanctions in regulating business. Businessmen abhor the idea of being branded a criminal. Society does not particularly care whether murderers and rapists like being branded as criminals, but businessmen, after all, form a large, respectable, and influential class in our society. Therefore, effectiveness of the penal sanction in this case leads to pressure against use of the sanction. The phenomenon is a general one: middle-class persons resent being "treated like a criminal," no matter what legal rule they may violate. But rules acquire legitimacy through being adopted in the regular processes utilized in society for making rules. The legitimacy of rules derives from the use of a standardized process of adoption, as much as or more than from the subject matter with which the rules deal. Americans in general accept the proposition that it is "wrong" to violate the law, even if they feel the law acts unwisely when it prohibits certain conduct. The very fact that a criminal statute has been enacted by the legislature is a powerful factor in making the proscribed conduct illegitimate in the eyes of a potential actor, even when the actor disagrees with the purpose of the law.

Lane has suggested that there are no generic differences between the factors which produce violations of economic regulatory law and the factors which produce other criminal acts.[20] If this is true, then economic regulation through the use of criminal sanctions poses a real dilemma for society and for the businessman. The businessman may find himself impelled toward crime; he recognizes the legitimacy of the laws which define the crime he is tempted to commit; yet he cannot concede that he is a criminal. We tend to view the criminal as a person who violates laws which we cannot see ourselves violating. In the phraseology of Harry Stack Sullivan, the criminal is that person whom we perceive from the standpoint of our own self-system as "not-me."[21] In other cases, the criminal is the person who violates rules which we can imagine ourselves violating (or have violated in the past) but which we see as part of our "bad-me"—"There but for the grace of God go I." We are willing to condemn the conduct of the "bad-me" as "wrong," but are not likely to agree to the imposition of sanctions we feel are too severe.

This attitude emerges toward such crimes as drunk driving and statutory rape (where the victim is a girl who looks much older than she is). Many people who condemn drunk driving and statutory rape have the uncomfortable feeling that these are crimes they have committed, are likely to commit, or could commit. The result is a tendency to distinguish between the conduct (which we condemn) and the person (with whom we readily sympathize). In the case of some economic crimes, juries have found it convenient to convict the corporation (a fictional entity) rather than the human conspirators. This seems to have occurred in some price-fixing trials, to the bewilderment of legal commentators.[22] The distinction between person and conduct is particularly important in economic crimes, since these are often crimes which the businessman can see himself violating, even when he admits that violation is wrong and ought to be prevented—if for no other reason than that the law ought to be obeyed.

Obviously, distinguishing between the person and the conduct depends upon whether one identifies with the person. A stern, church-going teetotaler cannot readily sympathize with drunk drivers. . . . Nonbusinessmen may similarly fail to understand business temptations. . . . An official of General Electric can understand more readily how it is possible to be tempted down the primrose path of price fixing than can a factory worker. The factory worker, particularly if he has leftist leanings, may classify price fixing and restraint of trade with theft, murder, and rape. We need not confine ourselves to factory workers. Sutherland, a distinguished academic, talks about restraint of trade as a crime in the same tone one might use in speaking of murder or theft; he does not seem to recognize that a roomful of Philadelphia lawyers cannot always advise a soap company whether it is criminal to buy another soap company, while any sane person would know that it is a crime to rob a stranger's house.

The difficulty of categorizing the behavior of businessmen as criminal or noncriminal does not mean that restraint of trade cannot be a "crime" in the same sense as burglary—the electrical price-fixing case, for one, proves that it can. The defendants, in effect, put on masks, jimmied open windows, and stole the people's money. There are crimes and there are crimes. For the mine-run economic crime, it is easy to see why the sanctions of the criminal law are not often employed. We have mentioned some reasons already; there are others. As Sutherland has pointed out, law enforcement is in the hands of members of a social class who are likely to sympathize with the businessman.[23] The nonuse of criminal sanctions to enforce antitrust laws, for example, is a consequence of the institutionalizing of a program which was originally the product of genuine popular outrage. The clamor against "the trusts" can be compared with the clamor against sex criminals, murderers, and those who plant bombs in airplanes. Ultimately, however, state and federal governments created enforcement and administrative agencies staffed with personnel who tended to treat with some understanding the problems of the businessmen whose businesses were regulated. Even when antitrust law is vigorously enforced through civil sanctions (e.g., cease and desist orders), the choice of such civil sanctions reflects the fact that the administrators are able to sympathize with the business position; they readily separate the "conduct" from the "person." This may well be another reason for the neglect of criminal sanctions in antitrust regulation, except for flagrant cases of willfulness and stealth. (This genuine sympathy is above and apart from another, admittedly potent, factor inducing sympathetic behavior; namely, the fact that regulators often end up in the employ of the companies they formerly regulated.)

Thus the "moral neutrality" of regulatory crimes arises out of a number of factors to which writers like Kadish may give insufficient weight. The businessman can hardly be blamed for failing to sense as an abhorrent crime the commission of an act which is forbidden in or pursuant to a regulatory statute in which criminal sanctions have been authorized but which historically have not been used except in flagrant cases. Nor can he be blamed for failing to sense as "criminal" acts made criminal only in order to socialize the remedial process. But tensions and conflicts arise because of lack of understanding of these facts by the broader public and because, as noted above, the authorization of criminal sanctions may initiate a process of interaction between law and prevailing morality.

Some general features of this process of interaction are worthy of note here. The aim of regulatory law is to secure compliance by the regulated. Criminal sanctions are a technique to ensure compliance. Compliance, however, can be viewed in two lights: short- and long-run compliance. When a program of economic regulation is adopted, the attention of the legislature is usually fixed on problems of short-run compliance. The symbolic value of law as law, the fact that most people want to obey the law and will do so, has important consequences for long-run compliance. American social scientists generally agree that social sanctions can be employed deliberately to modify modes of social action—not only overt behavior, but also cognitive, affective, and conative attitudes. Less technically put, social sanctions can be used to change beliefs, attitudes, and personal values and goals; they can effectuate policy considerations by influencing what a person thinks he ought to do or what he wants to do in a particular situation. . . . Legal institutions are therefore particularly appropriate vehicles for effecting changes in thoughts and emotions in the long run. The law may specify clear and unambiguous requirements, may provide a vigorous enforcement program, and can be equipped to maintain a long-continuing effort. Some authorities have suggested that administrative regulation is an especially useful tool for bringing about social change: it permits detailed specification of required conduct, it can modify the rules to plug loopholes as attempts at evasion appear, and it has great flexibility to adopt tactics and allocate resources toward enforcement of its regulations.[24]

Underlying these propositions is the assumption that people tend to think that what they do is the right thing to do, even if they began to do so because they were forced to. Eventually, they begin to expect similar conduct from others and, indeed, are eager to impose it upon others. As conduct becomes formalized, it lays an ideological basis for the extension of similar social norms to situations that are perceived in "analogous" terms. Ironically, some of the participants in the electrical price-fixing case reported that they first experienced price fixing when they served as industry representatives in federal price-control programs during World War II.[25] Less dramatically, filing income tax returns and carrying drivers' licenses have become so commonplace that the public probably accepts these "customs" and, by and large, believes strongly that they are proper.

Other social scientists, however, disagree with the proposition that people learn to want to do what they have to do. Bendix, for example, stresses how variable are the effects of coercion on personality.[26] How a person will react to a requirement that he do something he thinks wrong and does not want to do depends on his whole arsenal of psychological resources. Certainly people are not sheep; the countless revolutions and civil wars of human history are proof enough that law does not always convert its subjects. But surely there is some tendency for persons to provide "public justifications" for what they are actually doing.[27] Thus, the public morality must be under some pressure to correspond with required conduct. We should not be surprised to find an intergenerational "drift" toward increased moral justification of required conduct.

The phenomenon of intergenerational drift is probably particularly important in the case of "economic crimes." A major factor in determining whether this drift toward justification takes place is the extent to which public officials appreciate the distinction between criminal law as technique and criminal law as a reflection of popular morality. Again we may use the antitrust laws as an example of economic legislation which arose out of profound and passionate feelings of public outrage. The passion which attended the birth of the Sherman Antitrust Act has certainly subsided. Yet antitrust laws have not become dead letters, because they have been handed over to federal agencies which have increasingly buttressed the statutes with relatively precise regulations and have built up bureaucratic structures to enforce these laws. Business, for its part, has learned to live with the antitrust laws, whatever reservations business has as to the wisdom of these laws. The businessman knows generally that these laws exist; he is accustomed to consult lawyers who advise him on the legality of proposed mergers and acquisitions; he frequently modifies his behavior in ways which take the laws into account.

Some criminal statutes, however, have become dead letters because they have not become highly institutionalized. When the moral outrage which set them in motion subsides, they lose their vitality. The classic case is that of the colonial blue laws. These laws were vigorously enforced because the society which created them believed in them passionately: Men informed on their neighbors; local courts and magistrates rigorously enforced laws against Sabbath breaking, adultery, card playing, disobedience to parents, and fornication.[28] Formal administrative techniques were neither needed nor used; the whole society involved itself in seeking out violators and bringing them before the bar of public opinion and legal punishment. When the passion subsided, the laws ceased to be enforced, since there was no administrative structure charged with enforcement.

The electrical price-fixing cases are unusually interesting in that they seem to foreshadow a rebirth of passion in the relatively colorless field of antitrust law. The wide publicity, the newspaper harangues, the human interest stories and the rash of lawsuits which followed in their wake certainly dramatized the antitrust laws and disturbed many businessmen. In the price-fixing case—as in "show trials" in general—the criminal law was used, whether deliberately or not, to influence behavior by the use of the mechanisms of law enforcement most open to public view—the preachments of the prosecutors, the sermons delivered by the judge. The public participated in these trials, directly (on grand juries, for example) and indirectly as spectators, newspaper readers, and radio and television audiences. The effect sought in such cases is twofold: first, to warn and deter those who might violate the law; second, to rekindle in the public a sense of the immorality of the defendants' acts. But it was the quality of flagrancy and stealth, combined with the magnitude of the crime, which made a "crackdown" possible. And at the same time it alerted the business community and its apologists to the dangers inherent in the mere authorization of criminal sanctions. This danger lies in the discretion vested in the administrators—the danger of selective use of these powerful sanctions for reasons not justified on grounds of administrative efficiency. It is precisely the same danger which some have seen in the "misuse" of tax law to put gangsters in jail, the abuse of laws against fornication, the application of trespass laws against Negro sit-in demonstrators, and the "persecution" of Communists through the use of laws which originally had nothing to do with Communism. But these are problems not peculiar to regulatory crimes; they are problems of government generally and of bureaucracy generally, the general problem of fairness in the use of administrative discretion.

It is equally clear that these are not problems peculiar to the use of criminal sanctions, since similar problems are raised by the variable administration of zoning laws, the "unfairness" of the licensing process, and the inequities involved in government subsidies and penalties in general. The sanctions (positive and negative) which are available to a legal system range in a continuum from cash grants on one end to death in the electric chair on the other. Historical and social realities dictate the authorization and application of sanctions (criminal and civil) in legal regulations, depending upon the ends to be achieved, the class of persons to be affected, and the behavior sought to be influenced. At every point in the process of choosing and using sanctions questions are raised—moral questions, empirical questions, questions of ends and means. Criminology in general has given up the search for general theories of "crime" and general theories of "criminal sanctions." This is all to the good; what is needed is not a theory of "crime" (let alone a theory of "economic crime") but theories of human behavior. It is not likely (at least at this stage of the development of social science) that a theory will be found to describe and predict human behavior accurately enough to fit the murderer, the corporate monopolist, the mislabeler of baking powder, and the trespasser on public grass (to mention only "criminals"). Discussions of the use of sanctions in economic regulation—whether the discussants are lawyers or social scientists—ought properly to begin by delineating exactly what sanctions and types of economic regulation are under debate.

Notes

1. Richard A. Whiting, "Antitrust and the Corporate Executive," *Virginia Law Review*, 47 (October, 1961), p. 981.

2. "When the Story Broke," *New Republic*, 144 (February 20, 1961), p. 7.

3. Quoted in John Herling, *The Great Price Conspiracy* (Washington, D.C.: Robert B. Luce, 1962), pp. 291–297.

4. Quoted in John G. Fuller, *The Gentleman Conspirators* (New York: Grove Press, 1962), p. 14.

5. Sanford H. Kadish, "Some Observations on the Use of Criminal Sanctions in Enforcing Economic Regulations," *University of Chicago Law Review*, 30 (Spring, 1963), p. 423.

6. See Kenneth Carlston, *Law and Structures of Social Action* (London: William Stevens, 1956), p. 194; William L. Letwin, "Congress and the Sherman Antitrust Law, 1887–189," *University of Chicago Law Review*, 23 (Winter, 1956), pp. 240–247.

7. William Graham Sumner, "The Concentration of Wealth: Its Economic Justification," in Stow Persons, ed., *Social Darwinism: Selected Essays* (Englewood Cliffs, N.J.: Prentice-Hall, 1963), p. 153.

8. Sumner, "Democracy and Plutocracy," in *ibid.*, pp. 143–149.

9. See *Standard Oil Co.* v. *United States*, 221 U.S. 1, 60 (1911); *United States* v. *American Tobacco Co.*, 221 U.S. 106, 179 (1911); *United States* v. *Corn Prods. Ref. Co.*, 234 F.: 964 (So. Dist. N.Y. 1916).

10. *United States* v. *Aluminum Co. of America*, 148 F.2d 416, 446 (2d Circ. 1945).

11. John R. Commons and John B. Andrews, *Principles of Labor Legislation*, 4th ed. rev. (New York: Harper & Row, 1936), p. 97.

12. Alfred W. Jones, *Life, Liberty and Property: A Study of Conflict and a Measurement of Conflicting Rights* (New York: Octagon Books, 1964).

13. Henry M. Hart, Jr., "Aims of the Criminal Law," *Law and Contemporary Problems*, 23 (Summer, 1958), p. 437.

14. Graham Hughes, "Morals and the Criminal Law," *Yale Law Journal*, 71 (March, 1962), p. 682.

15. Karl N. Llewellyn, *Jurisprudence: Realism in Theory and Practice* (Chicago: University of Chicago Press, 1962), p. 403.

16. Robert E. Lane, *The Regulation of Businessmen: Social Conditions of Government Economic Control* (New Haven, Conn.: Yale University Press, 1954); Harry V. Ball, "Social Structure and Rent Control Violations," *American Journal of Sociology*, 65 (May, 1960), pp. 598–604.

17. See generally, Lawrence M. Friedman, "The Usury Laws of Wisconsin: A Study in Legal and Social History," *Wisconsin Law Review* (July, 1963), pp. 515–565.

18. See generally, Frank J. Remington and Victor G. Rosenblum, "The Criminal Law and the Legislative Process," *University of Illinois Law Forum* (Winter, 1960), pp. 481–499.

19. See Llewellyn, *op. cit.*, pp. 403–404.

20. Lane, *op. cit.*, p. 107.

21. Harry Stack Sullivan, *The Interpersonal Theory of Psychiatry*, ed. by Helen Swick Perry and Mary Ladd Gawel (New York: Norton, 1953), pp. 162–164.

22. See, for example, Alan M. Dershowitz, "Increasing Community Control over Corporate Crime," *Yale Law Journal*, 71 (December, 1961), pp. 292–293, fn. 50. See also Paul E. Hadlick, *Criminal Prosecutions Under the Sherman Antitrust Act* (Washington, D.C.: Ransdell, 1939), pp. 170–171.

23. Edwin H. Sutherland, *White Collar Crime* (New York: Dryden Press, 1949), pp. 247–248.

24. Arnold Rose, "The Use of Law to Induce Social Change," *Transactions of the 3d World Congress of Sociology*, 6 (1956), p. 52; Jack Greenberg, *Race Relations and American Law* (New York: Columbia University Press, 1959), pp. 1–30.

25. Richard Austin Smith, "The Incredible Electrical Conspiracy," *Fortune*, 63 (April, 1961), p. 136.

26. Reinhard Bendix, "Compliant Behavior and Individual Personality," *American Journal of Sociology*, 58 (November, 1952), p. 302.

27. See generally, Jack W. Brehm and Arthur R. Cohen, *Explorations in Cognitive Dissonance* (New York: Wiley, 1962).

28. See generally, George L. Haskins, *Law and Authority in Early Massachusetts* (New York: Macmillan, 1960).

SELECTED REFERENCES

There already exists for persons interested in further pursuit of material concerning white-collar crime that most useful of all tools, a thorough, intelligently drawn bibliography. It was prepared by Dorothy Campbell Tompkins of the Institute of Governmental Studies, University of California, Berkeley, and published by the institute under the title *White Collar Crime—A Bibliography* in February, 1967. Mrs. Tompkins undertook her compilation on assignment for the President's Commission on Law Enforcement and Administration of Justice.

The Foreword note to the Tompkins bibliography by Dwight Waldo, director of the Institute of Governmental Studies, provides a sense of its mission and importance:

> It is a probing, exploratory, and original effort. For "white-collar crime" has, since the coining of the term, been more a point of view, an accusation and hypothesis, than a recognizable and accepted area of criminality and criminal law. Mrs. Tompkins has wrestled with the problems of definition and has covered a wide-ranging literature in specifying and probing the relevant categories.

With a more than adequate and contemporaneous bibliography available, the following selected references are limited to the more prominent writings on white-collar crime, particularly those which have conceptual contributions to make. In addition, items that have appeared since the Tompkins bibliography, some foreign references, and publications on subjects beyond the boundaries of the Tompkins work have been especially favored for inclusion in the following reference list.

Anderson, David K., "Ambulance Chasing in Illinois: A Success Story," *University of Illinois Law Forum* (Summer, 1957), pp. 309–314.

Anthony, Robert N., "The Trouble with Profit Maximization," *Harvard Business Review*, 38 (November–December, 1960), pp. 126–134.

Apel, Hans, "The Scope and Significance of Economic Misrepresentation," *Journal of Economics and Sociology*, 21 (January, 1962), pp. 77–90, and 21 (April, 1962), pp. 173–188.

Bacon, Seldon D., "Review of Sutherland, *White Collar Crime*," *American Sociological Review*, 15 (April, 1950), pp. 309–310.

Bartenstein, Fred, Jr., "Research Espionage: A Threat to Our National Security," *Food Drug Cosmetic Law Journal*, 17 (December, 1962), pp. 813–827.

Bauer, Bertrand N., " 'Truth in Lending': College Business Students' Opinions of *Caveat Emptor*, Fraud, and Deception," *American Business Law Journal*, 4 (Fall, 1966), pp. 156–161.

Bayley, David H., "The Effects of Corruption in a Developing Nation," *Western Political Science Quarterly*, 19 (December, 1966), pp. 719–732.

Becker, Joseph M., *The Problem of Abuse in Unemployment Benefits* (New York: Columbia University Press, 1953).

Bernard, Viola W., "Why People Become the Victims of Medical Quackery," *American Journal of Public Health*, 55 (August, 1965), pp. 1142–1147.

Black, Hillel, *The Watchdogs of Wall Street* (New York: Morrow, 1962).

Bloch, Herbert A., and Gilbert Geis, *Man, Crime, and Society: The Forms of Criminal Behavior* (New York: Random House, 1962), pp. 379–404.

Bromberg, Walter, *Crime and the Mind* (New York: Macmillan, 1965), pp. 377–400.

Caplovitz, David, *The Poor Pay More: Consumer Practices of Low-Income Families* (New York: The Free Press, 1963).

Carlin, Jerome E., *Lawyer's Ethics: A Survey of the New York City Bar* (New York: Russell Sage Foundation, 1966).

Cavanaugh, Karl W., "Retail Credit Sales and Usury," *Louisiana Law Review*, 24 (June, 1964), pp. 822–849.

Childs, Marquis W., and Douglass Cater, *Ethics in a Business Society* (New York: Harper & Row, 1954).

Clinard, Marshall B., *The Black Market: A Study of White Collar Crime* (New York: Holt, 1952).

Cohen, Sheldon S., "Morality and the American Tax System," *George Washington Law Review*, 34 (June, 1966), pp. 839–845.

Cook, Fred J., *The Corrupted Land: The Social Morality of Modern America* (New York: Macmillan, 1966).

Cressey, Donald R., *Other People's Money: The Social Psychology of Embezzlement* (New York: The Free Press, 1953).

———, "Foreword," in Edwin H. Sutherland, *White Collar Crime* (New York: Holt, 1961), pp. iii–xii.

———, "The Respectable Criminal: Why Some of Our Best Friends Are Crooks," *Trans-action*, 2 (March–April, 1965), pp. 12–15.

Curran, Barbara A., *Trends in Consumer Credit Legislation* (Chicago: University of Chicago Press, 1965).

Dickens, Charles, " 'Smart' Dealings in America," in Lewis A. Coser, ed., *Sociology Through Literature* (Englewood Cliffs, N.J.: Prentice-Hall, 1963), p. 399.

Dickinson, William B., "Business Morality," *Editorial Research Reports*, 1 (June 12, 1961).

Dixon, Paul R., "Federal-State Cooperation to Combat Unfair Trade Practices," *State Government*, 39 (Winter, 1966), pp. 37–41.

Egan, Bowes, "Criminal Economic Law and Consumer Protection," *Journal of Business Law* (England), 26 (January, 1967), pp. 26-31.

Emerson, Thomas I., "Review of Sutherland, *White Collar Crime*," *Yale Law Journal*, 59 (January, 1950), pp. 581–585.

"Ethics in America: Norms and Deviations," *Annals of the American Academy of Political and Social Science*, 363 (January, 1966), pp. 1–136.

"Expense Accounts," *Harvard Business Review*, 38 (March–April, 1960), pp. 6–12 ff.

Farago, Ladislas, *It's Your Money: Waste and Mismanagement in Government Spending* (New York: Random House, 1964).

Findlay, Robert C., Frank J. Miele, and Robert M. Hanlon, "Consumer in the Marketplace: A Survey of the Law of Informed Buying Protection," *Notre Dame Lawyer*, 38 (August, 1963), pp. 556–613.

Finklestein, Louis, "The Businessman's Moral Failure," *Fortune*, 58 (September, 1958), pp. 116–117 ff.

Frank, Stanley B., "Beware of Home-Repair Racketeers," *Saturday Evening Post* (July 21, 1956), pp. 17 ff.

Fuller, John G., *The Gentlemen Conspirators: The Story of Price-Fixers in the Electrical Industry* (New York: Grove Press, 1962).

Fuller, Richard C., "Morals and the Criminal Law," *Journal of Criminal Law and Criminology*, 32 (March–April, 1942), pp. 624–630.

Geis, Gilbert, "Toward a Delineation of White-Collar Offenses," *Sociological Inquiry*, 32 (Spring, 1962), pp. 160–171.

Gentry, Curt, *The Vulnerable Americans* (Garden City, N.Y.: Doubleday, 1966).

Gibney, Frank, *The Operators* (New York: Harper & Row, 1960).

Goldman, M. M., *You Pay and You Pay: An Expose of the Respectable Racketeers* (New York: Howell, Soskin, 1941).

Goodman, Walter, *All Honorable Men: Corruption and Compromise in American Life* (Boston: Little, Brown, 1963).

Gross, Llewellyn, *Symposium on Sociological Theory* (New York: Harper & Row, 1959), pp. 531–561.

Grundfragen Der Wirtschafts Kriminalität (Wiesbaden: Bundes Kriminalant, 1963).

Hadden, Tom, "The Origins and the Development of Conspiracy to Defraud," *American Journal of Legal History*, 11 (January, 1967), pp. 25–40.

Hadlick, Paul E., *Criminal Prosecution under the Sherman Antitrust Act* (Washington, D.C.: Ramsdell, 1939).

Hall, Jerome, "Criminology," in Georges Gurvitch and Wilbert E. Moore, eds., *Twentieth Century Sociology* (New York: Philosophical Library, 1945), 342–365.

———, *Theft, Law, and Society*, 2d ed. (Indianapolis: Bobbs-Merrill, 1952).

———, "Criminology and Penal Theory," in *General Principles of Criminal Law*, 2d ed. (Indianapolis: Bobbs-Merrill, 1960), pp. 600–621.

Hartung, Frank E., "Common and Discrete Values," *Journal of Social Psychology*, 38 (August, 1953), pp. 3–22.

———, "White Collar Crime: Its Significance for Theory and Practice," *Federal Probation*, 17 (June, 1953), pp. 31–36.

Hazard, John N., "Soviet Socialism and Embezzlement," *Washington Law Review*, 26 (November, 1951), pp. 301–320.

Hazard, Leland, "Are Big Businessmen Crooks?" *The Atlantic*, 208 (November, 1961), pp. 57–61.

Herling, John, *The Great Price Conspiracy: The Story of the Anti-Trust Violations in the Electrical Industry* (Washington, D.C.: Robert B. Luce, 1962).

Hilt, Peter B., "Criminal Prosecution for Adulteration at Common Law," *Food Drug Cosmetic Law Journal*, 15 (June, 1960), pp. 382–398.

Hodges, Luther. *The Business Conscience* (Englewood Cliffs, N.J.: Prentice-Hall, 1963).

Hoover, J. Edgar, "FBI Investigation of Fraud," *Journal of Accountancy*, 120 (July, 1965), pp. 34–39.

Hopkinson, Tom M., "New Battleground—Consumer Interest," *Harvard Business Review*, 42 (September–October, 1964), pp. 97–104.

Insalata, S. John, "Deceptive Business Practices: Criminals in Cuff Links," *Vital Speeches of the Day*, 29 (May 15, 1963), pp. 473–475.

Irey, Elmer L., and William J. Slocum, *The Tax Dodgers* (New York: Greenberg, 1948).

James, Leslie, "Bribery and Corruption in Commerce," *International and Comparative Law Quarterly*, 11 (July, 1962), pp. 880–886.

Jaspan, Norman, and Hillel Black, *The Thief in the White Collar*. (Philadelphia: Lippincott, 1960).

Josephson, Matthew, *The Robber Barons: The Great American Capitalists, 1861–1901* (New York: Harcourt, Brace, 1934).

Kaleki, Michal, "An Attempt at the Elucidation of the Phenomenon of Economic Criminality," *Kulturai i Spoteczenstwo* (No. 3, 1962), pp. 73–77.

Kessler, Friedrich, "The Protection of the Consumer under Modern Sales Law," *Yale Law Journal*, 74 (December, 1964), pp. 262–284.

Keysor, Charles W., "Beware of Genteel Crooks," *Commerce Magazine*, 52 (April, 1955), pp. 20 ff.

Kline, George L., "Economic Crime and Punishment," *Survey*, 57 (October, 1965), pp. 67–72.

Kossack, Nathaniel E., " 'Scam': The Planned Bankruptcy Racket," *New York Certified Public Accountant*, 35 (June, 1965), pp. 417–423.

Lane, Robert E., *The Regulation of Business: Social Conditions of Government Economic Control* (New Haven, Conn.: Yale University Press, 1954).

Langer, Elinor, "Growing Old in America: Frauds, Quackery, Swindle the Aged and Compound Their Trouble," *Science*, 140 (May 3, 1963), pp. 470–472.

Lasagna, Louis, *The Doctors' Dilemma* (New York: Harper & Row, 1962).

Lefkowitz, Louis J., "New York: Criminal Infiltration of the Securities Industry," *Annals of the American Academy of Political and Social Science*, 347 (May, 1963), pp. 51–57.

Lever, Harry, and Joseph Young, *Wartime Racketeering* (New York: Putnam's, 1945).

Lynd, Robert S., "Our Racket Society," *The Nation*, 170 (August 25, 1951), pp. 150–152.

McMillen, Wayne, "Charitable Fraud: An Obstacle in Community Organizations," *Social Service Review*, 29 (June, 1955), pp. 153–171.

Mannheim, Hermann, *Comparative Criminology* vol. 2, (London: Routledge, 1965), pp. 469–498.

———, *Social Aspects of Crime in England between the Wars* (London: G. Allen, 1940), pp. 186–210.

Marecki, Yacek, "Economic Criminality: Mechanism and Remedies," *Kulturai i Spoteczenstwo*, (No. 3, 1962), pp. 57–72.

Mors, Wallace P., "State Regulation of Retail Installment Financing: Progress and Problems," *Journal of Business*, 23 (October, 1950), pp. 199–218, and 24 (January, 1951), pp. 43–71.

Mourant, François, "La Criminalites des Classes Superieres," *Bulletin, Societie de Criminologie de Quebec*, 3 (May, 1964), pp. 43–52.

Myers, Robert S., "The Rise and Fall of Fee-Splitting," *Bulletin of the American College of Surgeons*, 40 (November–December, 1955), pp. 507–509, 523.

Nelson, Walter H., *The Great Discount Delusion* (New York: McKay, 1965).

Newman, Donald J., "White Collar Crime," *Law and Contemporary Problems*, 23 (Autumn, 1958), pp. 735–753.

Normandeau, André, "Les Deviations en Affaires et la 'Crime en Col Blanc,' " *Revue Internationale de Criminologie et de Police Technique*, 19 (October–December, 1965), pp. 247–258.

President's Commission on Law Enforcement and the Administration of Justice, *The Challenge of Crime in a Free Society* (Washington, D.C.: Government Printing Office, 1967), pp. 47–49.

――――, *Crime and Its Impact—An Assessment* (Washington, D.C.: Government Printing Office, 1967), pp. 102–115.

"Quackery in California," *Stanford Law Review,* 11 (March, 1959), pp. 265–296.

Quinney, Richard, "The Study of White Collar Crime: Toward a Reorientation in Theory and Research," *Journal of Criminal Law, Criminology, and Police Science,* 55 (June, 1964), pp. 208–214.

"Regulation of Advertising," *Columbia Law Review,* 56 (November, 1956), pp. 1018–1111.

Riemer, Svend H., "Embezzlement: Pathological Basis," *Journal of Criminal Law and Criminology,* 32 (November–December, 1941), pp. 411–423.

Riis, Roger, and John Patric, *Repairmen Will Get You If You Don't Watch Out* (Garden City, N.Y.: Doubleday, 1942).

Rising, Nelson, "Contours of Conflict: Protection of the Defaulting Consumer," *U.C.L.A. Law Review,* 13 (January, 1966), pp. 348–365.

Ross, Edward A., *Sin and Society: An Analysis of Latter-Day Iniquity* (Boston: Houghton Mifflin, 1907).

Saden, George A., "Inquiry into Ambulance Chasing," *Connecticut Bar Journal,* 34 (June, 1960), pp. 117–122.

Seavey, Warren A., "*Caveat Emptor* as of 1960," *Texas Law Review,* 38 (April, 1960), pp. 439–449.

Sherwin, Robert, "White-Collar Crime, Conventional Crime and Merton's Deviant Behavior Theory," *Wisconsin Sociologist,* 2 (Spring, 1963), pp. 7–10.

Smigel, Erwin O., "Public Attitudes toward 'Chiseling' with Reference to Unemployment Compensation," *American Sociological Review,* 18 (February, 1953), pp. 59–67.

Smith, Richard Austin, "The Incredible Electrical Conspiracy," *Fortune,* 63 (April, 1961), pp. 132–137, and 63 (May, 1961), pp. 161–164.

Sorenson, Robert C., "Review of Sutherland, *White Collar Crime,*" *Journal of Criminal Law, Criminology, and Police Science,* 41 (May–June, 1950), pp. 80–82.

Steefen, Thomas L., "Truth in Lending: A Viable Subject," *George Washington Law Review,* 32 (April, 1964), pp. 861–892.

Stern, Philip M., *The Great Treasury Raid* (New York: Random House, 1964).

Stocker, Frederick D., and John C. Ellickson, "How Fully Do Farmers Report Their Incomes?" *National Tax Journal,* 12 (June, 1959), pp. 116–126.

Sutherland, Edwin H., "Crime and Business," *Annals of the American Academy of Political and Social Science,* 217 (September, 1947), pp. 112–118.

――――, *White Collar Crime* (New York: Dryden Press, 1949).

――――, "The White Collar Criminal," in Vernon C. Branham and Samuel B. Kutash, eds., *Encyclopedia of Criminology* (New York: Philosophical Library, 1949), pp. 511–515.

"Symposium on Consumer Protection," *Michigan Law Review,* 64 (May, 1966), pp. 1197–1466.

Tosun, Oztekin, "Economic Crimes in Turkey," *Istanbul Universitesi Hakuk Fakultesi Mecmuasi,* 26 (Nos. 1–4, 1961), pp. 3–15.

"Translating Sympathy for Deceived Consumers into Effective Programs for Protection," *University of Pennsylvania Law Review,* 114 (January, 1966), pp. 395–450.

Vold, George B., *Theoretical Criminology* (New York: Oxford University Press, 1958), pp. 245–261.

Wagner, Walter, *The Golden Fleecers* (Garden City, N.Y.: Doubleday, 1967).

Walton, Clarence C., and Frederick W. Cleveland, Jr., *Corporations on Trial: The Electrical Cases* (Belmont, Calif.: Wadsworth, 1964).

Weinberg, Arthur and Lila, *The Muckrakers* (New York: Simon and Schuster, 1961).

Weston, Glen E., "Decline of *Caveat Emptor,*" *Federal Bar Journal,* 24 (Fall, 1964), pp. 548–578.

Whitman, Howard, "Why Some Doctors Should Be in Jail," *Collier's*, 132 (October 30, 1953), pp. 23–27.

Willets, Harry, "The Wages of Economic Sin," *Problems of Communism*, 11 (September–October, 1962), pp. 26–32.

Willging, Thomas E., "Installment Credit: A Social Perspective," *Catholic University Law Review*, 15 (January, 1966), pp. 45–68.

Wraith, Ronald, and Edgar Simpkins, *Corruption in Developing Countries* (London: G. Allen, 1963).

Zirpins, Walter, and Otto Terstegen, *Wirtschafts Kriminalität* (Lübeck: M. Schmidt-Römhild, 1963).